An Introduction to

MODERN
EUROPEAN HISTORY
1890–1990

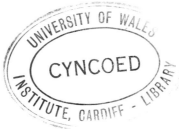

Alan Farmer

Hodder & Stoughton
A MEMBER OF THE HODDER HEADLINE GROUP

access to history

context

An Introduction to

MODERN
EUROPEAN HISTORY
1890–1990

Alan Farmer

Hodder & Stoughton
A MEMBER OF THE HODDER HEADLINE GROUP

ACKNOWLEDGEMENTS

The front cover shows French troops resting, 1916 by CRW Nevinson reproduced courtesy of the Imperial War Museum, © Mrs AC Patterson.

The publishers would like to thank the following individuals, institutions and companies for permission to reproduce copyright illustrations in this book: AKG Photo, London page 150 (left); Bildarchiv Preussischer Kulturbesitz page 33; British Library (Shelfmark LD6) © Solo Syndication/*Daily Mail* 6/3/1946 page 301 top; Will Dyson, *Daily Herald* 13/5/1919/Centre for the Study of Cartoons and Caricature, University of Kent, Canterbury page 106; David Low/*Evening Standard*/Centre for the Study of Cartoons and Caricature, University of Kent, Canterbury pages 230, 301 (bottom); Corbis page 9, 121 (top), 163, 220, 259, 274, 279, 294; David King Collection pages 27, 32, 84, 85 (bottom), 188; Hulton Getty pages 20, 85 (top), 96, 109, 121 (bottom), 150 (right), 172, 237; Imperial War Museum, London pages 73, 75, 156; Punch pages 231, 301 (middle).

The publishers would also like to thank the following for permission to reproduce material in this book:

The extract from *The Second World War: Volume I The Gathering Storm* by Winston S Churchill, Cassell Plc, 1948 is reproduced with permission of Curtis Brown Ltd, London, on behalf of the Estate of Sir Winston S Churchill. Copyright Winston S Churchill; The University of Exeter Press for extracts from *Nazism 1919–1945: A Documentary Reader, Volumes 1–4*, ed. J Noakes and G Pridham, published 1983–1998; Hodder Wayland for the extracts from Purnell's *History of the 20th Century*, 1969; Macmillan Press Ltd for the extract from *The Illusion of Peace: International Relations, 1918–33* by S Marks, 1976; Extracts from *Hitler 1889–1936: Hubris* by Ian Kershaw, Penguin Books, 1998, copyright © Ian Kershaw, 1998, reproduced by permission of Penguin Books Ltd.

Every effort has been made to trace and acknowledge ownership of copyright. The publishers will be glad to make suitable arrangements with any copyright holders whom it has not been possible to contact.

Orders: please contact Bookpoint Ltd, 130 Milton Park, Abingdon, Oxon OX14 4SB. Telephone: (44) 01235 827720, Fax: (44) 01235 400454. Lines are open from 9.00–6.00, Monday to Saturday, with a 24 hour message answering service. You can also order through our website at www.hodderheadline.co.uk

British Library Cataloguing in Publication Data
A catalogue record for this title is available from The British Library

ISBN 0 340 75366 8

First published 2000
Impression number   10   9   8   7   6   5   4
Year   2005   2004   2003

Copyright © 2000 Alan Farmer

Typeset by Wearset, Boldon, Tyne and Wear.
Printed in Great Britain for Hodder & Stoughton Educational, a division of Hodder Headline, 338 Euston Road, London NW1 3BH by J. W. Arrowsmith Ltd, Bristol.

CONTENTS

List of Figures

List of Profiles

List of Tables

PREFACE

Access to History Context

Structure

In some ways *Access to History Context* volumes are similar to most textbooks. They are divided into chapters, each of which is focused on a specific topic. In turn, chapters are divided into sections which have self-explanatory headings. As is the case with most textbooks, *Context* authors have organised the chapters in a logical sequence so that, if you start at the beginning of the book and work your way through to the end, everything will make sense. However, because many readers 'dip' into textbooks rather than reading them from beginning to end, care has been taken to make sure that whichever chapter you start with you should not find yourself feeling lost.

Special Features in the Main Text

Points to Consider – at the start of each chapter this shaded box provides you with vital information about how the chapter is organised and how the various issues covered relate to each other.

Issues boxes are a standard feature of each chapter and, like Points to Consider boxes, are designed to help you extract the maximum benefit from the work you do. They appear in the margin immediately following most numbered section headings. The question(s) contained in each issues box will tell you which historical issue(s) the section is primarily going to cover. If the section you intend to start with has no issues box, turn back page by page until you find one. This will contain the questions the author is considering from that point onwards, including the section you are about to read.

Boxed sections appear in both the margin and the main column of text. In each of the boxes you will find a self-explanatory heading which will make it clear what the contents of the box are about. Very often, the contents of boxes are explanations of words or phrases, or descriptions of events or situations. When you are reading a chapter for the first time you might make a conscious decision to pay little attention to boxed entries so that you can concentrate your attention on the author's main message.

Q-boxes appear in the margin and contain one or more questions about the item they appear alongside. These questions are intended to stimulate you to think about some aspect of the material the box is linked to. The most useful answers to these questions will often emerge during discussions with other students.

Activities boxes – as a general rule, the contents of activities boxes are more complex than the questions in Q-boxes, and often require you to undertake a significant amount of work, either on your own or with others. One reason for completing the task(s) is to consolidate what you have already learned or to extend the range or depth of your understanding.

Profiles – most of these are about named individuals who are central to an understanding of the topic under consideration: some are about events of particular importance. Each Profile contains a similar range of material. The two aspects you are likely to find most useful are:
▼ the dated timeline down the side of the page; and
▼ the source extracts, which provide you with ideas on what made the subject of the Profile especially notable or highly controversial

Profiles also provide useful points of focus during the revision process.

End-of-chapter Sections

The final pages of each chapter contain different sections. It is always worthwhile looking at the **Summary Chart** or **Summary Diagram** first. As their names suggest, these are designed to provide you with a brief and carefully structured overview of the topic covered by the chapter. The important thing for you to do is to check that you understand the way it is structured and how the topics covered inter-relate with one another.

The **Working on . . .** section should be studied in detail once you have finished your first reading of the main text of the chapter. Assuming that you read the Points to Consider section when you began work on the chapter, and that you followed any advice given in it when you read the chapter for the first time, the Working on . . . section is designed to suggest what form any further work you do on the chapter should take.

The **Answering extended writing and essay questions on . . .** sections, taken as a whole throughout the book, form a coherent body of guidance on how to tackle these types of examination questions successfully.

The same is true of the **Answering source-based questions on . . .** sections which have been carefully planned bearing in mind the ways you need to build on the skills you had already developed in this area. You may find these sections particularly helpful during the time you are preparing for an exam.

The last part of each chapter contains a **Further Reading** section. These are of vital importance to you in chapters covering topics you are expected to know about in some detail. To do well in any History course it is essential to read more than one book. However, it is possible to find individual books which can act as your guide and companion throughout your studies, and this is one of them. One of the major ways in which it fulfils this function is by providing you with detailed guidance on the way you can make the most effective use of your limited time in reading more widely.

This book is an integral part of the *Access to History* series. One of its functions is to act as a link between the various topic books in the series on the period it covers, by drawing explicit attention in the Further Reading sections to where, within the series, other material exists which can be used to broaden and deepen your knowledge and understanding. Attention is also drawn to the non-*Access to History* publications which you are likely to find most useful. By using material which has been written based on the same aims and objectives, you are likely to find yourself consistently building up the key skills and abilities needed for success on your course.

Revision

Context books have been planned to be directly helpful to you during the revision period. One of the first things many students do when starting to revise a topic for an examination is to make a list of the 'facts' they need to know about. A safer way of doing this (because it covers the possibility that you missed something important when you originally worked on the topic) is to compile your lists from a book you can rely on. *Context* volumes aim to be reliable in this sense. If you work through the chapter which covers the topic you are about to revise and list the events contained in marginal 'events lists' and in boxed lists of events, you can be confident that you have identified every fact of real significance that you need to know about on the topic. However, you also need to make a list of the historical issues you might be asked to write about. You can do this most conveniently by working through the relevant chapter and noting down the contents of the 'issues boxes'.

For almost everybody, important parts of the revision process are the planning of answers to all the main types of structured and essay questions, and the answering of typical questions (both those requiring extended writing and those based on source material) under exam conditions. The best way to make full use of what this book has to offer in these respects is to work through the two relevant sets of end-of-chapter sections (Answering extended writing and essay questions on . . . and Answering source-based questions on . . .) in a methodical manner.

Keith Randell

THE DOMESTIC SCENE: 1890–1914

CHAPTER *1*

POINTS TO CONSIDER

In 1890 Europe was the world's most successful continent and arguably became stronger and richer still between 1890 and 1914. Only the USA could (and increasingly did) pose a challenge to European dominance. However, it is difficult to generalise about Europe as a whole. There were major social, economic and political differences between the various countries. Different countries, therefore, faced different challenges. This chapter will examine the challenges facing Europe's four main powers (excluding Britain) in the period 1890–1914. It has been broken down into five sections. The first section deals with general European trends. The others deal with Germany, France, Austria–Hungary and Russia.

1 General European Trends

a) What were the Main Economic and Social Trends?

i) Population Growth

Between 1850 and 1914 Europe's population increased from 226 million to 468 million. Europe's poorest areas tended to experience the largest growth of population. Europe's population would have increased still further but for the emigration of over one million Europeans a year to the USA, South America and new colonies overseas.

ii) Industrialisation and Urbanisation

Western and northern Europe were far more industrialised than eastern and southern Europe. By the late nineteenth century Germany had overtaken Britain in coal and iron production and did even better in what is sometimes termed the 'Second Industrial Revolution' – the production of steel, chemicals and electricity. Although European industry was growing rapidly, Europe's share of world manufacturing output was decreasing – due to the massive expansion of the American economy.

> **ISSUES**
> How serious were the social, economic and political problems in France, Germany, Austria–Hungary and Russia in the years 1890–1914?

As industry grew, so did towns and cities. As towns and cities grew, so did service sector jobs – in health, education, transport, etc. New methods of retail distribution were necessary to meet the demands of urban consumers.

iii) Agriculture

Most Europeans still worked on the land. Farming methods in many parts of southern and eastern Europe remained the same as they had been for generations. While there was an increase in European food production, Europe imported more and more food.

iv) Communications

Cheap and rapid forms of transport – railways, trams, steamships – were increasingly available. Automobiles began to be produced in the 1890s and by 1914 aeroplanes were no longer a novelty. In 1901 Marconi sent the first radio signals across the Atlantic.

v) Education

By 1914 primary education was free and compulsory almost every-where in western Europe. Most of those who lived in industrial soci-eties were literate. This, coupled with technical advances, led to a great increase in sales of newspapers and magazines. The political and advertising power of the cheap popular press was immense.

vi) Women's Status

Women's status was slowly changing. Although very few women had the right to vote, upper- and middle-class women had more freedom. Many were limiting their childbearing, thus liberating themselves for other activities. The expansion of women's education enabled women to enter careers which had previously been an all-male pre-serve. Madame Curie, for example, became a world famous scientist. For those who did not reach the heights of Curie, there were new jobs as teachers or office workers. However, peasant and working-class women were still tied to the home or continued to work for very low wages in factories, on farms or as domestic servants.

b) What were the Main Political Trends?

i) Monarchy

The vast majority of countries still had a monarch. The only major exception was France. While some kings had relatively little political influence, the *Tsars* of Russia and the *Kaisers* of Germany and Austria–Hungary wielded colossal power.

RISING LIVING STANDARDS

Across Europe there were massive gaps between the 'haves' and 'have nots'. However, ordinary Europeans experienced a rise in living standards and a longer life expectancy.

▼ Industrial workers saw a reduction in the average hours of work.

▼ By 1914 several countries had introduced old age pensions and national insurance schemes for workers.

▼ Food prices were falling and Europeans could enjoy a wide range of overseas products.

▼ Medicine was increasingly scientific in both its methods of diagnosis and in its development of cures and anaesthetics.

▼ Industrial workers had more leisure time. Some families were able to afford a holiday and men (in particular) involved themselves in a variety of sports and hobbies.

ii) The Elite
In most countries, wealthy elites, whether traditional landowners or new industrialists, possessed great political power. They often dominated the leading positions in the army, judiciary and civil service.

iii) Parliamentary Democracy
▼ Only Russia, Turkey and Montenegro did not have a parliament in 1900. However, the power of the various parliaments varied enormously, with some being little more than a rubber stamp for the monarch's wishes.
▼ Only Finland and Norway allowed women to vote.
▼ Only Spain and Sweden shared Britain's two-party system. Elsewhere there was a spate of parties. Governments, therefore, were invariably coalitions of various groups.
▼ Not everyone favoured parliamentary democracy. Some on the right believed it led to weak government. Some on the left associated it with the middle class and attacked politicians for not representing the real interests of the people.

c) Problems and Challenges

i) The Nationalities Problem
The late nineteenth century saw an increase of nationalist feeling across Europe. Many minority ethnic groups lived within existing states and clamoured for home rule or complete independence.

ii) The Problem of Anti-Semitism
Anti-Semitism was strong in many parts of eastern Europe, not least in Russia where there was a large Jewish population. Russian Jews not only suffered segregation and discrimination but were also liable to face violent assault. Riotous outbreaks against Jews were known as pogroms. Tens of thousands of Russian Jews emigrated to the USA, Germany, Austria–Hungary, France and Britain. Meanwhile, new anti-Semitic tendencies were developing in western and central Europe. While anti-Semitism in the past had been essentially religious, during the late nineteenth century it became increasingly racial. Many German intellectuals extolled the virtues of the Aryan (which equated with, but was not quite the same as, the 'Germanic') race. These same writers were often anti-Semitic. By the 1890s, many Germans regarded the Jews – never more than one per cent of the German population – as a problem. In Austria–Hungary and France, Jews also became a convenient scapegoat for virtually everything perceived to be wrong in society.

iii) The Socialist Problem
By the late nineteenth century, most socialists were influenced by the

ideas of Karl Marx. Marx, a German Jew, spent most of his later life in Britain where he wrote *Das Kapital*, published in 1867. All history, Marx thought, was the history of class struggles. He claimed there was a growing gulf between the middle class (or bourgeoisie) who owned all the capital and the industrial working class (or proletariat). He believed that the exploited workers would inevitably rise up and overthrow the bourgeoisie and the capitalist system. The state, declared Marx, would then regulate the economy in the interests of the proletariat. Eventually there would be a classless society based on public ownership of the essential means of production.

Marx died in 1883 but his ideas lived on, becoming something of a substitute religion for many working men. Those workers who espoused Marxism and who felt themselves to be terribly exploited (as indeed many were) looked forward to ultimate victory and a socialist millennium. Marxist doctrines underpinned the policies of the various socialist parties which began to play an active role in most European countries in the late nineteenth century. However, socialist leaders (most of whom were middle-class intellectuals – not workers) were divided on how best to achieve Marxist ends. While some extremists advocated violent revolution, moderates believed the best way to improve the lot of the proletariat was to work within the system and to cooperate with other parties to bring about social reform.

Socialist trade unions were similarly divided. Some were mainly concerned with trying to get higher wages and to reduce the working hours of their members, others were more revolutionary. **Syndicalists**, strong in France, Spain and Italy, believed that the general strike was the weapon which would destroy the capitalist system. While general strikes occurred in several countries (notably Italy), government authorities invariably stood firm: they had no intention of surrendering power to militant workers. The effectiveness of the general strike was thus a myth – albeit an inspiring one for some workers and intellectuals.

iv) The Anarchist Threat

Anarchists posed another threat to the establishment. Frenchman, Pierre Joseph Proudhon, one of the founders of anarchism, had claimed that 'all property is theft'. He also opposed all traditional forms of government. His ideal society would consist of small communities running their own affairs with little or no central administration. In the late nineteenth century, Proudhon's influence spread and anarchists such as Bakunin in Russia supported the use of terror to sweep away existing institutions. Between 1893 and 1900 President Carnot of France, Empress Elizabeth of Austria–Hungary, and King Umberto of Italy were killed by anarchist terrorists. Such

SYNDICALISM

This was a militant labour movement, originating in France but also strong in Italy and Spain. Syndicalists believed in the inevitability of class warfare and thought the workers' strongest weapon was the general strike.

terrorist acts did little to win anarchist support. In many respects anarchism and socialism were in competition with each other. Their aims were incompatible: socialists aimed to capture the state while anarchists aimed to destroy it. However, anarchism and socialism were not totally separate movements. Some anarchists had socialist leanings while some socialists admired anarchist theory – and action. While the working class generally preferred socialism, anarchists gave the socialists a run for their money in Spain and Italy.

v) The Intellectual Challenge

By the late nineteenth century writers, composers, artists and architects questioned traditional assumptions and sought new forms of expression. Philosophers like Nietzsche preached the need for a fresh set of values appropriate to the new age. However, many Europeans were suspicious of the 'new' and remained loyal to the 'old'. Religion is a good example of the struggle between 'old' and 'new'. Most countries still had an established church. Southern Europe was mainly Catholic, northern Europe mainly Protestant, and Russia mainly Orthodox. While most Europeans remained devout Christians, religion was losing its power to shape and control behaviour, particularly in the growing towns. Some left-wing politicians, while not necessarily being anti-Christian, were vehemently anti-clerical and wished to reduce or destroy altogether the power of the established church. Churchmen, by contrast, tended to throw their weight behind the established order. The Catholic Church, in particular, was vehement in its opposition to socialism.

vi) Right v Left

In most countries there were deep political divisions. These divisions were often based on class. However, religion, race and nationality were similarly divisive. In an attempt to explain the divisions, historians brand particular groups as right or left wing. The 'left' (including anarchists, socialists, and radical liberals) wanted to change society, particularly in the interests of the 'have nots'. The 'right' tended to be nationalistic, conservative, and often favoured strong government (by a monarch, dictator or elite). However, this right–left divide is somewhat crude. In reality, there were many different brands of 'right' and 'left', and groups termed 'right' and 'left' often had little in common.

MARXIST MISCONCEPTIONS

By 1900 it was, or should have been, apparent that Marx had got most things wrong – not least the notion that the capitalist system was on the point of collapse.

▽ Marx assumed that the proletariat would be loyal to their class. This proved to be naive. In practice, many workers were indifferent or hostile to socialism.

▽ Marx believed that industrialisation and middle-class revolution must precede the proletarian revolution. Thus his ideas did not seem to have much potential in countries like Russia where there was little industry. Ironically, proletarian revolution achieved its greatest success in Russia.

▽ Marx believed that the proletariat would become poorer and poorer. Instead standards of living were rising for most workers.

ACTIVITY

Brainstorm three reasons why European governments were often prepared to take vigorous action against socialists and anarchists.

2 Wilhelmine Germany

In 1871 a collection of German states had formed the German Reich (Empire). The architect of German unification was the Prussian 'Iron Chancellor', Otto von Bismarck. By 1890 Germany seemed a united and powerful nation. Its economy was second only to the USA's. Yet many scholars regard its political system as backward. Kaiser Wilhelm II (who gave his name to the 'Wilhelmine era') still had autocratic powers. What was the nature of Wilhelmine Germany?

a) The Main Social and Economic Developments in Germany

In the late nineteenth century, Germany became a great industrial nation. Between 1870 and 1914 coal production increased by over 200 per cent while steel production rose an incredible 80-fold. After 1890 the electricity industry was perhaps Germany's greatest economic achievement, providing a third of the world's output by 1914. There were similar advances in the chemical industry.

However, despite growing industrialisation, over one third of the population continued to live and work in the countryside. Many farmers, great and small alike, were hostile to the values of industrial society.

b) How Strong was German Nationalism?

German nationalism was strong. Urbanisation, education, better communications, and military service all helped to promote a strong German identity. But Germany was not totally united. It remained a nation of 25 states, some of which were hostile to Prussia (the dominant state) and resisted assimilation into a national German culture. Moreover, over six per cent of the population were Poles, Danes and French who had little loyalty to Germany.

c) How was Germany Governed?

Germany was a federal state, its powers and functions divided between the federal (or Imperial) government and the 25 states which it comprised. While no longer sovereign or free to secede, the states preserved their own constitutions, rulers, parliaments and administrative systems. They were free to legislate on a wide variety of matters including education, health and police. The states' power in the central government was maintained through the Federal Council (Bundesrat). Prussia was easily the largest state, possessing

---

FACTORS ENCOURAGING GERMANY'S ECONOMIC EXPANSION

▼ **An excellent education system**.
▼ **Population growth**. The population grew from 49 to 65 million between 1890 and 1910.
▼ **Capital**. German banks were prepared to invest heavily in German industry.
▼ **Mineral resources**, especially coal and iron ore.
▼ **A good transport system**, including navigable rivers, railways and canals.
▼ **Cartels**. Many German industries were organised into cartels.

CARTELS
Cartels were large controlling companies that either owned the whole of a particular industry in one area or owned all the plants involved in one particular process. This enabled the companies to fix prices and do away with the hazards of competition.

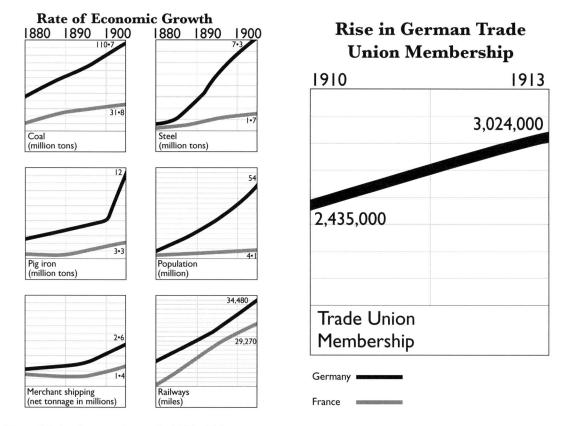

Figure 1 Rate of economic growth, 1880–1914.

two-thirds of German territory and 60 per cent of the population. Prussia had brought about German unification in 1871 and it was Prussia which dominated thereafter. Constitutionally, Prussian dominance was secured in two ways: first the King of Prussia was head of the Empire; and, second, Prussia had sufficient voting power in the Bundesrat to block any unwelcome constitutional amendment.

The Imperial government controlled the armed forces and was responsible for foreign policy, banking, and taxation for imperial purposes. The Kaiser appointed the Chancellor and was head of the army. The Chancellor and other Imperial ministers were responsible only to the Kaiser. The Chancellor presided over the Bundesrat, prepared legislation for the Reichstag (the Imperial parliament) and had the right, with the Kaiser's consent, to dissolve the body. From 1871 to 1890, Bismarck was Chancellor. His influence over Kaiser Wilhelm I ensured that he had virtually total authority in Germany.

The nature of the Prussian state government assisted authoritarianism. In Prussia the monarch's position was supported by the great landowners (*Junkers*) who dominated the Prussian parliament and held an important share of the leadership in the civil service and army. The army continued to play a key role in German politics and society. Many Germans saw the army as the symbol of German greatness, and extolled its virtues. Troops took an oath of personal loyalty to the Kaiser rather than to the state, and in many respects were independent of any control other than the Kaiser's. Social distinction in Wilhelmine Germany was measured almost entirely by military rank.

But democracy did exist in Germany. The Reichstag, elected by universal manhood suffrage every five years, had the power to make federal law, could withhold its consent to legislation, and had to approve the annual Imperial budget. In Bismarck's 'reign', politicians failed to exploit these powers. Nevertheless, the Reichstag was not a complete paper tiger. Even Bismarck found it necessary to ensure he had a majority in the Reichstag by close cooperation with one or more of the leading parties.

Table 1 State of the parties in the Reichstag, 1890–1914.

	1890	1893	1898	1903	1907	1912
Conservatives	73	72	56	54	60	43
Independent Conservatives	20	28	23	21	24	14
National Liberals	42	53	46	51	54	45
Liberal Progressives	66	37	41	31	42	42
German People's Party	10	11	7	9	7	–
Centre Party	106	96	102	100	105	91
Social Democrats	35	44	56	81	43	110
Nationalities: e.g. Poles, Danes	38	35	34	32	29	33
Others	7	21	41	22	33	19

How democratic was Germany? **Q**

The rise of the Social Democrats (the SPD) was the major political phenomenon of the era. How to treat the party and its ideas were to be crucial issues for Wilhelm and his Chancellors. While some SPD members wanted to smash the capitalist system, most were prepared to work with other parties to achieve social reform. Germany also experienced a growth of economic and ideological interest groups. By 1914 Germany had by far the largest trade union movement in Europe. Agriculturalists and industrialists also had pressure groups, while the Pan-German League, the Colonial Society and the Naval League all embraced a whole range of ultra-nationalist and expansionist demands.

d) How Important was Kaiser Wilhelm II?

Wilhelm II became Kaiser in 1888 and remained so until November 1918. Some historians think he was responsible for all the misfortunes of his 30-year reign. He can be seen as immature, self-assertive, erratic, and prone to errors of judgement. 'The Kaiser is like a balloon', said Bismarck. 'If you do not hold fast to the string, you never know where he will be off to.' He took a personal, interfering interest in almost every subject from ship design to theatrical productions. He surrounded himself at court with odd characters, including a homosexually-inclined spiritualist. The chief of the military cabinet died of a heart attack while performing for the Emperor dressed as a ballerina. Wilhelm frequently selected key officials for personal rather than political reasons: such men were often inadequate. However, it is possible to view Wilhelm more sympathetically. Some scholars see him as an intelligent, conscientious, energetic, and enthusiastic ruler. Others relegate him to the sidelines, arguing that his life was an endless whirl of state occasions, military manoeuvres, cruises, and hunting trips, and that his social duties meant that he did not have command of the detail of the government's work. They claim that while he may have occasionally meddled, he did not determine the course of German policy. However, most historians think Wilhelm played a vital role. Their view is that, since he appointed and dismissed all members of the Reich and Prussian executives, he determined the parameters of what was and what was not possible. No major decision could be taken without his agreement.

Figure 2 Kaiser Wilhelm II.

e) Germany: 1890–1914

Bismarck and Wilhelm II soon disagreed on several matters including how to deal with the socialists. Bismarck wanted to stand firm against them. Wilhelm, anxious to be seen as a 'People's Emperor', wanted to drop the repressive legislation. Bismarck finally resigned in 1890. None of his successors had his power and authority. Bismarck's immediate successor was Caprivi, a Prussian soldier with little political experience who wanted to stand above parties and particular interests. He quickly discovered that this was impossible. For a few years Wilhelm II continued his conciliatory policy towards socialism, in the hope that concessions would woo the moderates away from extremist policies. However, in 1894 Wilhelm, fearful of the growing strength of the SPD, changed his mind and determined to stand firm against socialism. Caprivi refused to support a new anti-socialist bill and resigned.

Caprivi's successor Chlodwig was 75 years old. He was not expected to oppose the Kaiser's policies and he lived up to this

WHAT WAS BISMARCK'S LEGACY?

Bismarck dominated Germany until 1890. In an attempt to unite the new state, he clashed with some of the main forces in German life or, as he saw them, 'enemies of the Reich'.

▼ He clashed with the Catholic Church.

▼ He clashed with socialism. In the 1880s all socialist associations, meetings and publications could be forbidden or dissolved. Such measures simply increased socialist solidarity and bitterness. Bismarck did not rely on repression alone. He also tried to 'kill socialism by kindness', introducing health and accident insurance and old age and disability pensions for many wage earners. However, this social security system, while being welcomed, did not wean the workers off socialism.

expectation. For several years Wilhelm was the most decisive figure in the government, dictating most aspects of policy. However, his efforts to take firm anti-socialist action met with little success. In 1900 Bülow became Chancellor. A courtier more than a statesman, he cultivated a close relationship with Wilhelm. Caprivi's policy of making concessions to the workers was revived. For example, workers' entitlements to pension and insurance benefits were extended.

A major crisis arose in 1908 following an article in the *Daily Telegraph* in which Wilhelm expressed his wish for closer relations with Britain. Reichstag members questioned Wilhelm's right to make such important policy statements. For some months there was talk of constitutional changes to reduce the Kaiser's power. But nothing was done since the Reichstag could not agree on any acceptable alternative. By 1909 Bülow, whose relations with Wilhelm had become increasingly strained, was unable to command a clear majority in the Reichstag and resigned. He was replaced by Bethmann-Hollweg.

In 1912 the SPD, with over 30 per cent of the vote, became the largest party in the Reichstag. However, the SPD found it difficult to cooperate with other parties and thus the government had a chance of passing its own legislation. In 1913 there was a crisis over an incident at Zabern, a town in Alsace. Soldiers had dealt roughly with townspeople and those who subsequently demonstrated against the army's actions were imprisoned. There were public and official protests. Only when the Alsace governor threatened to resign did Wilhelm act. Rather than punish the soldiers concerned, he ordered them to be sent away on manoeuvres. While the Zabern incident forcefully underlined the power of the army, it also showed that the Kaiser and army could not altogether ignore public opinion.

f) Modern or Backward?

By 1914 Germany was still in most respects an authoritarian monarchy, in which both Wilhelm II and the old elites retained their power. However, the Kaiser did not have everything his own way. German governments could not ignore the Reichstag and had to patch up working majorities in order to pass legislation. The Reichstag, with its ever-increasing SPD presence, extended its right to debate government policy. Criticisms of the Kaiser were commonplace and the German press had considerable freedom. Nor was Wilhelm in a position to take firm action against his critics. While he might dream of using the army to strike against the SPD, he did not dare unleash a decisive strike against the party. It is thus possible to argue that there was potential in Germany for future democratic development.

ACTIVITY

'To what extent was Germany economically "modern" but politically "backward"?'

Suggested line of response:
▼ Stress that Germany was economically 'modern' (by the standards of the time).
▼ The 'politically backward' is more difficult. You will first need to define 'backward'. For the sake of argument, assume that 'backward' means autocratic rather than democratic. Even then, the question is not easy! It needs a 'yes' and 'no' type response. Yes … Germany was autocratic … No … Germany was a democracy of sorts.

3 The Third Republic

In 1870–1 France had suffered two severe shocks: defeat by Prussia (and the loss of Alsace-Lorraine) and a short-lived civil war (the Commune). The Third Republic came into existence as a result of these events. Perhaps because of this it was never particularly popular. Yet it survived. Why – and how successful was it?

ISSUES
What problems did the Third Republic face? Why did it survive? How successful was it?

a) The Social and Economic Situation

i) On the negative side:
▼ French industrial progress was not as great as that of Germany.
▼ The loss of Alsace-Lorraine's iron ore deposits was a severe blow.
▼ The French population hardly grew. In 1871 there were 37 million people. In 1911 there were only 39 million.
▼ The proletariat was increasingly militant.

ii) On the positive side:
▼ The economy was diversified. Its traditional strengths, the production of food, wine, and luxury items, remained. Heavy industry grew rapidly and new industries (e.g. electricity and chemicals) also developed.
▼ High tariffs succeeded in protecting French producers.
▼ From 1897 France enjoyed a period of prosperity. (The period became known as '*la belle époque*' – the good old days.) The standard of living rose. So did life expectancy: it was higher than in Germany in 1914.
▼ Society was reasonably stable. More than half the French population still worked on the land. The old noble class was economically and politically insignificant. The mass of French farmers owned their own – small – farms. They provided a solid core to French society.

Table 2 A comparison of annual pig iron and steel production, 1890–1910 (1000 metric tonnes).

Pig iron	UK	Germany	France
1890	8,033	4,037	1,970
1900	9,003	7,549	2,714
1910	10,380	14,793	4,032

Steel	UK	Germany	France
1890	3,637	2,161	566
1900	5,130	6,645	1,565
1910	6,374	13,698	3,506

b) How was France Governed?

Instead of a king, France had a president. Elected by the National Assembly for seven years, he was largely a figurehead. He could not veto legislation or dissolve the National Assembly. The Assembly comprised the Chamber of Deputies and the Senate. The Senate was usually conservative. The 300 senators had to be at least 40 years old; 225 were elected for nine-year terms while the outgoing Assembly elected a further 75 life senators. The Chamber of Deputies was elected by universal adult male suffrage. It was here that real power lay: this was the body to which ministers held themselves responsible.

After 1871 there was a proliferation of political parties and a lack of party discipline. In consequence, the Chamber of Deputies was rarely able to produce a clear majority and governments changed with startling rapidity. The changes did not usually mean significant differences of policy: indeed most governments came and went without managing to carry out any major measures. However, there were important differences between right and left, which at times of crisis tended to polarise into two irreconcilable camps. These divisions were as much based on religion as class. The right, which generally had the support of the Catholic Church, tended to distrust democracy, preferring 'order' and strong government. The left defended the Republic and tended to be **anti-clerical**. While tensions between right and left often attracted attention, deputies in the centre usually held the balance of power.

> **ANTI–CLERICALISM**
> This was the opposition to the political, social and economic influence of the church, especially the Roman Catholic Church. Anti-clericalism was important in French, Italian and Spanish politics in the late 19th and early 20th century.

c) How Serious was the Right-Wing Threat?

i) General Boulanger

In 1886 Georges Boulanger was appointed Minister of War. He talked of a war of revenge against Germany and many on the right soon saw him as a new Napoleon, a pure patriot who rose above the sordid interests of politicians. When Boulanger lost his post in 1887, his popular support seemed to threaten the Republic. In 1888 he stood as candidate in a number of by-elections and won a series of spectacular victories. He demanded the establishment of a new form of government, essentially dictatorship, that would work for the 'unity, the greatness and the prosperity of the fatherland'. His electoral victories came to a climax in 1889 when he swept the board in a by-election in Paris. Had he put himself at the head of an enthusiastic mob, he might well have overthrown the government. However, his nerve failed him. When the government started proceedings against him for treason, he fled to Belgium and his support collapsed. The massive support that rallied behind Boulanger showed how powerful were the – mixed – forces which rejected the Republic.

ii) The Panama Scandal

In 1879 Ferdinand de Lesseps had tried to build a Panama Canal. His project ran into financial difficulties, so much so that in 1888 the Chamber voted for the Panama Canal Company to be helped by a large public loan. When investors did not come forward in sufficient numbers, the company was forced into liquidation. In 1892 it was revealed that the company's interests had been promoted by dishonest finance and bribing politicians. The scandal aroused great cynicism about those in public life. It also increased anti-Semitism in France, largely because two Jews had carried out much of the bribery. The Jewish community in France was small – only 80,000 strong in the 1890s. But right-wing nationalist groups, anxious to find a scapegoat for France's perceived problems, targeted the Jews, claiming they were deliberately undermining French values.

iii) The Dreyfus Affair

In 1894 Dreyfus, the first Jew attached to the French General Staff, was arrested and tried for passing secrets to Germany. Found guilty, he was sentenced to life imprisonment on Devil's Island. His conviction did not cause much stir at the time apart from those who thought he should have been shot. However, by 1897 it was clear that Dreyfus had been convicted on flimsy evidence. Army leaders, aware that the trial had been improperly conducted, resisted attempts to reopen the case. The case was finally reopened when Lieutenant-Colonel Picquart, the new Head of Intelligence, discovered evidence that the man who had really been selling military secrets to the Germans was Major Esterhazy. In 1898 Esterhazy demanded a trial to clear his name. Thanks to the forged evidence of Colonel Henry of the Intelligence Branch, he was rapidly acquitted.

The radical paper *L'Aurore* now printed an article by the novelist Emile Zola in which he accused individual army officers of perverting the course of justice. This caused a sensation. Dreyfus became a symbol, bitterly dividing the nation. The left generally supported Dreyfus. The right were generally against him. The 'anti-Dreyfusards' believed that the army's prestige was more important than the guilt or innocence of one man (especially a Jew!). Events now turned in Dreyfus's favour. Colonel Henry admitted incriminating Dreyfus and committed suicide. Esterhazy, realising the game was up, confessed his guilt. Although it was now clear that Dreyfus was innocent and that the army leadership had colluded in finding him guilty, anti-Dreyfusards still resisted the truth. Such was the passion generated by the affair that some feared an army coup. Instead, a strong Radical government, led by Waldeck-Rousseau, came to power determined to see justice was done. Unrest in the army was quelled and some officers were purged. In 1899 Dreyfus was brought home and re-tried by the army. Amazingly he was again found guilty but released because of 'extenuating circumstances'. The government now stepped in and gave Dreyfus a full pardon.

The Dreyfus affair embittered national life for many years. The right became more anti-Semitic: the left, blaming the Catholic Church for the affair, became more anti-clerical. The Radicals, who dominated politics down to 1914, passed a number of measures against the Church. In 1905 a Separation Law ended state support of the Catholic Church which now had to pay its own clerical salaries.

After 1900 the right-wing threat died down but did not entirely disappear. The members of Charles Maurras's Action Française were nationalist, anti-Semitic, and anti-parliamentarian, believing that the restoration of the monarchy was the way to France's salvation. Although little more than of nuisance value, Action Française drew on widespread disillusionment with politics and politicians.

d) How Serious was the Left-Wing Threat?

The French proletariat was relatively small and most French farmers had little time for the doctrines of Marx. Nevertheless socialist ideas spread. By 1900 there were several small squabbling socialist parties. In 1904–5 the main socialist groups agreed to form a united party. Although the new party reaffirmed its commitment to 'socialising the means of production', it was prepared to work within the parliamentary system. It had some success, winning 54 seats in 1906 and 103 seats in 1914.

The main trade union organisation (the CGT) advocated revolutionary syndicalism, believing that a general strike was the best way to destroy the capitalist system. After 1906 there was a spate of violent strikes. Troops were sometimes used against the strikers and some union leaders were imprisoned.

e) Conclusion

At first glance it may seem surprising that the Third Republic survived. Few Frenchmen seemed to have had much affection for it. Many on the right wanted stronger leadership, while revolutionary socialists on the left wanted to 'smash' the system. The Republic seemed to totter from one crisis to another. Yet it survived. Arguably, it did so because it was the form of government which divided people the least. When faced with a choice, the majority preferred the Republic to the prospect of a more right or a more left-wing regime. By 1914 the right-wing threat had subsided and on the left syndicalists represented only a minority of the population.

Did the Third Republic's successes outweigh its failures? Arguably they did. The fact that it survived was itself an achievement. On the economic front, France had made sound progress and there had been a measure of social reform in areas of public health, working conditions and national insurance. France was successful in other ways. Many French men were proud of their artistic, cultural and intellectual achievements, and of their empire – second only to that of Britain.

ACTIVITY

To test your understanding, consider the following question: 'Why did the politics of the Third Republic appear so unstable?'

Suggested line of response:
▼ France was divided politically. The Third Republic reflected the left–right divisions.
▼ There were a large number of parties. Governments thus found it hard to obtain an overall majority.
▼ Examine the right- and left-wing threats.
▼ Was the Republic more stable than it sometimes seems?

---

4 Austria–Hungary

ISSUE
How serious was the nationalities problem?

By 1890 Austria–Hungary (the Habsburg Empire) contained over 40 million people made up of 11 different nationalities (see Figure 3). In 1867, faced with demands for Hungarian independence, Emperor Franz Joseph had agreed to the so-called Compromise whereby the Empire was divided into two, with an Austrian half and a Hungarian half. After 1867, in domestic matters Austria–Hungary was really two states rather than one. However, the two countries shared the same monarch: Franz Joseph was Emperor of Austria and King of Hungary. Austria–Hungary is thus sometimes called the Dual Monarchy. What were the main problems facing the Dual Monarchy?

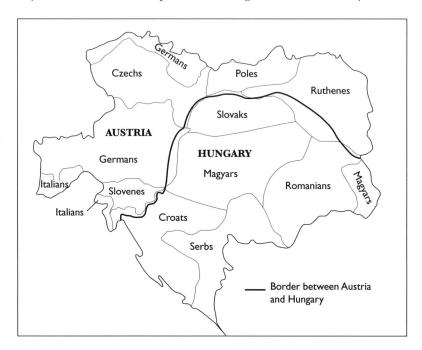

Figure 3 Locations of nationalities within the Austro-Hungarian Empire.

The Nationalities of the Austro–Hungarian Empire

The figures are based on the 1910 census.

Germans
Number: 12,000,000 (23 per cent of population)
The Germans tended to see the Empire as primarily German and themselves as the dominant race. German was the language of court, state and army.

Magyars
Number: 10,000,000 (20 per cent of population)
The largest single ethnic group in Hungary but they comprised less than half the population.

Czechs
Number: 6,500,000 (12 per cent of population)
Strongest in Bohemia and Moravia, most wanted a federal constitution in which they had similar status to the Magyars.

Poles
Number: 5,000,000 (10 per cent of population)
The Poles had considerable rights of self-government in Galicia. While some wanted an independent Poland, they realised it was unlikely to happen. Most were loyal to the Habsburg Empire.

Ruthenians
Number: 4,000,000 (9 per cent of population)
Most lived in Galicia and were dominated by the Poles. There was no strong sense of Ruthenian nationalism.

Croats
Number: 2,500,000 (5 per cent of population)
Croats lived in both Austria and Hungary and enjoyed rights of self-government. Some Croats hoped to create an independent South Slav state consisting of Croatians, Serbs and Slovenes.

Serbs
Number: 1,500,000 (3 per cent of population)
By 1914 many Serbs looked to Serbia as their homeland.

Slovenes
Number: 1,250,000 (2.5 per cent of population)
Mainly Catholic peasants, most did not want independence.

Slovaks
Number: 2,000,000 (4 per cent of population)
There was little cooperation between the Slovaks (who lived in Hungary) and the Czechs (who lived in Austria).

Italians
Number: 750,000 (1.5 per cent of population)
Living on the Italian borders, they were too few in number to cause a major problem.

Romanians
Number: 3,250,000 (6.5 per cent of population)
Unlike Serbia or Italy, Romania did not seek to 'redeem' the Romanian areas of the Empire.

Jews
Number: 2,250,000 (Under 5 per cent of population)
Concentrated in the larger cities, they played an important economic, cultural and financial role.

Muslims
Number: less than 500,000 (1 per cent of population)
Most lived in Bosnia-Herzegovina. Allowed religious freedom, they were generally loyal to the Empire.

Table 3 Austro-Hungarian coal and pig iron production before the First World War.

Coal production per head of population (tons) in 1913	
USA	5.10
Great Britain	4.01
Germany	3.85
France	1.59
Austria–Hungary	**1.17**
Italy	0.35
Russia	0.32

Pig iron consumption (millions of tons) in 1910	
USA	27.8
Germany	14.1
Great Britain	9.1
France	4.1
Russia	3.0
Austria–Hungary	**2.1**
Italy	0.6

a) The Multi-national Problem

Many historians have contended that so many nationalities made the break-up of the Habsburg Empire inevitable. The First World War is seen as simply accelerating the process. Indeed, some see the war itself arising from the failure of Austria–Hungary to deal with the problems posed by South Slav nationalism. But not all historians are convinced. Alan Sked, for example, has said: 'the truth is that there was no internal pressure between 1876 and 1914 for the break-up of the Monarchy'. 'The fact that the Monarchy fell does not logically imply any decline at all,' says Sked. However, even Sked would probably admit that many of the major events in both Austria and Hungary after 1890 were related to problems posed by the various nationalities.

b) The Main Social and Economic Problems

Hungary was still predominantly agricultural. Much of the land was owned by great landowners and farming methods were generally backward. In Austria industrialisation was developing. In Bohemia, which had large coal and iron deposits, almost a third of the population was employed in industry. However, the extent of industrialisation should not be exaggerated. Only 20 per cent of Austrians lived in towns of over 5,000 people in 1890. As everywhere, the Austrian proletariat suffered from low wages, poor housing and long working hours. Most people within the Empire were poor peasants. In eastern Hungary illiteracy was the norm and infant mortality rates were among the highest in Europe.

c) How was Austria–Hungary Governed?

The constitutional arrangements of the 1867 Compromise were complex.
  ▼ The Emperor still had great powers: he could summon or dissolve parliament, appoint ministers, and rule by decree in an emergency.
  ▼ There was a single Imperial army and three Joint Ministers who controlled foreign policy, defence and finance. The Joint Ministers were responsible to Delegations from Austria and Hungary. The Delegations' approval was required in order to provide the necessary finance.
  ▼ Austria and Hungary each had their own ministers and parliaments with control over all matters within their respective boundaries. On paper both Austria and Hungary had some aspects of democracy.
  ▼ In Austria there was an Upper House (composed of nobles, churchmen and Emperor-appointees) and an elected Lower House (Reichsrat). Prior to 1896 most people could not vote. The 1896 reforms

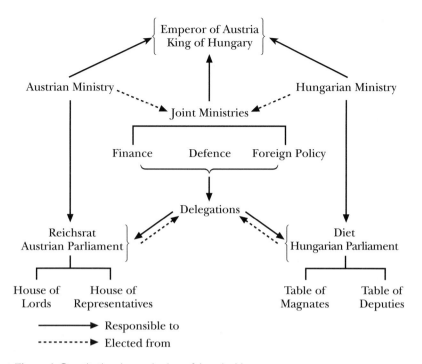

Figure 4 Constitutional organisation of Austria–Hungary.

increased the electorate by over 5 million but ensured that the upper and middle classes remained dominant. Moreover, the Reichsrat's power was minimal. Ministers owed their loyalty more to the Emperor than to a parliamentary majority.

▼ In Hungary arrangements were similar. Again there were two houses: an elite Upper House and an elected Lower House. Until 1908 only Magyar taxpayers could vote.

d) What were the Main Political Crises?

The domestic history of Austria–Hungary is complex because it is not the history of a single nation. It is certainly the history of two nations – and arguably many more.

i) Austria

Austrian governments were plagued by the constant rivalries between the nationalities. Count Taaffe, Prime Minister from 1879–93, maintained the support of German, Pole and Czech conservatives (a coalition known as the Iron Ring) by a series of minor concessions for Czechs and Poles. However, demands for Czech home rule increased: in the 1891 election the nationalistic 'Young Czechs' won all the Bohemian seats. In 1893, following Czech riots against Aus-

FRANZ JOSEPH

Franz Joseph became Emperor in 1848 at the age of 18. Since he believed he was Emperor by grace of God, he thought he had no responsibility to obey the general will of the people. The older he got, the more set in his ways he became, refusing, for example, to use new inventions such as the telephone. He was generally a stickler for tradition and correct behaviour. The only exception was his lechery: he was still capable of rape in his sixties. It is easy to criticise Franz Joseph for failing to deal with the problems besetting the Dual Monarchy. However, in his defence, he was both conscientious and hard-working, and he did inspire loyalty among many of his people. Indeed, in many ways, it was he, and he alone, who embodied the political unity of the Empire.

trian rule, Taaffe considered extending the franchise, believing that the Czech masses would be less nationalistic than the Czech middle class. Taaffe's idea so alarmed his conservative supporters that his bill was voted down and Franz Joseph dismissed him. In 1895, after two years of confusion, Count Badeni, a Pole, became prime minister. His efforts in 1897 to extend language rights for Czechs led to his downfall. Germans objected to the fact that to hold government posts in Bohemia they would have to be bilingual. Badeni fell and his bill was withdrawn. His successor, von Korber, ruled by decree – that is by passing laws without referring to parliament for approval – until 1907.

In 1907 universal manhood suffrage was introduced. This measure was pushed through by Franz Joseph despite considerable opposition from the landed gentry. The Emperor's aim seems to have been to try to bring the Czech middle classes to heel. Like Taaffe, he hoped that the working class would be more concerned with social reform than with demands for home rule, and thought the spectre of Marxism might scare the Czech middle classes into supporting the Empire. His hopes were only partially fulfilled. Working-class movements remained less important than national movements. No real attempt was made to form a united socialist party. The Czech Social Democratic Party, for example, was more concerned with the rights of Czech workers than with the rights of all workers. After 1907 the political situation was even more confusing and unmanageable. In 1911 over 50 parties – some nationally based, others class based – competed for 516 seats. There were so many small parties it was impossible to form a coalition with a majority of seats.

ii) Hungary

In 1902–3 the Hungarian parliament refused to support an increase in the size and budget of the joint army unless Magyar words of command were authorised for Magyar regiments. This was tantamount to demanding a separate Hungarian army and was rejected by Franz Joseph. The Independence Party, which demanded independence from the Habsburg Empire, won the 1905 election. Since the Hungarian parliament still refused to approve an increase in the army, the Emperor appointed his own prime minister, sent troops to disperse the parliament, and ruled by decree. Although these actions fuelled the flames of Magyar nationalism, the Independents were unable to mobilise enough support to oppose this 'royal dictatorship'. By 1910 they had lost much of their credibility.

If the Magyars were divided on the independence issue, they were united in their determination to maintain Magyar dominance within Hungary. The Magyar language was made compulsory in all schools, and local traditions, festivals and costumes were suppressed. Only

Figure 5 Franz Joseph.

the Croats were allowed some aspects of home rule and had their own courts, schools and police. Magyar control was assured by electoral laws which effectively banned most other ethnic groups from voting. Although universal suffrage was supposedly introduced in 1908, only people who passed a Magyar literacy test could vote. In the 1910 elections, non-Magyars won only eight seats out of over 400.

The Magyars have sometimes been seen as a repressive ruling class trying to keep the lid firmly on Slav nationalist aspirations. It has been argued that this oppression built up massive tensions within the Empire as a whole. However, this view does not quite fit the facts. While the minority races were discriminated against, there was little organised opposition to Magyar rule. The Magyars did not see themselves as racially exclusive. If people wanted to better themselves, they simply had to learn the Hungarian language. Some groups were content to be assimilated. Only in the outlying rural villages of Slovakia, Ruthenia and the South Slav lands did Magyarisation fail to make much impact. But the semi-literate peasants in these areas, resistant to many forms of change, posed no serious threat.

e) Was the Habsburg Empire on the Point of Collapse in 1914?

In 1908 Franz Joseph celebrated 60 years on the throne. *The Times* reported the climax of celebrations in Vienna as follows:

> On June 12 there passed before the Emperor, in a procession which lasted more than three hours, 12,000 of his subjects, of all races and tongues, in costumes of historic periods, shouting their loyal greetings . . . the people . . . cheered each race and clan, in the consciousness that not only common loyalty to a common dynasty personified in a venerable Sovereign, but also a common history, common interest, common enemies and a common destiny, all unite them.
>
> *Source A*

This does not imply that the Habsburg Empire was on the point of disintegration. In 1914 the Czechs wanted home rule, not independence. The South Slavs – Croats, Serbs and Slovenes – were divided amongst themselves. The assassination of Franz Ferdinand at Sarajevo in June 1914 (see page 53) can be seen as the action of a small group which was not representative of Bosnian Serbs as a whole. The most convincing evidence that most people were still loyal to the Empire is the First World War. For most of the war, most peoples fought loyally in the Habsburg army. Possibly they had little alternative. However, more rebellions and more signs of defeatism ought to have occurred if the Empire had been under real threat from nationalist conflict within its borders.

ISSUES

What problems faced Russia? How successful was the government in dealing with these? Was Russia on the verge of revolution in 1914?

5 Russia

In the late nineteenth century Russia lagged behind most other powerful countries in Europe. This backwardness was even apparent in Russia's calendar which was 13 days behind that of the rest of Europe. While it is often assumed that backwardness somehow caused the Revolutions of 1917, backwardness does not inevitably lead to revolution. Indeed, it usually does not. Precisely how backward Russia was is also debatable. Nevertheless, there is no doubt that Russia faced many problems.

a) The Problem of Size

Russia was the world's largest country in area in 1890, comprising one sixth of the world's land surface. By 1900 there were about 129 million people within the Russian empire. Russia's size might appear to be a strength. It was also a weakness. One problem was the sheer difficulty of communication. Orders from the government in the

Table 4 The major nationalities of the Russian Empire, 1897 (millions).

Great Russian	55.6	Lithuanian	1.2
Ukrainian	22.4	Armenian	1.2
Polish	7.9	Romanian/Moldavian	1.1
White Russian	5.8	Estonian	1.0
Jewish (defined by faith)	5.0	Mordvinian	1.0
Kirgiz/Kaisats	4.0	Georgian	0.8
Tartar	3.4	Tadzhik	0.3
Finnish	3.1	Turkmenian	0.3
German	1.8	Greek	0.2
Latvian	1.4	Bulgarian	0.2
Bashkir	1.3		

Figure 6 The Russian Empire in 1905.

capital, St Petersburg, often never found their way to remote corners of the empire. The fact that Russia was an empire was another problem. Less than half of the people within the empire actually considered themselves Russian and some of the nationalities wanted independence. In the late nineteenth century Russian governments tried to force non-Russian people to adopt the Russian language and Russian customs. This policy was known as Russification.

b) Economic and Social Problems

i) The Economic Situation

Russia was essentially an agricultural country – and a country which in many areas had still not had an agricultural revolution. There was little in the way of crop diversification or new methods. Most peasants belonged to a *mir* (a type of commune) in which land was collectively, not individually, held. Land was regularly redistributed, according to a family's influence or size. Thus farmers had no incentive to be efficient. If they farmed their land well, their strips might be taken over by another family. An additional problem was that

RUSSIA'S INDUSTRIAL PROGRESS

▼ In the late nineteenth century, a series of ministers, especially Sergei de Witte (1892–1903), promoted industrialisation.

▼ Russian governments supported the building of railways. By 1905 some 40,000 miles had been constructed, including the 4,000-mile long Trans-Siberian railway (built between 1891 and 1904) which ran from St Petersburg to Vladivostok.

▼ Railway building helped open up Russia's huge mineral wealth and also encouraged industries like coal, iron and steel.

▼ Russia attracted considerable investment from abroad.

▼ Russian industry was protected by high tariffs.

there were too many peasants and not enough land to go round. Between 1877 and 1917 Russia's population grew by 50 per cent: the amount of additional land increased by only 10 per cent.

The solution to the agricultural problems was for Russia to industrialise. The surplus population could then move into the towns and industry would produce the fertilisers and machines that farmers needed. Unfortunately Russia, while rich in natural resources, was industrially backward. However, it is important not to over-stress Russian industrial backwardness.

ii) The Social Situation

Marxist historians once described Russian society as *feudal*. Feudal is a difficult term to define. By one definition a feudal society has a weak ruler, a strong nobility, a weak middle class, large numbers of serfs, and no proletariat. By this definition late nineteenth-century Russia was *not* feudal.

▼ Russia's tsars were far from weak.

▼ Russian nobles were far from strong. While some nobles were incredibly rich, the nobility was under the thumb of the tsar – not the reverse. Nor was the nobility united. By no means all were Russian (many were Polish) and not all were great landowners. By 1905 over half the hereditary nobility owned no land. Nor were all the nobility hereditary. Many were service nobility. They had a title simply because of the job they held. Lenin's father, for example, was a noble because he was a school inspector.

▼ There was a growing, and increasingly influential, middle class.

▼ Over 80 per cent of Russians were peasants – not serfs. In 1861 Alexander II had freed (or emancipated) the serfs. However, after 1861 peasants were not totally free and equal. They had a separate legal status. Moreover they had to pay (over a 49-year period) for the land they had been 'given'. The *mir* was responsible for collecting the repayment. All peasants were thus effectively tied to the *mir* and were not allowed to leave unless they had the permission of the village elders. Most peasants had a very low standard of living. Nevertheless, some, by luck or hard work, were bettering themselves, usually by obtaining more land. By 1905 some three quarters of Russia's cultivated land was under peasant control. Moreover in the 1890s the legislative discrimination started to come to an end.

▼ As Russian industry developed, so the proletariat developed. Russian workers suffered similar conditions to workers in every other industrialising country, working long hours for low wages. Living conditions in the growing towns were dreadful.

c) Russia's Political Problems

The tsar held total power. In 1890 Russia had the dubious distinction of being one of only three European countries without a parliament. The tsar in 1890 was Alexander III. He ruled with the assistance of his personally chosen ministers, a large army, a small secret police (the Okhrana), and the support of the Orthodox Church. Russia was an autocracy. However, it was not as restrictive as is sometimes implied.

▼ Russia's bureaucracy was inefficient. The lack of government at grass roots level limited the government's effectiveness.

▼ Although Russia was seen as a police state, it had relatively few police. While revolutionaries were sent to Siberia, conditions there were much better than under Stalin.

▼ Democracy of sorts did exist in Russia. In 1864 local government councils (Zemstvos) were set up to control, among other things, education and health. In 1870 municipal councils were set up.

d) Russian Revolutionaries

In the late nineteenth century, revolutionaries demanded change. In the 1870s idealistic students had 'gone to the people' preaching that the peasants should demand personal rights. These *narodnik* or populist students had no popular success. Bemused peasants usually handed them over to the police. Some revolutionaries then turned to violence, assassinating key government figures. In 1881 terrorists succeeded in assassinating Alexander II. His murder solved nothing. His son Alexander III, an uncompromising autocrat, hit back at the revolutionaries. So did his son Nicholas II. All thoughts of creating a parliament ended. Revolutionary groups were forced underground. But they did not disappear. By the early twentieth century there were several such groups.

> **SOCIAL REVOLUTIONARIES (SRs)**
> The SRs, the largest revolutionary group, pinned their hopes on the peasants. The only thing that all SRs had in common was opposition to the tsarist system and a belief in land redistribution. Some SRs supported terrorist means to achieve their ends.

e) Why was there a Revolution in 1905?

A series of bad harvests led to rising discontent in the early 1900s. In 1904 Russia went to war with Japan. The conflict was essentially about which country would control Manchuria and Korea. Russia had major difficulties in fighting in the Far East and her forces were defeated on both land and sea. The Russo-Japanese war exacerbated Russia's economic problems and destroyed confidence in the government. In the autumn of 1904 middle-class liberals launched a campaign demanding a parliament. On 22 January 1905 Father Gapon led a peaceful demonstration of some 200,000 people to the Winter Palace, hoping to present a petition to Tsar Nicholas II asking for a redress of workers' grievances. Troops opened fire on the marchers and

Was there a revolution in 1905?

BOLSHEVIKS AND MENSHEVIKS

In 1903 the SDs split. At a meeting in London a majority of the delegates supported Lenin. Lenin's 'party' thus became known as Bolsheviks (majority men). Lenin's opponents – including Plekhanov who accused him of dictatorial ambitions – were called Mensheviks (minority men).

Q Why did middle-class Russians often join revolutionary groups?

Social Democrats (SDs)

Some revolutionaries based their hopes on the proletariat. The first Russian Marxist was Plekhanov. In 1898 he founded the Social Democratic Party. 'Party' was a grand name. Only nine delegates – none of them workers – were present at the party's launch. Plekhanov was opposed to the use of terror. He accepted Marx's view that proletariat success was inevitable: it was simply a question of waiting for it to happen. Some of his followers were less patient, not least Vladimir Ilyich Ulyanov who, when in hiding, adopted the name Lenin. Son of a prosperous middle-class family, Lenin became a revolutionary while still a student. After being arrested and spending a few years in Siberia, Lenin went into exile in Switzerland and London where he became editor of the Marxist newspaper *Iskra* (the Spark). In 1902 he published a pamphlet *What is to be Done?* He concluded that Russian Marxists should try to 'push' history in the right (i.e. left!) direction. He envisaged that an elite group of well-led revolutionaries (with himself as leader) could do the pushing.

hundreds of people were killed or wounded on Bloody Sunday. Until now, most Russians had blamed Nicholas's ministers for the troubles. Now many blamed Nicholas himself. (Ironically Nicholas had not been in the Palace nor had he ordered the 'massacre'.)

Over the following months, discontent in Russia grew. There were more assassinations, liberals kept up their demands for a parliament, strikes became commonplace, peasants seized land, and in non-Russian areas there were calls for independence. As law and order broke down, Nicholas could not count on the loyalty of the armed forces. His best troops were fighting against Japan. Crews in the Black Sea fleet actually mutinied. In July the SRs set up an 'All Russian Peasant Union'. In October workers' leaders formed councils (or soviets), the most important of which was in St Petersburg, to try to coordinate strike action. Many leading revolutionaries, such as Lenin, were in exile when the disturbances began. The revolution, if that is what it was, occurred in spite of – rather than because of – them.

Russia seemed to be falling apart. However, Nicholas now handled matters with some skill. Dismissing a number of unpopular ministers, he brought back Witte. Witte first made peace with Japan. The Treaty of Portsmouth was far from glorious (Japan won most of the disputed land) but at least loyal troops could now return to deal with the troubles at home. Witte then insisted that Nicholas must agree to set up a parliament. In the 1905 October Manifesto Nicholas reluc-

NICHOLAS II

In 1894 Nicholas II succeeded his father Alexander III. He has usually had a bad press. He is often seen as a weak, indecisive man, very much under the control of his German-born wife – Alexandra. In fairness to Nicholas, he inherited a difficult situation. He tried to do his job conscientiously and did appoint some capable ministers. In some respects he was just unlucky. His bad luck was shown at his coronation when, through no fault of his own, hundreds of people were crushed to death. He was unlucky that his only son Alexis suffered from haemophilia. However, Nicholas brought some of the bad luck on himself. 'I shall defend the principle of autocracy as unswervingly as my deceased father', he said in January 1895. He continued the repressive policies of Alexander III, including Russification measures.

The following description of Nicholas II was written in 1912 by Count Witte, Minister of Finance from 1892 to 1903 and Prime Minister in 1905:

A ruler who cannot be trusted, who approves today what he will reject tomorrow, is incapable of steering the ship of state into a quiet harbour. His outstanding failing is his sad lack of willpower. Though he means well and is not unintelligent, this shortcoming disqualifies him totally as the unlimited autocratic ruler of the Russian people.

Source B

ACTIVITY

Why might Witte's evidence be considered a) reliable b) unreliable?

Nicholas disliked and distrusted Witte, sacking him in 1903 and again in 1905.

tantly agreed to do so. He also granted a host of civil liberties (including the rights of free speech and free assembly). These concessions, while pleasing many of the liberals, did not end the 'revolution'. In November 1905 there was a general strike in St Petersburg and in December an armed uprising in Moscow. What finally brought the troubles to an end was force. In December 1905 the St Petersburg soviet was dispersed and most of its leaders arrested. The Moscow rising was crushed: 500–1,000 people were killed in the fighting. Over the winter of 1905–6 loyal troops brutally restored order in the countryside. The revolution had failed. However, it did bring about one major change. Henceforward Russia would have a parliament, the Duma.

f) Was Russia becoming a Constitutional Monarchy?

Between 1906 and 1914 there were four Dumas. Arguably, however, there was little that amounted to real democracy in Russia.

▼ The Fundamental Laws of May 1906 declared that the Tsar still controlled the armed forces. He had the power to dissolve the Duma and could rule by decree when it was not in session. Moreover he still chose his own ministers.

▼ The Duma was merely the lower house of a two-chamber legislative body. The upper house was mainly appointed by the Tsar.

▼ The first two Dumas, too radical for Nicholas's taste, were quickly dissolved. The Tsar's government now tampered with the electoral laws, essentially disenfranchising peasants and industrial workers. The conservative-dominated third Duma, which met in late 1907, was prepared to work with Peter Stolypin, Nicholas's new chief minister. The fourth Duma, elected in 1912, was even more conservative.

However, while Russia was still an autocracy, it had embarked on the democratic road. After 1907 the Duma had some influence on ministerial decision-making. It exerted its right to question ministers and to discuss state finances. Arguably the Duma had made a promising start which might, given time, have blossomed into a more representative and powerful parliamentary system.

g) Was Russia a Repressive Police State?

Repression continued after 1905. Between 1905–9 over 2,500 people were executed. Trade Unions were harassed and striking workers sometimes shot, for example at the Lena goldfields in 1912. Censorship continued and the Okhrana was still active. Revolutionary leaders like Lenin and Trotsky remained in exile rather than risk imprisonment in Siberia. However, the extent of the repression can be exaggerated. There was surprisingly little censorship. Moreover, left-wing parties could and did contest Duma elections, even though the odds were stacked against them. Tough action against revolutionaries was in response to equally tough action by the revolutionaries. In 1908 alone, some 1,800 police were killed by terrorists. In 1911 Prime Minister Stolypin was assassinated.

h) Land Reforms

Stolypin was determined to create a class of prosperous peasant farmers (*kulaks*) who, he hoped, would support the tsar and be a barrier to future revolution. After 1906 the government encouraged peasants to buy their own land from the *mirs* or from rich landowners. A Land Bank was set up to loan funds to peasants. By 1914 over 30 per cent of peasants had separated from the *mir* and owned their own land. By 1914 revolutionary activity among the peasants seemed to be at a low level. Lenin was not alone among revolutionaries in fearing that the land reforms might achieve their political ends.

However, the impact of the land reforms should not be rated too highly. The relative prosperity of the peasants after 1910 was due to a rise in agricultural prices, not to Stolypin's reform. Most peasants were still tied to the *mir*. Moreover, while some peasants prospered, they did so at the expense of others. Poorer peasants, some of whom became landless labourers, resented the wealth of the *kulaks*. By European standards, most peasants remained dreadfully poor.

i) How Important was Russia's Industrial Development?

Russian industrial development, aided by huge foreign loans, continued after 1905. The country had a trade and budget surplus and the living and working conditions of most workers were improving.

(a)

Russian grain production (millions of tons)*

	Grain
1890	36
1900	56
1910	74
1913	90

*European Russia only

(b)

Foreign investment in Russia (roubles)

1893	2,500,000
1897	80,000,000
1898	130,000,000
1913	2,200,000,000

(c)

Industrial growth rate 1880–1914 (average % per year)

Russia	3.5
Germany	3.75
USA	2.75
UK	1

(d)

Industrial production 1914 (millions of tons)

	Russia	France	Germany	USA	Great Britain	Russian ranking
Coal	36	40	190	517	292	5th
Pig iron	4.6	5.2	16.8	31	10.4	5th
Steel	4.8	4.6	18.3	31.8	7.8	4th

Russia also ranked second in world oil production, fourth in goldmining.

(e)

The growth of Russian railways (in kilometres)

1881	1891	1900	1913
21,228	31,219	53,234	70,156

Table 5 Russia's economic performance.

However, in 1914 Russia was still essentially an agrarian society. While living conditions were improving, most workers were still poor. From 1912 there was growing industrial discontent. The fact that the proletariat was increasing meant that there was more potential for Marxist revolution.

j) Was Russia on the Verge of Revolution in 1914?

It is hard to believe that revolution was imminent in 1914. Lenin was increasingly despondent – and with good reason. The Bolsheviks had only between 5,000 and 10,000 members and the movement was riddled with police informers. SR and Menshevik leaders were similarly despondent. Nicholas II seemed to have recovered his popularity. In 1913 he and his family celebrated the tercentenary of the Romanov family and wherever they went they were greeted with apparent affection. However, while revolution was not the inevitable fate of tsarist Russia, there were still serious social, economic and political problems. 'Of the major governments of Europe none had so little credit with the people it would shortly have to lead in war as that of Nicholas II', says historian Hans Rogger.

ACTIVITIES

Examine Table 5. Answer the following questions:

1. In what way do the statistics suggest that Russia's economy by 1914 was a) strong, and b) weak? **[20 marks]**
2. Why might these statistics not tell the whole truth about Russia's economic performance? **[10 marks]**

▼ Working on The Domestic Scene: 1890–1914

Your reading of the chapter should enable you to come up with answers to the following questions. Note that there are no right or wrong answers. Have the confidence to reach your own conclusion (which should, of course, be based on good evidence).

1. Which of Germany, France, Austria–Hungary and Russia faced the most serious problems in the period 1890–1914? (Russia and Austria–Hungary must surely be in the frame. Were Russia's economic and social problems greater than Austria–Hungary's nationalities problem?)

2. Which country was most successful at dealing with its problems? (Germany and France seem to have been reasonably successful. Can a case be made that Russia and Austria–Hungary faced greater problems which they had gone some way to overcoming?)
3. Which regime was most in danger of collapse in 1914?

Answering Extended Writing and Essay Questions on The Domestic Scene: 1890–1914

Consider the following question: 'By 1914 the collapse of Austria–Hungary was likely if not inevitable'. Do you agree?

Do not worry about the fact that the question is based on a quote. Such questions are often easier to answer than non-quote questions. Do not think that you must automatically agree with the quote. You don't! A good way to approach such a question is to consider the factors that might have made Habsburg collapse likely/inevitable. The nationalities problem was such that Austria and Hungary were already effectively two separate countries. Other nationalities (particularly the Czechs and the South Slavs) were clamouring for home rule. In 1918 the Habsburg Empire did disintegrate. However, arguably Habsburg collapse was not imminent in 1914. Few of the national groups were demanding independence. Had the Czechs or South Slavs caused more trouble, the Empire might well have reformed itself as it had done in 1867. Arguably the Empire collapsed simply because Austria–Hungary lost the First World War (and this was by no means inevitable.) You need to present both sides of the case before summing up and giving your considered answer.

Answering Source-Based Questions on The Domestic Scene: 1890–1914

> Sire – We, working men and inhabitants of St Petersburg, our wives and our children and our helpless old parents, come to You, Sire, to seek for truth, justice and protection. We have been made beggars; we are oppressed; we are near to death ... The moment has come for us when death would be better than the prolongation of our intolerable sufferings. We have stopped work and have told our masters that we shall not start again until they comply with our demands. We ask but little: to reduce the working day to eight hours,

Source C An extract from Gapon's petition in 1905.

to provide a minimum wage of a rouble a day, and to abolish overtime ... Officials have brought the country to complete ruin and involved it in shameful war. We working men have no voice in the way the enormous amounts raised from us in taxes are spent ... Destroy the wall between Yourself and Your people. Give orders that elections to a Constituent Assembly be carried out under conditions of universal, equal and secret suffrage.

Source D Alexandra Kollontai, a female Bolshevik, who marched with the demonstrators and reached the square in front of the Winter Palace.

I noticed that mounted troops stood drawn up in front of the Winter Palace itself, but everyone thought that it did not mean anything in particular. All the workers were peaceful and expectant. They wanted the Tsar or one of his highest, gold-braided ministers to come before the people and take the humble petition ... At first I saw the children who were hit [by rifle fire] and dragged down from the trees ... We heard the clatter of hooves. The Cossacks rode right into the crowd and slashed with their sabres like madmen. A terrible confusion arose.

Source E Nicholas II's diary entry for 22 January 1905.

A painful day! There have been serious disorders in Petersburg because workmen wanted to come up to the Winter Palace. Troops had to open fire in several places in the city; there were many killed and wounded. God, how painful and sad! Mama arrived from town, straight to Mass. I lunched with the others. Went for a walk with Misha. Mama stayed overnight.

Source F A photograph of Bloody Sunday.

Source G German cartoon of 1905 showing the events of Bloody Sunday.

▼ QUESTIONS ON SOURCES

1. According to Source C why were the people marching? **[5 marks]**

2. To what extent is Source D a reliable source? **[5 marks]**

3. What does Source E suggest about Nicholas II's attitude? **[5 marks]**

4. Examine Sources F and G. Who do you think 'made' them and why? **[15 marks]**

5. To what extent do the sources a) agree? b) disagree? **[10 marks]**

6. Using all the sources and your own knowledge explain what happened on 'Bloody Sunday'. **[20 marks]**

Points to note about the questions

Question 1 This is a straightforward comprehension-type question. Everything you need is in the extract.

Question 2 The source seems to be 'primary' in that it was written by someone who was there. Presumably the writer was keen to damn the government. If nothing else it provides evidence of the Bolshevik attitude to Bloody Sunday.

Question 3 It is easy to say that this source indicates that Nicholas was not particularly troubled by the massacre. However, that may not be the case. He does express regret at the occurrences. How much did he usually write in his diary? Is this longer or shorter than his usual comments? Did he normally comment on personal or political events? You would need to read his diaries to answer such questions. But that should not stop you from asking the questions!

Question 4 Photographs are taken and cartoons drawn by someone – and usually for a reason. Think about where the photograph was taken from. Think about the views expressed in the cartoon.

Question 5 Note that while the sources may appear to be disagreeing about the types of troops involved in the massacre, they may all be giving a 'true' perspective.

Question 6 This is the occasion to show what you know about Bloody Sunday. In such questions where you are asked to use your own knowledge, it is a good rule of thumb to assume that half the marks will be awarded for extracting information from the sources and half the marks will be given for extra information.

Further Reading

Books in the Access to History *series*

On France read *France: The Third Republic 1870–1914* by Keith Randell. On Germany start with the relevant chapters in *From Bismarck to Hitler: Germany 1890–1933* by Geoff Layton. For Austria–Hungary and Russia *The Habsburg Empire* by Nick Pelling and *Reaction and Revolutions: Russia 1881–1924* by Michael Lynch both provide excellent introductions.

General

On Europe: 1890–1914, the relevant chapters in the following books are particularly good: *Years of Change: Europe 1890–1945* by Robert Wolfson and John Laver (Hodder & Stoughton) and *Europe 1880–1945* by J.M. Roberts, 1962 (Longman). On France, try *France 1870–1919* by R. Gildea, 1988 (Longman) and *France 1814–1914* by R. Tombs, 1996 (Longman). On Germany try *Imperial Germany: 1871–1918* by S. Lee, 1998 (Routledge) and *Bismarck and the German Empire* by L. Abrahams, 1995 (Routledge). For Austria–Hungary, *The Decline and Fall of the Habsburg Empire 1815–1918* by A. Sked, 1989 and *The Dissolution of the Austro-Hungarian Empire 1867–1918* by J.W. Mason, 1996 (both published by Longman) are essential reading. On Russia, try *Russia in the Age of Modernisation and Revolution 1881–1917* by H. Rogger, 1983 (Longman), *The Origins of the Russian Revolution* by A. Ward, 1993 (Routledge), *The End of Imperial Russia, 1855–1917* by P. Waldron, 1997 (Macmillan) and *The Russian Revolution* by R. Service, 1999 (Macmillan).

THE ORIGINS OF THE FIRST WORLD WAR

CHAPTER 2

POINTS TO CONSIDER

This chapter examines the causes of the First World War. The introduction sets the scene. The first two sections deal with the deep-seated causes of the war. Sections 3 and 4 deal with the medium-term causes while section 5 deals with the events in July/August 1914 which finally sparked off war. Sections 6 and 7 try to apportion responsibility. Proceed slowly, section by section, and by the end you should have your own answer to the key question: who or what was to blame for the outbreak of the First World War?

On 28 June 1914, Archduke Franz Ferdinand, heir to the throne of Austria–Hungary, was assassinated in the Bosnian town of Sarajevo. Within six weeks most of Europe was at war. Since 1914 historians have held many different views about the origins of the war. Some think that such a great event must have had great causes. But others have seen the war as simply an accident, triggered by a series of unfortunate events in July 1914. The question of responsibility for the war continues to divide historians. In 1919 the victorious Allies blamed the war on German aggression. However, British wartime leader, Lloyd George, was soon arguing that no country was wholly to blame for the war. This chapter will try to explain why Franz Ferdinand's murder sparked off war.

ISSUES
Was the First World War an accident or an accident waiting to happen? Which country or countries were most responsible for the war?

The European Powers

Germany
Germany was Europe's strongest power. German power was based on its industrial strength and excellent army.

France
France made a rapid recovery after its defeat in the Franco-Prussian war (1870–1). By 1890 it had a similar sized army to Germany and a navy second only to that of Britain. It also had a large overseas empire. While some French statesmen still

dreamed of recovering Alsace–Lorraine (lost to Germany in 1871), most were more concerned with winning allies to provide some security against Germany.

Russia
Russia's population was twice that of Germany and its army was the largest in Europe. Industrially, however, Russia was weak.

Austria–Hungary
Austria–Hungary's had no great economic strength and was the only European power without an overseas empire.

Britain
Britain considered itself more a world, than a European, power. Her empire was over 20 per cent of the world's land surface and Britain also had the world's strongest navy. Its army, however, was small: it was the only European power that did not have conscription.

Italy
Italy, the weakest of the great powers, had ambitions in Africa and the Mediterranean.

Figure 7 Europe in 1890.

1 Colonial Rivalry

For much of the nineteenth century, European powers had relatively little interest in colonies. In the period 1815–70 only France and Britain were involved in overseas expansion. While Britain annexed large territories, it did so somewhat reluctantly. Many British statesmen regarded colonies as 'millstones round our necks'. However, in the last three decades of the century things changed. European states extended their control over huge parts of Africa and Asia. Almost any territory was considered worthy of annexation. 'Expansion is everything', said British imperialist Cecil Rhodes. 'I would annex the planets if I could.' Between 1870 and 1900 Britain added 4.25 million square miles and 66 million people to her empire; France added 3.5 million square miles and 26 million people; Russia added 0.5 million square miles and 6.5 million people. Germany acquired a new empire of 1 million square miles and 13 million people. Belgium and Italy also acquired territory in Africa.

a) What Caused the 'New Imperialism'?

i) Economic Motivation

As early as 1902 J.A. Hobson, an English radical, argued that the 'disastrous folly' of imperialism was the result of certain interests – armament firms, big business, bankers – promoting the growth of empire for their own selfish ends. The Russian revolutionary Lenin went further, claiming that imperialism arose out of modern capitalism which had become dominated by huge combines. These combines, anxious to invest capital abroad and to control raw materials, supported the acquisition of colonies. Hobson's and Lenin's arguments are not convincing. The export of capital seems to have had little connection with imperial expansion. France, for example, invested less than seven per cent of her foreign capital in her colonies. Lenin's view that European industry was dominated by huge combines also does not square with reality. Britain (which had the largest empire) had few large combines. European combines that did exist did not have much influence over, nor even always support, their countries' imperial policies.

This is not to say there were no economic motives underpinning imperial expansion. In the late nineteenth century, the search for markets became increasingly competitive. Most countries (except Britain) had high tariffs protecting their trade. Britain feared it might be shut out of potential markets if other countries acquired too much of the colonial cake. Interestingly, European countries obtained only a fraction of their raw materials from their colonies and colonial trade was a small part of their total foreign commerce.

THE QUEST FOR SECURITY

Control over an area had its own consequences, not least a desire to control neighbouring districts in the interests of security. Britain, apprehensive of France's colonial ambitions after 1871, took measures to safeguard its own interests. Its concern for the security of the route to India, for example, led it to occupy Egypt. Occupation of Egypt led to a desire to control the Sudan in order to protect Egypt's southern border and the source of the River Nile.

Nevertheless, at the time most assumed there would be future economic advantages in colonies.

ii) Nationalism

Imperialism became closely linked to national prestige. Colonies were seen as status symbols. It was not just governments and the elite who were enthusiastic about colonies. The nationalistic masses applauded and generally backed imperial expansion. The popular press, best-selling authors and song writers all reflected and/or created enthusiasm for empire. Many imperialists were Social Darwinists. They took Charles Darwin's ideas on evolution and applied them to international relations. Countries were in a perpetual struggle for existence: only the strongest and 'fittest' survived. States must increase their empires or be overtaken by others. The following is part of a speech by British Prime Minister, Lord Salisbury, in 1898:

Source A

> You may roughly divide the nations of the world as the living and the dying. On one side you have great countries of enormous power growing in power every year, growing in wealth, growing in dominion, growing in the perfection of their organisation. Railways have given to them the power to concentrate upon any one point the whole military force of their population and to assemble armies of a magnitude and power never dreamed of in the generations that have gone by. Science has placed in the hands of those armies weapons ever growing in their efficacy of destruction ... By the side of these splendid organisations, of which nothing seems to diminish the force and which present rival claims which the future may only be able by a bloody arbitrament to adjust – by the side of these are a number of communities which I can only describe as dying.

iii) Humanitarian Concerns

Many Europeans believed it was the duty of the 'advanced' peoples to bring civilisation to those less fortunate. In terms of pressure groups, missionary societies played as important a role as financial interests. About 40,000 Catholic and 20,000 Protestant missionaries went to Asia and Africa with the aim of Christianising and civilising.

iv) Accident

In the colonial stampede, actions were often simply reactions to particular circumstances – not clearly rationalised policies. The impetus for expansion frequently came from men on the spot, missionaries, soldiers, explorers and businessmen, rather than from political leaders in Europe. The creation of a vast French empire in

West Africa, for example, was largely the work of the French colonial army, often acting contrary to instructions from Paris.

b) The Scramble for Africa

In 1880 only about one tenth of Africa had been annexed by European states. By 1900 only one tenth had not fallen under European rule. European powers staked out claims to territory, usually without much concern for the realities of tribal relationships.

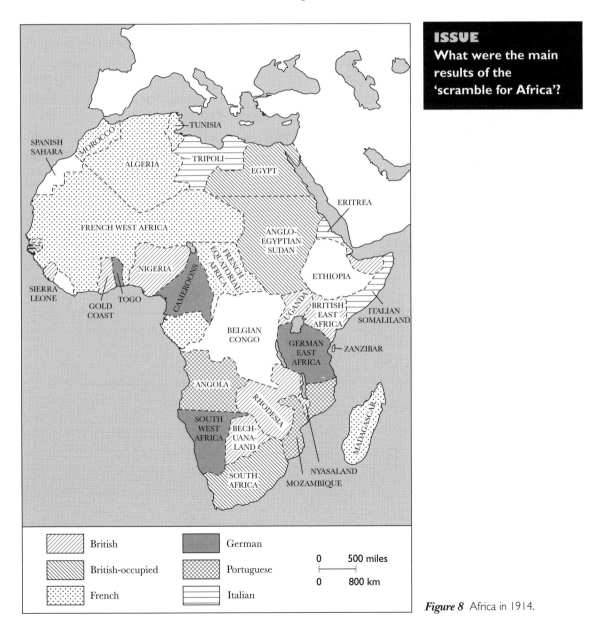

ISSUE
What were the main results of the 'scramble for Africa'?

Figure 8 Africa in 1914.

The main African troublespots in the 1890s

▼ **Anglo-French rivalry in West Africa**. A clash between over-zealous commanders of rival forces was always possible.

▼ **Anglo-French rivalry over the Sudan**. In 1898 there was a confrontation between a French expedition and a much larger British army at Fashoda. The French eventually had to back down and give up all claims to land along the Nile.

▼ **Italian ambitions in Ethiopia**. These ambitions were dashed in 1896 when an Italian army of 25,000 men was defeated at the battle of Adowa.

▼ **The Boer War**. In 1899 Britain went to war against the Boers in Transvaal. The war ended in British victory in 1902.

ISSUE

What were the main results of the 'struggle' for China?

c) The 'Struggle' for China

Between 1895 and 1905 China became the main focus of international rivalry. With a population of over 400 million, China seemed to offer tremendous economic potential. European, American and Japanese businesses competed fiercely for railway contracts and for mining rights. Success in securing economic concessions was seen as a reflection of political influence. The 'struggle for China' thus became a battle for prestige as much as for material gain.

In the case of Japan and Russia, political considerations went beyond mere prestige. Russia, for a variety of economic and strategic reasons, was determined to win control over the Chinese provinces of Manchuria and Korea. Japan also had ambitions in Korea. In the late nineteenth century, Japan had modernised rapidly and by the 1890s possessed a strong army and navy. Her victory in a war against China in 1894–5 had major repercussions. Russia protested that Japan's gains threatened its own interests and Japan was forced to abandon its claims to the Liaotung peninsula. Russia now looked to become China's protector. In return, the Chinese government agreed to allow Russia to build a railway across Manchuria. In 1898 China also granted Russia a 25-year lease on the Liaotung peninsula.

Other European powers also sought to carve out 'spheres of interest'. In 1897 Germany seized Kiaochow. France was most active in the south in areas adjacent to its empire in Indo-China. Britain sought to preserve its long-established position in central China. In 1900 anti-foreigner riots (known as the Boxer Rebellion) swept through China. European rivalry was – temporarily – forgotten and an international force marched on Peking, relieving the besieged embassies and taking harsh reprisals against the rebels. It seemed that China might now be partitioned amongst the powers. However, Britain and

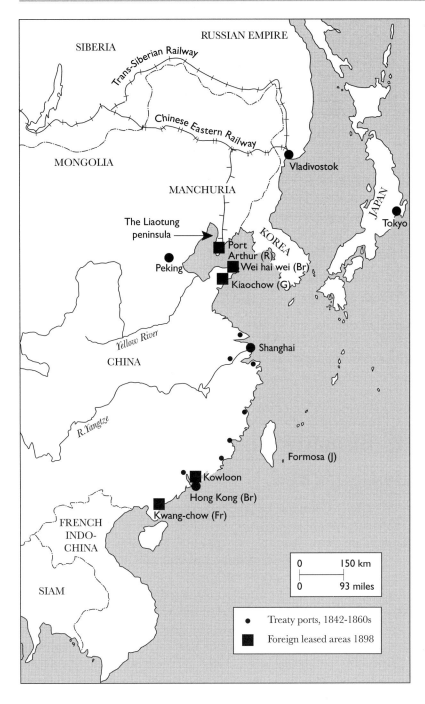

Figure 9 China and the Far East.

the USA were opposed to carving up China, supporting instead an Open Door policy by which all the powers would give up demands for exclusive rights in their spheres of interest.

Russia, still hoping to create a 'special relationship' with China, obtained even more economic concessions in Manchuria in 1900–1.

Japan, concerned at Russian policy, offered Russia a free hand in Manchuria in exchange for a free Japanese hand in Korea. Russia rejected this. When further negotiations proved fruitless, Japan launched a surprise attack on the Russian fleet at Port Arthur in February 1904. This was the start of the Russo-Japanese War. The Japanese quickly occupied Korea and besieged Port Arthur. The town was finally captured in January 1905 and the Japanese went on to defeat the main Russian army at Mukden. In May 1905, the Russian Baltic fleet, which had sailed halfway round the world, was destroyed at the battle of Tsushima. Russia was now forced to make peace, accepting that Korea was a Japanese sphere of influence. The Russo-Japanese war brought to an end the possibility of Russian domination of northern China. After 1905 China's territorial integrity ceased to be of major concern to the great powers.

ACTIVITY

Study Lord Salisbury's speech (Source A). What seems to have been his view of the nature of imperialism?

d) How Serious were the Colonial Rivalries?

Colonial rivalries, on occasions, seriously damaged relations between the European powers. Arguably, however, these rivalries provided a safety valve through which the great powers could let off steam, at a safe distance, without harming each other too much.

ISSUE
What was Bismarck's main legacy in 1890?

2 Bismarck's Legacy

a) Bismarck's Aims

After 1871, Germany dominated Europe. Having created the German Empire, Bismarck's main objective was now its security. He thought the best guarantee was peace. The possibility of a French war of revenge (to recover Alsace-Lorraine) posed an obvious threat to peace. However, France by itself was not a serious danger. Danger would only arise if France managed to ally with either Austria–Hungary or Russia. Then Germany would face the prospect of a war on two fronts. If Austria–Hungary and Russia went to war over their competing interests in the Balkans, France might have the opportunity of allying with either powers. Bismarck, therefore, worked to maintain good relations with Russia and Austria–Hungary and to reduce friction in the Balkans.

b) The Balkan Problem

The Ottoman (or Turkish) Empire was the 'sick man of Europe'. The extensive multi-national empire had been in decline throughout the nineteenth century. The Turkish government's authority in many areas was only nominal – not least in the Balkans. Here, peoples of various races and religions coexisted in a state of mutual animosity. Given that the great powers had conflicting interests, there was no simple solution to the 'Eastern Question': what to do about the Ottoman Empire.

▼ Russia, traditionally anti-Turkish, sought to assist the European areas still under Turkish rule to obtain independence (as Greece, Serbia, and Romania had already done). Many Russians supported **Pan-Slavism**. Russia also sought to profit from Turkey's weakness. In particular, it hoped to win control of the Straits, ensuring free passage for its ships from the Black Sea through to the Mediterranean.

▼ Austria–Hungary, while not averse to profiting from Turkish weakness, was opposed to the expansion of Russian power in the Balkans. It was also suspicious of Slav nationalism, a threat to its own multi–national empire.

▼ Greece, Bulgaria and Serbia longed to annex Turkish territory but lacked the military strength to do so. Their competing ambitions made it hard for them to ally.

> ### PAN-SLAVISM
> This was a movement which extolled the virtues of the Slav race and the Orthodox Church. Pan-Slavists thought Russia's historic mission was to protect and liberate the Slav people in the Balkans.

c) Bismarck's Policies

In 1872–3 Bismarck supported the creation of the Three Emperors' League (or *Dreikaiserbund*) of Germany, Russia and Austria–Hungary. The Balkan crisis of 1875–8 made it difficult for Bismarck to maintain good relations with both Austria–Hungary and Russia. He chose to work more closely with Austria–Hungary. By the terms of the 1879 Dual Alliance, Austria–Hungary and Germany promised to give each other full support if either were attacked by Russia. The treaty created a sort of 'Germanic' bloc in Europe. However, Bismarck did not view the alliance as necessarily anti-Russian. Indeed, he hoped that a more secure Austria–Hungary might be more prepared to cooperate with Russia. He also thought that the Dual Alliance might frighten Russia into improving relations with Germany. This calculation proved correct. In 1881 Germany, Russia and Austria–Hungary signed a new *Dreikaiserbund*, agreeing that each country could count on the neutrality of its partners if it was at war with another power. In 1882 Italy joined Germany and Austria–Hungary in the Triple Alliance.

So secure was Germany's position in the mid-1880s that Bismarck was able to indulge in the luxury of colonial ventures, which he had previously opposed. As a result, Germany acquired an African empire comprising South West Africa, Togoland, the Cameroons and East Africa. Bismarck's first concern, however, was German security in Europe. In 1890 he asserted that a good understanding with Britain was more important than the whole of East Africa.

Another crisis in the Balkans in 1887 threatened Bismarck's alliance system. Fearing that Russia might ally with France, Bismarck secured a secret Russo-German alliance – the so-called Reinsurance Treaty. Wilhelm II, who came to power in 1888, questioned the need for the Reinsurance Treaty and disagreements over its renewal led to Bismarck's resignation in 1890.

d) Conclusion

Opinions are still divided about Bismarck's achievements in foreign policy. His critics claim that his success was limited. Although he had kept France isolated, it remained embittered. By 1890 his elaborate alliance system appeared to be fragile. Arguably the Reinsurance Treaty was both contradictory and dangerous. The Dual Alliance, far from being a mechanism by which Germany could control Austria–Hungary, limited Germany's diplomatic options, eventually dragging it into war in 1914. Bismarck's African adventures also had undesirable long-term results, whetting the German public's appetite for colonies and worsening relations with Britain. Bismarck can thus be seen as bequeathing serious problems to his successors.

However, Bismarck's admirers make a stronger case. They approve of his aims and claim that he achieved most of them. He managed to cooperate with both Austria–Hungary and Russia and was generally on good terms with Britain. Given astute handling, his 'system' was workable. Russia, for example, was eager to renew the Reinsurance Treaty in 1890. Under Bismarck, Germany enjoyed security and Europe was blessed with twenty years of peace. His successors threw away his legacy. Unlike him, they failed to control both their own (and Austrian) ambitions. It is unfair to blame Bismarck for their failure.

BISMARCK'S FOREIGN POLICY: 1871–90

1871 creation of the German Empire;
1879 the Dual Alliance;
1882 the Triple Alliance;
1887 the Reinsurance Treaty;
1890 Bismarck resigned.

ACTIVITY

To test your understanding, consider the following question: 'How successful was Bismarck's foreign policy in the period 1871–90?'

Suggested lines of response:
▼ What were Bismarck's main aims? Were these aims rational?
▼ What did he do to try to achieve his aims?
▼ How successful was he in achieving his aims?

3 European Relations: 1890–1907

ISSUE
What impact did Germany have on international relations post-1890?

a) Germany's 'New Course'

The 'New Course' which Bismarck's successor Caprivi pursued 1890–94 was intended to simplify German policy by eliminating the complex commitments contained within the Bismarckian system. The most crucial decision – to reject Russia's proposal to renew the Reinsurance Treaty – was taken on the grounds that it was incompatible with Germany's commitment to Austria–Hungary and that it would anger Britain, whom Germany hoped to persuade to join the Triple Alliance. In 1890 an Anglo-German agreement was reached by which Germany gained Heligoland (an island in the North Sea) in return for giving up rights in Zanzibar and East Africa. Russia and France, fearing that a secret Anglo-German alliance existed, felt even more isolated. This fear gradually drew them together. The process was slow and was certainly not inevitable, if only because Tsar Alexander III was reluctant to ally with republican France.

b) The Franco-Russian Alliance

The initiative for a Franco–Russian alliance came from France. French financial assistance helped smooth relations and in 1891 serious negotiations began. A major difficulty was that France wanted a specific alliance directed against Germany while Russia wanted a general agreement directed against Britain. Eventually two separate agreements were made. The 1891 political agreement was anti-British in intent, aligning France with Russia in imperial disputes. In the 1892 military convention, France and Russia promised mutual support if either were attacked by Germany. France had at last broken out of the quarantine imposed on her by Bismarck, and Germany now faced the prospect of a war on two fronts.

c) Anglo-German relations: 1890–6

At the time the German government did not regard the Franco-Russian alliance as particularly dangerous. Indeed it hoped that the alliance might force Britain to join the Triple Alliance. The prospects of an alliance seemed good. Britain, generally anti-French and anti-Russian, felt somewhat isolated. However, fearing being drawn into a European war in defence of German interests, Britain wanted German friendship – not a full-blown alliance. Having failed to secure a British alliance, German leaders resorted to pressure and coercion. This was a mistake. The bullying tone of German

THE JAMESON RAID
In December 1895 Dr Jameson, administrator for the British South Africa Company, led a force of 470 men from Bechuanaland into Transvaal, intending to overthrow the Boer government. The raid was a total failure. Cecil Rhodes, Prime Minister of Cape Colony, was forced to resign because of his connivance at the escapade.

diplomacy simply irritated British statemen. So too did German policy, especially when Germany began to interfere in imperial matters. The culmination of this type of diplomacy was the Kruger Telegram in January 1896, following the **Jameson Raid**. Wilhelm's telegram to Kruger, the Boer president, supporting Transvaal's independence, was seen as a gross interference in British imperial affairs. By 1896 Anglo-German relations had deteriorated badly.

d) Weltpolitik

ISSUE
What were the main aims of *Weltpolitik*?

In 1896 Wilhelm II proclaimed that 'Nothing must henceforth be settled in the world without the intervention of Germany and the German Emperor'. This is often seen as the start of a new 'world policy' (*Weltpolitik*) which was, by intent, a rejection of Bismarck's 'continental policy'. The emphasis was now on overseas expansion. Bülow, the new German foreign minister, declared in 1897: 'We don't want to put anyone else in the shade, but we too demand a place in the sun'. Wilhelm desperately wanted Germany to be a world power like Britain. Many Germans agreed with him. By the late 1890s there were three powerful organisations devoted to the promo-

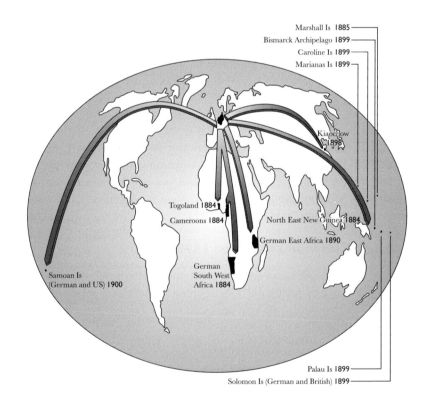

Figure 10 Weltpolitik: *German overseas expansion.*

tion of German world power – the Pan-German League, the German Colonial League, and the Navy League.

German historian Fritz Fischer claimed that there was a sort of masterplan to *Weltpolitik*. He detected three main elements in it: one was the navy which would demonstrate Germany's status as a world power, thereby rallying popular support behind the Kaiser; the second was the plan for a great Central African empire comprising the Congo and the Portuguese colonies of Angola and Mozambique; and the third was the scheme for a German-dominated central European economic zone comprising Austria–Hungary, the Balkan states, and the Ottoman Empire. Related to this scheme was the plan to link the whole area together by a railway from Berlin to Baghdad.

However, Fischer's critics think that behind the pursuit of *Weltpolitik* there lay no more than a vague longing to be a world power. Bülow's basic aim seems to have been to impress both public opinion and the Kaiser by a few cheap successes, in which appearances counted for more than realities. Thus, German foreign policy after 1897 was largely an opportunist 'public relations' exercise.

Contemporary observers tended to attribute the vagaries of German diplomacy to the Kaiser. In this they were partly correct. Wilhelm was a complex character whose moods were liable to change very rapidly. (This changeability was very evident in his love–hate relationship with Britain.) However, while the Kaiser did have considerable powers, he did not devote himself solely to foreign policy. Foreign ministers had much more day-to-day control of affairs. Thus, Wilhelm was not the only one to blame for the lack of clear aims in German diplomacy.

> ### THE GERMAN NAVY
> If Germany was to be a great world power, Wilhelm believed it needed a great navy. Thus, in 1898 and 1900, Germany passed two Navy Laws designed to create a powerful battle fleet. This fleet was to be used as 'the lever of *Weltpolitik*'. If Germany could 'influence' (i.e. threaten) Britain, it could influence the entire world.

e) British Policy: 1898–1902

German imperial ambitions and the creation of a big German navy were bound to be seen as challenges by Britain. For Germany, a fleet was a luxury: for Britain it was essential. Determined to maintain its naval supremacy, Britain commenced a major ship-building programme. The German naval threat inevitably increased suspicion and worsened relations between Britain and Germany. British and German public opinion, influenced by and influencing, the popular press, echoed government feeling and became a significant factor in Anglo-German relations. In Germany, Anglophobia probably reached its height during the Boer War. By 1902 the British public had become increasingly anti-German.

Disappointed with Germany, Britain turned to Japan to help check Russian ambitions in China. The 1902 Anglo-Japanese alliance seemed to mark the end of a British policy of avoiding 'entangling alliances' in peace time. Nevertheless, Britain was still isolated from

THE BOER WAR

From 1899 to 1902 Britain was at war with the Boers of the South African republics of Transvaal and Orange Free State. 300,000 British troops eventually defeated 60,000 Boers. Most of Europe sympathised with the Boer underdogs. There was even talk of a Continental League against Britain. Suddenly Britain's 'splendid isolation' seemed less than splendid. In these circumstances, Colonial Secretary Joseph Chamberlain proposed an Anglo-German alliance. Chamberlain's attempts to secure an alliance failed. Britain would still not join the Triple Alliance (Germany's objective). Germany would not join an anti-Russian alliance (Britain's objective).

its continental rivals. Indeed, with the Japanese alliance in the bag it seemed Britain could stay safely aloof of European ties.

f) The Anglo-French Entente

The Anglo-Japanese alliance, however, acted as a catalyst for improved Anglo-French relations. Given the mounting tension between Russia and Japan, both Britain and France feared they might be drawn into this conflict as allies of the main protagonists. An agreement of some kind thus seemed necessary. This came in April 1904 when both countries settled most of their outstanding colonial problems. In return for France accepting British supremacy in Egypt, Britain accepted that Morocco was a French sphere of influence. The *entente* was not an alliance: no enemy was singled out and no joint action was planned. However, the *entente* did indicate a mutual desire to end past friction and a willingness to cooperate in the future. Although not anti-German in intent, the *entente* had serious implications for Germany.

g) The First Moroccan Crisis, 1905–6

German ministers were prepared to provoke a crisis over France's hope of making Morocco a French sphere of influence. In March 1905 Wilhelm II landed at the Moroccan port of Tangier and dramatically declared his intention of upholding Morocco's independence. In April the German government demanded an international conference to review the question of Morocco. German policy was operating on two levels. On the surface the Germans were demanding 'fair shares for all' and the right to be consulted about Morocco's fate. But their hidden aim was to weaken, if not destroy, the Anglo-French *entente*. This was to be achieved by demonstrating that Britain was not a reliable or worthwhile ally. France, it was assumed, would be outvoted at the international conference since other nations would prefer the principle of 'open door' to French predominance in Morocco. France would be so humiliated that its leaders would recognise that cooperation with Germany, not Britain, was essential. To accomplish this, it was necessary to keep up tension until the French government gave in to German demands. This aggressive policy was pursued through the summer of 1905, backed by the unspoken threat of war.

The French Cabinet accepted German demands for a conference that would meet in 1906 at Algeciras. Germany had thus won a diplomatic victory. However, the Algeciras Conference itself was far from a triumph. Britain, as it had done throughout the crisis, backed France. Only Austria–Hungary supported Germany and France secured a strong position in Morocco, effectively controlling both the economy and the police. Algeciras was thus a severe blow to German prestige. Moreover, far from weakening the Anglo-French *entente*, the Morocco crisis strengthened it. Friendship with France became a basic principle of Britain's new Liberal government. In 1906 Sir Edward Grey, the Foreign Secretary, authorised 'military conversations' to consider how Britain might aid France if it was attacked by Germany.

h) The Triple Entente

Grey, convinced that Germany was a potential threat, determined to improve relations with Russia. Negotiations for an Anglo-Russian agreement began in 1906. They covered three disputed regions: Persia, Tibet and Afghanistan. Agreement was reached in 1907. Persia was divided into three zones: a northern Russian zone; a southern British zone; and a neutral zone separating the two. Both countries agreed not to meddle to the disadvantage of the other in the internal affairs of Tibet and Afghanistan. Although Russia cheated persistently on the Persian agreement, Grey strove hard to maintain good relations. This was a sign that Europe, not the Empire, was now the focal point of British policy.

i) The Situation in 1907

By 1907, Europe was divided into two blocs. This meant that Germany was far less secure than it had been in 1890. German policy-makers were largely to blame for this state of affairs. Between 1897 and 1907 Bülow and the Kaiser had conducted an ill-judged and often provocative policy. *Weltpolitik* had added little (except a few Pacific islands) to Germany's overseas empire. The construction of a large fleet had alienated Britain. By 1907 Germany's only firm ally was Austria–Hungary. Although the Triple Alliance was regularly renewed, Germany had little faith in Italy – with good cause. In 1902 Italy and France had reached an agreement whereby each assured the other of neutrality if either were attacked.

**THE MAIN EVENTS:
1890–1907**

1894 Franco-Russian Alliance;
1898 first German Navy Law;
1899
–1902 Boer War;
1904 Anglo-French Entente;
1905 first Moroccan Crisis;
1906 Algeciras Conference;
1907 Triple Entente.

ACTIVITY

To test your understanding consider the following question: 'How successful was German foreign policy in the period 1890–1907?'

Suggested line of response:
▼ What were Germany's aims after 1890? Were the aims rational?
▼ How did Germany set about realising its aims?
▼ To what extent had Germany achieved its aims by 1907?

ISSUE

How serious were the
tensions between the
main European powers
1908–13?

4 Increasing Tension, 1908–13

a) The 1908 Bosnian Crisis

An agreement between Austria–Hungary and Russia in 1897 helped lessen tension in the Balkans for over ten years. However, the situation in Serbia was a major concern for Austria–Hungary. Many Serbian politicians dreamed of uniting all Serbs in a Greater Serbia. Since there were twice as many Serbs in the Habsburg Empire and in Bosnia-Herzegovina (a province still in theory Turkish, but administered by Austria–Hungary since 1878) as there were in Serbia itself, Serbian ambitions could only be realised at Austria–Hungary's expense. In 1903 the pro-Austrian Serbian dynasty was overthrown and replaced by a pro-Russian regime. Austria–Hungary tried to bring economic pressure to bear on Serbia, worsening relations between the two states.

Meanwhile, Russia, after failure in the Far East, turned its attention back to the Balkans. It was particularly keen to ensure that its

Figure 11 The Balkans in 1900 and 1914.

warships had access from the Black Sea to the Mediterranean via the Straits. In September 1908 Izvolsky, the Russian foreign minister, met Aehrenthal, the Austro-Hungarian foreign minister. Aehrenthal was receptive to the idea of a 'deal' with Russia since he hoped to annex Bosnia-Herzegovina. A new regime, **the Young Turks**, had just come to power in Turkey. Restoring Bosnia-Herzegovina to full Turkish rule was one of the Young Turks' objectives. Austrian annexation of the provinces would prevent this and also end Serbia's hopes of winning them. In return for Austrian support on the Straits' issue, Izvolsky agreed to Austria's annexation of Bosnia.

When Austria–Hungary jumped the gun and announced the annexation of Bosnia in October 1908 the Russian government denied any knowledge of Izvolsky's 'deal' and instructed him to support Serbia and oppose Austria–Hungary's action. Izvolsky, claiming that he had been tricked by Aehrenthal, called for an international conference to discuss the situation. Austria–Hungary rejected this call. Tension mounted when Turkey demanded compensation and Serbia threatened war. In January 1909 Germany promised Austria–Hungary full support. Tension continued until March 1909 when Russia reluctantly recognised the annexation of Bosnia. Its hopes of securing free passage through the Straits came to nothing and it was left humiliated and angry.

b) Anglo-German Naval Rivalry

In 1906 Britain launched *Dreadnought,* a new battleship superior to everything else afloat in terms of speed, firepower and strength. Germany soon had its own *Dreadnought* programme and Britain's massive naval supremacy seemingly no longer counted. Britain now had to reconstruct its lead from scratch. In 1908 the Liberal government, after proposing to reduce naval expenditure was forced to yield to public pressure and accept the demand for eight new battleships. Attempts to reach agreement with Germany on reducing naval building failed. Thus the expensive naval race continued, seriously damaging Anglo-German relations.

c) The Second Moroccan Crisis, 1911

In May 1911 French troops occupied the Moroccan capital, Fez, following the outbreak of a revolt. A French takeover of Morocco, which would contravene the 1906 Algeciras agreement, seemed imminent. In July 1911 a German gunboat, the *Panther,* arrived at the Moroccan port of Agadir, ostensibly to protect German lives and property. Its real aim was to 'persuade' France to give Germany territorial compensation in return for German recognition of a French

---

THE YOUNG TURKS
This was a party within the Ottoman Empire. Its leaders hoped to reform, modernise and strengthen the Empire.

THE RESULTS OF THE 1908–9 CRISIS
▼ Serbia had no option but to back down and recognise Bosnia's annexation. Although the Serbian government promised to be a good neighbour, secret organisations linked Serbian patriots in Bosnia with nationalists in Serbia.
▼ The fact that Germany had given full backing to Austria–Hungary ensured that relations between Germany and Russia deteriorated rapidly. By 1909 Bismarck must have been turning in his grave. Germany had not prompted the Bosnian crisis but felt it had no alternative but to support its only ally: it now seemed that the Austrian tail was wagging the German dog.

protectorate over Morocco. The German foreign minister Kiderlen hoped to pull off 'a great stroke', winning both a prestige victory for Germany and also French goodwill.

The French government was conciliatory: it hoped to improve relations with Germany and was prepared to pay what it considered a fair price for Germany's goodwill. Kiderlen's demand for the whole of the French Congo, however, made an amicable settlement impossible. His main miscalculation, however, was in ignoring Britain. Worried that German power was being used to blackmail France, Britain was not prepared to ignore the *Panther* incident. In late July, Lloyd George, a powerful Cabinet member, hitherto noted for his pro-German sentiments, declared that Britain was ready to support France to the hilt. The British fleet was put on alert and war between Britain and Germany seemed a possibility. The crisis soon ended. A Franco-German accord was signed in November by which Germany obtained two meagre strips of territory in the French Congo. Kiderlen's heavy-handed methods had resulted in limited German gains and only at the price of increasing tension.

d) The Balkan Wars

In 1911 Italy, in pursuit of its ambitions in Tripoli (modern Libya), went to war with Turkey. Italian success encouraged the expansionist ambitions of the small Balkan states. In the spring of 1912 Serbia allied with Bulgaria. Greece and Montenegro joined the alliance (called the Balkan League) in the autumn. The Balkan League states had virtually nothing in common except a desire to drive the Turks out of Macedonia and divide the spoil amongst themselves. In October 1912 the Balkan League went to war against Turkey. The Turks were quickly defeated and driven out of Europe (except Constantinople). An armistice was signed in December 1912. The peace treaty had only just been signed (in London in May 1913) when Bulgaria, angry at being cheated out of some of its gains, attacked Serbia. Greece, Romania and Turkey now joined the Second Balkan War on Serbia's side. Bulgaria was swiftly defeated and forced to surrender most of its gains from the First Balkan War.

The main results of the Balkan Wars

▽ Although it managed to keep a toehold in Europe, Turkey had lost the bulk of its European territory. Facing the prospect of attack from Greece and Bulgaria, it looked for a strong protector and found one in Germany. After 1913 German advisers wielded considerable influence in Turkey.

▽ Bulgaria was left weakened and resentful.

▼ The Balkan Wars had been an unexpected and dangerous crisis for the great powers. They had tried to defuse the crisis by influencing the peace settlement. The main source of great power tension was Austria–Hungary's determination to create an independent Albania to prevent Serbia acquiring an outlet on the Adriatic. By threatening war, Austria–Hungary achieved its aim.

▼ By 1913 Serbia had doubled its population and was nearer realising its aim of creating a Greater Serbia.

▼ Many Austro-Hungarian leaders thought it was essential to 'smash' Serbia if the Habsburg Empire was to survive.

e) The Arms Race

In 1912, Germany embarked on a more ambitious naval programme and the Reichstag also agreed to increase the German army by more than 30 per cent with plans for further increases. Not surprisingly this provoked the *entente* powers into reviewing their own military strength. In 1913 France extended military conscription from two to three years. Russia also embarked on an ambitious army expansion programme.

MAIN EVENTS:
1908–13

1908	Bosnian Crisis;
1911	Second Moroccan Crisis;
1912	First Balkan War;
1913	Second Balkan War.

ACTIVITY

Consider the following question: 'Why were events in the Balkans so threatening in the period 1908–13?'

Suggested line of response:
▼ Stress that there were two power blocs in Europe.
▼ Stress that the great powers had conflicting aims in the Balkans.
▼ Examine the 1908 crisis.
▼ Examine the Balkan wars of 1912–13.

5 The July Crisis

a) The Sarajevo Assassination

Few people in early 1914 envisaged the outbreak of a major war. The Balkan Wars had passed without triggering great power conflict. Then, on 28 June Archduke Franz Ferdinand, heir to the Austro-Hungarian throne, visited Sarajevo in Bosnia. The trip was ill-con-

ISSUE
Why did the assassination of Franz Ferdinand lead to war?

ceived. Serb terrorists, who had known months in advance of the visit, had plenty of time to make assassination plans. On 28 June there were at least half a dozen Bosnian terrorists in Sarajevo hoping for an opportunity to kill Franz Ferdinand. The first assassination attempt – a bomb attack on the Archduke's car – failed. However, a wrong turning by the royal chauffeur resulted in Gavrilo Princip being in a position (through sheer chance) to shoot Franz Ferdinand and his wife.

The assassination shocked Europe. A showdown between Austria–Hungary and Serbia now seemed inevitable. Although Princip was Bosnian and therefore an Austrian subject, it was suspected that he and the other terrorists had received both their weapons and encouragement from Serbia. The assassination thus provided Austria–Hungary with a perfect excuse for military action against Serbia. Hotzendorf, chief of the Austrian general staff, Count Berchtold, the foreign minister and Emperor Franz Joseph all agreed that Austria–Hungary's prestige (and perhaps survival) demanded that severe reprisals be taken against Serbia – even if this meant risking war with Russia.

b) The 'Blank Cheque'

On 5–6 July both the Kaiser and his Chancellor, Bethmann-Hollweg, promised full German support for Austria–Hungary in whatever measures it took against Serbia. This was the so-called 'blank cheque'. Indeed Wilhelm and Bethmann-Hollweg went further: both recommended immediate action against Serbia. They assumed that Nicholas II would not support the assassination of a senior member of a fellow royal family. The German government, hoping to achieve a great diplomatic victory, was thus prepared to risk – although it did not expect – a general European war. Despite being urged by Germany to 'act at once', Austria–Hungary did nothing. Indeed, for three weeks there was little indication that Europe was moving towards a major crisis. The Kaiser departed for a yachting holiday. There was no frantic planning for war in Germany. Nor was there any alarm in Britain, France or Russia. Indeed, there was no real crisis until 23 July.

c) The Ultimatum

The ultimatum, presented by Austria–Hungary to Serbia on 23 July, shocked several foreign ministers by its severity. The ten demands (which Austria–Hungary was certain Serbia would not accept) had to be accepted in their entirety within a 48-hour time limit. The Serbian government's cleverly worded reply on 25 July seemed conciliatory –

Why did it take Austria–Hungary so long to act?

▽ Austria–Hungary had hoped to find clear evidence that the Serbian government was involved in the assassination. It failed to find such evidence. Ironically, the complicity of Serb officials, if not the Serbian government, is undeniable. Colonel Dimitrijevic, the Serbian military intelligence chief, was aware of the assassination plan (but did not expect it to succeed!). Serbian officials also allowed the – armed – assassins to cross into Bosnia. However, Serbian Prime Minister Pasic was not implicated in the murder. Indeed, there was bitter enmity between himself and Dimitrijevic.

▽ Not until 16 July did the Austrians persuade Hungarian ministers of the need for military action.

▽ A state visit to Russia by French President Poincaré and French Prime Minister Viviani was scheduled to take place between 20 and 23 July. Austria–Hungary did not want to give Russian and French leaders the opportunity to plan together. Not until Poincaré and Viviani were safely embarked on board ship for their return journey to France did the Habsburg government act.

even to Wilhelm II. However, the Serbs rejected the key demand – to let Habsburg officials into Serbia to participate in an enquiry into Franz Ferdinand's death. Boosted by assurances of Russian support, Serbia's government was prepared to risk, and indeed expected, war. Since Serbia had not unconditionally accepted the ultimatum, Austria–Hungary immediately severed diplomatic relations and ordered the mobilisation of most of its army.

d) The Worsening Crisis

On 24–25 July Russia announced that it would support Serbia. This was crucial. Sazonov, the Russian Foreign Minister, interpreted the Austrian ultimatum as a deliberate provocation. A fellow Slav state was apparently being threatened by the 'Germanic' powers. Russian prestige in the Balkans was at stake: if Serbia was abandoned, Russia's position in the Balkans would 'collapse utterly'. Determined to stand firm, the Russian government agreed to begin extensive military measures. Sir Edward Grey, realising the seriousness of the situation, sent a series of desperate appeals to Berlin on 27 July, hoping to secure German support for an international conference to try to resolve the crisis. Germany and Austria–Hungary rejected these appeals: Austria had no faith in great power conferences and no intention of allowing Britain to mediate. On 28 July Austria–Hungary declared war on Serbia and the next day her gunboats bombarded Belgrade.

Both the Kaiser (who had just returned from his cruise) and Bethmann-Hollweg now showed signs of having second thoughts. On 29–30 July Bethmann-Hollweg made some short-lived efforts to restrain Austria–Hungary. But events were now moving too fast for statesmen to control them. Military leaders began taking over the decision-making.

On 28 July Russia ordered partial mobilisation to deter Austria–Hungary. The Russian general staff, aware that partial mobilisation would hamper the effectiveness of a general mobilisation should this become necessary, pressed for full mobilisation. Russia's leadership, still hoping to avert war with Germany, hesitated. Nicholas II sent a telegram to Wilhelm on 29 July appealing for his help in avoiding war. While Wilhelm's reply was friendly, the German ambassador made it clear that any Russian mobilisation, however partial, would provoke German mobilisation. On 29–30 July Nicholas and his ministers debated whether to order a full or partial mobilisation. There was really no debate. One of the main aims of

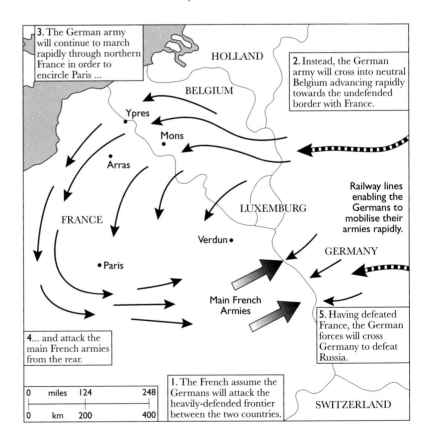

Figure 12 The Schlieffen Plan.

partial mobilisation had been to appease Germany. Now that Germany had refused to be appeased, the alternatives were full mobilisation or nothing. On 30 July Nicholas II, with French support, agreed to full mobilisation. Neither Russia nor France fully appreciated that this decision made war inevitable. They still hoped that Germany and Austria–Hungary might be prepared to negotiate a settlement. German military plans scuttled these hopes.

Amazingly Germany had only one plan to deal with a major war. This plan had been devised by Schlieffen, Chief of the General Staff, 1891–1908. As a solution to the problem of fighting a two fronts war, Schlieffen had planned a massive opening assault on France (via Belgium) with only a holding action on the eastern front. His plan sought to capitalise on Russia's slowness in mobilising. By the time the Russian army was ready to move, the Germans hoped to have defeated France so that troops could be transferred eastwards. If Russia was allowed to mobilise, the success of the Schlieffen plan was endangered.

e) War!

Germany now demanded that Russia cease all military activities aimed against Germany and Austria–Hungary within 12 hours. In the absence of a reply, Germany declared war on Russia on 1 August and began to mobilise her troops. France was asked for a promise of neutrality. When no such promise was received, Germany declared war on France on 3 August. Meanwhile, on 2 August, the German government demanded free passage for its troops through Belgium. The Belgian government refused Germany's 'request'. German troops therefore invaded Belgium. The violation of Belgium's neutrality (guaranteed by the great powers in 1839) had a major impact on Britain. While Grey and Prime Minister Asquith wanted Britain to support France, at least half the cabinet were opposed to intervention. However, virtually all the cabinet agreed that Britain should fight to defend Belgium. The 'left' were concerned about upholding small countries and international law. The 'right' appreciated that Belgium was strategically important. For centuries, it had been a prime objective of British policy to ensure that no strong power controlled the Low Countries. Britain now demanded the withdrawal of German troops from Belgium. When this ultimatum was disregarded, Britain declared war on Germany on 4 August.

Not until 6 August did Austria–Hungary declare war on Russia and not until 12 August did Britain and France declare war on Austria–Hungary. By then, all the great powers of Europe, save Italy, were at war. (Italy, fearful of the British fleet, found good excuses for not honouring her Triple Alliance commitments.) Everyone

MAIN EVENTS: SUMMER 1914

28 June assassination of Franz Ferdinand;
5–6 July German 'blank cheque' to Austria–Hungary;
23 July Austro-Hungarian ultimatum to Serbia;
28 July Austria–Hungary declared war on Serbia;
1 Aug Germany declared war on Russia;
3 Aug Germany declared war on France;
4 Aug Britain declared war on Germany.

expected that the war would be short. The German Crown Prince looked forward to a 'bright and jolly war'.

ISSUES
Did Germany will the war? Were other countries more or equally to blame?

6 Which Country Was Most to Blame for the First World War?

a) German Responsibility

In 1919 Germany was forced to accept Article 231 of the Versailles Treaty (the so-called War Guilt clause):

Source B

> The Allied and Associated Governments affirm and Germany accepts the responsibility of Germany and her allies for causing all the loss and damage to which the Allied and Associated Governments and their nationals have been subjected as a consequence of the war imposed upon them by the aggression of Germany and her allies.

After 1919 most Germans argued that this was unfair. German historians generally concluded that no single power was responsible for the war. However, in the 1960s German historian Fritz Fischer stirred up a hornet's nest when he blamed Germany for starting the war.

Fischer's main claims:
▼ Fearing the success of socialism in Germany, the traditional ruling classes pursued a prestige policy on a world scale. Their aim was to distract opinion from domestic tensions and to rally people behind the established order.
▼ Germany pre-1914 had expansionist aims not dissimilar to those of Hitler.
▼ A War Council in December 1912 determined that Germany should launch an expansionist war at the first favourable opportunity.
▼ Germany hoped and expected that war would result from its backing of Austria–Hungary in July 1914.

Criticisms of Fischer's thesis:
▼ Both Bülow and Bethmann-Hollweg explicitly dismissed war as a solution to the internal socialist problem.
▼ Germany did not pursue a coherent policy in the years before 1914.
▼ The German government did not decide on war in December 1912. The War Council was an irregular one, at which the Chancellor was not present.

▽ Germany made no concerted preparations for war after 1912. She gave surprisingly little support to Austria–Hungary in 1912–13.

▽ By focusing only on Germany, Fischer distorts the picture of the diplomatic situation in July 1914. Policy-making in other countries was equally important.

However, even if Fischer's thesis is rejected, it is still possible to hold Germany responsible for the war.

▽ Germany's aggressive policies increased tension and soured international relations after 1897, frightening France, Russia and Britain into a defensive alignment.

▽ Germany encouraged Austria to take a tough line in July 1914.

▽ In 1914 some German military leaders favoured a preventive war.

▽ As a result of the Schlieffen Plan, German mobilisation meant war.

▽ By invading Belgium, Germany brought Britain into the war.

b) Austrian Responsibility

▽ The Habsburg government exaggerated the Serbian threat. Serbia had only a tenth of Austria–Hungary's population. It had suffered heavy casualties in the Balkan Wars and both its army and finances were in a terrible state.

▽ Austrian leaders pursued a belligerent policy. In 1913–14 the Austrian chief of staff Hotzendorf urged war against Serbia.

▽ Austria–Hungary sought to benefit from the Sarajevo murder. It needed little prompting from Germany.

▽ Austria–Hungary contributed to the crisis by the delay between the Sarajevo murder and the ultimatum to Serbia. A rapid strike against Serbia might have averted war.

▽ Austria–Hungary was the first power to resort to force.

c) Russian Responsibility

▽ Russia was unable (and perhaps unwilling) to restrain or control Serb/Slav nationalism.

▽ Russia's promise of support influenced Serbia's decision to reject the Austrian ultimatum.

▽ Russia's decision to mobilise had terrible consequences.

d) French Responsibility

It is hard to blame France for the outbreak of war. By 1890 agitation to win back Alsace-Lorraine had subsided and thereafter France showed no desire for a war of revenge. While France did promise Russia support in 1914 (a sort of French 'blank cheque'), it did not encourage Russia to fight. The French president and prime minister were both literally at sea from 23 to 29 July and played a minor role in events.

e) British Responsibility

Grey has been blamed for not doing more to work for peace. But it is difficult to see what more he could have done. The view that he might have restrained German action by making it clear that Britain would support France is a red herring. German leaders expected – and were not too concerned about – British intervention! The British Expeditionary Force was only 150,000 strong (half the size of the Belgian army) and seemed unlikely to disrupt the Schlieffen Plan.

f) Serbian Responsibility

▼ Serbia's aggressive expansionism unsettled the Balkans prior to 1914.
▼ The Serbian government could have accepted the Austrian ultimatum.

g) Conclusion

It seems unlikely that any country planned or wanted a general war in 1914. Fischer's view – that the war was deliberately begun by Germany – is unconvincing. (Bethmann-Hollweg, asked by Bülow soon after the outbreak of the war, how it had come about, replied: 'If only I knew'.) However, while not being entirely responsible for the war, it does seem that Germany was more to blame than any other power. Opportunism, so often a feature of German diplomacy after 1890, marked German statesmanship in July 1914. The 'blank cheque' to Austria–Hungary indicated that Germany was willing to risk a general war. German leaders embarked upon this extraordinarily dangerous strategy with an almost nonchalant attitude. Thus, by late July Germany had to choose between war or diplomatic humiliation. This dilemma was very much of Germany's own making.

ACTIVITY

Divide into six teams – Germany, Austria–Hungary, Russia, Britain, France and Serbia. The job of each team is twofold: a) to prepare the defence case for their country, and b) to devise a number of questions they would like to put to the opposing teams/countries. Each country should then take its turn in the 'dock'. The captain of each team should first read out the defence statement. Questions from the other teams then follow. The teams take it in turn to bat.

At the end, each team should decide who was most to blame, giving a mark of 6 to the country they consider most responsible for the war, 5 for the next, etc. Take a vote to see which country gets the highest vote and thus is seen as most to blame for the war.

7 What Were the Main Causes of the War?

a) How Important was the Balkan Situation?

Austria–Hungary and Russia's conflicting Balkan ambitions had heightened tensions for many years. However, by 1914 the crucial issue was the conflict between Austria and Serbia. Serbian nationalism was a potential threat to the Habsburg Empire. Serbia's sense of grievance at the Austrian annexation of Bosnia-Herzegovina was matched by Austrian alarm at Serbia's expansion as a result of the Balkan Wars. In the final analysis, the First World War began as a fight for the future of the Balkans. Austria–Hungary and Germany made a bid for control: Russia resolved to stop them.

b) How Important was the Alliance System?

The fact that an Austro-Serbian dispute escalated into a general war had something to do with the alliance system. This can be seen as both a reflection of insecurity and a contribution towards it. Arguably, the alliance system reduced the flexibility of the great powers' response to crises. Germany's lack of a flexible response in 1914 ensured that its reply to a threat from Russia was to invade France.

However, it is possible to exaggerate the rigidity of the alliance system. In August 1914, Italy, for example, refused to support her partners in the Triple Alliance. The Triple Entente was not even an alliance. Britain had no precise commitments. In 1914 no one knew for certain what Britain's response to the crisis would be. This is hardly surprising: until Germany invaded Belgium the British cabinet was deeply divided over Britain's course of action. Interestingly, while many historians after 1914 argued that the alliance system made war inevitable, many contemporaries believed that, by creating a balance of power, it helped maintain peace.

c) How Important was 'International Anarchy'?

After 1918 politicians as far apart as Lenin and American President Woodrow Wilson believed that the existence of nation states, pursuing their own interests rather than collaborating in the interests of Europe as a whole, was bound eventually to lead to war. However, so-called 'international anarchy' had been a fact of life in European affairs since at least 1871, during which time Europe had enjoyed over 40 years of peace. Old-style diplomacy had partitioned Africa peacefully and resolved the situation in China. Moreover, pre-1914 European powers tended to act in 'concert' to avert the threat to peace: there was a tradition of responding to crises by convening international conferences to seek collective solutions. (Conferences had met in 1906 and 1912–13.) The breakdown of the 'concert' in 1914 was more a symptom than a cause of the growing tension .

d) How Important was the Arms Race?

It has been claimed that there was a European arms race pre-1914 and that this led inevitably to war. However, if arms races led inevitably to war, the world would not have survived the Cold War. Arguably the wealth of arms in Europe in 1914 might have acted as a deterrent. Moreover, most powers did not actually increase the size of their armies until after 1912. However, there is no doubt that Russia's army reforms, due to be completed in 1917, caused great anxiety in Germany, so much so that a preventive war against Russia made sense to some German military leaders. Nor is there any doubt that Anglo-German naval rivalry helped poison relations between the two countries. Britain's willingness to go to war in 1914 owed much to the anti-German feelings generated by the naval race.

e) How Important was Military Mobilisation?

Military mobilisation – or 'war by timetable' as A.J.P. Taylor called it – played a vital role in bringing about war in July/August 1914. Taylor argued that the outbreak of war was provoked almost entirely by rival plans for mobilisation. The Schlieffen Plan could not be put into effect if Germany allowed Russia time to mobilise. Germany's chance of victory depended on speed. To enable quick mobilisation, elaborate railway timetables had been calculated: these could not be easily amended without throwing everything into total confusion. German mobilisation plans meant almost immediate war. Germany's plans – albeit especially crucial – were not unique: the war plans of all the great powers hinged upon railway timetables and rapid deployment of men. It was assumed – wrongly – that the side which mobilised quickly and struck the first blow would triumph. In late July, therefore, as mobilisation got underway, diplomats found they had little freedom of manoeuvre.

f) How Important was Capitalist Competition?

Marxist historians' claims:
▼ Politicians were puppets of great industrialists and financiers.
▼ Industrialists, especially armaments manufacturers, had a vested interest in provoking war to increase their profits.
▼ Frenzied competition amongst commercial rivals for markets and for raw materials inevitably brought about an 'imperialist war'.

The anti-Marxist view:
▼ There is no evidence that industrialists and financiers were pressing for war. Indeed, well aware that they stood to lose rather than to gain, most were opposed to war.
▼ The view that capitalist states were bound to become involved in wars over access to colonial raw materials does not fit the facts. For much of the period the main rivalries were between Britain and France and Russia – not between Britain and Germany. The fact that Britain's imperial rivalries with France and Russia were resolved makes untenable all general assertions about such rivalries leading to war. Indeed, by 1914 most of the imperial issues had been settled.

g) How Important was Nationalism?

Nationalism was a powerful force in virtually every European country. It was fostered by mass education, the popular press and by right-wing pressure groups. Social Darwinist theories about the survival of the fittest spilled over into nationalist thinking. Many Germans, for example, assumed that they were the fittest race. Some dreamed of uniting all Germans in a Greater German state and then dominating 'inferior' races in eastern Europe. Pan-Slavism also had racist overtones. Balkan nationalism – especially the fact that frontiers did not correspond to national groups – was also a major problem. Ironically, most people in Europe voted for socialist and liberal – not nationalist – parties pre-1914, and across Europe there was a strong international peace movement. However, peace demonstrations in European cities ended in late July 1914 – to be replaced by cheering, patriotic crowds as national loyalty replaced class solidarity. The overwhelming impression in August 1914 is of nations united and of men going cheerfully to war. Apparent national consensus helped mobilise support which sustained (and possibly trapped) governments in 1914.

h) How Important were Domestic Crises?

It has been suggested that Germany, Austria–Hungary and Russia – faced with serious problems at home – wanted war to unite their nations and avoid revolution. This view is unhelpful. It was the worsening international situation, not domestic developments, that explains why the war came when it did. The threat perceived by governments was not revolution from within but invasion from outside.

i) Was the War an Accident or an Accident Waiting to Happen?

Some historians see Europe in 1914 as a powder keg waiting to explode. Others are sceptical. A.J.P. Taylor saw few great causes of the war. He claimed that it was an accident: if anything was to blame, it was simply railway timetables. Certainly deep-rooted explanations, by themselves, fail to explain why war broke out when it did. If Franz Ferdinand had not been assassinated in 1914 there would not have been a war. However, only by understanding developments prior to 1914 is it possible to understand why that assassination resulted in a general European war. The war may have been an accident but it was also an accident waiting to happen.

j) Conclusion

In 1914 all the great powers thought that their vital interests were at stake – interests for which it was worth risking war. All claimed they were fighting a war of self-defence and so in a sense they were: all were motivated more by insecurity and by fear of others expanding than by a desire to expand themselves. All believed that the war would be short and that attack was the best form of defence. All got it wrong: the war was not short and defence was to prove the best form of defence. Had European leaders realised the horrors that lay ahead, they surely would not have acted as they did in 1914.

▼ Working on The Origins of the First World War

In trying to work out what caused anything in history, it is always useful to consider:
▼ What were the main long-term causes (preconditions)?
▼ What were the main medium-term causes (precipitants)?
▼ What were the main short-term causes (triggers)?

There may well be debate about what exactly is a precondition (as opposed to a precipitant) and what exactly is a precipitant (as opposed to a trigger). Don't worry about this. The divisions are partly cosmetic. The main thing is that they should help structure your thoughts. Try to work out what you think were the main preconditions, precipitants and triggers which resulted in the First World War. Did any of the preconditions mean that war was likely or inevitable? To what extent did war seem imminent by early 1914? Could/should the war have been averted in 1914?

Answering Extended Writing and Essay Questions on The Origins of the First World War

Consider the following question: 'To what extent should Germany be held responsible for the start of the First World War?'

One way to approach this question is first to consider the historiographical debates. What have been historians' views about German responsibility? (Fischer's views are particularly important.) Then you might use the plan outlined in the previous section and examine Germany's policy in the long, medium, and short term. You will also need to say something about the responsibility of other countries. If Germany was not responsible, who – or what – was? Finally you will have to reach a conclusion. Have the courage to say what you think. What is your main evidence for arguing as you do?

Answering Source-Based Questions on The Origins of the First World War

... the Kaiser authorised me to inform our gracious majesty that we might in this case, as in all others, rely upon Germany's full support ... he did not doubt in the least that Herr von Bethmann-Hollweg would agree with him. Especially as far as our action against Serbia was concerned. But it was the Kaiser's opinion that this action must not be delayed. Russia's attitude will no doubt be hostile, but for this he had for years prepared, and should a war between Austria–Hungary and Russia be unavoidable, we might be convinced that Germany, our old faithful ally, would stand at our side. Russia at the present time was in no way prepared for war, and would think twice before it appealed to arms ... if we had really recognised the necessity of warlike action against Serbia, he [the Kaiser] would regret if we did not make use of the present moment, which is all in our favour.

Source C a report of the conversation between Wilhelm II and the Austrian ambassador Count Szogyeny in Berlin on 5 July 1914 which Szogyeny sent to Berchtold, the Austrian Foreign Minister.

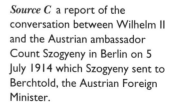

Austria no longer intends to tolerate the sapping activities of the Serbians, and just as little does she intend to tolerate longer the continuously provocative attitude of her small neighbour at Belgrade ... She fully realizes that she has neglected many opportunities, and that she is still able to act, though in a few years she may no longer be able to do so. Austria is now going to force a showdown with Serbia, and has told us so ... Nor have we at the present time forced Austria to her decision. But we neither could nor should attempt to stay her hand. If we should do that, Austria would have the right to reproach us (and we ourselves) with having deprived her of her last chance of political rehabilitation. And then the process of her wasting away and of her internal decay would be still further accelerated. Her standing in the Balkans would be gone forever. You will undoubtedly agree with me that the absolute establishment of the Russian hegemony in the Balkans is, indirectly, not permissible, even for us. The maintenance of Austria ... is a necessity for us both for internal and external reasons.

We must attempt to localise the conflict between Austria and Serbia. Whether we shall succeed in this will depend first on Russia, and secondly on the moderating influence of Russia's allies. The more determined Austria shows herself, the more energetically we support her, so much the more quiet will Russia remain. To be sure, there will be some agitation in St Petersburg, but, on the whole, Russia is not ready to strike at present. Nor will France or England be anxious for war at the present time. According to all competent observation, Russia will be prepared to fight in a few years. Then she will crush us by the number of her soldiers: then she will have built her Baltic Sea fleet and her strategic railroads.

Source D written by Jagow, the German secretary of state, to Prince Lichnowsky, the German ambassador in London, on 18 July 1914.

▼ QUESTIONS ON SOURCES

1. Examine Sources C and D. To what extent do they agree?
[10 marks]
2. To what extent can Source C be trusted? **[10 marks]**

Points to note about the questions

Question 1 Both sources suggest that Germany supported Austria–Hungary taking action. To what extent do the sources differ in emphasis?

Question 2 Note that Wilhelm's words are being reported. Might Szogyeny have changed the emphasis of what Wilhelm said?

Further Reading

Books in the Access to History series
A very useful treatment will be found in *Rivalry and Accord: International Relations 1870–1914* by John Lowe. It is also worth reading the relevant sections on foreign policy in *Reaction and Revolutions: Russia 1881–1924* by Michael Lynch, *From Bismarck to Hitler: Germany 1890–1933* by Geoff Layton, *France: The Third Republic 1870–1914* by Keith Randell and *Britain and the European Powers 1865–1914* by Robert Pearce.

General
The literature on the origins of the war seems never-ending. *The Origins of the First World War* by R. Henig, 1993 (Routledge) is a good short introduction. Try also *The Outbreak of the First World War: 1914 in Perspective* by D. Stevenson (Macmillan). More detailed studies include *The Origins of the First World War* by J. Joll, 1992 (Longman), *Decisions for War, 1914* by K.Wilson (ed.), 1995 (UCL Press) and *The Origins of the First World War* by H.W. Koch (ed.) 1984 (Macmillan). F. Fischer's *Germany's War Aims in the First World War*, 1967 and *War of Illusions*, 1972 (both published by Chatto & Windus) need to be treated with care.

CHAPTER **3**

THE IMPACT OF THE FIRST WORLD WAR

POINTS TO CONSIDER

In this chapter you will be studying the course and consequences of the First World War. Although the war was fought all over the globe and involved many non-European nations, it was essentially a European conflict. It began – and most of the fighting took place – in Europe. Its impact on Europe was colossal. The chapter has been divided into an introduction and five sections. It may be that you are concentrating on one of – rather than all – the sections. Those sections which only provide background to your main area of interest can be read through quickly. However, it would be unwise to ignore them altogether. The ability to set your knowledge in a rounded context is an advantage when studying any topic in history. For example, you cannot really understand what happened in Russia in 1917 or the 1919 peace settlement, unless you have some knowledge of the war.

In August 1914 all of Europe's great powers (except Italy) went to war. Few wars in history have been so popular at their outset. Across Europe young men clamoured to enlist. Virtually everyone thought it would be short. However, the war did not meet expectations. It degenerated into a war of attrition on a scale without precedent. Millions of men were killed or badly wounded. Historians debate many aspects of the war. The first key question is why it lasted so long. Had it ended before 1916, it is unlikely that Tsar Nicholas II would have been overthrown in March 1917. Had the March Revolution not occurred it is inconceivable that the Bolsheviks would have come to power in November 1917. One of the first actions of the Bolshevik government was to pull Russia out of the war, which could easily have changed its outcome. However, in 1917 the USA joined the war on the Allied side. Does the USA's entry explain the victory of the Allies in 1918? Having won the war, the victors had to make peace. The results of their labours – the Versailles peace settlement – have divided historians ever since.

1 Why Did the War Last so Long?

a) The Failure of the Schlieffen Plan

In August/September 1914 the Schlieffen Plan came close to success. The French put their own Plan XVII into effect: this was designed to recapture Alsace-Lorraine. In the Battle of the Frontiers, French troops were mown down by German machine guns and artillery. In three weeks, the French suffered 300,000 casualties. Meanwhile 1.5 million German troops pressed on through Belgium. However, not everything went well for the Germans. The Belgians and the 150,000 strong British Expeditionary Force put up stiff resistance and slowed down the German advance. More seriously, the Russians mobilised their forces faster than anticipated and Moltke (the German Chief of Staff) sent troops from France/Belgium to East Prussia to help check the Russian offensive. This weakened the German attack in the west. French troops from Lorraine were rushed to defend Paris. (Ironically, if the French had had more success in the Battle of the Frontiers, Paris would probably have been lost!) On 5 September, Joffre, the French commander, attacked the German exposed flank. The fighting, which lasted over the next week, is known as the Battle of the Marne. Moltke finally lost his nerve and ordered his troops to retreat to the river Aisne. Here they dug in. Although the French had won a vital battle, they were unable to exploit it. All their efforts to break through the German lines failed. Both sides now tried to outflank each other in a race for the Channel ports. Dogged French and British resistance at the first battle of Ypres ensured that the Allies retained control of the key ports. After this, both sides dug in and by the end of 1914 a system of trenches ran from the Channel to Switzerland.

b) Developments on the Eastern Front in 1914

Responding to French pleas, the Russians attacked both the Germans in East Prussia and the Austrians in Galicia. The Russian 'steamroller' could feasibly have captured Berlin and won the war for the Allies. (The Russians outnumbered the Germans by three to one.) However, German generals Hindenburg and Ludendorff defeated one Russian army at Tannenburg (in August) and another at the Masurian Lakes (in September). The Russians had far more success against the Austrians, winning the Battle of Lemburg in August/September, destroying half the Austro-Hungarian army in the process, and driving deep into Galicia. The first months of the war went badly for Austria–Hungary. By December 1914 its forces

---

ISSUE
Why did the First World War not end in 1914, 1915 or 1916?

THE SCHLIEFFEN PLAN
German forces would sweep through Belgium and Luxemburg, capturing Paris and knocking out France in 42 days. German troops would then recross Germany and deal with the Russians. The Plan was amazingly risky. As the bulk of the German army moved west, Germany was largely unprotected from Russian attack. Moreover seven-eighths of the German forces in the west were committed to the Belgian sweep; only one-eighth were left in Germany to counter expected French offensives.

MAIN EVENTS OF THE WAR: 1914

August	Battle of the Frontiers;
August	Battle of Tannenburg;
September	Battle of the Marne;
September	first trenches dug on the River Aisne; Battle of the Masurian Lakes;
October– November	'The race to the sea'; first Battle of Ypres.

Figure 13 The war in Eastern Europe.

Table 6 The balance of power in 1914.

	Great Britain	France	Russia	Germany	Austria–Hungary
Population	46,407,037	39,601,509	167,000,000	65,000,000	49,882,231
Soldiers available on mobilisation	711,000[1]	3,500,000	4,423,000[2]	8,500,000[3]	3,000,000
Merchant fleet (net steam tonnage)	11,538,000	1,098,000	486,914	3,096,000	559,784
Battleships (built and being built)	64	28	16	40	16
Cruisers	121	34	14	57	12
Submarines	64	73	29	23	6
Annual value of foreign trade (£)	1,223,152,000	424,000,000	190,247,000	1,030,380,000	198,712,000
Annual steel production (tons)	6,903,000	4,333,000	4,416,000	17,024,000	2,642,000

[1]Including empire [2]Immediate mobilisation [3]Emergency maximum

Figure 14 The combatants of the First World War.

	1914	1915	1916	1917	1918
The Central Powers					
Austria–Hungary	July				Nov
Bulgaria		Oct			Sept
Germany	Aug				Nov
Turkey	Nov				Oct
The Allied Powers					
France	Aug				Nov
Belgium[1]	Aug				Nov
Great Britain	Aug				Nov
Greece				June	Nov
Italy		May			Nov
Portugal			March		Nov
Japan	Aug				Nov
Montenegro[2]	July				Nov
Romania			Aug Dec		Nov
Russia	July			March	
Serbia[2]	July				Nov
USA				April	Nov

[1] Virtually the whole of Belgium was under German occupation from the autumn of 1914.

[2] Montenegro and Serbia were destroyed as independent states in the winter of 1915–16, but guerilla warfare continued and both states had governments in exile.

had also been driven out of Serbia. Turkey, anti-Russian and confident of German victory, entered the war in October 1914.

c) Equal Strength

Allied strengths:
▽ The Allies had more men. The Russian army was the largest in Europe. Britain and France could also call on their empires for men.
▽ Britain possessed the world's strongest navy. Its fleet blockaded Germany.
▽ Britain and France were able to acquire resources worldwide.

Central Power strengths:
▽ Germany had the finest army in Europe, with many trained reserves.
▽ Germany had a powerful navy. If Britain lost control of the seas, it lost the war because it would soon be starved into submission.
▽ The **Central Powers** had the advantage of interior lines of communication. They could move men from one front to the other using their excellent railway systems.
▽ Although the Allies had more men, Russian forces were not well-equipped and the large British volunteer army would not be ready for action until 1916.
▽ Germany was Europe's strongest industrial power.
▽ As a result of the German advance in 1914, France lost its main industrial area.

THE CENTRAL POWERS

The term used to describe Germany and Austria–Hungary (and later the Ottoman Empire and Bulgaria).

Why did Moltke think Germany had lost the war after the battle of the Marne?

d) The Nature of the War

i) The War on Land

In August 1914 both sides were committed to the offensive. In the event attack proved to be terribly costly. This was largely because of the increased range, volume and accuracy of fire-power provided by the magazine rifle, the machine gun and artillery. On all fronts, but especially on the Western Front, both sides dug in. Conditions in the trenches were hellish. Soldiers suffered from trench foot, lice, rats, shelling, snipers and enemy raids. The trench systems became more elaborate, especially on the German side, as the war progressed. In general the Germans adapted better to trench warfare. They made better use of barbed wire, developed better machine guns, and built huge bunkers deep enough to withstand the heaviest artillery pounding.

The first response of commanders on all sides to the trench stalemate was to call for more heavy artillery. Massive artillery bombardment, however, did not end the stalemate. It rarely destroyed barbed-wire entanglements, did not kill troops in deep bunkers, warned the enemy of a forthcoming attack, and simply churned up the ground across which the infantry was supposed to advance.

Most Allied generals continued to believe in the offensive. (It was politically difficult for the French to remain on the defensive given that ten per cent of their territory was in German hands.) Common

Figure 15 Conditions on the Western Front.

NEW METHODS OF WARFARE

▽ Poison gas was first used by the Germans in 1915 at the second battle of Ypres. Gas simply made trench conditions even more dreadful.

▽ Tanks (a British invention), used for the first time in battle in September 1916, did not – initially – have much effect. The early tanks' top speed was only 4 mph and they were prone to break down. Germany built only a handful of tanks. Only in 1918 did tanks have a considerable impact on the war.

▽ Aircraft played an increasingly important role. At first they were used for reconnaissance. However, they were soon equipped with bombs and machine guns and were able to attack ground forces. Both sides developed 'fighter' aircraft to defend their airspace. By 1918 the RAF had some 22,000 aircraft and nearly 300,000 personnel. Yet, despite this, aircraft did not significantly affect the outcome of any battle.

sense seemed to suggest that if enough men were put in a small place where they vastly outnumbered the enemy they should be able to break through. However, it was not as straightforward as this. If troops attacked in close order they were mown down. If they advanced in open order, officers lost control of them. Even if they broke through the first defence line, there was invariably a second line and it was relatively easy for defending generals to move in reserves and so quickly plug gaps. Attacking generals, dependent on telegraph wire, primitive wireless, or runners, had little contact with a battle once it had begun and keeping moving men who had broken-through the enemy lines proved difficult.

Warfare on the Eastern Front was less static than in the west. Attacking armies were able to smash their way through enemy lines. However, they usually suffered heavy casualties in doing so. Advancing troops invariably ground to a halt because they could not be supplied. Meanwhile the retreating troops established new positions.

It is easy to blame the leaders on all sides for their failure to come up with ideas to break the deadlock. However, even today, it is hard to see what could have been done. During the war all armies experimented with new tactics and new weapons. Few of these experiments were totally successful.

ii) The War at Sea

Before 1914 Britain and Germany had spent millions constructing powerful navies. In 1914 a great naval battle seemed inevitable. However, it did not happen. There were some minor naval engagements early in the war as the British navy successfully cleared the seas of German merchant and fighting ships. The Germans were unwilling to risk their High Seas fleet against the (larger) British Grand Fleet. The laying of mines, a relatively new and cheap means of sea warfare, also made it difficult for German ships to venture forth. The main German naval threat came from U-boats, which sank Allied merchant ships in an attempt to starve Britain into surrender. The U-boat campaign, however, also resulted in the sinking of neutral ships. The USA – Britain's greatest trading partner – protested. The sinking of the liner *Lusitania* in May 1915 which resulted in the loss of over 1,100 lives (including 128 Americans) led President Woodrow Wilson to issue an ultimatum to Germany. Rather than risk war with the USA, Germany agreed to abandon unrestricted submarine warfare. However, it continued building more U-boats so that, if needs be, it could conduct a more concerted campaign in the future.

e) Total War

Could the high casualties of the war have been avoided?

The First World War was not fully 'total'. Although there was some aerial bombing and some long-distance shelling, most civilians, escaped attack. However, it was a 'total war' in the sense that it touched the lives of virtually everybody in Europe's warring states.

i) Mobilisation

Huge numbers of men served in the armed forces. Britain (which introduced conscription in 1916) mobilised 12.5 per cent of its men for the forces, Germany 15.4 per cent and France 16.9 per cent.

ii) The Economic Front

Given that the side which produced the greater quantities of guns and munitions stood the greater chance of victory, all governments extended power over their economies. Everywhere there was a short-age of manpower. Armies demanded men but so did industry and agriculture. Substitute workers, particularly women, helped indus-tries cope with the labour shortage. However, the war increasingly became an exercise in striking the correct balance between meeting the needs of the fighting front and ensuring that the civilian popu-lation had enough resources to prevent morale being undermined by serious hardships. Each nation responded differently to the eco-nomic demands of the war.

Price controls, subsidies for farmers, food rationing and even a limit on the opening hours of pubs were all eventually introduced in Britain. Britain's wartime production – 240,000 machine guns, 25,000 artillery pieces, 3,000 tanks and 55,000 aircraft – was impres-

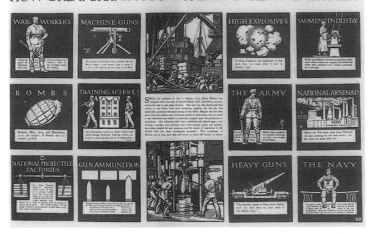

Figure 16 The war of munitions.

sive. It was achieved without setting up state-run factories or the wholesale drafting of civilian labour. To increase war production, the French government in 1914 had to demobilise about 500,000 skilled workers from the army and control of labour was introduced in 1915. France managed to increase war production in spite of losing much of its industrial heartland. By 1918 French industry had produced 50,000 aircraft and 4,800 tanks.

In Germany the War Raw Materials Department exercised vast power – directing labour, controlling the railways, introducing rationing and price controls, and allocating resources to industries competing for scarce raw materials (as a result of the Allied blockade). From 1916 all German males between the ages of 17 and 60 were subject to war service, whether in the military or industrial sector. However, the German government did not actually take over the factories. Instead, big business worked with the government (making huge profits in the process). While war production soared, German consumers were hit hard: there were soon shortages of almost everything. This led to steep inflation.

Britain and France were more successful than the Central Powers and Russia in coping with the economic war, largely because they had access to the world's resources. In particular, they were able to purchase huge quantities of materials from the USA. By 1916 American trade with the Allies reached a staggering $3,214 million (compared with $280 million with the Central Powers.

In general, the war led to mounting suffering on the home front. Across Europe, real wages of workers did not keep pace with prices. More seriously, food was often in short supply. This was the result of a series of poor harvests, problems of transportation, a shortage of farm labourers, the commandeering of horses, and a lack of chemicals for fertilisation. Ironically Britain, which was most dependent on imports, fared best. As the war continued, economic difficulties had a severe impact on civilian morale.

iii) Propaganda and Censorship

All governments appreciated the need to use propaganda (and censorship) to maintain morale. Posters, newspapers, and the cinema were used to convince people that the war was going well and that the sacrifices were justified. The enemy were depicted as villains. Britain, for example, accused German soldiers of atrocities in Belgium – raping nuns and impaling babies on bayonets. These were blatant (but effective) lies. In reality, there were relatively few atrocities in areas occupied by the enemy. In this respect, the First World War was different to the Second World War.

f) Stalemate: 1915

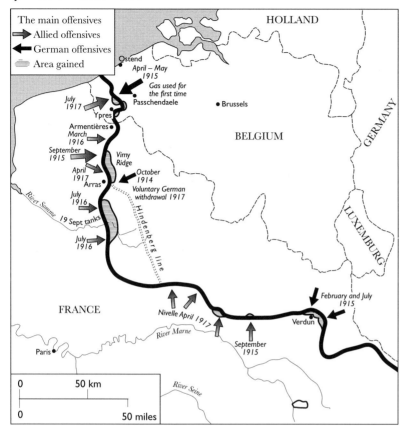

Figure 17 The Western Front, 1915–18.

▼ For the most part, the Germans remained on the defensive on the Western Front. France and Britain launched a series of major – unsuccessful – assaults throughout the year.

▼ In Britain several important men (especially Winston Churchill) were convinced that the best way to win the war was to open up new fronts in the Balkans. Their initial aim, however, was to knock Turkey out of the war. The Straits could then be opened to Allied shipping, thus providing Russia with a much needed supply line. Unfortunately the Dardanelles (or Gallipoli) campaign was a series of missed opportunities. By the time an Allied army arrived in April, Turkish defences had been well prepared. Allied forces, pinned down on a narrow beachhead, suffered over 200,000 casualties before the enterprise was abandoned in January 1916.

▼ Italy joined the war on the side of the Allies in May 1915. By the secret Treaty of London it was promised, at Austria–Hungary's expense, Trentino, the Tyrol, Trieste, Istria and North Dalmatia. While Italian forces enjoyed a two to one superiority, they failed to break formidable Austrian defences along the Isonzo River.

MAIN EVENTS OF THE WAR: 1915	
April	Allied landings at Gallipoli;
May	sinking of the *Lusitania*;
May	Italy entered the war;
May–September	German offensive in Poland;
September–October	failure of Allied attacks on the Western Front.

▼ In 1915 the Germans launched a major offensive in the east, forcing the Russians into headlong retreat. However, Germany failed to knock Russia out of the war.

▼ Bulgaria, promised Serbian Macedonia, now joined the war and in October German, Austrian and Bulgarian troops mopped up Serbia. An Anglo-French force landed at Salonika, hoping to help the Serbs, but was quickly pushed back when it tried to advance.

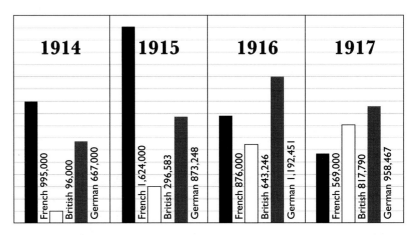

Figure 18 Losses on the Western Front.

g) The Stalemate Continues: 1916

i) Verdun

The German commander Falkenhayn decided to attack Verdun, a symbolically important fortress, which could be attacked from several sides. His aim was not really to make a breakthrough. Gambling on French determination to defend the place at any cost, he was rather hoping to bleed the French army 'white'. The German attack was launched in February: 1,400 guns fired over 100,000 shells an hour on French positions. French troops – starved, gassed, bombarded – would not yield. 'They shall not pass', became the French rallying cry. This was as Falkenhayn had hoped. However, as more and more German troops were sucked into the fighting, they too suffered heavy casualties. French commander Petain rotated the divisions which had to endure the German shelling: thus almost 75 per cent of all French infantry endured the horrors of Verdun.

ii) The Somme

By 1916 a British army of over one million men was trained and ready to fight. In an effort to help the French, General Haig launched a great assault on the Somme. A ten-day preliminary bombardment had little impact and on the first day of the battle (1 July) the British lost nearly 60,000 casualties. The fighting continued for five more months. Allied forces advanced a maximum of seven miles.

iii) The Brusilov Offensive

In June the Russian commander Brusilov launched a major offensive. To achieve surprise, his attack was not preceded by a long artillery barrage and his forces went forward in strength at several points, making it hard for the enemy to shift resources. The attack broke through the Austro-Hungarian lines but had less success against the Germans. Romania, exaggerating the extent of Russian success and hoping to gain Transylvania, joined the war on the Allied side. Its forces were swiftly defeated. The fall of Bucharest in December marked the end of Romania's war effort.

iv) The Situation by the End of 1916

1916 ended, as it had begun, in stalemate. American efforts to mediate came to nothing. In Britain Lloyd George replaced Asquith as prime minister. In Germany, generals Hindenburg and Ludendorff replaced Falkenhayn. They became effectively (if not effective) military dictators. French General Nivelle, who claimed he knew how to win the war, replaced Joffre. In November Habsburg Emperor Franz Joseph died. His successor Karl, aware that Austria–Hungary was likely to disintegrate if the war continued, put out secret peace feelers. War weariness, however, was most apparent in Russia.

MAIN EVENTS OF THE WAR: 1916	
February– August	Battle of Verdun;
May–June	Battle of Jutland;
June– October	the Brusilov offensive;
July– November	Battle of the Somme.

ACTIVITY

Test your grasp of Section 1 by answering the following question: 'Why had the First World War not ended by 1916?'

Brainstorm the main points you might wish to include in your answer. Work out eight to ten headings which might be suitable paragraphs for the essay. Then write a conclusion of no more than eight to ten sentences which summarises your answer.

---

2 The March Revolution in Russia

a) How Effective was the Russian War Effort, 1914–17?

The outbreak of war was greeted in Russia, as elsewhere, with a wave of patriotic hysteria. But with social divisions, a weak economy and a narrow base of political support, the tsarist regime was deeply vulnerable to the strains of a long conflict. Historians still debate the effectiveness of Russia's war effort.

ISSUE
Why was Nicholas II overthrown in March 1917?

RASPUTIN

Alexandra believed that this self-professed holy man had the power to help her only son Alexis who suffered from haemophilia. She took Rasputin's advice on political matters, sometimes appointing and sacking ministers at his suggestion. Rasputin's antics – especially his displays of drunken and sexual debauchery – alienated the nobles and professional classes whose support the government desperately needed. In December 1916 Rasputin was assassinated in bizarre fashion by a group of right-wing nobles who claimed that they hoped to save the name of the royal family.

i) The Negative View

▼ The army did not perform well. In 1914 the Russians were defeated at Tannenburg and at the Masurian Lakes. In 1915 Russian forces were driven out of Poland and the Baltic states. By the end of 1916 the badly-led army had suffered some 7 million casualties. Not surprisingly troop morale fell disastrously.

▼ Russian industry was unable to cope. Both the army and civilians suffered from shortages of most items. Workers' wages did not keep pace with prices and strikes increased.

▼ Agriculture was unable to cope. By 1917 there were food shortages in the main towns.

▼ The Russian government was unable to cope. During the war there was considerable ministerial instability. Between August 1915 and February 1917, for example, Russia had four prime ministers and three ministers of war. The Duma became increasingly critical of the way the war was being handled. In September 1915 Nicholas made himself Commander-in-Chief of the army. This was a mistake. Henceforward he was identified directly with the failures of his forces. Moreover, he now spent little time in Petrograd (the new name of the capital – St Petersburg sounded too German). Nicholas left his autocratic – and German (!) – wife Alexandra in control. She brought the royal family into disrepute because of the influence of Rasputin.

ii) The (More) Positive View

▼ Historian Norman Stone has claimed that the Russsian army fought pretty well. In 1914 it was successful against Austria–Hungary and Turkey. In 1915 it was not overwhelmed by the Germans. It did what Russian armies have frequently done, trading land for time. The 1916 Brusilov offensive helped relieve pressure on other fronts. As supreme commander, Nicholas generally promoted competent officers. Russian casualties were proportionately no greater than those of other countries. The army was not in a state of mutiny in early 1917.

▼ Russian industry coped remarkably well. By 1916 shell production had risen by 2,000 per cent and rifle production by 1,100 per cent. Russia, dependent totally on its own resources, managed to mobilise and equip over 14 million men.

▼ The agricultural situation was not disastrous. Although many peasants went off to war, women, children, and older men were able to maintain production. Before 1914, much of Russia's cereals had been exported: this no longer happened. Consequently there was probably more food in Russia after 1914 than before. The main problem was transporting the food to the towns.

▼ The Russian government coped reasonably well. There was more democracy in Russia during the war than before. At local level Municipal and War Industries Committees worked in collaboration with the government. The Duma was in session for much of the war and had some influence on the Tsar's choice of ministers. Both Alexandra's and Rasputin's influence have been greatly exaggerated.

b) The March Revolution

By 1916–17 the Tsarist government was in danger. In Petrograd and Moscow there were increasing numbers of strikes and demonstrations in protest at food and fuel shortages. There was also concern about the loyalty of the 340,000-strong Petrograd garrison. Cold and hungry (like most of the Petrograd population), the troops were not the best disciplined in the army.

Nicholas's fall, however, was not inevitable. There was little unrest in the countryside. Most of the revolutionary leaders were in exile. Although liberals in the Duma might criticise Nicholas, they feared trying to replace him in the midst of war. If Nicholas had got through the winter (when food and fuel shortages were at their worst) he might have survived. But events in March 1917 brought about his downfall.

ISSUE
Was the March Revolution spontaneous?

March 1917

3 March Steel workers went on strike.

7 March Nicholas left Petrograd for army headquarters at Mogilev 400 miles away.

8 March International Women's Day brought more workers out on the streets.

9 March Clashes between the police and strikers.

10 March Petrograd paralysed by a general strike. Some army units mutinied and joined the strikers. The Petrograd army commander was unable to identify which units were still loyal.

11 March Petrograd was in chaos. By now more than 100,000 troops had gone over to the rioters. The Tsar's cabinet resigned.

12 March Duma members set up a Provisional Committee to try to control events. Meanwhile workers set up a Soviet.

13 March Nicholas tried to return to Petrograd. Striking railway workers diverted his train to Pskov. Duma officials and top army commanders (who said that the army could not be relied on) called upon Nicholas to abdicate.

15 March Nicholas abdicated for himself and (unexpectedly) for Alexis his son. Duma officials had assumed that Alexis would become the new Tsar.

16 March Grand Duke Michael (Nicholas's brother) refused to accept the crown, unless it was offered him by a Constituent Assembly. The Romanov monarchy was at an end.

c) Conclusion

The war was crucial in bringing about Nicholas's downfall. Inflation, food shortages, high casualties, and a sense of hopelessness sparked off a near-spontaneous revolution. Petrograd factory-floor activists played an important role in bringing workers out on the streets but they were not carrying out a coherent policy. (They belonged to various revolutionary parties). Duma officials, while not in any way orchestrating the revolution, did not rally to Nicholas's defence. Military dissatisfaction was also vital. While there was no great army mutiny, the unreliability of units of the Petrograd garrison was crucial. So was the failure of the leading generals to support Nicholas in his hour of need.

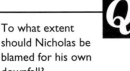

To what extent should Nicholas be blamed for his own downfall?

ACTIVITY

Consider the following question: 'Why did the Romanov dynasty come to an end in March 1917?'. Re-read Chapter 1 (section 4) to find the long-term Russian problems. Then write two paragraphs summarising the situation from 1914–17: one should be on the impact of the war; the other on the events of March 1917.

ISSUE

Why were the Bolsheviks able to seize power in November 1917?

3 The November Revolution

a) The Provisional Government

In March 1917 a Provisional Government came to power. While its authority was accepted by the Army High Command, it had little real legitimacy: it was simply a group of self-appointed Duma members. The government was to be provisional until elections could be organised to produce a Constituent Assembly. The first Provisional Government was headed by the liberal Prince Lvov. (Alexander Kerensky was the only socialist in the new government.) Lvov's government quickly displayed its liberal credentials, abolishing the death penalty, freeing political prisoners, ending discrimination on the basis of class, nationality or religion, and allowing freedom of speech. Overnight Russia became the freest of all the warring states.

b) What Problems did the Provisional Government Face?

The Provisional Government's honeymoon period quickly ended. It was soon clear that it faced massive problems, not least those which had helped bring down Nicholas II.

i) Great Expectations

The March Revolution had heightened expectations among the Russian people. These expectations would be hard to realise – certainly in the midst of war. Elections to the Constituent Assembly were postponed several times: organising elections in the middle of war was not easy. The Provisional Government was also reluctant to embark on a major programme of land reform before the Assembly met and while the war continued. It believed it had little alternative but to continue the war. Russia's honour was at stake. Moreover, the entry of the USA into the war in April 1917 gave hope of victory. Massive Allied loans were an added inducement to keep fighting.

ii) Dual Power

From the start the Provisional Government's power was challenged by the soviets (councils). Representing workers, peasants and soldiers, these emerged spontaneously in March 1917 and swiftly mushroomed. (By April there were 67 soviets in Siberia alone.) The most important soviet was that in Petrograd. Dominated initially by Mensheviks and Social Revolutionaries (SRs), it was more left-wing than the Provisional Government. It also had a more popular mandate. The Petrograd garrison, factory committees (which also mushroomed) and trade unions recognised soviet ahead of Provisional Government authority. Without the permission of the soviets, few initiatives could be taken. (Historians talk of 'Dual Power'.) Soviet power was shown as early as 15 March when the Petrograd Soviet issued Order Number 1. This called for the setting up of soldiers' committees in every military unit: these would send deputies to the Petrograd Soviet and take political orders only from that body.

However, the tensions between the Provisional Government and the Petrograd Soviet can be exaggerated. Most Soviet members thought it was necessary to support the Provisional Government to prevent a right-wing backlash, particularly an army coup. The Soviet actually approved most of the Provisional Government's actions, including the continuation of the war. Some men (like Kerensky) had considerable influence within both the Provisional Government and the Petrograd Soviet.

iii) The Breakdown of Law and Order

As the summer wore on, rural disturbances increased. Great landowners were unable to prevent their estates being seized by peasants. Elsewhere various national groups (for example, the Finns) effectively won independence from Russia.

iv) Problems in the Towns

The economic crisis in the towns worsened. Workers demanded an eight-hour day, higher wages, and worker control of factories. They did so in an atmosphere of crisis. There was a growing shortage of raw materials, resulting in falling industrial output and the closure of factories. Worsening inflation led to more discontent. Fierce clashes ensued between factory committees and employers.

v) Problems in the Army

The influence of soldiers' committees undermined the structure of command in the army. Officers' authority began to collapse.

vi) Divisions

The Provisional Government was divided between those on the left (who wanted social reform) and those on the right (who wanted the restoration of law and order). By May a more left-wing Provisional Government had formed. It faced an uphill struggle to maintain its authority in the face of direct action by workers and peasants. It also faced a serious challenge from the Bolsheviks.

LENIN

The following description of Lenin comes from John Reed, an American journalist (and socialist) in Petrograd in 1917. His book, *Ten Days that Shook the World*, is a classic:

A short, stocky figure with a big head set down on his shoulders, bald and bulging. Little eyes, a snubbish nose, wide, generous mouth and heavy chin. Dressed in shabby clothes, his trousers much too long for him. Unimpressive, to be the idol of the mob, loved and revered as perhaps few leaders in history have been. A strange popular leader – a leader purely by virtue of intellect; colourless, humourless, uncompromising and detached, but with the power of explaining profound ideas in simple terms. His great mouth, seeming to smile, opened wide as he spoke; for emphasis he bent forward slightly. No gestures. And before him a thousand simple faces looking up in intent adoration.   *Source A*

Figure 19 Lenin speaking in public in Petrograd, 1917. Trotsky is to his left, leaning against the rostrum.

1870 born Vladimir Ilyich Ulyanov (Lenin was a pseudonym) to middle-class parents;
1893 joined a revolutionary group in St Petersburg where he practised as a lawyer;
1897 exiled to Siberia where he married Nadezhda Krupskaya, a fellow Marxist;
1900 left Russia: did not return until 1917 (except for a few weeks in 1905);
1902 published *What Is to Be Done?* in which he emphasised the role of an elite party in effecting revolution;
1903 brought about split between the Bolsheviks and the Mensheviks;
1914 settled in Switzerland;
1917 returned to Russia and organised the Bolshevik Revolution;
1917 communist dictator of
–24 Russia;
1924 died.

Figure 20 A communist painting showing Lenin's arrival at the Finland Station, Petrograd, April 1917.

c) The Return of Lenin

In March 1917 the Bolsheviks did not seem to have much chance of winning power. The party had fewer than 20,000 members and most of its leaders were abroad. While a general amnesty enabled

Bolsheviks to return from exile, this posed problems for Lenin (in Switzerland). The Germans came to his assistance. Anticipating that he would do his utmost to end Russia's involvement in the war, the German government arranged for him to cross Germany in a special train. He arrived in Petrograd in mid-April.

The April Theses

Lenin's April Theses laid down a new Bolshevik strategy.

▼ Lenin looked forward to the immediate implementation of the proletariat revolution.
▼ There must be no cooperation with the Provisional Government or with moderate socialists. The soviets must rule and the Bolsheviks must win power in the soviets.
▼ Once in power, the Bolsheviks would end the 'imperialist' war.
▼ Lenin proclaimed 'all land to the peasants'. (By this he meant granting land to the *mirs* – not individual peasants.)

MILITARY FAILURE

In late June 1917, a new Russian offensive ended in disaster. Discipline within the Russian army broke down. Troops disobeyed (and sometimes killed) officers and deserted in large numbers. Army leaders demanded the restoration of the death penalty and a curb on the influence of the soldiers' committees.

Bolshevik support began to grow. Aided by German funds, the Bolsheviks launched an effective poster and newspaper campaign. More important than propaganda, however, was the fact that the Bolshevik programme (summed up by the slogans 'Peace, Bread, Land' and 'All Power to the Soviets') was popular. The Bolsheviks were the only party promising an end to the war and the only socialist party untainted by any association with the Provisional Government. Bolshevik support was particularly strong among factory workers. However, the Bolsheviks remained a minority group. When the first All-Russian Congress of Soviets met in Petrograd in June 1917, the Bolsheviks had 105 delegates, the SRs 285 and the Mensheviks 248.

d) The July Days

In July Lvov resigned and a third and even more left-wing Provisional Government, headed by Kerensky, assumed power. It faced an immediate challenge. In mid-July there were serious riots in Petrograd. Whether these riots were Bolshevik-inspired is debatable. Lenin certainly did not orchestrate them. However, many of the rioters were undoubtedly Bolshevik sympathisers. While Lenin prevaricated and the rioters fell out among themselves, troops loyal to Kerensky restored order. Kerensky blamed the Bolsheviks for the disturbances and published evidence indicating that Lenin was a German agent. Bolshevik leaders were imprisoned (Lenin fled to Finland to escape arrest) and Bolshevik newspapers were suppressed.

e) Kerensky

Kerensky faced massive problems. The Germans were advancing, the Russian army seemed on the point of collapse, and the economic situation was deteriorating. Given the situation, it is possible to view Kerensky sympathetically. Arguably no liberal or moderate socialist could have controlled events at this time. However, it is also possible to see him as a lightweight – a devious politician with limited ability.

f) The Kornilov Affair

Kerensky now appointed General Kornilov as Commander-in-Chief with a brief to restore order in the army. Kornilov believed that Russia generally needed stronger government. He therefore demanded the banning of strikes and the imposition of tougher discipline on workers. While Kerensky hesitated (he seems to have had some sympathy with Kornilov's views), Kornilov, claiming he was acting on Kerensky's authority, began to deploy troops in the direction of Petrograd, intending to impose order in the capital. Kerensky, however, denounced him as a traitor and called on all loyal citizens to take up arms to defend the city. Seeing Kornilov's move as the start of the long-predicted right-wing backlash, left-wing forces united. Bolshevik leaders were released from prison, and the Petrograd Soviet and factory committees formed their own Red Guard units (many with Bolshevik sympathies) to deal with the threat. Railway workers tore up tracks ahead of Kornilov's army while other workers went out to fraternise with his troops. Kornilov's army quickly withered away and he was arrested.

The Kornilov affair had important results. It left the army leadership totally demoralised. Most officers regarded Kerensky as spineless: they were unlikely to go to his assistance in the future. The affair weakened Kerensky's position in other respects – not least in helping resurrect the Bolsheviks. Leading Bolsheviks (including Trotsky who only now threw in his lot with Lenin) had been instrumental in rousing support to defend Petrograd. It was the Bolsheviks who reaped the praise for averting Kornilov's coup. Moreover, many Bolshevik supporters were now armed.

g) The Situation in October 1917

By September the Bolsheviks had a majority in the Petrograd soviet. Trotsky played a crucial role. Chair of the Petrograd Soviet, he also headed the Military Revolutionary Committee (MRC), set up in October to organise resistance to future threats from the right. The MRC, strongly but not exclusively Bolshevik, had important links with the Petrograd garrison and with the sailors of the Baltic fleet.

It seemed certain that the Bolsheviks would be the largest party in the second All-Russia Congress of Soviets, scheduled to meet in November 1917. Given that this body could declare the Provisional Government's authority null and void, it seemed that all the Bolsheviks had to do was wait for power to fall into their lap. However, Lenin wanted the Bolsheviks to seize power in their own right *before* the meeting of the Congress and before the November elections for the Constituent Assembly (which Kerensky had finally ordered). In late October, Lenin returned to Petrograd and convinced the Bolshevik central committee that the 'time was perfectly ripe' for a Bolshevik coup. Lenin then went back to Finland, leaving it to Trotsky to make the plans. Bolshevik planning was not as well-organised as later propaganda implied. (Lenin had not set a date for the coup!) Even Lenin and Trotsky did not see exactly eye to eye. Rather than seize power before the opening of the Congress, Trotsky's aim was to synchronise the Bolshevik uprising with that opening.

h) The November Revolution

In early November, Kerensky tried to close Bolshevik newspapers and arrest leading Bolsheviks in a pre-emptive strike. This action prompted Bolshevik counter-action. On 7 November Trotsky ordered MRC troops to occupy strategic points in Petrograd. There was virtually no opposition. Indeed most people in Petrograd were unaware that anything unusual was happening. The Winter Palace, home of the Provisional Government, was not immediately attacked: it was defended by only a few hundred officer cadets and female soldiers. Not until late in the evening did the cruiser *Aurora* fire on the Palace. Bolshevik propagandists depicted this as an event of heroic proportion: the prelude to the storming of the Winter Palace by the Red Guard early on 8 November. However, in reality the *Aurora* fired blanks and the storming of the Palace was a damp squib. Kerensky had fled from Petrograd hours before in a vain attempt to find loyal troops. By nightfall most of his ministers had also fled and the Winter Palace's defenders had gone home. The Palace's seizure was purely symbolic.

When the Congess of Soviets met late on 7 November, Lenin proclaimed that the Provisional Government had been overthrown. The Congress, in which the Bolsheviks had a 60 per cent majority, recognised the legality of a new government – the Council of People's Commissars – headed by Lenin. All the Commissars were Bolsheviks. 'All Power to the Soviets' in practice meant 'All Power to the Bolsheviks'. Menshevik and SR deputies left the Congress in disgust.

i) The Treaty of Brest-Litovsk

Lenin immediately began peace negotiations with Germany. Peace terms were finally signed in March 1918. By the terms of the Treaty of Brest-Litovsk Russia lost her Polish territories, the Ukraine, the Baltic States and Finland (Figure 21).

j) Conclusion

After 1917 most Marxist historians claimed that the November Revolution was a popular workers' revolution. However, most Western historians argued that a small clique of well-organised Bolsheviks managed to win power by hoodwinking the masses. Most historians (whether Marxist or Western) saw Lenin as a strategic genius, fulfilling his plans for revolution along lines laid down in 1902. Neither the conspiracy nor the populist explanations entirely hold up. The Bolsheviks were not the most popular party in Russia in 1917. This was proved in the Constituent Assembly elections in November: the Bolsheviks won only 25 per cent of the vote. Nevertheless, by November 1917 the Bolsheviks were undoubtedly popular in both Petrograd and Moscow. By November 1917 the party had at least 250,000 members: it was no longer the small, disciplined group of elite revolutionaries which Lenin had once thought essential to win power. In truth the Bolsheviks in 1917 were not particularly well-disciplined or well-led. Apart from establishing a few guiding principles, Lenin did remarkably little. For most of the eight months between March and November he was not even in Russia. (Trotsky, a better organiser and orator, played a more significant role in October/November.) However, the Bolsheviks were better led than the other socialist parties. Given the unpopularity of the Provisional Government, there was a power vacuum in Russia. Lenin recognised this. He knew just what he wanted: power for himself and the Bolsheviks, not power-sharing. In the event, the Bolshevik seizure of power proved easy. Keeping power would prove more difficult.

4 Why Were the Central Powers Defeated?

a) The USA Enters the War

In January 1917 the German High Command believed that the Central Powers were losing the war. It seemed that their civilian populations were being starved into surrender while their armies were being worn down by attrition. Hindenburg and Ludendorff decided that the U-boat was Germany's last hope of victory. Aware that the

RUSSIA: MARCH–NOVEMBER 1917

April	return of Lenin to Petrograd;
July	the July Days: Kerensky became Prime Minister;
September	the Kornilov affair;
November	Bolshevik Revolution.

ACTIVITY

Consider the following question: 'How important was Lenin's role in bringing about the November Revolution?' Think of four or five points you might make a) stressing the importance of Lenin's role, and, b) claiming he did not play a significant role.

ISSUE
Why and how were the Central Powers defeated?

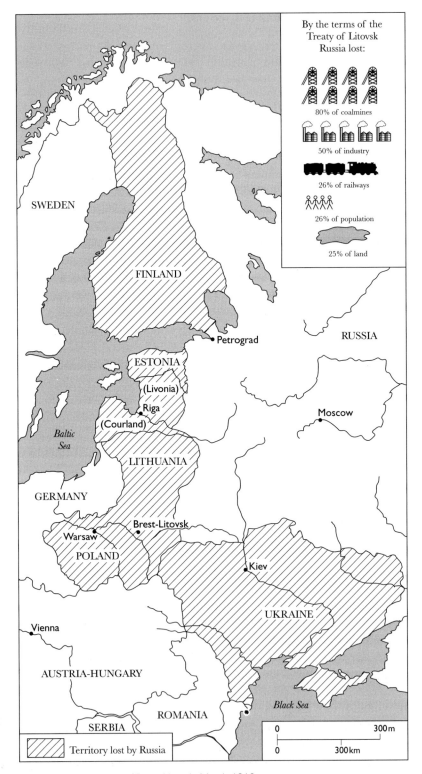

Figure 21 The Treaty of Brest-Litovsk, March 1918.

reintroduction of unrestricted submarine warfare might well bring the USA into the war, they gambled that the U-boats would starve Britain into surrender before significant American military aid could reach Europe. In February 1917, therefore, Germany announced that its U–boats would again sink all ships in Allied waters.

President Wilson immediately severed diplomatic relations with Germany. Some American politicians and newspapers urged a declaration of war. Wilson hesitated. His sympathies had always been with the Allies but he was still anxious to avoid war. Events, however, conspired against him. In March a telegram from the German Foreign Secretary Zimmermann to the German minister in Mexico (promising that Mexico would receive Texas, New Mexico and Arizona if she declared war on the USA) was intercepted by British intelligence and published in the USA. The telegram caused a wave of anti-German sentiment in the USA. The March Revolution in Russia removed a further obstacle to US entry into the war: the war now did seem like a struggle between autocracy and democracy. Late in March three American ships were torpedoed. This seems to have been the last straw. On 6 April the USA declared war on Germany.

The USA entered the war as an 'associated power' – not as an ally of Britain and France. This reflected Wilson's determination to distance the USA from what he saw as the selfish ambitions of the old European powers. In Wilson's view the war was a crusade for democracy and freedom – not a sordid struggle for land and colonies. Despite this difference of emphasis, American entry into the war gave the Allies a tremendous morale boost. However, it would take many months before the USA was able to mobilise its forces. This gave the Central Powers some hope of victory.

b) Allied Problems in 1917

▼ In April General Nivelle's efforts to break through the strong Hindenburg lines failed. A large part of the French army mutinied. Order was restored by Petain (the hero of Verdun) who now replaced Nivelle.
▼ In July British forces launched the third battle of Ypres (also known as Passchendaele). In the four-month offensive, British casualties numbered over 500,000: Britain gained five miles of mud. Passchendaele came to symbolise the war's apparently pointless slaughter.
▼ On the Eastern Front Russia no longer posed a serious military threat. Germany was thus able to transfer large numbers of men to the west.
▼ In October German and Austrian forces defeated the Italians at Caporetto, forcing the Italians into a 50-mile headlong retreat.
▼ The German U-boat gamble came close to success. In April one in four ships heading for British ports was sunk and Britain was threatened with starvation.

THE MAIN EVENTS: 1917

April	USA entered the war;
April–May	Nivelle's Offensive;
July–November	Battle of Passchendaele;
October–November	Battle of Caporetto;
November	Clemenceau became French Prime Minister

c) Central Power Problems in 1917

▼ In June Greece joined the Allies. Allied troops at Salonika could now move against Bulgaria.

▼ The Turks faced a serious Arab revolt. Meanwhile a British advance from Egypt captured Jerusalem.

▼ At sea Britain adopted the convoy system. Fewer ships were sunk and improved 'spotting' methods led to more U-boat losses.

▼ Food shortages helped undermine civilian morale in Germany and Austria–Hungary.

d) The German Spring Offensive: 1918

The outcome of the war was delicately balanced in early 1918. Germany's position on the Eastern Front was secure. But its allies were a source of concern and there was the prospect of a huge American blood transfusion to help the Allies. The longer the war lasted, the worse the situation would become. Germany's military leaders therefore determined to launch a great spring offensive in the west. The offensive was well-planned. In March German troops smashed through British lines on the Somme. A second offensive in April in Flanders was similarly successful. In May/June a third German attack broke through French lines on the Aisne river and advanced to within 37 miles of Paris. But German troops were short of support and supplies and the attack ground to a halt at the river Marne (as in 1914).

Faced by a critical situation, the Allies reorganised their command structure: General Foch was appointed single overall commander. Foch did not lose his nerve. Rather than throw men into battle, he held troops in reserve so that he could counter-attack. This came in July 1918 and was brilliantly successful. The German army was pushed back. On 8 August British forces with more than 600 tanks broke through the German lines at Amiens. The Allied advance continued remorselessly through early September along the entire front.

e) The Defeat of Germany's Allies: 1918

▼ On 30 September Bulgaria surrendered.

▼ British forces continued their advance in the Middle East. On 30 October Turkey agreed to an armistice.

▼ In October the Italians smashed the Austrians at Vittorio Veneto. In late October Czech leaders took over Prague, Serb and Croat leaders proclaimed the establishment of a Yugoslav state, and Hungary declared its independence. The Austrian government finally signed an armistice on 3 November.

f) German Surrender

In late September Hindenburg and Ludendorff, realising the war was lost, abdicated their power, leaving the Reichstag in control. In this way, they hoped that Germany might obtain better peace terms. Moreover the new government (and not the army leaders) would be blamed for Germany's defeat. Led by Prince Max of Baden, the new government asked Wilson for an armistice on the basis of the 14 Points (see page 95). Rejected in January 1918 (when first proposed) because German leaders still thought victory was within their grasp, the 14 Points now seemed to offer a more lenient peace than British or French demands. British and French leaders, though far from happy with the situation, agreed that negotiations should go ahead. (They feared that the USA might otherwise make a separate peace.) The only obstacle to peace now was the Kaiser, whose removal from power Wilson insisted on as a precondition for an armistice. Several weeks of secret negotiation followed. However, by early November Germany was falling apart. Rumours that the High Seas fleet was going to be sent out on a last do-or-die mission against the British fleet led to a mutiny among the sailors at Kiel on 28 October. Mutineers joined up with striking workers and soviets began to spring up on the Russian model. Civil war threatened Germany. On 9 November Wilhelm II abdicated and fled to Holland. On 11 November the new German socialist government agreed to the Allies' armistice terms and the First World War ended at 11.00 a.m.

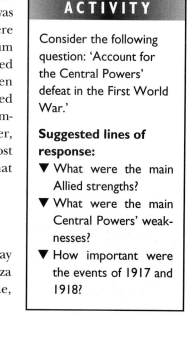

THE MAIN EVENTS: 1918

March	Treaty of Brest-Litovsk;
March–July	Ludendorff offensive;
July–November	Allied counter-offensive;
October	mutiny of German sailors at Kiel;
November	armistice between Allies and Germany.

g) The Armistice

The armistice terms were designed to remove Germany's ability to fight. German troops were ordered to withdraw beyond the Rhine. The Germans were also deprived of large quantities of war material, including all their submarines and much of their surface fleet and air force. Finally, the blockade of Germany was to continue until peace terms had been drawn up and accepted. The armistice was greeted with shock by many Germans who thought they were winning the war. (German troops still controlled most of Belgium and huge areas of eastern Europe.) After 1918 nationalists claimed that the German army might still have won the war had it not been for the 'November criminals' – socialists and Jews – who 'stabbed Germany in the back'. Certainly, the mutinies and strikes in November 1918 made continuation of the war almost impossible. However, the armistice came about because Hindenburg and Ludendorff lost their nerve or, perhaps more accurately, saw sense, appreciating that German defeat was inevitable.

h) The Cost of the War

About 10 million men died in total. A further 5 million civilians may have died from diseases related to food shortages. A great influenza epidemic in 1918–19, which killed millions of people worldwide, added to the misery.

ACTIVITY

Consider the following question: 'Account for the Central Powers' defeat in the First World War.'

Suggested lines of response:
▼ What were the main Allied strengths?
▼ What were the main Central Powers' weaknesses?
▼ How important were the events of 1917 and 1918?

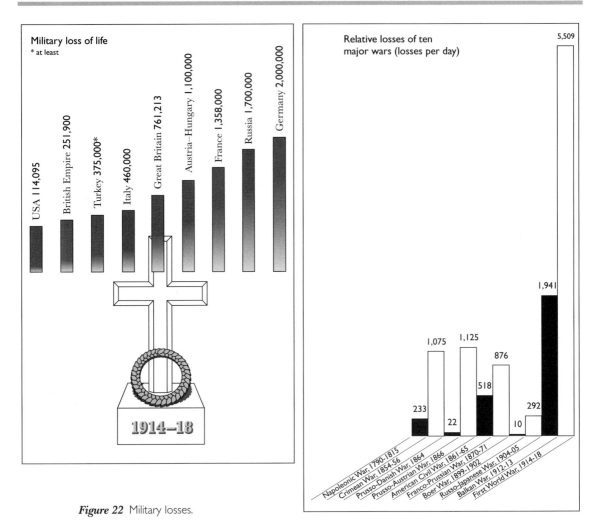

Military loss of life
* at least

USA 114,095
British Empire 251,900
Turkey 375,000*
Italy 460,000
Great Britain 761,213
Austria–Hungary 1,100,000
France 1,358,000
Russia 1,700,000
Germany 2,000,000

1914–18

Relative losses of ten major wars (losses per day)

5,509
1,941
1,125
1,075
876
518
292
233
22
10

Napoleonic War, 1790-1815
Crimean War, 1854-56
Prusso-Danish War, 1864
Prusso-Austrian War, 1866
American Civil War, 1861-65
Franco-Prussian War, 1870-71
Boer War, 1899-1902
Russo-Japanese War, 1904-05
Balkan War, 1912-13
First World War, 1914-18

Figure 22 Military losses.

5 The Peace Settlement

a) Allied War Aims Pre-1919

In August 1914 none of the Allied powers had clearly stated war aims. However, as the war progressed, they formulated some specific (and often secret) aims. Britain and France, for example, agreed which parts of the Ottoman Empire each would annexe. Italy and Romania were both promised Austro-Hungarian territory as a way of persuading them to join the Allied side. Ironically, a war waged mainly against Germany thus became a war for the dismemberment of the Ottoman and Habsburg Empires!

Woodrow Wilson had outlined his war aims – his 14 Points – in January 1918. Wilson thought he knew why the war had started: by eliminating those causes (for example, secret alliances and frustrated nationalism) he hoped that in future war would be avoided. In his view, the peace should contain 'no annexations, no contributions, no punitive damages'. The 14 Points were regarded as idealistic pipe-dreams by many hard-headed British and French statesmen. But they needed to retain US support and could not reject Wilson's proposals out of hand. Interestingly, Wilson's attitude had hardened somewhat by November 1918: he now insisted – and the Germans accepted – that Germany should make compensation 'for all damage done to the civilian population of the Allies'.

b) The Peacemaking Process

In January 1919 the leaders of 32 countries assembled in Paris to make peace. (Wilson had arrived in Europe – ominously for those who were superstitious – on Friday 13 December 1918.) The Conference quickly settled down into some kind of routine. The bulk of the detailed work was done by 58 commissions and committees set up to deal with specific matters. The main decisions were taken by a Council of Ten comprising the prime ministers and foreign ministers of the USA, Britain, France, Japan and Italy. However, Japan played only a minor role. Its main concern was to win territory in Asia. Once this was achieved, it took little interest in other negotiations. In March the Council of Ten was replaced by a Council of Four comprising Wilson, Lloyd George, Clemenceau and Orlando (the Italian leader). Orlando, however, was on the fringes of the game: Lloyd George, Clemenceau and Wilson were the key men.

c) The Problems of Peacemaking

▽ The sheer immensity of the task of reconstructing Europe was appalling. There was political and economic chaos (including famine) across much of central and eastern Europe.
▽ The Habsburg Emperor, Karl, had abdicated and in the last weeks of the war several of the Empire's nationalities had declared independence. The dozen or so nationalities within the old Empire lived uneasily side by side and in some areas there were no clear-cut boundaries between them. Various national groups were actually fighting over boundaries as the peacemakers met. Another Europe was thus taking shape beyond the control of the Paris peacemakers.
▽ There was the fear that Bolshevism might spread westwards from Russia. By 1919 the red flag already waved over government buildings in Munich and Budapest.

THE 14 POINTS

1. 'Open covenants of peace, openly arrived at'.
2. Freedom of navigation on the seas.
3. Removal of economic barriers between nations.
4. Reduction in armaments, 'to the lowest points consistent with domestic safety'.
5. Colonial problems to be settled with reference to the interests of colonial peoples.
6. Evacuation of all Russian territory.
7. Evacuation of Belgium.
8. Evacuation of French territory and the return of Alsace-Lorraine to France.
9. Readjustment of Italy's boundaries along 'clearly recognizable lines of nationality'.
10. Autonomy for the peoples of Austria–Hungary.
11. Evacuation of Romanian and Serbian territory.
12. Autonomous developments for the peoples of the Ottoman Empire.
13. Creation of an independent Poland made up of all those areas 'indisputably Polish': the new Poland to have secure access to the sea.
14. Establishment of a 'general association of nations'.

Figure 23 The 'Big Three' at Versailles: David Lloyd George, Georges Clemenceau and Woodrow Wilson.

SELF-DETERMINATION

The right of people of a particular nation (normally defined as people speaking the same language) to rule themselves.

THE LEAGUE OF NATIONS

The League of Nations, Woodrow Wilson's obsession, was written into the Treaty of Versailles. Interestingly, the Americans had come to Paris with only rather woolly ideas whereas Britain had prepared a concrete scheme for the League. This became the framework for the League.

▼ Commitments made during the war added to the complexity of the negotiations. For example, promises made to Italy to entice it into the war (including areas with large German populations) were clearly at odds with Wilson's principle of **self-determination**.

▼ The Big Three were under considerable pressure from their respective countries. Most people in Britain and France demanded vengeance. One British politician urged the victors to 'squeeze the German lemon until the pips squeak'.

▼ Lloyd George, Clemenceau and Wilson held different views about how best to ensure a durable peace settlement.

i) Clemenceau's Aims

Clemenceau wanted German power permanently reduced so that never again would it be able to threaten France. In demanding a harsh peace, he was seeking no more than every Frenchman expected.

ii) Wilson's Aims

Wilson was primarily concerned with establishing a just and lasting system of international relations. He intended to set up an international body – a **League of Nations** – to ensure the peaceful settlement of future disputes. Wilson had two other related goals: the extension of democracy and the application of self-determination.

iii) Lloyd George's Aims

During the December 1918 election campaign, Lloyd George had given the impression that he would impose a harsh peace on Germany. However, he was not as anti-German as the British electorate hoped and expected. Realising the danger of leaving an embittered Germany, Lloyd George was inclined to leniency. He also feared that a humiliated Germany might be driven into the arms of the Bolsheviks. Thus, while he 'talked hard' for home consumption, on most key issues he stood with Wilson against Clemenceau.

d) The Treaty of Versailles

i) The Territorial Terms

Negotiations about Germany's frontiers were highly contentious. At first the French demanded that Germany's western frontier be fixed on the River Rhine. The area on the left bank would go to France or become an independent state. Lloyd George and Wilson both opposed this idea, believing it would become a cause of constant German resentment. The settlement of Germany's eastern border was even more contentious. The 14 Points had promised to create an independent Poland which would have secure access to the sea. However, there was no clear-cut division between areas of German and Polish population. Clemenceau wanted a strong Poland and supported the most extreme Polish territorial claims. But Lloyd George feared incorporating millions of embittered Germans within the new state. As a result of his pressure, the German port of Danzig (today Gdansk) was made a Free City and **plebiscites** were held in Upper Silesia and Allenstein, ensuring that Germany retained some disputed areas. Even so, virtually all Germans were outraged by the loss of land to Poland, especially the loss of the Polish corridor which separated East Prussia from the rest of Germany.

> **PLEBISCITE**
> A kind of referendum. All the adults of an area vote on a particular issue or set of questions.

In the south, Germany was forbidden to unite with Austria. Had it been allowed to do so, Germany would have been stronger in 1919 than in 1914. This meant that Germans could claim that the principle of self-determination was not extended to them.

Germany also lost all her colonies. On Wilson's insistence Germany's ex-colonies were to be ruled as mandates. This meant that the ruling powers had to bear in mind the wishes of the colonial inhabitants who should be prepared for self-government.

ii) German Disarmament

Germany was to have no tanks or aeroplanes and its army was limited to 100,000 men. It was to have no large battleships and no submarines. Most of its fleet was to be surrendered to the Allies. (In fact,

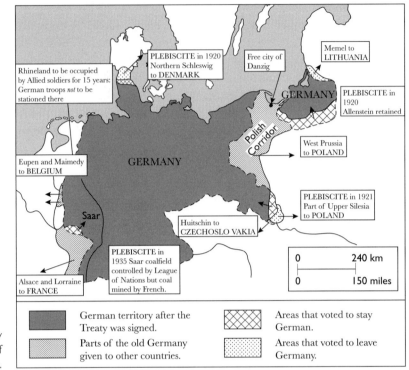

Figure 24 Territory lost by Germany at the Treaty of Versailles.

the crews, in a last act of defiance, scuttled their ships at Scapa Flow in the Orkneys in June 1919.)

iii) Reparation and War Guilt

By article 231 Germany had to accept full responsibility for causing the war. This war guilt clause – hated by the Germans – provided a moral base for the Allied demands for Germany to pay reparations. The main difficulty was deciding how much Germany could and should pay, and how this money should be divided among the Allies. No single issue caused more acrimony. Wilson wanted a reparations settlement based on Germany's ability to pay. However, the French and British publics wanted to extract huge payments which would help the Allied countries meet the cost of war and also weaken Germany financially for years to come. Lloyd George was pulled several ways. He was determined that Britain should get its fair share of reparations, insisting (successfully) that 'damage' should include merchant shipping losses and the costs of pensions to those disabled, widowed or orphaned by the war. But, like Wilson, he thought that Germany should only pay what it could reasonably afford and he was impressed by the view that if Germany was hit too hard it would no longer be a good market for British goods. However, he could not afford to ignore the prevailing mood in Britain or the fact that he

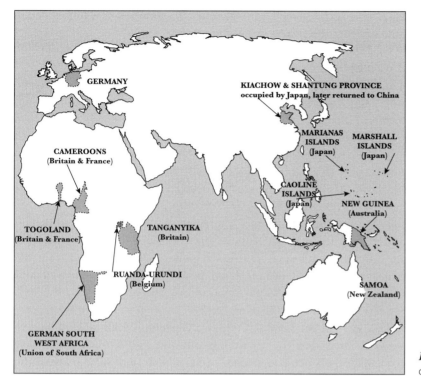

Figure 25 Loss of German colonies.

himself had promised to screw Germany 'to the uttermost farthing'. A Reparations Commission was eventually set up to determine the amount Germany should pay. In 1921 it recommended a sum of £6,600 million. Although this was far less than originally envisaged, some economists and most Germans claimed (probably wrongly) that it was more than Germany could afford.

The Treaty of Versailles was completed in great haste at the end of April 1919. The Germans, allowed only three weeks to make written observations, attacked nearly every provision. In the end, however, Germany had no option but to accept the treaty or face the threat of invasion. The Treaty was finally signed in the Hall of Mirrors at Versailles on 28 June 1919 – the same place in which the German Empire had been proclaimed in 1871.

e) Criticisms of Versailles

Arguably the problems facing Europe by 1919 were so great that, even if the Big Three had agreed upon everything, it would have been virtually impossible to construct a lasting peace settlement. Gilbery White, a member of the American delegation, said of the peacemakers: 'It is not surprising that they made a bad peace: what is surprising is that they made peace at all'. However, it is highly debatable whether the peace was, in fact, 'bad'.

i) Contemporary Views

The Big Three were not unaware of the deficiencies in their handiwork. But this was precisely why, so far as Wilson and Lloyd George were concerned, the League of Nations was created. In 1919 Lloyd George said that it would 'be there as a Court of Appeal to readjust crudities, irregularities, injustices'. This was perhaps putting too much faith in an organisation which lacked enforcement powers. Moreover the League was also to lack the USA. The US Senate refused to ratify the Treaty of Versailles and thus the USA did not join the League. In contrast, the treaty was well received in Britain and passed through parliament with overwhelming majorities. On the whole, Britain seemed to have gained what it wanted from the peace settlement. German naval power had been destroyed and Germany had agreed to pay reparations. The prevailing British view was that the treaty was firm but just.

This was not the view in Germany. Germans of all political persuasions claimed that the treaty was punitive and a major departure from Wilson's 14 Points. Radical opinion in Britain soon reached the same conclusion. In 1919 the economist J.M. Keynes wrote a devastating critique of the treaty, particularly its reparation clauses, in an influential book, *The Economic Consequences of the Peace*. He argued that a naive Wilson had been forced by a vindictive Clemenceau and a scheming Lloyd George to agree to an over-harsh peace. It soon became apparent that even Lloyd George had doubts about the treaty, suspecting that Germany had been treated unfairly. These doubts were echoed by many British politicians after 1919.

However, most Frenchmen considered the treaty far too soft. After a costly war, for which it was largely to blame, Germany had lost only 13 per cent of its pre-war territory and 10 per cent of its population. Surrounded by small, unstable states on its southern and eastern borders, it remained potentially Europe's strongest state. Clemenceau had been prepared to accept the Versailles terms only because Wilson and Lloyd George had offered France a defensive alliance. The Senate, however, refused to ratify this guarantee and Britain then did likewise. Most Frenchmen, in consequence, felt betrayed.

ii) Historians' Views

Historians have echoed the contemporary criticisms. Many think the treaty was the worst of all worlds – too severe to be acceptable to most Germans, and too lenient to constrain Germany. Arguably the peacemakers' failure to solve the German problem in 1919 laid the foundations of the Second World War. Versailles left Germany with grievances and also with the latent potential to make trouble.

However, it is possible to defend the peacemakers. Even with hind-sight, it is difficult to suggest realistic solutions to the German problem. Certainly, when compared to the Treaty of Brest-Litovsk, Versailles was lenient. Virtually all of the German territory lost (except Danzig and the Polish Corridor) was justified on the grounds of nationality. (More Poles were left under German rule than Germans under Polish rule.) Most of the Germans who were outside Germany (e.g. in Czechoslovakia) had been Austrian.

f) The Settlement of South and Eastern Europe

Once the Treaty of Versailles had been signed, the Big Three returned home and the completion of treaties with Germany's allies was left to less eminent representatives. They had a difficult job, given the disintegration of the Habsburg Empire and the fact that Russia was in the throes of civil war. Some British and French states-men would have liked to retain the Habsburg Empire in some form, if only as a counterweight to Russia and Germany. But given the intense nationalist feeling amongst the peoples of the former empire this was impossible. Most Allied statesmen supported the principle of self-determination and efforts were made to redraw frontiers along ethnic lines. All the defeated countries were ordered to pay reparations and reduce their armed forces.

The eastern treaties, combined with various settlements along the Russian borders, ultimately created a string of new states from Finland to Yugoslavia. Disputes over frontiers continued well into the 1920s. Although the peacemakers did their best to apply the principle of self-determination, so mixed were the various nationalities that all over eastern Europe large communities found themselves governed by people of a different ethnic group. Czechoslovakia, for example, had a population of about 14,500,000 made up of Czechs, Slovaks, Germans, Hungarians, Ruthenians and Poles. The Czechs were a minority in what they saw as their own country. Few countries were happy with the settlement. Bulgaria, Hungary and Austria were left bitter and resentful. Many of the new states were at odds among themselves over disputed boundaries. Even Italy was unhappy. Although it had gained territory from Austria, most Italians thought these gains were derisory, given that some 600,000 Italians had died. Nor had it gained all the land promised in 1915.

ACTIVITY

The Treaty of Versailles is a good topic for debate. Half the group should prepare an argument defending the treaty: the other half should argue that the treaty was a failure.

TREATY OF ST GERMAIN

Signed with Austria in September 1919. Austria lost the Trentino, much of South Tyrol and Istria with Trieste to Italy, and large amounts of land to Czechoslovakia, Poland, Yugoslavia and Romania. The population of Austria was reduced from 22 m to 6.5 m.

TREATY OF NEUILLY

Signed with Bulgaria in November 1919. Bulgaria lost territory to Yugoslavia, Greece and Romania.

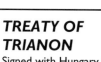

Figure 26 The Balkan and Turkish settlement, 1919–23.

TREATY OF TRIANON

Signed with Hungary in June 1920. Two-thirds of Hungary's pre-war territory was given to Czechoslovakia, Yugoslavia and Romania. Hungary's population was reduced from 21 m to 7.5 m.

TREATY OF SEVRES

Signed with Turkey in August 1920.

▼ The Straits, linking the Black Sea and the Mediterranean, were to be demilitarised and placed under international supervision.

▼ The Arab areas of the Ottoman Empire were given as mandates to Britain and France. France acquired Syria and Lebanon. Britain acquired present – day Israel, Jordan and Iraq.

▼ Greece gained East Thrace, Smyrna and several Aegean islands.

g) Some Other Effects of the War

i) Political Consequences

▼ After 1919 Europe was divided into states which wished to uphold the peace settlement (notably France) and those which were determined to revise it (notably Germany).

▼ By 1919 there was a power vacuum in central and eastern Europe. It was unlikely that the new states would be strong enough to withstand future challenges from embittered German or Russian governments.

▼ The settlement reduced the number of people living in a state in which they were not the dominant nationality from 60 to 30 million. However, the 1919 minorities were probably more discontented than those in 1914 and many looked to neighbouring states for aid.

ii) Economic and Social Consequences

▼ The war had been incredibly expensive. Most countries had borrowed to pay for it. Many countries were in debt to Britain. Britain, in turn, was in debt to the USA. Germany owed reparations to Britain and

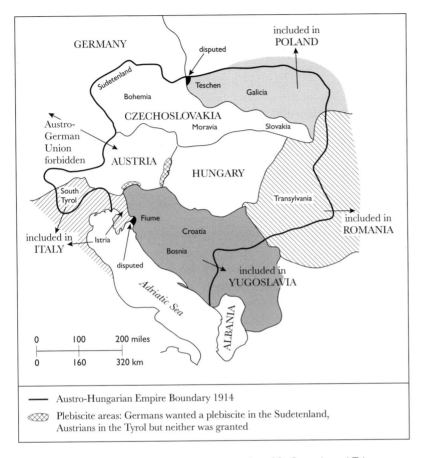

Figure 27 The former Habsburg Empire: the treaties of St Germain and Trianon.

France but received loans from the USA. The financial situation was thus chaotic.

▼ During the war most governments had printed paper money, encouraging inflation.

▼ European economic growth was retarded by the war. European firms lost markets abroad to American and Japanese companies.

▼ Millions of men were left physically or psychologically disabled. There were also huge numbers of widows and orphans.

▼ Debate rages about the effect that the war had on women's roles. During the war some women had done men's jobs – and done them as well as men. It is thus possible to claim that women as a whole gained both respect and self-confidence which was reflected in their successful demands for the vote post-1918. However, arguably women were little more than cheap labour during the war. After 1918 most women returned, quite gladly in most cases, to their previous domestic role.

TREATY OF LAUSANNE

In 1919–20 Mustafa Kemal led a national uprising and overthrew the Ottoman family. Turkey defeated Greece in 1921–2 and a new agreement, the Treaty of Lausanne, was signed in 1923. This was the first significant revision of the peace settlement.

▼ Turkey regained much of the land lost to Greece.

▼ It no longer had to pay reparations.

▼ Working on The Impact of the First World War

Your reading of this chapter should ensure that you have a view on which country contributed most to Germany's defeat.

▼ The Russians suffered the most casualties.

▼ France played a major role from first to last. She lost twice as many men as Britain.

▼ The British navy's blockade of Germany was vital. The British army (perhaps the best in Europe by 1918) played a major role in defeating both Turkey and Germany.

▼ The USA's contribution was crucial. While Americans did not actually do much fighting, the prospect of fresh troops, arriving at the rate of 300,000 a month by August 1918, terrified the Germans. US intervention thus encouraged the Allies and demoralised the Germans. In Ludendorff's view: 'America became the deciding factor in the war.' Do you agree?

Answering Extended Writing and Essay Questions on The Impact of the First World War

Consider the following question: 'Why was the first Revolution in Russia in 1917 followed so soon by a second one?'

The first point to notice is that this question is about the November – not the March – Revolution. Historians are divided about whether the November Revolution was the result of the weaknesses and mistakes of the Provisional Government or the strengths and successful policies of the Bolsheviks. The debate is rather like discussing the outcome of a soccer match. Given the situation in March 1917 was it always likely that the Bolsheviks would 'win'? Did the Provisional Government 'play' badly? Was it let down by some of its key 'players' (e.g. Kerensky)? Did the Bolsheviks 'play' well? How important were Lenin and Trotsky? Taking all the evidence into account, explain why you think the November Revolution occurred.

Answering Source-Based Questions on The Impact of the First World War

> It must be a peace without victory ... Victory would mean peace forced upon the loser, a victor's terms imposed upon the vanquished. It would be accepted in humiliation, under duress as an intolerable sacrifice, and would leave a sting, a resentment, a bitter memory upon which terms of peace would rest, not permanently, but only as upon quicksand.

Source B President Wilson's Address to the Senate, 22 January 1917.

> I cannot imagine any greater cause for future war than for the German people who have proved themselves one of the most powerful and vigorous races of the world, should be surrounded by a number of small states, many of them consisting of peoples who have never previously set up a stable government for themselves, but each containing large masses of Germans clamouring for reunion with their native land ... You may strip Germany of her colonies, reduce her armaments to a mere police force and her navy to that of a fifth rate power; all the same in the end if she feels that she has been unjustly treated ... she will find means of exacting retribution.

Source C Lloyd George in the Fontainbleu Memorandum, March 1919.

> The military and naval conditions are undeniably severe, but not in our opinion, a whit more stringent than the safety of Europe and the world requires ... The articles on reparations may not seem so satisfactory. The principle that Germany is to accept responsibility for all the loss and damage she has done appears to be accepted. At the same time we are told that the Allies recognise her inability and inability of her confederates to make this loss and damage good.

Source D The Times, May 1919.

> The last time I had the opportunity of addressing the House upon this Treaty its main outlines had been settled. I ventured to call it a 'stern but just Treaty'. I adhere to that description. The terms are in many respects, terrible terms to impose upon a country. Terrible were the deeds that it requites. Terrible are the consequences that were inflicted upon the world. Still more terrible would have been the consequences had they succeeded. What do these terms mean to Germany?
> Take the territorial terms. In so far as territories have been taken away from Germany, it is a restoration. Alsace-Lorraine, forcibly taken from the land to which its population were deeply attached. Is it an injustice to restore them to their country? Schleswig-Holstein, the

Source E Lloyd George speaking to the House of Commons in June 1919.

meanest of the Hohenzollern frauds; robbing a small, poor, helpless country and then retaining that land against the wishes of the population for fifty to sixty years. I am glad the opportunity has come for restoring Schleswig-Holstein. Poland, torn to bits, to feed the carnivorous greed of Russian, Austrian and Prussian autocracy. This Treaty has re-knit the torn flag of Poland.

PEACE AND FUTURE CANNON FODDER

Source F Will Dyson's cartoon about the Peace Conference.

The Tiger: " Curious! I seem to hear a child weeping ! "

▼ QUESTIONS ON SOURCES

1. What concerns are expressed in Sources B, C and F about the peace settlement? **[10 marks]**

2. Examine Sources D and E. How do they justify the peace settlement? **[10 marks]**

3. Using your own knowledge, explain which of these sources was the most accurate in its analysis of the peace settlement and its likely consequences. **[25 marks]**

Points to note about the questions

Question 1 All the Sources express similar concerns but Source C is rather more explicit.

Question 2 You will probably need to refer to Figure 27 to make yourself familiar with some of the areas mentioned in Source E.

Question 3 The 1919 peacemakers are sometimes blamed for causing the Second World War. Was Germany left so aggrieved that a second conflict was likely or inevitable? Or did the peacemakers do a good job in very difficult circumstances? Note that there is no right or wrong answer to this question. It is the quality of your argument that matters, not the source you select.

Further Reading

Books in the Access to History series

On The First World War and the peace settlement, try the first chapters in *War and Peace: International Relations 1914–45* by David Williamson. On the Russian Revolution, Chapters 5 and 6 in *Reaction and Revolutions: Russia 1881–1924* by Michael Lynch are excellent.

General

Try *The Great War 1914–18* by S.C. Tucker, 1997 (UCL Press) as a starter. *The Great War* by M. Ferro, 1973 (Routledge) and *The First World War* by A.J.P. Taylor, 1963 (Penguin) are still good accounts. Among the best recent texts are *The Oxford Illustrated History of the First World War* by H. Strachan, ed., 1998 (OUP) and *The First World War* by J. Keegan, 1998 (Hutchinson).

On the peace settlement, try *Versailles and After* by R. Henig, 1995 (Routledge) and the first chapter of *The Lost Peace: International Relations in Europe 1918–39* by A. Adamthwaite, 1980 (Edward Arnold).

For the Russian Revolution, a good place to start is Chapter 13 of *Years of Change: Europe 1890–1945* by Robert Wolfson and John Laver. Try also *Russia 1914–41* by John Laver in the History at Source series (Hodder & Stoughton). Chapters 3–8 in *The Russian Revolution 1917–1921: A Short History* by J.D. White, 1994 (Edward Arnold) and Chapter 5 of *The End of Imperial Russia 1855–1917* by P. Waldron, 1997 (Macmillan) are well worth reading. So are Chapters 1 and 2 in *The Russian Revolution* by S. Fitzpatrick, 1986 (OUP).

CHAPTER 4

THE SOVIET UNION: 1917–41

POINTS TO CONSIDER

Following the November 1917 Revolution first Lenin and then Stalin controlled Russia. Their actions dominate this chapter. Although historians tend to shy away from using the words 'good' and 'bad', there is a moral dimension to history and you will have to make up your own mind whether you approve or disapprove of what Lenin and Stalin aimed to do and did. The chapter has been divided into an Introduction and seven sections. You need to read it all. If you are only studying Lenin you need to have some notion of what happened after his death. (To what extent was he responsible for Stalinism?) If you are only studying Stalin, you need to know something about Lenin. (Was he Lenin's heir – as he claimed?)

ISSUE

How successful were Lenin and Stalin?

Given the situation in Russia in November 1917, it was probably easier to achieve power than to keep it. The Bolsheviks now had to tackle the problems which had helped bring them to power. In 1918–19, as Civil War tore Russia apart, it seemed unlikely that Lenin's regime would survive. Yet survive it did. Why it did so is one of the key issues. Another is Lenin's role and the extent of his success before his death in 1924. Many people assumed that Trotsky, hero of both the Revolution and the Civil War, would succeed Lenin. Instead the power struggle was won by Stalin. The effects of his collectivisation and industrialisation programmes still generate massive debate. So do his purges which resulted in millions of deaths. The system that Lenin established and Stalin built upon lasted for fifty years after 1941. 1941, however, is a good place to take stock. In that year Russia was attacked by Nazi Germany. To what extent was the country prepared for the challenge? To what extent had Lenin and Stalin, in accordance with their Marxist aims, created a workers' state in which everything was run by the state on behalf of the workers?

1 Bolshevik Rule, 1917–18

a) The Situation in November 1917

In November 1917 Lenin's government faced several problems.
▼ The Bolsheviks had little support outside the main cities.
▼ Industrial production was falling, inflation had reached uncontrollable heights, the transport system was crippled and there were severe food shortages in the towns.
▼ Some areas, such as Finland, had declared independence from Russia.
▼ Suspicious of Bolshevism, the Allied countries were set to intervene in Russia if Lenin made peace with Germany.

b) Repression and Dictatorship

Lenin's government immediately resorted to dictatorial methods. All non-Bolshevik newspapers were banned and leading opponents arrested. A new secret police force – the Cheka – was set up and given sweeping powers. Lenin was not a democrat. He believed that the workers needed the 'enlightened leadership' of the Bolsheviks to guide them towards socialism. Disregarding the results of the Constituent Assembly elections, in which the Bolsheviks won only a quarter of the seats, he ordered the Assembly to be dissolved at gun point in January 1918, after only one day in session. Scores of Bolshevik opponents were shot in subsequent street demonstrations. But while Bolshevik Russia was a dictatorship, central intervention in the provinces was limited. Lenin's government simply telegraphed its revolutionary decrees to towns across Russia hoping that local groups would act on them. Some did. Many did not.

Figure 28 Lenin.

	Votes	Seats
SRs	17,490,000	370
Bolsheviks	9,844,000	175
National minority groups	8,257,000	99
Left SRs (pro-Bolshevik)	2,861,000	40
Kadets (Constitutional Democrats)	1,986,000	17
Mensheviks	1,248,000	16
Total	41,686,000	717

Table 7 Elections for the Constituent Assembly, 1917.

c) Bolshevik Economic Policy

▼ Church lands and the estates of rich landlords were confiscated. Local peasant soviets were instructed to oversee land redistribution. In effect, this officially sanctioned what had been happening since March

1917. By allowing the peasants to keep the occupied land, Lenin won peasant approval.

▼ The 'commanding heights' of industry – large factories, railways, mines and banks – were nationalised. While small factories were exempted from government takeover, workers often took them over anyway.

▼ The Supreme Council of the National Economy (Vesenkha) was set up. It was intended to oversee the entire economy.

These measures did little to improve Russia's economic plight. In the towns, factory output continued to collapse while the food-supply problem worsened.

Other significant developments: November 1917–March 1918

▼ All class privileges, ranks and titles were abolished.
▼ The separation of church and state was proclaimed.
▼ Divorce was made easy.
▼ Minority nationalities were offered more independence.
▼ Russia adopted the modern calendar.
▼ The Bolshevik Party became known as the Communist Party.
▼ The Russian capital was moved to Moscow – much easier to defend than Petrograd.

---

d) The Treaty of Brest-Litovsk

Lenin had promised an immediate peace with Germany. Trotsky was given the task of peacemaking. Hoping that the Central Powers would collapse and revolution would follow, he preferred delaying tactics to immediate surrender. Frustrated by Trotsky's tactics, German forces again advanced. Aware that Russian forces were too weak to prevent Germany taking whatever territory it wanted, Lenin accepted the Treaty of Brest-Litovsk in 1918 (see page 90). The Treaty was both a humiliation and an economic disaster. Russia lost areas containing 26 per cent of Russia's population, 27 per cent of its arable land, and over 70 per cent of its iron and coal industry. Lenin still hoped that the Bolshevik revolution would spark off workers' risings across Europe. He thus calculated that Brest-Litovsk would be only temporary: in the aftermath of a European proletarian revolution, he expected that Germany and Austria–Hungary would renounce their ill-gotten war gains.

ACTIVITY

Brainstorm four or five reasons which might explain the mounting opposition to the Bolsheviks by 1918.

2 The Civil War

Large numbers of Russians did not accept Bolshevik ('Red') rule. By late-1918 Lenin only controlled Petrograd and Moscow and the land between. Elsewhere a confusion of opponents were in the process of establishing anti-Bolshevik ('White') governments. The Whites comprised tsarist supporters, liberals, Mensheviks and SRs – groups which had little in common except a hatred of the Bolsheviks. The Bolsheviks presented the Civil War as a class war but it was far more complex than this. As well as the (multi-toned) Whites, there were also the 'Blacks' (anarchists) and the 'Greens' (peasant groups who opposed both Reds and Whites). The sheer size of Russia often meant that local matters predominated over national issues. Some national groups who had declared independence from Russia were ready to fight to maintain their independence.

a) The Start of the War

The actions of the Czech Legion, a force of 40,000 Czechs who had volunteered to fight for Russia as a way of gaining independence from Austria–Hungary, brought troubles to a head in May 1918. After Russia made peace, the Czechs set out to Vladivostok, aiming to rejoin the Allies on the Western Front. En route, they met resistance from local Bolshevik forces. The Czechs fought back, winning control of much of the trans-Siberian railway. Czech success encouraged Bolshevik opponents to come out openly against Lenin. By November, White leader Admiral Kolchak controlled much of Siberia.

b) Foreign Intervention

In March 1918, Allied forces landed at Murmansk and Archangel. In April Japanese troops occupied Vladivostok and were soon joined by American troops. In 1918–19 British troops entered parts of southern Russia while British warships sailed into Russian Baltic waters and into the Black Sea. The French established a major base around the Black Sea port of Odessa. The appearance of foreign forces encouraged the formation of other White governments, for example that of General Yudenich in Estonia.

c) Red Victory

The decisive battles of the Civil War were fought in 1919. Red forces drove back the advancing troops of Denikin, Kolchak and Yudenich

REASONS FOR FOREIGN INTERVENTION
▼ The Bolsheviks had nationalised a large number of foreign companies, frozen all foreign assets, and declared that they had no intention of honouring Russia's war debts.
▼ White regimes promised to continue to fight against Germany if they gained power.
▼ The Allies were determined to stop vital war supplies, previously loaned to Russia and still stockpiled there, from falling into German hands.
▼ The Allies hoped to destroy Bolshevism (a perceived threat).
▼ Some countries (like Poland and Romania) hoped to win land at Russia's expense.

THE FATE OF NICHOLAS AND ALEXANDRA

After the March Revolution, ex-Tsar Nicholas II and his family were held prisoner. By mid-July 1918 they were under house arrest in Ekaterinburg, which seemed set to fall to the Whites. The Romanov family (and some of their servants) were last seen alive on 16 July. Despite Lenin's announcement that local Bolsheviks had executed them, doubts remained about the Romanovs' fate. White forces captured Ekaterinburg on 25 July and found signs of a mass execution in the basement of the house in which the royal family had been prisoners. A White investigative team claimed to have discovered their bodies but many doubted the reliability of its findings. For many years it was suspected that one or more of the royal family might have survived. In 1991 bones were found in a forest near Ekaterinburg. DNA tests indicated that they were those of the Romanovs.

Source A

and recaptured Murmansk and Archangel after Allied troops pulled out in the autumn. Railways were crucial in transporting troops to critical points. It was no accident that key battles took place near rail-heads, or that Trotsky, the Red commander, used a heavily-armed special train as his headquarters.

In April 1920 Polish forces drove deep into the Ukraine, capturing Kiev. However, the Polish invasion was repulsed and the Red Army in turn advanced into Poland, hoping to incite a communist revolt. But most Poles rallied behind their government and the Russians were driven out of Poland, losing parts of Belorussia and the Ukraine in the process. (The Treaty of Riga, which defined the Russian-Polish frontier, was signed in 1921.) In late 1920 White forces in the Crimea were evacuated by the British navy. Although some fighting continued in Georgia and Siberia, the Reds had won the Civil War.

d) Why did the Reds Win?

i) The Red Army

Trotsky ensured that the Red Army was a formidable force. Ignoring the objections of many Bolsheviks, he enlisted some 40,000 ex-tsarist officers to train and lead the army. As a precaution, political commissars (dedicated Party workers) were attached to the army to report on the officers' reliability. The practice of electing officers was abandoned. The Red Army soon outstripped its opponents in terms of numbers, fighting efficiency and morale.

ii) Red Terror

The Reds used terror more effectively than the Whites. The chief instrument was the Cheka. Historian Martin McCauley gives some idea of Cheka methods:

> In Kharkov, Chekists scalped their prisoners and took the skin, like gloves, off their hands ... In Poltava they impaled 18 monks and burnt at the stake peasants who rebelled. In Odessa they boiled officers and ripped them in half.

iii) White Divisions

The Whites distrusted each other and quarrelled amongst themselves. The Reds, by contrast, were relatively united.

iv) Leadership

As Commissar for War, Trotsky's contribution to Bolshevik victory was crucial. Lenin, who decided high policy, also played a vital role. No White leader of the stature of Trotsky or Lenin emerged.

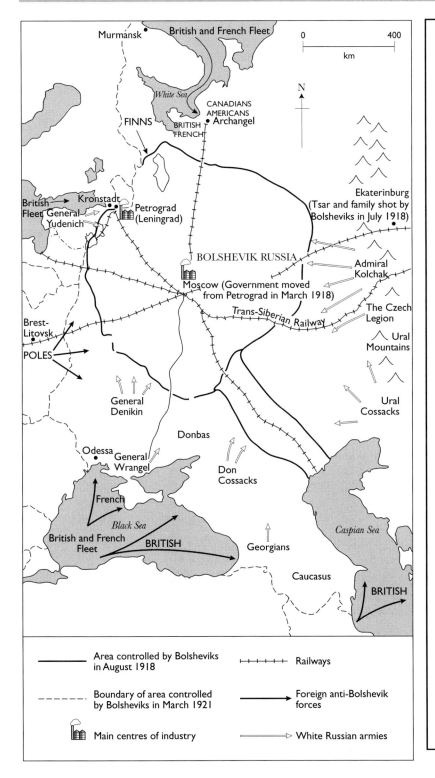

Figure 29 The Russian Civil War, 1918–20.

WAR COMMUNISM

▼ All industry was brought under state control.

▼ The dislocated transport system, the shortage of manpower resulting from conscription into the Red Army, and the flight of townsfolk into the countryside in search of food, led to a steep fall in industrial production.

▼ Industry's problems deepened by hyperinflation. Bolshevik policy of printing paper money destroyed the rouble's value.

▼ For Lenin the most pressing reason for introducing war communism was the critical food shortage. He blamed the richer peasants (or *kulaks*), accusing them of hoarding their grain stocks in order to keep prices high. (In reality, the peasants thought that it was not worth selling their produce until they received a fair price.) From 1918–21 Cheka and Red Army units were sent to requisition grain by force. The result was disastrous. Knowing that any surplus would be confiscated, peasants produced only the barest minimum. By 1921 the grain harvest was less than half that of 1913. The result was a terrible famine in which some five million people died.

v) White Unpopularity

The majority of Russians were peasants. While most did not particularly like the Reds, they disliked the Whites even more, fearing that they might lose the land they had gained if the Whites triumphed.

vi) Foreign Intervention

Foreign assistance was not as effective as the Whites expected. Most countries sent only a few troops and few of these ever fought the Reds. With the end of the First World War, the Allies had less reason to continue the fight. Those leaders who favoured an anti-Bolshevik crusade were a minority. The war-weary Allies had no stomach for another long campaign. Moreover, there were many Red sympathisers in both Britain and France. Overall, foreign intervention may ultimately have been counter-productive. Patriotic Russians resented the foreign presence and this may have increased Red support.

vii) Geography

The Reds controlled the most densely populated areas, rail network and the main industrial areas. The Whites, scattered geographically, found it hard to coordinate their attacks.

e) What were the Main Results of the Civil War?

i) The Economic Results

In 1918 Lenin introduced a series of economic measures collectively known as 'war communism'. Henceforward, every aspect of economic life was subordinated to the task of winning the civil war.

ii) The Political Results

In July 1918 a new constitution was introduced. In theory the supreme authority was the All-Russian Congress of Soviets. However, in reality, all the important decisions were made by Lenin and a small circle of comrades who controlled the Communist Party. This was made official in 1919 when power at the Party's apex was devolved from the several-hundred strong Central Executive Committee to two major sub-committees: the Politburo decided high policy; and the Orgburo oversaw internal administration. Increasingly decisions only went in one direction – from the top downwards.

iii) Other Results

▼ Russia had lost land on her western borders – Finland, the Baltic States, Bessarabia (to Romania) and territory to Poland.
▼ Most of Russia's leaders after 1920 had fought in the Civil War. They were accustomed to using terror and violence to achieve their ends.

The Communist Party
The Communist Party was not the government but it made all the important decisions

Politburo
decided

Secretariat (Civil Service)
selected and appointed people to carry out the Party's decisions

Orgburo
organised

Central Executive Committee
ran the Communist Party

Party Congress
• approved candidates elected from Regional and District branches
• the Congress elected members of the Central Executive Committee

The Government
The government appeared to represent the Soviet people. However, the Communist Party controlled it

Sovnarkom (Council of Peoples Commissars)
• up to ten members
• carefully chosen by Lenin (the Chairman) and by the Communist Party
• the Commissars led the Government departments

All Russian Central Committee
• 200–300 members
• senior government posts
• chosen from 'elected' representatives of the All Russian Congress

All Russian Congress of Soviets
• 2,000 members
• a form of parliament, containing only members of the Communist Party

Figure 30 Communist control.

ACTIVITY

Consider the question: 'Why did the Bolsheviks win the Civil War?' Make a list of the points which you would include in answering the question. Put these reasons in order of importance. Explain your top two reasons to the rest of the class.

3 Russia: 1920–4

a) The Situation in 1920–1

The defeat of the Whites did not mark the end of open opposition to the Bolsheviks. Indeed such opposition grew in 1920–1. The basic cause was economic discontent.

i) Peasant Unrest
As the Red Army was demobilised, peasant uprisings broke out across Russia. (The peasants were opposed to grain requisitioning.) Thousands of troops were killed before order was restored.

ii) Worker Unrest
There was increasing unrest (reflected in a growing wave of strikes) among workers. In February 1921 thousands of Petrograd workers crossed to the naval base on Kronstadt and linked up with the sailors to demand greater freedom. The demonstrators elected leaders and issued a manifesto listing their demands including new soviet elec-

ISSUES
Why – and to what extent – did Lenin retreat from Communism?

tions, freedom of speech, rights for trade unions, and the release of political prisoners. Frightened by the scale of opposition, 60,000 Red Army troops brutally crushed the Kronstadt rising in March.

b) The New Economic Policy

Lenin determined to replace war communism with a New Economic Policy (NEP). He told the Tenth Party Congress in March 1921:

> We are living in such conditions of impoverishment and ruin that for a time everything must be subordinated to this fundamental consideration – at all costs to increase the quantity of goods . . . We know that so long as there is no revolution in other countries, only agreement with the peasantry can save the socialist revolution in Russia . . . We must try to satisfy the demands of the peasants who are dissatisfied, discontented, and cannot be otherwise. In essence the small farmer can be satisfied with two things. First of all, there must be a certain amount of freedom for the small private proprietor; and secondly, commodities and products must be provided . . . Let the peasants have their little bit of capitalism, as long as we keep power. The Proletarian government is in no danger as long as it firmly holds transport and large-scale industry in its hands.

Source B

NEP was primarily aimed at keeping the peasants' support and giving them an incentive to produce more food. The seizure of surplus food ended. Peasants could now trade any surplus for profit – at first only at local markets but then through middlemen (known as **Nepmen**) to the towns. This was not the only retreat from communism. In an effort to improve industrial production, NEP permitted small-scale production by up to 20 workers. Conscious of the unease of many Party members, he was at pains to stress that NEP was only a temporary concession to capitalism. His authority and the depressed economic situation ensured that the Congress approved NEP.

NEPMEN
The term used to describe merchants, tradesmen, businessmen and shopkeepers who made money as a result of NEP.

---

c) What were the Results of NEP?

Lenin's realism had resulted in political theory taking second place to economic necessity. Inevitably there was less equality as traders and small manufacturers made money, and *kulaks* employed poorer peasants as hired labourers. While the state 'superstructure' was socialist, its base consisted of millions of capitalist peasant farmers. By 1923 Trotsky was condemning the 'flagrant errors' of economic policy which had subordinated proletarian needs to the interests of the Nepmen.

	1913	1921	1922	1923	1924	1925	1926
Grain (million tons)	81.6*	37.6	50.3	56.6	51.4	72.5	76.8
Iron (million tons)	4.2	0.1	0.2	0.3	0.75	1.5	2.4
Electricity (million kWh)	1.9	0.5	0.8	1.1	1.5	2.9	3.5
Steel (million tons)	4.2	0.2	0.4	0.7	1.1	2.1	3.1
Cotton fabrics (million metres)	2,582	105	349	691	963	1,688	2,286
Average monthly wage of urban worker (in roubles)	30.5	10.2	12.2	15.9	20.8	25.2	29

Table 8 Production in Russia, 1913–26.

* 1913 was a particularly good year for the harvest.

Note: the statistics shown in this (and other) tables should be taken as very approximate. The data was often unscientifically measured and then distorted for political ends.

However, statistics suggest that by 1924 the Soviet economy had made a marked recovery. By the mid-1920s grain and industrial production had increased and the value of money had stabilised. The rise in living standards meant that there was less discontent. Once the requisition squads stopped raiding their farms, most peasants lost interest in rebellion. There were also far fewer industrial strikes. (This was hardly surprising: trade union leaders were exclusively Communists and did not sanction strikes in state-owned concerns.) But NEP was not a total success. Arguably it shelved rather than solved the agrarian crisis. While farms remained small, the levels of production would not be high. How long NEP would continue to operate and whether it genuinely represented Party aspirations were questions that remained unsettled at Lenin's death.

d) What was the Political Situation by 1924?

While there was now some economic freedom there was little political freedom. Lenin never wavered from his insistence on the supreme authority of the Party. In 1921 all political parties other than the Communists were outlawed. Although the secret police (now called the GPU) was slimmed down, opponents of the regime continued to be punished and a new network of labour camps opened in remote parts of Russia. The Tenth Party Congress even tried to prevent criticism of the government from within the Party. Any two people who disagreed with the Politburo could be declared a faction and expelled. The Politiburo ruled – and Lenin ruled the Politiburo.

In 1917 the Bolsheviks had said that nationalities which wanted to break free from Russia could do so. In the Civil War, however, many

ACTIVITY

Read the extract from Lenin's March 1921 speech and examine Table 8. Then answer the following questions:

1. What are the main reasons Lenin gives for introducing the NEP? **[5 marks]**
2. Why might the statistics in Table 8 not be accurate? **[10 marks]**
3. 'By 1924 the Soviet economic performance matched the tsarist performance.' Do the statistics bear this out? **[10 marks]**

parts of the old empire had been reconquered. These areas were made Soviet Republics. In 1922 the Russian, Ukrainian, Byelorussian and Transcaucasian Republics signed a treaty of union. Henceforward they were known as the Union of Soviet Socialist Republics (USSR). The republics maintained some control over local matters but most of the important decisions were made in Moscow.

e) Religion Under Communism

Lenin's government was atheist but many Russians remained deeply religious. Lenin feared that if he left the Orthodox Church alone it would become a centre of organised resistance to communism. However, he also realised that if he made an all-out attack on religion he would stir up a hornet's nest, among Jews and Muslims as well as Christians. He dealt with this situation by allowing people freedom of belief and worship while destroying the wealth of the Church. Church property was seized by the state and the clergy had to pay high taxes. Religious instruction was banned in schools.

THE USSR: 1918–24

1918 March: Moscow became the new capital; Treaty of Brest-Litovsk; May: start of the Civil War
1920 end of the Civil War;
1921 Kronstadt rising; introduction of NEP;
1922 formation of the USSR.

f) Foreign Policy

After 1917 the Bolsheviks could look for little help from foreign powers: most were deeply suspicious of communism. Nor did Lenin seek friendship. Instead he talked in terms of fomenting revolution across the globe. In March 1919 the Communist International (Comintern) was set up in Moscow with just this intent. However, after 1920 Lenin adopted a more realistic approach to foreign policy. The failure of communist revolts in Germany and Hungary convinced him that the time was not ripe for world revolution. Notwithstanding the existence of the Comintern, Soviet policy was now marked by a desire to avoid conflict. In 1921 trade links were re-established with Britain and several other countries. Russia also set out to protect itself by playing on the differences that divided the capitalist powers. In 1922 Russia and Germany signed the Treaty of Rapallo. The two 'pariah nations' (as Lloyd George called them) agreed to cooperate economically.

4 Lenin: An Assessment

ISSUE
How successful was Lenin?

Contemporaries held different views about Lenin. Stalin said:

> For 25 years Comrade Lenin moulded our Party and finally trained it to be the strongest and most highly steeled Workers' Party in the world ... Ours is the only country where the crushed and labouring

masses have succeeded in throwing off the rule of the landlords and capitalists and replacing it by the rule of workers and peasants ... The greatness of Lenin lies above all in this, that by creating the Republic of Soviets he gave a practical demonstration to the oppressed masses of the world that the rule of landlords and capitalists is short lived ... he thus fired the hearts of the workers and peasants of the whole world with the hope of liberation.

Source C

Historians are similarly divided about Lenin.

i) The Negative View

▼ Lenin was a ruthless dictator. The state he created was more tyrannical than the tsarist state. His secret police killed more than 250,000 people between 1917–24.

▼ He was wholly unprincipled in the methods he used to achieve his ends.

▼ Given the conditions prevailing in Russia after 1917 it is hard to see the Revolution as a triumph for the workers.

▼ Lenin's rule paved the way for that of Stalin. Stalin's brutal totalitarianism was a logical development of the system established by Lenin.

ii) The (More) Positive View

▼ The desperate struggle for survival after 1917 explains the harshness of Lenin's actions.

▼ Lenin was a skilled opportunist. His political realism was evident with the NEP.

▼ He sincerely intended to improve the lot of the working class.

▼ It is unfair to blame Lenin for Stalin's crimes.

5 The Emergence of Stalin

a) The Power Struggle

From late 1921 Lenin suffered a series of strokes, the third of which in March 1923 left him permanently speechless. The result was a power struggle within the seven-man Politburo. Four men, Trotsky, Stalin, Zinoviev and Kamenev, were seen as potential successors to Lenin. Trotsky seemed the most likely candidate. He had played a prominent role in 1917 and in the Civil War, and was a powerful speaker and a talented writer. However, he had many opponents who disliked his arrogance and feared that he might set himself up as a military dictator. Stalin, who Trotsky regarded as 'an eminent mediocrity', was in a strong position:

The British *Times* reported as follows in January 1924:

A man of iron will and inflexible ambition he had no scruple about means and treated human beings as mere material for his purpose ... This is not the place to describe in detail the terrible achievements of Bolshevism – the shameful peace with Germany, the plundering of the educated and propertied classes, the long continued terror with its thousands of innocent victims ... Never in modern times has any great country passed through such convulsion ... Both the Communist Party and the Council of People's Commissaries were completely under Lenin's control ... The Communist experiment brought Russia to economic ruin, famine, and barbarism.

Source D

ACTIVITY

Which of the following statements do you agree with: 'Lenin deserves praise for his aims and his achievements' or 'Lenin was a disaster for Russia'? Explain your answer.

ISSUE
Why and how did
Stalin assume absolute
power?

▼ As General Secretary of the Party he had enormous power. Responsible for the appointment of thousands of officials, he filled key posts with his own supporters.

▼ As well as being an able administrator (particularly skilful on committees), Stalin was a superb politician, possessing an excellent sense of timing and an apparent (and totally misleading) joviality. He presented himself as a moderate figure in the centre of the Party, working for consensus.

Although increasingly distrustful of Stalin, Lenin's ability to influence matters in the last months of his life was limited. Zinoviev, Kamenev and Stalin joined forces against Trotsky. A letter by Trotsky to *Pravda* in 1923 in which he condemned the bureaucratic control over the party exercised by 'secretaries' such as Stalin, brought the conflict within the Politburo into the open. At the Thirteenth Party Congress in January 1924 Trotsky and his supporters were condemned for factionalism. Lenin died a few days later. He was eventually laid to rest in a glass coffin in a mausoleum in Moscow's Red Square and Petrograd was renamed Leningrad in his honour.

Lenin's *Testament*, critical of Stalin, was hushed up. Instead Stalin gave the impression that he and Lenin had been close comrades. Trotsky, alone of all the Party leaders, did not attend the funeral, giving the impression that he was insulting the dead hero. (He was actually away from Moscow, recuperating from illness. He later claimed that Stalin had deliberately misinformed him about the date of the funeral.) Trotsky now clashed with Zinoviev, Kamenev and Stalin on a number of major issues, not least the question of permanent revolution. Trotsky's view was that the USSR, as well as building up its industrial strength, should help communists in other countries to overthrow their governments. Most Party members believed that this policy stood little chance of success. They preferred Stalin's policy of building up socialism in the USSR – 'Socialism in one country'.

In 1925 Trotsky – totally isolated – was dismissed from his post as War Commissar. He soon discovered he had two unexpected allies – Kamenev and Zinoviev. Stalin cut his ties with these two left-wingers as soon as he had defeated Trotsky, allying instead with the right-wing of the party led by Bukharin, Tomsky and Rykov. In 1926 Trotsky, Kamenev and Zinoviev were expelled from the Politburo. In 1927 Trotsky was expelled from the party and exiled to Central Asia. In 1929 he was expelled from Russia. The three new members of the Politburo – Molotov, Voroshilov and Kalinin – were all Stalin's supporters. Stalin, therefore, was now in a position to move against Bukharin, Rykov and Tomsky: all three men were stripped of their

STALIN AND TROTSKY

STALIN 1879–1953

1879 born Joseph Djugashvili (Stalin was a pseudonym meaning 'man of steel') in Georgia: his father was a cobbler; his mother, a deeply religious woman, made great sacrifices to ensure he had a good education;

1894 entered the theological college at Tiflis where he became more interested in revolutionary ideas than in joining the priesthood;

1904 joined the Bolsheviks;

1905–17 rose gradually in the Party as a result of his hard work and willingness to participate in raids to seize money for the Party's cause;

1912 helped found the Party newspaper *Pravda* (Truth);

Nov 1917 became Commissar for Nationalities;

1918–21 organised the Caucasus region for the Bolsheviks in the Civil War;

1922 became General Secretary of the Communist party.

TROTSKY 1879–1940

1879 born in the Ukraine, the son of a Jewish farmer;

Late 1890s educated at Odessa University where he became interested in Marxism; imprisoned for participating in revolutionary activities;

1902–5 lived in western Europe;

1905 played a major role in the 1905 Revolution as leader of the Petrograd Soviet;

1907 escaped abroad: something of a maverick but more a Menshevik than a Bolshevik;

August 1917 finally threw in his lot with the Bolsheviks;

Nov 1917 played a major part in the November Revolution;

March 1918 negotiated the Treaty of Brest-Litovsk;

1918–25 Commissar for War: created the Red Army and led it to victory in the Civil War.

An extract from Lenin's *Testament* (dictated in December 1922):

> Since he became General Secretary, Comrade Stalin has concentrated enormous power in his hands and I am not sure that he will always know how to use that power with sufficient caution. On the other hand Comrade Trotsky ... is distinguished not only by his outstanding qualities (personally he is the most capable man in the present Central Committee) but also by his excess of self-confidence and a readiness to be carried away by the purely administrative side of affairs. **Source E**

Postscript (added in January 1923)

> Stalin is too rude, and this fault, entirely supportable in relations amongst us Communists, is insupportable in a General Secretary. Therefore I propose to the comrades to find a way to remove Stalin from that position and to appoint another man who will be more patient, more loyal, more polite, less unpredictable and more considerate to his comrades. **Source F**

ACTIVITY

1. What reservations does Lenin have about a) Stalin and b) Trotsky? **[10 marks]**
2. Why do you think Lenin made these observations? **[10 marks]**

**THE POWER
STRUGGLE: 1924–9**

1924 death of Lenin;
1925 January: Trotsky dismissed
as Commissar for War;
April: the party adopted
'Socialism in One Country';
1927 Trotsky, Zinoviev and
Kamenev expelled from
the Party;
1929 Trotsky banished from the
USSR.

power. Thus, by 1929 Stalin controlled the Politburo. He was now addressed simply as *vozhd* – the leader.

It is perhaps too simplistic to reduce the power struggle to Stalin's completely cynical manoeuvrings to reach the top. He did not change policy simply for the sake of discrediting his rivals. There is no doubt that he was concerned about Russia's economic progress. He was also committed to the cause of communist revolution. His egotism persuaded him that he was indispensable to that cause.

b) Stalin's Totalitarianism

From the start Stalin identified himself as Lenin's heir, claiming that all he did was in the Leninist tradition. (After 1924 Lenin, in the eyes of the Party faithful, became virtually a god whose words and actions were 'law'.) By the late 1930s, however, Stalin had built up a more complete totalitarian state than Lenin had ever envisaged. The media gave the impression that Stalin was endowed with wisdom, iron resolution and genial paternal qualities. The propaganda campaign reached into every area of life. Artists, writers and film-makers had to produce work in praise of Stalin and his achievements (or simply not produce). There were statues of Stalin in every town and pictures of him in every factory. Every success was put down to his genius. Failures were blamed on others. While the media gave the impression that he was a benign leader, in reality (especially as his power grew) he was secretive, suspicious and vindictive. The secret police (renamed the NKVD in 1934) extended its work, arresting independent minds, keeping watch on industry and the armed forces, and running the growing number of prison camps. Terror and mass indoctrination were not totally successful: many people retained their religious faith and/or a sense of (non-Russian) identity. This suggests that Stalin could not bend the country entirely to his will. Moreover, in some respects he was dependent on popular support. Much of what he did had the approval of many Party members. Stalinism, therefore, was not simply the product of one man.

Q Why do you think many Russians supported Stalin's – often brutal – actions?

ISSUE
How successful were Stalin's economic measures?

6 The Economic Changes

a) What was the Situation in 1928?

i) The Economic Situation
Russia's recovery under NEP had been rapid. However, while agricultural and industrial production by 1928 exceeded their 1913 levels, technological progress had been limited. Peasants continued to culti-

vate their small plots by traditional methods. (Nearly a third of farms had no horses or oxen, let alone tractors.) On the industrial front, Russia lagged far behind other nations in terms of output and productivity levels and remained overwhelmingly a rural country in which over four-fifths of the population earned their livelihood from farming. Ironically, the so-called workers' government had precious few workers. The necessity of developing industry was accepted by nearly all shades of opinion within the Communist Party. Marx, after all, held that an industrial society was essential for the establishment of a socialist society. While virtually all Soviet leaders thought the state must lead the industrialisation process, there was massive debate about precisely how this was to be done. Those involved in the 1920s power struggle had very different views. Trotsky believed that industrialisation could succeed only if the state strengthened nationalised industry. Bukharin, on the other hand, anxious not to antagonise the peasants, had supported the continuation of NEP.

ii) The Peasant Problem

The biggest beneficiaries of the Revolution were the peasants who had achieved their long-held goal of acquiring more land. They were essentially capitalists and showed little interest in socialism. Although agricultural production had recovered, the amount of food sold on the market was substantially lower than before 1914. Even in the best year of NEP, grain exports amounted to only one quarter of the 1913 level. More seriously, not enough grain was reaching the towns. Matters reached crisis point in 1927 when peasants sold only half as much grain to state agencies as in 1926. With this amount of grain the towns could not be fed. While low grain prices were the main cause of the problem, the government blamed the grain crisis on the failure of NEP. In response to the crisis, Stalin ordered draconian requisitioning methods to seize grain.

b) The First Five-Year Plan

In December 1927 the Fifteenth Party Congress supported the creation of a Five-Year Plan (FYP) for the development of the whole economy. This marked the official end of NEP. The state would now take control over every aspect of economic life. The bulk of workers, rural and urban, would become employees of state-run enterprises. The aim of the plan was clear: the USSR was to be industrialised. The FYP's goals were staggering. They included a 250 per cent rise in industrial production and a 150 per cent rise in farm production. A major start was to be made on the collectivisation of peasant farms. The term 'Plan' is misleading. While detailed targets were produced for every industry, a set of (ideal) targets is not quite the same thing

---

WHY DID STALIN SUPPORT THE SO-CALLED 'SECOND REVOLUTION'?

▼ In 1927–8 he feared attack (for no good reason!) from Britain, France and Poland. Only a strong industrial economy (he believed) could ensure success in war.

▼ He saw himself as a modern Ivan the Terrible or Peter the Great who would modernise Russia and make it a great power.

▼ A growing proletariat would broaden support for communism.

▼ A successful Soviet economy would impress workers around the world and increase the appeal of communism.

▼ Many party members supported the 'modernisation' of the Soviet economy.

as a plan. There was in fact very little planning, as such, from the top. Stalin's government exhorted and terrorised the workforce into ever greater efforts towards ever greater production. But such planning as there was occurred not at national but at local level as regional and site managers struggled desperately to make sense of the instructions they were given.

ISSUE
How successful was collectivisation?

c) Collectivisation

i) Why did Stalin Introduce Collectivisation?
Stalin knew that means would have to be found to finance industrialisation. If Russia could export more farm produce this would help it buy essential machinery. To export more (as well as feed more industrial workers), Russian agriculture to produce more. The existing system was unlikely to produce more food: peasant farms were too small to utilise modern equipment. Unless the situation changed, Stalin faced the prospect of annual grain crises and of being held to ransom by peasant farmers, particularly the *kulaks*, who had little sympathy with communism. He was determined to control – rather than be controlled by – the peasantry. It would be much easier for the state to control thousands of large farms rather than millions of smaller ones. As well as producing more food, **collective farms**, using modern methods, would require less labour. This would release people to work in industry. In short, collectivisation seemed to kill many birds with one stone.

COLLECTIVE FARM
Peasants gave up their land in return for joining, and sharing the produce of, a collective farm (or *kolkhoz*). Each *kolkhoz* was run by a committee under local Party control and had to deliver a fixed amount of produce to the state at fixed (low) prices.

ii) War on the Kulaks
Voluntary collectivisation did not prove successful. The 15,000 collective farms in existence in 1927 had only increased to about 57,000 collectives by 1929. This meant that over 90 per cent of peasants had still not joined collective farms. Moreover, in 1928–9, the amount of grain reaching the towns was lower than ever. Stalin now decided on a policy of compulsion. Twenty-five million peasant families were to be forced to form 240,000 collective farms. At the same time the *kulaks* were to be destroyed. In December 1929 mass collectivisation and 'dekulakisation' began. Inevitably collectivisation met with violent opposition, especially from *kulaks* who had the most to lose. Resistance was particularly strong in the Ukraine. Opposition was ruthlessly crushed. Secret police and army units surrounded villages and machine-gunned the inhabitants into surrender, transporting those left alive to remote regions where many died from hunger and disease.

By March 1930 over half the peasants had joined collective farms. But the results in productivity were appalling. Many peasants preferred to slaughter their animals rather than let collectives have them. Moreover, many of the collectives proved to be hopelessly inefficient and crop yields dropped alarmingly. It was clear that collectivisation would disrupt the vital spring sowing of grain. Faced with the prospect of a disastrous famine, Stalin back-tracked. In March 1930, blaming local Party leaders for the excesses, he said that peasants who wished to leave collectives could do so. More than half did so, taking back most of their land. To counter this unexpected turn of events, Stalin ordered a resumption of forcible collectivisation in the summer of 1930. By 1935, 94 per cent of the crop area of land was collectivised.

iii) The Results of Collectivisation

Arguably Stalin achieved his aims. Farming became more mechanised. In 1930 there were fewer than 25,000 tractors and 1,000 combine harvesters on Russian farms. By 1940 there were 525,000 tractors and 182,000 combines. By 1940 the wheat crop was 80 per cent higher than in 1913. Collectivisation thus ensured that the growing towns had a regular supply of food, that there was grain to export, that labour was released for use in industry, and that life in the countryside was closer to communist ideals.

	1928	1929	1930	1931	1932	1933	1934	1935
Grain (m. tons)	73.3	71.7	83.5	69.5	69.6	68.6	67.6	75.0
Cattle (millions)	70.5	67.1	52.5	47.9	40.7	38.4	42.4	49.3
Pigs (millions)	26.0	20.4	13.6	14.4	11.6	12.1	17.4	22.6
Sheep and goats (millions)	146.7	147.0	108.8	77.7	52.1	50.2	51.9	61.1

Table 9 Agricultural production in Russia, 1928–35.

The figures are Western estimates based on Soviet statistics.

However, Stalin's polices can be seen as disastrous. The human cost was horrendous. Between 1931 and 1933, over ten million people (especially Ukrainians) died of famine. So bad was the situation that some parents killed and ate their children. Stalin's wife committed suicide in 1932, blaming her husband for the misery he had brought to the USSR. By 1933 livestock production had fallen to half the 1928 figure. Nor were collective farms very efficient: they suffered from government interference and there was little incentive for farmers to work hard. The much-heralded mechanisation of farming was slow in arriving. The peasants reaped little reward. They were poorly paid and the promised schools and clinics rarely materialised.

ISSUE

How successful were
the Five-Year Plans?

It is sometimes asked
whether it is not possible
to slow down the speed of
change ... No comrades it
is not possible! The speed
must not be reduced! On
the contrary we must
increase it as much as is
within our powers and
possibilities. This is
dictated to us by our
obligations to the working
class of the whole world.
To slacken the pace would
be to lag behind; and
those who lag behind are
beaten ... Russia has too
often been beaten ...
because of her military,
cultural, political, industrial
and agricultural
backwardness ... We are
fifty to one hundred years
behind the advanced
countries. We must make
up this gap in ten years.
Either we do this or they
crush us.

Source G Stalin speaking in
1931.

d) Industrialisation

i) The First Five-Year Plan

The overall aim of the first FYP was to triple production in the heavy industry sector (coal, iron, steel and oil) and double it in other sectors. Just how successful the first FYP was is difficult to say. Soviet propaganda certainly boasted that it had been a success, and Stalin claimed in mid-course that it had already achieved its targets and so would end a year early. But local officials and managers tended to exaggerate their production figures in order to give the impression of success, so all statistics have to be treated warily. However, there seems little doubt that the first FYP was an extraordinary achievement. Some of the projects like the great new metallurgical centre created at Magnitogorsk were huge. (Historian Sheila Fitzpatrick has termed the economic schemes 'gigantomania' – the worship of size for its own sake.) A propaganda campaign encouraged the workers to take pride in carrying out the Plan because it would strengthen the USSR and make life better for everyone. Millions of young workers took this message seriously, working long hours in 'shock brigades'.

However, the first FYP was far from being an unqualified success. The Plan put emphasis on quantity at the expense of quality. By deliberate design, the production of consumer articles was given a low priority and little attention was given to living and working conditions. Unemployment relief was ended. People could lose their jobs if they were sick. The simplest errors, such as accidentally damaging tools, were denounced as 'sabotage'. At a higher level, those factory managers who were unable to meet their targets might find themselves on trial as enemies of the state. Secret police were sent into factories to spy on managers and to report on their performance.

There was no let up in the speed of the industrialisation process (See Source F).

ii) The Second and Third Five-Year Plans

The second FYP was more realistic than the first. The planners, learning from some of their mistakes, now called for production increases of 14 instead of 20 per cent a year. Nevertheless, problems remained. Over-production occurred in some parts of the economy and under-production in others. The struggle to obtain an adequate supply of materials often led to fierce competition between regions and sectors of industry, all of them anxious to escape the charge of not achieving their targets. The result was considerable unproductive hoarding of resources. The reluctance to criticise openly also had serious repercussions. Since no one was willing to admit that an error in planning or production had occurred, faults went unchecked until they reached proportions that could no longer be hidden. There then followed the inevitable search for scapegoats.

What successes there were occurred in heavy industry where the second FYP began to reap the benefits of the creation of large-scale plants under the first Plan. There were excellent growth rates, in the engineering and metal-working sectors while the output of tractors trebled. The third FYP, launched in 1938, placed more emphasis on the production of 'luxuries' like radios and bicycles. But the plan was overshadowed by the growing threat of Germany and the need for rearmament. Thus defence spending, only 4 per cent of the industrial budget in 1933, reached 33 per cent by 1940.

iii) Slave Labour

People accused of being *kulaks*, saboteurs or enemies of the state were sent to a host of new labour camps often set up in the most inhospitable parts of the USSR. About 12 million people may have been working in labour camps by 1939. Prisoners, who were usually sentenced to ten or 25 years, rarely lived for more than two years: food and medical supplies were scarce, and camp discipline harsh. The great economic advantage of the camps was that prisoners could be forced to work on dangerous projects in areas where ordinary workers did not want to go.

iv) Was Russian Industrialisation a Success?

Behind the propaganda and dubious statistics there lay real achievement. By 1937 industrial production was probably some four times higher than it had been in 1928. By 1939 only half of Russia's population lived and worked on the land. Many Russians seem to have been proud of their achievements. The fact that Russia was able to defeat Nazi Germany after 1941 can be seen as justification for Stalin's methods. Moreover, in some aspects, life in Russia did improve. A rudimentary health service began to emerge and education improved, providing the opportunity for upward social mobility.

However, beyond the fact that they were engaged in a great national enterprise, there was little in material terms to help people endure the severity of these years. It is somewhat ironic that in a reputedly proletarian state the living standards of the workers should have been given the lowest of priorities. By 1935 only one in 20 Moscow families had more than one room to themselves. In the new towns the accommodation problem was worse: factories were always built before homes. For most Russians the FYPs meant hard work, poor conditions and the loss of freedom, both inside and outside the workplace. Living standards in 1941 were probably lower than in 1928. Arguably the industrialisation process was not based on a real-

THE STAKHANOVITE MOVEMENT

In August 1935 Alexei Stakhanov, a miner, produced nearly 15 times his required quota of coal. (The fact that he was helped by a team of auxiliaries was kept secret.) His example was seized on by the Party. He was hailed as a national hero and other workers were encouraged to emulate him. Those who did were rewarded with higher pay and honours.

THE GULAG

In 1930 the secret police set up a special department to run the labour camps. It was called Gulag. The camps are sometimes known as the gulag.

THE FIVE-YEAR PLANS

1928 start of First FYP;
1929 collectivisation speeded up
-30 and the *kulaks* smashed;
1933 start of Second FYP;
1938 start of Third FYP.

istic understanding of Russia's needs. While it was concentrating on mass employment in heavy industry, Western nations were abandoning heavy industries, moving to modern technology, and responding to consumer demands. Thus, Stalin's economic revolution may have committed the USSR to a form of development that made it impossible for it to realise its main objective of catching up with the world's advanced nations. Certainly the speed of the industrialisation process often led to inefficiency. Given the shortage of qualified personnel, the deportation of many thousands of skilled men to labour camps was a serious loss. Nor was the USSR as well-prepared for war as it might have been. Many Soviet citizens had endured so much that they were prepared to welcome Nazi troops as deliverers. Moreover, most Soviet industry was still sited west of the Urals, the area most vulnerable to German attack.

Stalin had done little for equality. Incentives in the workplace resulted in the creation of a new elite who were highly favoured in matters of pay, housing and medical treatment. Stalin also did little for female emancipation. Given that industrialisation required an ever-increasing workforce, he made it more difficult for women to get a divorce or have an abortion. Many women found themselves doing the same job as men during the day (although rarely in senior posts) and bringing up a family as well.

7 The Purges

Lenin had accepted the need to use terror to destroy opposition and the need for purges to purify the Party, removing members whose ideas or behaviour were considered dangerous. Stalin's purges, however, were different in scale to those of Lenin. Starting in 1934, he began the systematic terrorising of colleagues and Party members. The reign of terror was at its height from 1936 to 1938. No one was safe. Anyone considered a threat to Stalin's authority was destroyed.

a) The Early Purges

In 1932 Ryutin, a Party member who had published an attack on Stalin was publicly tried and expelled from the Party with some of his followers. In 1933–4 nearly one million Party members, a third of the total membership, were purged. This had serious implications because purged members were likely to lose their jobs and their ration-cards. However, these purges rarely involved imprisonment or execution.

b) The 1936 Show Trial

In August 1936 Kamenev and Zinoviev and 14 others were put on public trial charged with involvement in Kirov's murder and with conspiring to overthrow the government. Vyshinsky, the Chief Prosecutor, hurled abuse and false allegations at the accused. Amazingly (to many at the time) they all pleaded guilty (knowing that the sentence was death) and read out their abject confessions in court. This is part of Zinoviev's last plea:

> I should like to repeat that I am fully and utterly guilty. I am guilty of having been the organiser, second only to Trotsky, of that bloc whose chosen task was the killing of Stalin. I was the principal organiser of Kirov's assassination. The party saw where we were going and warned us, Stalin warned us scores of times, but we did not heed these warnings. We entered into alliance with Trotsky.
>
> *Source H*

All 16 men were executed. Why did Kamenev, Zinoviev and other 'Old Bolsheviks' confess? Some think the men may have regarded their admission of guilt as a last act of loyalty to the Party to which they had dedicated their lives. More likely, constant beatings, starvation, deprivation of sleep and threats against their families were used to extract confessions. They may also have been promised that their lives would be spared if they confessed. Why Stalin insisted on a policy of public trials is a mystery. He could simply have had the men killed. Perhaps he was intent on revealing the scale of the conspiracy against him, thus proving the need for the purging to continue.

c) The 1937 and 1938 Show Trials

In 1937, 17 Communists, denounced collectively as the 'Anti-Soviet Trotskyist Centre', were charged with spying for Germany. The accused included Radek and Pyatakov, former favourites of Lenin. Radek's grovelling confession, in which he incriminated colleagues, including his friend Bukharin, saved him from the death sentence imposed on all but three of the other defendants. He died two years later in a labour camp. In 1938, in the third major show trial, Bukharin, Rykov and 18 other 'Trotskyite-Rightists' were charged on a variety of counts, including spying, and conspiracy to murder Stalin. By 1939 the only member of Lenin's Politburo still alive (Stalin apart) was Trotsky. He was murdered in Mexico in 1940 by one of Stalin's agents who buried an ice-pick in his skull.

THE KIROV MURDER

In December 1934 Kirov, the Party Secretary in Leningrad, was murdered. This may have been done on Stalin's orders. (Soviet leader Khruschev stated this to be the case in 1956.) Kirov was a popular figure in the Party and was thus a potential rival. Stalin used the excuse of Kirov's murder to move against his enemies. After giving the NKVD new powers and introducing the death penalty for all terrorist acts, Stalin claimed that Kirov's death had been organised by a wide circle of 'Trotskyites and Leftists', who must all be brought to account. Thousands were arrested, including Kamenev and Zinoviev. Many were shot.

d) The Purge of the Army

In May 1937 Vyshinsky announced that 'a gigantic conspiracy' had been uncovered in the Red Army. Marshal Tukhachevsky, Chief of the General Staff, was arrested along with seven other generals. The men, accused of having spied for Germany and Japan, were tried in secret. After ritual confession, all were shot. A major purge of the armed forces followed.

e) Mass Terror

The main target of the purges initially were Party members. Of the 1,996 delegates who attended the 1934 Party Congress, 1,108 were executed in the next three years. The Moscow show trials with their catalogue of accusations, confessions and death sentences were copied in all the USSR republics. But the greatest impact of the purges was on the middle and lower ranks of society. Anyone related to – or friendly with – any previous victim was in danger. Suspects were usually arrested in the middle of the night and tortured until they confessed to ridiculous crimes. Most were sent to labour camps but at times in 1937–8 up to 1,000 people a day were shot in Moscow alone. In the rush to uncover more conspiracies, interrogators themselves became victims. In 1936 Yagoda, head of the NKVD, was removed from his post and shot. Yezhov, his successor, lasted two years. Between 1934 and 1939 some 12 million people may have died in the camps or been executed.

f) What were Stalin's Motives?

It is possible to argue that Stalin's motives were logical. Perhaps he believed there was a real plot to overthrow him. The purges ensured that the Party was brought entirely under his control. They were also a useful way of terrorising people into obeying orders and provided an abundant source of slave labour. However, it is easier to claim that the purges were totally irrational. Historian Edward Acton has described Stalin as 'a singularly repulsive concoction of power lust, megalomania, cynicism and suspicion'. He bore terrible grudges, distrusted everyone around him and had no scruples about using violence. The killing did not take place behind his back: he personally checked and signed execution lists.

Without seeking to deny that Stalin was ultimately responsible, some historians have questioned whether he was solely to blame for the purges. They point out that many Party members supported the purges. At every level of the Party, there was a fear of counter-revolution. Purges also left posts to be filled which improved chances of

Table 10 Purge victims.

Date	The victims	What happened to them	Crimes accused of
	Senior Party Leaders		
1932	Ryutin Group	Expelled from Party, exiled	Treason, plotting against Stalin
1936	Zinoviev and Kamenev	Show trial, shot	Kirov's murder, links with Trotsky
1937	Pyatakov, Serebryakov	Show trial, shot	Spying for Germany and Japan
	Radek, Sokolnikov	Sent to labour camps	Spying for Germany and Japan
1938	Bukharin, Rykov, Krestinsky	Show trial, shot	Treason
	Other Party Officials		
	Almost every party and state leader in every one of the republics of the USSR	Shot or sent to labour camp	'Bourgeois nationalism', treason
	The Armed Forces		
1937–	3 out of 5 Marshals (including Tukhachevsky),	All executed	Treason
	14 out of 16 Army commanders,	All executed	Treason
	8 out of 8 Admirals,	All executed	Treason
	60 out of 67 Corps commanders,	All executed	Treason
	11 out of 11 deputy Commissars for defence,	All executed	Treason
	78 out of 80 members of Supreme Military Council	All executed	Treason
	Half of the officer corps (35,000)	Shot or imprisoned	Treason
	The Security Services		
1937	Yagoda – head of NKVD	Show trial (with Bukharin), shot	Treason, murder, corruption
	Most senior police officials	Shot or imprisoned	Treason, murder, corruption
1939	Yezhov (Yagoda's replacement)	Shot	British agent, killing innocent people
	Others		
1929–39	Up to 24 million people	Transported to labour camps, 13 million died	Kulaks, criminals, wreckers, failure to inform on others

promotion. Moreover, Stalin may not have been totally in control of events. While he made the decision to launch the purges, how that decision was put into effect largely depended on local Party organisations: some may have exceeded their 'duties'. In the end the terror acquired a momentum of its own. Once the machinery of secret police, informers and prison camps had been set up, it was difficult to stop the process.

▼ Working on The Soviet Union: 1917–41

According to Bolsheviks then (and Marxist supporters since) what took place after November 1917 was nothing less than the taking of power by the people and the creation of a new state in which the workers ruled. However, it seems more reasonable to claim that the result of the Bolshevik Revolution was a seizure of power not by but from the masses. Certainly the Stalinist system was a far cry from the socialism which many Russians had aspired to achieve in 1917. The state had become overbearing and coercive, operated by a Party elite and a mushrooming bureaucracy. Lenin must surely shoulder much of the blame for the direction Russia took after 1917. While many historians have rejected the idea that Lenin would have sanctioned Stalin's terror policies, others have shown how violent Lenin's rule was. Arguably Stalinism was more a logical extension of the system Lenin had established than a perversion of it.

It is difficult to say anything very positive about Stalin. Today even Marxist historians condemn him (as did Trotsky) for being 'the grave-digger of the Revolution'. Perhaps he did succeed in dragging Russia into the twentieth century. But as historian E.H. Carr observed: 'Seldom perhaps in history has so monstrous a price been paid for so monumental an achievement'. You must decide for yourself how monumental you think Stalin's economic achievements were. The price, in terms of mass butchery, enslavement and impoverishment, was surely monstrous.

Answering Extended Writing and Essay Questions on The Soviet Union: 1917–41

Consider the following question: '"Criminality enthroned". Is this a fair description of Stalin's rule?'

Brainstorm a list of the positive and negative features of Stalin's rule.

Does one outweigh the other? Now write an essay (of no more than 1,000 words) saying whether you agree with the quote or not – and why.

Answering Source-Based Questions on The Soviet Union: 1917–41

Magnitogorsk was a city built from scratch. Within several years, half a billion cubic feet of excavation was done, forty two million cubic feet of reinforced concrete poured, five million cubic feet of fire bricks laid, a quarter of a million tons of structured steel erected. This was done without sufficient labour, without necessary quantities of the most elementary materials. Brigades of young enthusiasts from every corner of the Soviet Union arrived in the summer of 1930 and did the groundwork of railroad and dam construction necessary before work could begin on the plant itself. Later, groups of local peasants and herdsmen came to Magnitogorsk because of the bad conditions in the villages, due to collectivisation. Many of the peasants were completely unfamiliar with industrial tools and processes. A colony of several hundred foreign engineers and specialists, some of whom made as high as one hundred dollars a day, arrived to advise and direct the work.

From 1928 until 1932 nearly a quarter of a million people came to Magnitogorsk. About three quarters of these new arrivals came of their own free will seeking work, bread-cards, better conditions. The rest came under compulsion . . .

In early April it was still bitter cold, everything was frozen. By May the city was swimming in mud. Bubonic plague had broken out not far from Magnitogorsk. The resistance of the population was very low because of undernourishment and consistent overwork. Sanitary conditions were appalling.

Source I John Scott, an American Communist working in Russia.

The following data are drawn from the work of the economic historian, E. Zaleski, whose findings are based on careful analysis of Soviet and Western sources:

	1927	1930	1932	1935	1937	1940
Coal (million tons)	35	60	64	100	128	150
Steel (million tons)	3	5	6	13	18	18
Oil (million tons)	12	17	21	24	26	26
Electricity (million kWh)	18	22	20	45	80	90

Source J Russian industrial production 1927–40.

▼ QUESTIONS ON SOURCES

1. Examine Source I. What has Scott to say a) positively and b) negatively about Magnitogorsk? **[10 marks]**
2. Is Scott a reliable source for conditions in Magnitogorsk? Explain your answer. **[10 marks]**
3. Why are the statistics in Source J not necessarily accurate?
[10 marks]

Points to note about the questions

Question 1 Scott provides a graphic description of the harsh conditions. He also indicates the mixture of idealism and coercion that characterised the early stages of industrialisation.
Question 2 Scott was there! This is important. However, he was both American and Communist. To what extent might he be biased?
Question 3 Think about who compiled the statistical information.

Further Reading

Books in the Access to History series

The last chapters in *Reaction and Revolutions: Russia 1881–1924* by Michael Lynch are excellent on Lenin. The first chapters of *Stalin and Khruschev: The USSR 1924–64* by Michael Lynch contain excellent material on Stalin.

General

Try Chapter XIII in *Years of Change: Europe 1890–1945* by Robert Wolfson and John Laver (Hodder & Stoughton). *Russia 1914–1941* by John Laver (History at Source series, Hodder & Stoughton) contains useful advice on answering essay and source-based questions. Try also *The Russian Revolution 1917–32* by S. Fitzpatrick, 1986 (OUP), *A History of the Soviet Union* by G. Hosking, 1985 (Fontana) and *The Soviet Union 1917–1991* by M. McCauley, 1993 (Longman). On Lenin try *Leninism* by N. Harding, 1996 (Macmillan). On Stalin try *Stalin's Russia* by C. Ward, 1993 (Edward Arnold), *Stalin and Stalinism* by A. Wood, 1990 (Routledge), and *Stalinism* by G. Gill, 1998 (Macmillan). Read *The Great Terror* by R. Conquest, 1997 (Hutchinson) for an account of Stalin's terror and *Into the Whirlwind* by E.S. Ginzburg, 1967 (Collins) for a personal account of suffering.

GERMANY: 1918–39

CHAPTER 5

The Weimar Republic was born out of Germany's defeat in 1918. The Republic experienced two periods of crisis. It survived the first (1919–23). The second (1929–33) destroyed it. Whether the Weimar Republic (and with it democracy) expired in 1930 or 1933 is debatable. A more important issue, however, is not when but why the Republic collapsed. Linked to that question is another: why did Adolf Hitler, leader of the National Socialist German Workers' Party (NSDAP) or Nazi Party, come to power in 1933? After 1933 Hitler established a one-party state in which he appeared to hold total power. But how total was his power? Was he a 'weak' rather than a 'strong' dictator? Was the **Third Reich** a well-run state or something of a shambles? What was the nature of Nazism?

> **THE THIRD REICH**
> The Nazis called their regime the Third Reich. The Second Reich was the name for the period 1871–1918 when Germany was ruled by Kaisers Wilhelm I and II.

1 The Weimar Republic: 1919–23

a) Was there a German Revolution?

By November 1918 it was clear that Germany was losing the First World War. A sailors' revolt at Kiel spread to other ports. Troops sent to deal with the trouble joined the rebels and workers', soldiers' and sailors' councils sprang up across Germany. There was a general strike in Berlin and armed workers roamed the streets. It seemed that Germany was about to go the way of Russia. On 9 November, Kaiser Wilhelm II abdicated. Ebert, leader of the Social Democratic Party (SPD), became Chancellor of the new republic. On 11 November Germany signed an armistice with the Allies.

Ebert and his SPD colleagues were moderates and wanted to operate within a democratic system. By contrast, the Spartacists, led

THE FREIKORPS

These were paramilitary units, made up mainly of right-wing ex-soldiers. Their formation was encouraged by the High Command, anxious to keep order in the border regions and to prevent a communist takeover.

by Rosa Luxemburg and Karl Liebknecht, wanted to emulate the Bolsheviks in Russia. When a Spartacist rebellion broke out in Berlin, Ebert called in the army and **Freikorps**. By mid-January, after a week of street fighting, the rising had been put down and Luxemburg and Liebknecht murdered. Over the next few months the Freikorps crushed left-wing uprisings in other cities and suppressed a short-lived Bavarian Soviet Republic. Ebert's strong action ensured that the infant Republic survived the traumas of its birth.

Whether the so-called 'German Revolution' amounted to a real revolution is debatable. The Kaiser had gone and parliamentary democracy had been introduced. But the defeat of the Spartacists meant there was no social revolution. The structure of land ownership remained the same and big business was not nationalised.

GERMANY'S PROBLEMS IN 1919

▽ Food shortages continued. The Allied blockade continued until mid-1919.
▽ Germany had little option but to accept the Treaty of Versailles (see pages 97–9). Virtually all Germans condemned the Treaty and nationalists blamed the Weimar politicians for signing it.

b) The Weimar Constitution

In January 1919 Germans elected a new national assembly. Over 75 per cent of the votes went to the three parties which supported Ebert

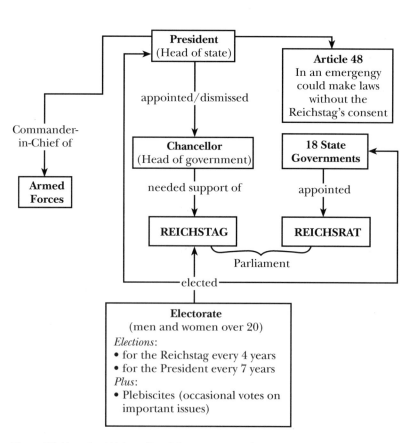

Figure 31 How the Weimar Republic was governed.

– the SPD, the Centre Party, and the Democrats. Because law and order had broken down in Berlin the assembly met in Weimar. Once the Spartacist rebellion had been crushed, it moved back to Berlin. The new government, however, retained its name – the Weimar Republic. The assembly approved a new constitution – finally adopted in July 1919 (see Figure 31).

Historians have criticised two aspects of the Constitution:

▽ In a state of emergency the president could rule by decree.
▽ Proportional representation, whereby a party received the same percentage of Reichstag seats as it received votes, encouraged a proliferation of parties making it impossible for one party to obtain a majority. Therefore it was necessary to form coalition governments. Such governments were usually short lived, (see Table 11).

Date	Party of Chancellor	Chancellor	President
1919	SPD	Scheidemann	Ebert (SPD)
1919–20	SPD	Bauer	
1920	SPD	Müller	
1920–1	Centre Party	Fehrenbach	
1921–2	Centre Party	Wirth	
1922–3	Non-party	Cuno	
1923	DVP	Stresemann	
1923–5	Centre Party	Marx	
1925–6	Non-party	Luther	Hindenburg (Non-party)
1926–8	Centre Party	Marx	
1928–30	SPD	Müller	
1930–2	Centre Party	Brüning	
1932	Non-party	Papen	
1932	Non-party	Schleicher	
1933	Nazi	Hitler	

Table 11 The governments of the Republic, 1919–33: parties, Chancellors and Presidents.

However, it is possible to defend the Constitution.

▽ It was the most democratic in Europe at the time.
▽ The fact that the president could issue decrees ensured that the government could function in a crisis.
▽ The system of proportional representation was fair. Whether it encouraged the emergence of political extremism is debatable.

c) The Threat from Left and Right

i) The Left-wing Threat

Efforts to spark communist revolt in 1920–1 were crushed by the army (see Figure 32).

ii) The Right-wing Threat

While far from united, right-wingers agreed on a number of issues.

▼ They favoured strong government and disliked parliamentary democracy.

▼ They believed that the German army had been 'stabbed in the back' in 1918 by unpatriotic forces within Germany – pacifists, socialists and Jews. These 'November Criminals' had then accepted the shameful Versailles Treaty.

The right posed a threat to the Republic in a number of ways:

▼ Right wing parties won Reichstag seats. The Nationalists (DNVP) got 15 per cent of the vote in 1920.

▼ Some state governments (such as Bavaria) were controlled by the right.

▼ The right had the support of the Freikorps.

▼ Right-wing army officers, judges and civil servants retained positions of power.

iii) The Kapp Putsch

In 1920 the need to reduce the size of the army created great unease within the ranks of the army and the Freikorps. Dr Kapp and General Luttwitz tried to exploit the situation. Marching on Berlin with 5,000 men, they declared that the Weimar government was overthrown. Army leaders refused to crush the **putsch**. However, when workers in Berlin went on strike in support of the government, Kapp panicked and fled abroad. The putsch collapsed. The fact that it had occurred at all highlighted the right-wing threat to the Republic.

PUTSCH
A German word meaning an armed attempt to seize power.

---

iv) Right-wing Terrorism

Freikorps units were disbanded in 1920. But some ex-members formed murder squads to carry on the fight against the left. Judges usually condoned their crimes. Between 1919 and 1922 there were 376 political assassinations – 22 by the left and 354 by the right. Ten left-wingers were sentenced to death. Not a single right-wing assassin received the death sentence. Of the 354 right-wing assassinations 326 went unpunished.

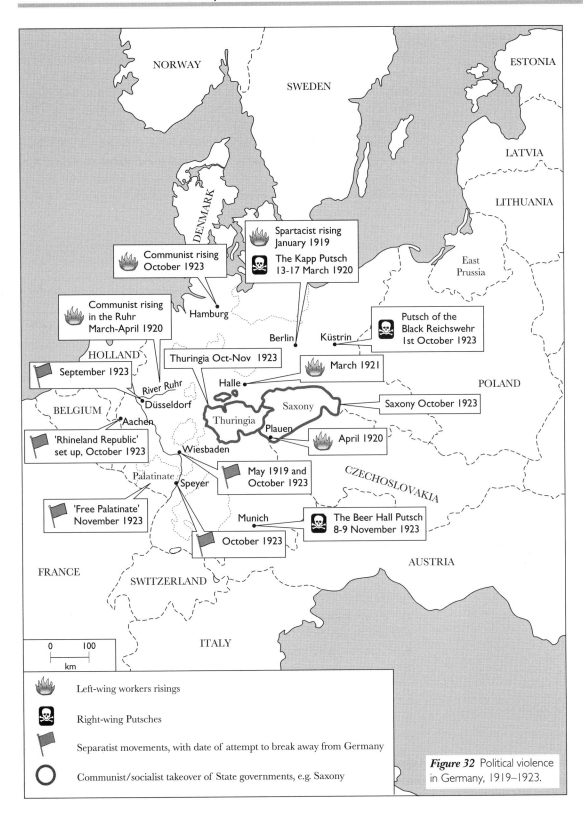

Figure 32 Political violence in Germany, 1919–1923.

ECONOMIC PROBLEMS ARISING FROM THE WAR
▼ Germany had lost important industrial regions.
▼ In 1921 the Allies ordered Germany to pay £6,600 million in reparations.

d) Economic and Financial Problems

By 1919 Germany's finances were in a mess. Weimar governments worsened the situation by printing more money, thus fuelling inflation (see Table 12). Those on fixed incomes suffered badly, and workers claimed that wages did not keep up with rising prices. But not all were losers. Those who were able to pay off their debts with inflated money benefited. So did farmers as a result of high food prices. Nor did industry suffer. The mark's devaluation meant that German goods were cheap abroad while foreign goods were expensive in Germany. The resultant high demand for German goods meant that there was little unemployment.

Table 12 Dollar quotations for the mark.

Month	Marks/dollar
July 1914	4.2
January 1919	8.9
July 1919	14.0
July 1921	76.7
January 1922	191.8
July 1922	493.2
January 1923	17,972.0
July 1923	353,412.0
August 1923	4,620,455.0
September 1923	98,860,000.0
October 1923	25,260,208,000.0
15 November 1923	4,200,000,000,000.0

e) The 1923 Crisis

In January 1923 French and Belgian troops invaded the Ruhr (Germany's most important industrial region) to collect reparations still owing to them. Too weak to take military action, the Weimar government ordered 'passive resistance' and Ruhr workers downed tools. With the economy paralysed, the government printed vast quantities of paper notes. The result was hyperinflation. By autumn 1923 people were paid by the day. In cafés a cup of coffee increased in price as people drank it. The middle classes saw their savings destroyed. Those on fixed incomes (like pensioners) were ruined. The economic crisis led to political crisis:
▼ Communists took over Saxony and Thuringia. Ebert, now President, acted firmly and the insurgency was quickly suppressed.

▼ An attempted right-wing putsch in Munich also failed (see page 146).

In August 1923 the leader of the People's Party the (DVP), Gustav Stresemann, became chancellor. Calling off passive resistance in the Ruhr, he promised to resume reparation payments and introduced a new currency. These actions helped stabilise the currency and led (eventually) to French forces quitting the Ruhr. In 1924 the Allies introduced the Dawes Plan. This extended the reparation repayment period and provided for a large loan to help German recovery.

THE YEARS OF CRISIS: 1918–23

1919 January – Spartacist uprising; election of national assembly; June – Treaty of Versailles;

1920 Kapp putsch;

1923 January – occupation of Ruhr; hyperinflation; August – Stresemann appointed chancellor; end of 'passive resistance'.

ACTIVITY

Brainstorm the positive and negative aspects of the period 1919–23 from the point of view of a) a supporter of Weimar, b) a right-wing extremist, c) a left-wing extremist.

2 The Weimar Republic: 1924–32

ISSUE
How successful was the Weimar Republic between 1924 and 1932?

a) 1924–9: a 'Golden Age'?

The period 1924–9 is usually seen as the high point of the Republic. Its (apparent) success coincided with the influence of Stresemann, Chancellor for a few months in 1923 and then Foreign Minister until 1929. However, some historians question the extent of Weimar's health, bearing in mind that it disintegrated so soon after 1929.

i) Economic and Social Success?

Positive points:

▼ The Dawes Plan did much to restore confidence in the economy and investment poured in, especially from the USA. New houses, roads, and public facilities were built.

▼ Factories were equipped with new machinery. German industrial output more than doubled between 1923 and 1929.

▼ Wages rose in real terms every year from 1924 to 1930. Working hours were shortened and social insurance was improved.

▼ Women had more equality. Some were elected to the Reichstag: others took up professional jobs.

Negative points:

▼ Germany's recovery was dangerously dependent upon US loans.

▼ German farmers – one third of the population – did not prosper. Farm prices fell and farmworkers' earnings in 1929 were only half the national average.

▼ Even in the peak year of 1928 unemployment stood at 1.3 million.

▼ Germany's balance of trade was consistently in the red.

▼ Not all Germans favoured female emancipation. Ironically, most women supported the parties emphasising traditional roles.

ii) Political Success?

Positive Points:

▼ There were no further attempts to overthrow the government.

▼ In the 1924 and 1928 elections the extremist parties of right and left lost ground.

▼ In 1925, on Ebert's death, 78-year-old Field Marshal von Hindenburg was elected President. Hindenburg seemed a useful figurehead.

Negative points:

▼ The political situation remained unstable. Between 1924 and 1930 there were seven governments. The longest survived 21 months.

▼ By the late 1920s the moderate parties were finding it harder to ally.

▼ Many Germans were cynical of party politics.

▼ Hindenburg's election was a potential threat. A right-wing conservative, he did not identify with the Republic or its values.

iii) Cultural and Artistic Success?

Positive points:

▼ The 1920s can be seen as a very creative period with experimentation in art, architecture, drama, film, literature and music. Lively debate flourished in an atmosphere of free expression. Berlin, with 120 newspapers and periodicals, 40 theatres and hundreds of night clubs, seemed to have replaced Paris as the cultural centre of Europe.

Negative points:

▼ The left regarded much of the experimentation as bourgeois – in no way reflecting the needs of the working class. The right saw the new developments as decadent and a threat to traditional values. Many Germans thought Berlin was sleazy, corrupt and sex-obsessed.

b) The Years of Crisis: 1929–32

i) The Economic Crisis

In October 1929 disaster struck the New York stock exchange on Wall Street. The value of shares collapsed and many people were ruined. Americans pulled their investments from Germany, ruining thousands of businesses in the process. As the world slid into depression, even those businesses which had managed without American loans were badly affected. By 1932 at least 6 million Germans were unemployed). Millions of others had to accept low wages and short-

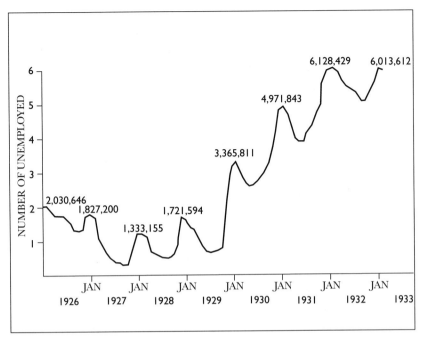

Figure 33 Unemployment in Germany, 1925–33.

time working. The situation was just as bad in the countryside where the agricultural depression deepened.

ii) Political Crisis

The onset of the depression discredited the Weimar Republic. Stresemann died in October 1929 and there was no politician of his calibre to replace him. The various parties in the 1928 'Grand Coalition' soon found themselves at loggerheads. SPD Chancellor Müller refused to agree to cuts in unemployment benefit which the Centre Party and the DVP argued were essential in order to balance the budget. Brüning, the Centre Party leader, replaced Müller as chancellor. Brüning's cabinet, lacking SPD support, did not have a majority in the Reichstag. In 1930 President Hindenburg dissolved the Reichstag when it refused to approve the budget. The 1930 election saw Germans – in desperation – turning to extreme parties. The Communists (KPD) won 77 seats. The Nazis did even better, winning 107 seats and becoming the second largest party. Henceforward, no moderate coalition could be formed.

Brüning remained as chancellor from 1930–2. Lacking a Reichstag majority, he was dependent on Hindenburg issuing emergency degrees. Arguably democracy in Germany thus ended in 1930. Brüning can be seen as a semi-dictator. His economic policies – he cut government spending and increased taxes – also contributed to the rising unemployment. His only success was negotiating an end to Germany's reparation payments in 1932.

WEIMAR REPUBLIC: 1924–30

1924 Dawes Plan;
1925 Hindenburg elected President;
1929 death of Stresemann: Wall Street Crash;
1930 Brüning became chancellor.

ACTIVITY

Discussion: Would Weimar have collapsed even if there had been no Great Depression?

ISSUE
What part did Hitler play in the rise of the Nazis?

3 The Rise of the Nazis, 1919–30

a) Adolf Hitler's Early Life

Hitler was born in Austria in 1889. From 1908 to 1913 he lived as something of a down-and-out in Vienna, making a living selling posters and postcards. In 1913 he moved to Germany. Enlisting in the German army in 1914, he quickly found his vocation, fighting in many of the major battles on the Western Front. There are two remarkable facts about his army career: first he survived; and second he only rose to become corporal. (His superiors thought he had no leadership qualities!) He was a good soldier, winning the Iron Cross for bravery. For Hitler the war was a crucial experience. He enjoyed the comradeship of the trenches and the fact that his life had a purpose. He was horrified when, recovering in hospital from a gas attack, he heard news of Germany's surrender. He wrote later:

Source A

> So it had all been in vain. In vain all the sacrifices. In vain the hours in which, with mortal fear clutching at our hearts we did our duty. In vain the death of two millions. Had they died for this, so that a gang of wretched criminals could lay hands on the fatherland?

On leaving hospital, Hitler returned to Munich. Impressing army authorities with his speaking talents and his nationalist views, he was given two jobs: lecturing troops in political education; and keeping an eye on extremist groups. In September 1919 he was sent to investigate the German Workers' Party – founded in January 1919 by Anton Drexler. Drexler's intention was to win working-class support for nationalist ideas. His 'party' (it only had 55 members) was one of many such groups springing up in Munich. Hitler accepted Drexler's invitation to join the party. He was soon its leading member.

b) Hitler's Ideology

Hitler can be seen as a cynical opportunist who simply wanted power for power's sake. However, most historians now see him as a genuine idealist who held very strong principles to which he clung until his death. He certainly could be pragmatic, seizing the main chance when it presented itself, even if this meant putting his long-term plans on ice. But belief in principles and skill at tactical manoeuvring are not mutually exclusive.

While Hitler's ideology has been described as 'a vast system of bestial, Nordic nonsense', his views – which were by no means new – had a certain (brutal) logic. He saw life as a struggle (his book *Mein*

Kampf translates as 'My Struggle') in which only the strongest nations, races and individuals survived. He believed that Germany was – or should be – the world's greatest nation and that the Germans were – or should be – the master race. For Hitler the opposite of the German was the Jew. He blamed Jews for all Germany's ills and saw them plotting to take over the world. Hitler did not believe in equality. Just as some nations and races were superior to others, so some individuals were superior. Germany needed a heroic leader who would express the popular will. That leader should work to ensure that Germany dominated Europe. This meant expanding eastwards, acquiring land from the inferior Slav races and destroying the evil of communism in the USSR. The fact that this might lead to war did not worry Hitler. In his view, war was the highest form of 'struggle'.

c) Why was the Nazi Party able to launch itself in Munich after 1919?

i) National Conditions
Defeat in war, the Spartacist rising, the continuing left-wing threat, the Treaty of Versailles, and economic problems, all encouraged the rise of right-wing extremism.

ii) The Situation in Bavaria
In early 1919 far-left revolutionaries declared Bavaria a communist republic and there was a 'red' terror. In May 1919 Freikorps and army units kicked out the communists, killing hundreds in a 'white' terror. By 1920 Bavaria, under the control of a right-wing government (led by Gustav Kahr), was a haven for right-wing extremists.

iii) Hitler's Role
Hitler played a vital role in ensuring that the Nazis were more successful than other right-wing groups in Bavaria. Resigning from the army, he threw himself into politics, soon proving himself a brilliant speaker in the Munich beer halls.

In 1920 Hitler announced a 25 Point Programme (see Source F) – a mix of nationalism and socialism – to a 2,000 strong audience at the Hofbrauhaus beer cellar. The German Workers' Party now adopted a new name – the National Socialist German Workers' Party (NSDAP). In 1921 Hitler became party leader. By 1922 the party, helped by Bavarian army officers who provided recruits and money, was the biggest and best organised right-wing group in Bavaria. Attracting support from all types of people, especially ex-soldiers and young idealists, it seemed to be a party of action. In 1921 Hitler

My critical faculty was swept away. Leaning from the rostrum as if he was trying to impel his inner self into the consciousness of all these thousands, he was holding the masses, and me with them, under an hypnotic spell by the sheer force of his conviction . . . I forgot everything but the man; then glancing around, I saw that his magnetism was holding these thousands as one.

Source B Kurt Ludecke describing how he was affected by one of Hitler's speeches in 1922.

THE SA (STURM-ABTEILUNG OR STORM TROOPERS)

Founded in 1921 as the Nazi paramilitary organisation, it was banned after the Beer Hall Putsch but re-established in 1925. Its members wore brown shirts. Its leader from 1931–4 was Ernst Röhm. By 1932 it had hundreds of thousands of members. As well as defending Nazi Party meetings from attack, it was also used to beat up political opponents and disrupt their meetings.

Q Was the Beer Hall Putsch a fiasco or a well-conceived bid for power?

created the **SA** (*Sturm-Abteilung* or storm troopers). By 1923 Hitler was well-known in Bavaria (but not in the rest of Germany).

d) The Beer Hall Putsch

In November 1923 Hitler attempted to seize power. The situation in Germany was certainly favourable, with the French occupying the Ruhr and hyperinflation destroying the economy. Within the NSDAP, Hitler had built up excitement to such a degree that he had to do something to maintain his credibility. What he did made sense. In September he was instrumental in forming a Battle League of right-wing groups. War hero General Ludendorff gave his support. The plan was to win control of Bavaria and then to march on Berlin. Preparations were reasonably thorough. Kahr, the Bavarian leader, had indicated that he might support the putsch. When, at the last minute, he backed down, Hitler decided to go ahead anyway.

On 8 November Kahr was addressing a large meeting at the Burgerbraukellar in Munich. SA men surrounded the beer cellar and Hitler burst in brandishing a revolver. Announcing that the national revolution had begun, he 'persuaded' Kahr to support him. The beer cellar roared its approval. After this things went wrong. Ludendorff allowed Kahr and other officials to escape. Warned of the situation, the Weimar government ordered the Bavarian authorities to crush the putsch. On 9 November Hitler led some 3,000 men into Munich, hoping for a show of mass support. Instead, armed police opened fire and 16 marchers died. Hitler, lucky to survive, was arrested. In February 1924 he and Ludendorff were tried for treason. The trial made Hitler a national figure. Claiming that he had only been acting as a patriotic German, he turned the trial into a propaganda victory. He was found guilty and was sentenced to five years imprisonment. Serving less than a year of his sentence, he was released in December 1924.

f) Nazi Strategy, 1925–9

Hitler was now convinced that the Nazis must win power by democratic means. He wrote the following letter from prison:

> When I pursue active work, it will be necessary to pursue a new policy. Instead of working to achieve power by an armed coup, we will have to hold our noses and enter the Reichstag against Catholic and Marxist members. If outvoting them takes longer than outshooting them, at least the result will be guaranteed by their own Constitution. Sooner or later we shall have a majority, and after that – Germany!

Source C

In 1925 Hitler re-established control over the NSDAP in Bavaria. However, the party had begun to win recruits in north Germany. North German Nazis, led by Gregor Strasser who wanted to make the Nazi programme more socialist, were less loyal to Hitler. Hitler saw off Strasser's challenge. Demanding total loyalty, he won over most of his critics in 1926. In the late 1920s Hitler reorganised his party. A host of new departments – for example, for youth and for women – were set up. Elaborate Nazi ritual was established and the party's first Nuremberg rally was held in 1927. Hitler now developed a new image for himself. No longer the revolutionary fanatic, he appeared instead as a calm, reasonable man awaiting the call of history – which must surely come.

Failing to win mass support from industrial workers, the Nazis turned their attention to the distressed farmers in north Germany. This strategy came too late for the 1928 election in which the Nazis won only 12 seats – 2.6 per cent of the vote.

HITLER AND THE NAZIS: 1919–28

1919 Hitler joined the German Workers' Party;
1921 formation of the SA;
1923 Beer Hall Putsch;
1924 Hitler imprisoned;
1928 the Nazis won 12 seats in the Reichstag.

ACTIVITY

Consider the question, 'How important was Hitler in the rise of the Nazi Party, 1919–28?'

Key points to develop:
▼ the situation in Germany and Bavaria;
▼ the power of Hitler's personality, ideas and leadership;
▼ the significance of the Beer Hall Putsch;
▼ Hitler's strategy post-1924.

---

4 The Nazis Win Power, 1930–4

ISSUE
Why did the Nazis win power in Germany?

a) The Nazi Breakthrough

A Nazi surge began in late 1928 as the party's focus on northern peasants began to pay dividends. By 1929 the Nazis were winning 10–20 per cent of the vote in state elections across northern Germany. Increasing unemployment led to increasing Nazi support. In the September 1930 election the Nazis won 107 seats – 18 per cent of the vote. Overnight they became Germany's second largest party. As the depression worsened, Nazi support continued to grow. In March 1932 Hitler challenged Hindenburg for the presidency. Although he lost, he won nearly 37 per cent of the vote.

In May 1932 Hindenburg dismissed Brüning. Papen, an obscure, right-wing conservative, became chancellor. Having no popular

		Jan 1919	June 1920	May 1924	Dec 1924	May 1928	Sept 1930	July 1932	Nov 1932	March 1933
Right	Nazis **(NSDAP)**	–	–	32	14	12	107	230	196	288
(AGAINST THE REPUBLIC)	National Party **(DNVP)**	44	71	95	103	73	41	37	52	52
(FOR THE REPUBLIC)	People's Party **(DVP)**	19	65	45	51	45	30	7	11	2
(FOR THE REPUBLIC)	Centre **(Z)**	91	64	65	69	62	68	75	70	74
(FOR THE REPUBLIC)	Democratic Party **(DDP)**	75	39	2	32	25	20	4	2	5
(FOR THE REPUBLIC)	Social Democrats **(SPD)**	165	102	100	131	153	143	133	121	120
(AGAINST THE REPUBLIC)	Independent Socialists **(USPD)**	22	84	–	–	–	–	–	–	–
Left	Communists **(KPD)**	–	4	62	45	54	77	89	100	81

Table 13 The results of national elections to the Reichstag, 1919–33.

support, Papen made some effort to come to terms with the Nazis, hoping to form a broad right-wing government. One of his first measures was to lift the ban imposed by Brüning on the SA. The consequences were predictable: there was increased violence (86 people died in street fights in July). Papen's efforts to win over Hitler failed and new elections were called. In July 1932 the Nazis won 230 seats (37 per cent of the vote), becoming the largest party in Germany.

b) What was the Nazi Appeal?

- At a time of misery, they seemed to offer strong, decisive leadership.
- They were strongly anti-Marxist.
- They pledged to unite the country, replace the class system and get everyone pulling together for the common good. They did not represent a narrow sectional interest group.
- They stressed traditional values while also having an image of youth and dynamism.
- Nazi economic ideas were better thought out than many of their critics claimed. They promised to give subsidies to farmers and create jobs for unemployed workers.
- The extent to which anti-Semitism helped win support is a subject of debate. Some historians suggest that the Nazis played down the tone of their anti-Semitic message in the early 1930s. However, many Germans were undoubtedly anti-Semitic. Nor did the Nazis really play down their anti-Semitism. They depicted the Jews (and communists who they saw as one and the same) as being responsible for all Germany's problems.

Which Germans voted Nazi?

Hitler claimed that the NSDAP was a *Volk* party – a movement above class. Was it?

▼ The NSDAP won considerable support from the lower middle class, for example, teachers, artisans, civil servants and farmers who, while rarely unemployed themselves, felt threatened by the depression.

▼ While some historians claim that workers were unlikely to vote Nazi, there is plenty of evidence to suggest that large numbers did vote Nazi. Most of the SA – over 1 million strong by 1933 – were working class.

▼ Nazi support was strong in country areas and small towns in north Germany. However, the party did attract support in some big towns and in parts of the south.

▼ While Nazi voters were more likely to be Protestant, many Catholics voted for Hitler.

▼ The Nazis won a large proportion of young, first-time voters – but many old people also voted Nazi.

▼ Men were more likely to vote Nazi than women. The NSDAP offered little for women of a feminist disposition. The Nazi view was that women's concerns were *Kinder, Kirche, Küche* (children, church and kitchen). However, given that the majority of the electorate were women, the Nazis clearly won substantial female support. Many women approved of the Nazi stance on traditional values and were actively involved in NSDAP organisations. Female voters tended to be more conservative than men and so were less hostile to – even if they did not necessarily vote for – the NSDAP.

In short, the Nazis did win support from significant numbers of Germans of all types and classes. In that sense the NSDAP was a genuine *Volk* party as Hitler claimed.

---

c) How Effective was Nazi Propaganda?

The Nazis set great store by propaganda. Goebbels, who orchestrated Nazi election campaigns, used a host of new and old techniques. Well coordinated press campaigns targeted specific interest groups with specific messages. The party sent some of its main speakers, prepared to address local issues, into rural districts – usually neglected by other parties. Nazi rallies added to the excitement.

Frau Solmitz, a school teacher, described a 1932 Nazi rally:

> The hours passed, the sun shone, the expectations mounted . . . It got to 3 o'clock. 'The Führer's coming!' A thrill goes through the masses. Around the platform hands could be seen raised in the Hitler greeting . . . There stood Hitler in a simple black coat, looking expectantly over the crowd. A forest of swastika banners rustled upwards. The jubilation of the moment gave vent to a rousing cry of 'Heil'. Then Hitler spoke. Main idea: out of the parties a people (Volk) will emerge, the German people. He castigated the 'system' . . . For the rest he refrained from personal attacks and also unspecific and specific promises. His voice was hoarse from speaking so much in

Source D

previous days. When his speech was over, there were roars of jubilation and applause. Hitler saluted . . . the 'Germany Anthem' sounded over the track. Hitler was helped into his coat. Then he went. How many look to him in touching faith as the helper, saviour, the redeemer from overgreat distress.

Figure 34 This poster claimed that the Nazis were building for the future with three foundation stones – ARBEIT (work), FREIHEIT (freedom), BROT (bread). The Jews and Communists offered only 'promises, breakdown of law and order, unemployment, emergency decrees, social decay, corruption, terror, propaganda, lies'.

Figure 35 Nazi election poster, 1932. 'Women! Millions of men out of work. Millions of children without a future. Save our German families. Vote for Adolf Hitler!'

ACTIVITY

Examine the two election posters in Figures 34 and 35 and the account of the Nazi rally. What do these sources tell us about the nature of the Nazi appeal?

d) Was Hitler the Puppet of Big Business?

Marxist historians claimed that Hitler was the puppet of big business and that big business support explains Hitler's rise to power. However, there is little evidence that big business financed Hitler to any great extent pre-1933. Many businessmen mistrusted him if only because he led a party that was socialist in name (at least). Most NSDAP money came from the efforts of its own members – from subscriptions, jumble sales, etc. If money alone could have bought political success, the DNVP – which received large sums from business – would have won every election after 1918.

e) How Important was Hitler's Role, 1930–2?

Hitler's messianic leadership was crucial in attracting and maintaining support. His charismatic authority served to ensure that the disparate groups within the party – not least the often unruly SA – held together. However, he was not totally successful. His failure to win the confidence of President Hindenburg – the key to political power – was particularly important. After Nazi success in the July 1932 election Hitler expected that Hindenburg would appoint him chancellor. Instead, Hindenburg allowed Papen to remain in control. Hitler's actions over the summer of 1932 can be seen as intransigent or complacent. He refused to unleash a putsch, despite the fact that he probably now had the strength to seize power. He also made no effort to ally with the DNVP.

In September, after a decisive vote of no confidence in the Reichstag, Papen called for new elections. The Nazi party was short of funds and Goebbels found the going hard. 'The organisation is as jaded as a battalion which has been too long in the front trenches', he wrote. The November 1932 elections were a major blow for Hitler. The NSDAP vote slipped (to 33 per cent) and it won only 196 seats. It seemed that the myth of invincibility had been exposed.

f) How did Hitler become Chancellor?

In December General Schleicher told Hindenburg that the army no longer had confidence in Papen. Hindenburg reluctantly dismissed Papen. Schleicher, assuring Hindenburg he could command a majority in the Reichstag, now became chancellor. Failing to win Hitler's support, he approached the Nazi leader Gregor Strasser who showed some interest in a deal. Although nothing came of Schleicher's efforts, it seemed that the NSDAP was falling apart. (Strasser was forced to quit the party.) But events now came to Hitler's rescue. In early January 1933, Papen, angry at his dismissal, began secret negotiations with Hitler and Hugenberg, the DNVP leader. The DNVP and the NSDAP shared many views – nationalism, anti-communism and hatred of Weimar. In mid-January the Nazis threw everything into elections in the state of Lippe to show that they were still a major force. The strategy worked. Winning 39 per cent of the vote, Hitler could boast that his party was back on the road. On 28 January Schleicher resigned. Hindenburg finally agreed to accept Hitler. On 30 January Hitler was sworn in as Chancellor with Papen

THE OTHER PARTIES, 1930–2
▼ The Centre Party retained its Catholic support.
▼ The communist KPD increased its vote.
▼ The SPD retained the support of most workers.
▼ The liberal DDP and DVP parties collapsed. Their votes went almost entirely to the Nazis.
▼ The nationalist DNVP still won the support of its traditional voters.

as Vice-Chancellor. His cabinet comprised three Nazis and ten conservatives. In Berlin, the Nazis celebrated with a huge torchlight parade. 'It is almost like a dream', wrote Goebbels, 'a fairy tale ... The New Reich has been born ... The German Revolution has begun.'

g) The March 1933 Election

The revolution had several weeks to wait. Hitler had become Chancellor legally – but only because of Hindenburg and a deal with the 'old gang'. Hugenberg and Papen, confident they could control Hitler, underestimated his talents. Within six months he had succeeded in making himself dictator. Those who see Hitler as simply an opportunist think this occurred almost by accident. Others think it was all part of a master plan. Most likely, Hitler had clear ideas about where he wanted to go in 1933 but was not altogether sure how to get there. His first move was certainly planned. Against the wishes of his DNVP allies, he called for new elections, hoping to gain a Nazi majority in the Reichstag.

In the March 1933 election campaign the Nazis had two important advantages. First the DNVP alliance ensured that Nazi coffers were full. Goebbels was thus able to mount an impressive campaign. Second, Goering recruited 50,000 SA as special police, ensuring that the Nazis could terrorise their opponents legally.

Then on 27 February, the Reichstag building was burned down. Van der Lubbe, a Dutch communist, was found inside the Reichstag. He admitted starting the fire and denied that anyone else was involved. The Nazis, however, claimed that the fire was a communist plot – a signal for a revolution. The communists then (and later) blamed the Nazis, claiming that the fire provided them with an excuse to move against the KPD. The fire was certainly very convenient for the Nazis. Hindenburg, convinced that the KPD was involved, issued a decree suspending freedom of the press, of speech and association. Leading KPD and left-wing SPD members were arrested and socialist newspapers closed down. On 5 March 1933 the Nazis won 43.9 per cent of the vote. The DNVP won 8 per cent. Between them the two parties had a majority.

h) How did Hitler Assume Full Power?

i) The Enabling Act

Hitler was determined to increase his power and to appear to do so legally. To change the constitution, he needed a two-thirds majority. He obtained this by preventing the 81 KPD members taking their seats in the Reichstag, and by winning Centre Party support. He was thus able to pass the Enabling Act. This allowed him to pass laws without the Reichstag's consent. The Act passed by 441 votes to 94.

ii) 'Bringing into Line'

The Nazis now 'brought into line' those parts of the political system that were anti-Nazi.

▼ Hitler reorganised the state parliaments so that each now had a Nazi majority. In 1934 all state parliaments were abolished.

▼ In May 1933 trade unions were abolished. Workers' interests were now protected by the Nazi-controlled Labour Front.

▼ In late May 1933 the Nazis occupied the offices of the SPD and the KPD, confiscating their funds and closing down their newspapers.

▼ In June–July 1933 the other parties dissolved themselves and Germany became officially a one-party (Nazi) state.

iii) The Night of the Long Knives

However, Hitler was still not totally in control.

▼ Hindenburg remained as President.

▼ The army remained outside Nazi control.

▼ The two million-strong SA was a potential threat. While it had played a crucial role in helping Hitler win power, its violent methods proved something of an embarrassment after 1933. Moreover, many SA men, disappointed at the pace of change, were critical of Hitler – not least the SA leader, Ernst Röhm. Röhm wanted to merge the SA with the army, with both under his control. This alarmed both Hitler and army leaders. Hitler did his best to appease Röhm – without success. Fearing that Röhm was planning a putsch, Hitler struck first. On the night of 30 June/1 July 1934 – 'The Night of the Long Knives' – he used detachments of the SS to purge the leaders of the SA and settle scores with other enemies. Some 200 people were killed, including Röhm, Gregor Strasser and Schleicher. Hindenburg and the army leadership supported Hitler's action. At one stroke he had wiped out one threat to his power and gained the support of the other – the army.

> ### THE FÜHRER
> When Hindenburg died in August 1934, Hitler combined the offices of Chancellor and President. Henceforward he was known as the **Führer** (leader). Civil servants and members of the armed forces now took a personal oath of loyalty to him.

i) Who or What was to Blame for Nazi Success?

Historians have long debated who or what was to blame for Nazi success. Marxist historians once claimed, unhelpfully, that it had something to do with Germany's industrial development. The view that Nazism was the logical culmination of German history and that there was a flaw in the German character is similarly unhelpful. In reality, Nazism was the product of the situation in Germany after 1918: defeat in war, the creation of the Weimar Republic, the Versailles Treaty, economic crises and the communist threat.

Some historians blame flaws in the Weimar Republic for Hitler's success. But arguably proportional representation stopped Hitler becoming Chancellor sooner – as did President Hindenburg. The DNVP can be blamed for allying with the Nazis. But at the time it seemed rational to do so: coalition government was the way that the Weimar system worked. It is possible to blame the SPD and the KPD for failing to cooperate against the Nazis. Instead the two socialist parties spent as much time fighting each other. But even if they had united, it is unlikely that they would have prevented the Nazi take-over. While it is possible to blame the German people for voting Nazi, less than half actually did so in March 1933.

5 The Nature of Nazi Rule, 1933–9

a) What was Hitler's Leadership Style?

The spirit of the Third Reich was embodied in Hitler's remark that there could be only one will in Germany, his own, and that all others had to be subservient to it. He saw politics essentially as the actions of great men and the solving of problems as a matter of will-power. Decision-making in the Third Reich was thus inspired by Hitler's personal whim rather than by administrative procedures. While he was the only source of real authority, he was rarely involved in the day-to-day discussions which led to the formulation of policy. Cabinet meetings became less frequent (there was just one in 1938) and he did not see some of his ministers for months at a time. His preference for his home in Bavaria instead of Berlin and his aversion to systematic work, meant that decision-making was often a chaotic process.

b) 'Authoritarian Anarchy'?

Most historians now think that the Third Reich was not efficiently governed. They particularly stress the fact that there was a proliferation of bureaucracies and agencies and no precise relationship between them. No attempt was made, for example, to fuse the institutions of the Nazi party and the state administrations. They functioned uneasily alongside each other at every level, competing to implement policies which Hitler did little more than outline. The situation was further complicated by the fact that the party itself was by no means a unified whole. It consisted of a mass of organisations like the Hitler Youth and the SS, which were keen to uphold their own interests. Hitler's tendency to create new agencies, with the job of speeding up particular projects, added to the confusion. Powerful leaders, like Goering and Himmler, soon built up their own empires, largely ignoring everyone except Hitler.

Historians Broszat and Mommsen have gone further, claiming that the anarchic system controlled Hitler, rather than he the system. In consequence, they believe that historians should focus upon the structure of the Nazi state rather than upon Hitler himself. In this **'structuralist'** or **'functionalist'** view, many of the Nazi regime's measures, rather than being the result of long-term planning or even deliberate intent, were simply knee-jerk responses to the pressure of circumstance. Mommsen has even suggested that Hitler was a 'weak dictator' who took few decisions and who had difficulty getting these implemented.

However, the functionalists have probably exaggerated the 'authoritarian anarchy' of the Third Reich. In reality, there was not always confrontation between party and state bureaucrats. Moreover, the men who staffed both the party and state machinery conducted their business with reasonable efficiency. The special agencies were able to get things done quickly. Indeed, the idea of 'authoritarian anarchy' does not fit the remarkable success of the Third Reich up to 1941. To view Hitler as a 'weak dictator' is to misconstrue the situation. He was ultimately in control of Nazi Germany. He did not – could not – concern himself with everything. However, in those areas he considered vital, he made the strategic decisions; subordinates hammered out the details. Historians have often underestimated him. He did have some impressive qualities, including an excellent memory and real firmness of purpose.

> **FUNCTIONALISTS (OR STRUCTURALISTS)**
> These are terms used to describe historians who believe that Hitler did not have as much control over events as 'intentionalist' historians believe.

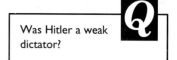

> Was Hitler a weak dictator?

c) To what Extent was Nazi Germany a Police State?

i) The Schutzstaffel (SS)

The SS, formed in 1925 as an elite bodyguard for Hitler, was a minor section of the SA until Heinrich Himmler became its leader in 1929. Efficient and ambitious, Himmler envisaged the SS taking over the business of policing Germany. By 1936 all the police (including the **Gestapo**) were unified under Himmler's control. SS men were drafted into the police and police officers were encouraged to join the SS. However, Himmler was determined that the SS should be more than a security service. He intended it to become a racial elite, providing Germany with a new nobility. Would-be SS recruits had to go before a Racial Selection Board which imposed strict criteria. Obsessed with racial purity, Himmler accepted only perfect Aryan specimens, preferably tall, blond, blue-eyed and intelligent. SS men were only allowed to marry women of 'good' German blood. The SS's guiding principle was unquestioning obedience to Hitler.

> **GESTAPO**
> The Prussian secret police which was allowed to use torture to extract information and confessions.

Figure 36 Henrich Himmler.

ii) Concentration Camps

In March 1933 Himmler established the first concentration camp (for political opponents) at Dachau. By the summer of 1933 almost 30,000 people had been taken into 'protective custody' without trial and without the right of appeal. Dachau became the model camp, imposing a system intended to break the spirit of the inmates. The camp guards – men of the SS Death Head units from 1936 – had total power. Corporal punishment was routinely administered and the barely-fed prisoners were also expected to do hard physical labour. By 1937 the three main camps, Dachau, Sachsenhausen and Buchenwald, held only a few thousand communists, Jews, and 'asocials' (beggars, habitual criminals and homosexuals). Some inmates had died. Others had been 'reformed' and released. However, the takeover of Austria and the Sudetenland in 1938 led to an increase in arrests. By September 1939 there were some 25,000 prisoners and three new camps – Flossenburg, Mauthausen and Ravensbruck.

iii) What Was the Extent of the Terror?

'Terror is the most effective instrument', Hitler declared. 'I shall not permit myself to be robbed of it simply because a lot of stupid, bourgeois mollycoddlers choose to be offended by it.' His regime repressed its enemies with thoroughness and brutality. However, it is possible to exaggerate the extent of Nazi terror prior to 1939.

▼ The SS's influence was limited pre-1939.
▼ The concentration camps were not extermination camps pre-1939.
▼ The understaffed Gestapo was not very efficient at a local level.
▼ Those who disliked the Nazi regime were able to leave Germany.

d) How did Hitler Control the Church and the Army?

Hitler preferred cooperation to conflict with the churches. Given that he seemed to be upholding traditional values, both the Protestant and Catholic churches were prepared to cooperate with him. In 1933 Protestants agreed to unite to form a 'Reich Church', electing a Nazi as their 'Reich Bishop'. Some members of the Reich Church – they called themselves 'German Christians' – wore Nazi uniforms: their slogan was 'the swastika on our chests and the Cross in our hearts'. In July 1933 Hitler made a Concordat with the Pope. In return for the Catholic Church staying out of German politics, Hitler guaranteed religious freedom for Catholics. In general, throughout the 1930s Church leaders sought to avoid conflict with the Nazi regime. A Nazi anti-clerical campaign in 1936–7 generated some opposition. But most Christians continued to accept, many wholeheartedly, the Nazi regime.

The army posed no real threat to Hitler. Leading officers, even if

ACTIVITY

Discussion: What exactly is a totalitarian state? Was Nazi Germany more totalitarian than Stalin's Russia or Mussolini's Italy?

they disliked Nazi rule, shared many of its aims. Hitler did not altogether trust the 'old guard' generals. In 1938 he removed War Minister Blomberg and Commander-in-Chief Fritsch.

6 The German Economy

Many scholars have been critical of the Nazis' economic performance.

▼ They are seen as being simply lucky. The depression was at its worst in 1932. By 1933 there was a worldwide economic upturn. Hitler benefited from this.

▼ Arguably there was not much of an economic upturn. Some claim the German economy was so much in crisis in 1939 that Hitler was forced into a war of expansion.

However, the Nazis' economic performance can be defended:

▼ In 1933 they had specific plans to improve the economic situation. In the short term they intended to create jobs by spending money on public works. They also aimed to protect farmers by raising tariffs and granting subsidies. In the longer term, Hitler envisaged an economy geared to the demands of war and planned to win 'living space' (*lebensraum*) in eastern Europe. These plans were put into action after 1933.

Table 14 The strength of the German economy.

(a) Index of industrial and consumer goods (1928 = 100)		
	Industrial goods	Consumer goods
1928	100	100
1933	56	80
1934	81	91
1936	114	100
1938	144	116

(b) Index of wages (1936 = 100)	
1928	125
1933	88
1934	94
1936	100
1938	106

(c) Comparative military expenditure: Germany and Britain (% of GNP)	Germany	Britain
1935	8	2
1936	13	5
1937	13	7
1938	17	8
1939	23	22

(d) National income (million marks)	
1928	125
1933	88
1934	94
1936	100
1938	106

▼ Hitler was not bound by economic 'theory': he was prepared to experiment.

▼ There *was* a considerable upturn in the economy after 1933. Between 1933 and 1939 German industrial production more than doubled and its unemployment record was the best in Europe. After 1936 it was actually short of workers. The economy was strong enough to provide 'guns' (for war) and 'butter' (an improved standard of living). There is no convincing evidence that the economy was in severe crisis in 1939.

Figure 37 Unemployment in Germany, 1933–9.

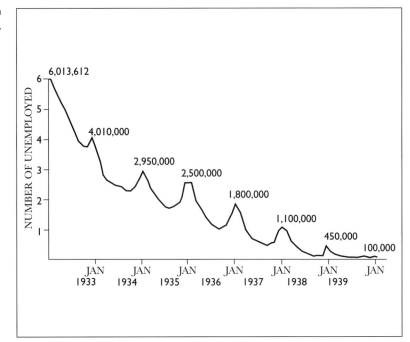

a) Schacht and the New Plan

Nazi economic policy 1933–7 was largely under the control of the Economics Minister, Dr Schacht. Under Schacht's guidance, money was provided for various employment schemes. New roads, homes, schools, and hospitals were built. A National Labour Service ensured that young Germans were found work. (After 1935 all men aged 18–25 had to spend six months in the Labour Service.) The fact that the Nazis encouraged women to stay at home meant that there were more jobs for men. These measures helped to reduce unemployment to 1.7 million by 1935. Schacht's 'New Plan' (1934) provided for control of all aspects of trade, and encouraged the signing of trade treaties with countries of south-east Europe and South America.

b) The Four-Year Plan

The main aim of the Four-Year Plan, begun in 1936, was to prepare Germany for war. A key objective was to make Germany self-sufficient in raw materials by the development of synthetic substitutes. The Plan, under Goering's control, had mixed success. Arms production did not reach the levels desired by the armed forces and production of 'synthetic' rubber and oil fell short of target. However, Germany was reasonably self-sufficient by 1939 and, given its success in 1939–40, it is hard to argue that its forces were not ready for war. The fact that more money was spent on arms led to a boom in the late 1930s.

c) Who Benefited from Nazi Economic Policies?

i) The Proletariat
Statistics suggest that workers' real wages were lower in 1938 than they had been in 1928. However, by the late 1930s most workers were better off than they had been in 1932. The German Labour Front improved working conditions through its 'Beauty of Work' programme while 'Strength through Joy' provided a wide variety of activities which took place outside working time.

ii) Peasants and Small Farmers
While small farmers remained the lowest paid group in Germany, import controls and a setting of higher farm prices offered some relief. Nazi propaganda portrayed farmers as the backbone of the nation. Ironically the number of farmers decreased after 1933 as people left the countryside to earn higher wages in the towns.

iii) Business Interests
Big business, while concerned at the increasing amount of government interference, made huge profits.

> **ACTIVITY**
>
> Examine Table 14 and Figure 37. What evidence suggests that Nazi economic policies were a) successful? b) unsuccessful?

7 | Nazi Society: The Racial State

> **ISSUE**
> To what extent did the Nazis carry out a social revolution between 1933 and 1939?

a) Eugenics

According to Nazi doctrine, a purified Aryan race, embodying all that was positive in humanity, was bound to triumph in the world struggle. While good 'blood' was to be encouraged, racial aliens and the mentally and physically handicapped, were to be eliminated. A 1933 law permitted the compulsory sterilisation of anyone suffering from a hereditary disease and/or deemed to be mentally or physically unfit. Doctors and directors of hospitals, homes and prisons

EUGENICS
Only those who have 'desirable' characteristics should be allowed to breed.

THE NUREMBERG LAWS
In September 1935 Hitler introduced two new laws at the annual Nuremberg rally:
▼ Marriage and sexual relations between Jews and Germans were prohibited.
▼ Jews lost their German citizenship.

The question of defining just who was Jewish remained a major problem. Not until November 1935 did party and ministry experts finally manage to reach a compromise. A 'full Jew' was defined as someone who had three Jewish grandparents or someone who had two Jewish grandparents and was married to a Jew. This definition of 'Jewishness' excluded some 250,000 half-Jews from much of the anti-Jewish legislation.

KRISTALLNACHT (THE NIGHT OF BROKEN GLASS)
On 7 November 1938 a German official in Paris was shot by a Polish Jew. On 9 November Goebbels delivered a bitter attack on the Jews and called for the official's death to be avenged. Nazi activists took

submitted nearly 400,000 names during 1934–5. Over 80 per cent of the cases (which went to new health courts) resulted in sterilisation. A 1935 law prohibited a marriage if either party suffered from a mental derangement or had a hereditary disease.

b) The Treatment of German Jews, 1933–9

In 1933 there were some 500,000 Jews in Germany, less than one per cent of the population. Anti-Semitism was an article of faith for Hitler. While he had not prepared a step-by-step anti-Jewish programme, he certainly had in mind the major lines of future action. These included the exclusion of Jews from public office, a ban on Jewish-German marriages, and efforts to force Jews to emigrate.

i) The Situation, 1933–5
In March 1933 Nazi mobs beat up large numbers of Jews and destroyed Jewish property. While officially opposing violence (which soured relations with Hindenburg and other conservatives), Hitler supported anti-Semitic legislation. From April 1933 there was a flood of laws excluding Jews from specific jobs. Anti-Semitic measures were also taken by local authorities and by professional organisations. Jews also faced the anti-Semitic rabble-rousing of the Nazi press. By making their lives difficult, the Nazis hoped to encourage Jews to emigrate. However, many Jews, barred from taking any of their assets out of Germany, were reluctant to leave. Moreover, there were few countries willing to accept them. Few Germans (not even church leaders) spoke out against the anti-Jewish measures.

ii) The Situation, 1936–9
In 1936 Germany staged the Olympic Games. Concerned that overt anti-Semitism might induce several countries to withdraw their teams, the government adopted a more moderate line. However, in 1937, Goering began issuing decrees which shut down a wide variety of Jewish businesses. The hardening of anti-Semitic activity was possibly accelerated by the Nazi takeover of Austria in March 1938 (see page 216). Nazis beat up and humiliated many of Austria's 200,000 Jews, and looted Jewish homes and businesses. In August 1938 Eichmann set up a Central Office for Jewish Emigration in Vienna. This allowed would-be emigrants in one day to complete procedures which in Germany took many weeks. Jews left the Office with an emigration visa and little else. Virtually all their property was confiscated. By November 1938 about 50,000 Austrian Jews had emigrated.

Over the winter of 1938–9, many new laws against Jews came into effect. For example, from 1 January 1939 Jews were forbidden to undertake any form of independent business activity. They were also banned from visiting theatres, cinemas, concerts and circuses. In January 1939 Goering commissioned Heydrich, Himmler's right-hand man, to bring the 'Jewish question to as favourable a solution as present circumstances permit'. The solution was forced emigration. Heydrich, aiming to rid Germany of Jews within ten years, copied Eichmann's methods. In the twelve months after November 1938 about 150,000 Jews left Germany.

iii) Conclusion

Functionalist historians see Nazi anti-Jewish policy between 1933 and 1939 as erratic and improvised. They think that Hitler simply accepted whatever 'solution' to the Jewish problem was currently in vogue. But **intentionalist** historians believe, more persuasively, that Hitler was the principal – if not always the sole – driving force of anti-Semitism. Party activists, who urged him to take radical action against the Jews, urged him in a direction he wanted to go. Arguably Nazi goals had been systematically pursued and rapidly achieved: by September 1939 about 70 per cent of Germany's Jews had been driven to emigrate. Just where Hitler's policy was leading is debatable. In a speech to the Reichstag in January 1939, he said:

> Today I will once more be a prophet: if the international Jewish financiers in and outside Europe should succeed in plunging the nations once more into a world war, then the result will not be the Bolshevizing of the earth, and thus the victory of Jewry, but the annihilation of the Jewish race in Europe.

him at his word. On 9/10 November (*Kristallnacht*) 8,000 Jewish businesses were destroyed, 200 synagogues burned, hundreds of Jews beaten up and over 90 killed. Some 30,000 Jews were herded into concentration camps. Most were later released but only after agreeing to leave Germany. As a result of *Kristallnacht*, a huge fine was levied on the Jewish community (as compensation for the Paris murder!).

INTENTIONALISTS
Intentionalist historians believe that Hitler was a strong dictator who was in a position to realise his intentions.

Source E

The fact that Hitler expressed such intentions cannot be taken as proof that he was already set on **genocide**. Indeed, given the emphasis on emigration, it seems unlikely that he was yet contemplating mass murder.

GENOCIDE
The extermination of a race of people.

ACTIVITY

1. Comment on the phrase: 'the result will not be the Bolshevizing of the earth, and thus the victory of Jewry'. **[7 marks]**
2. What may have been Hitler's purpose for speaking as he did in 1939? **[7 marks]**

c) The Creation of a People's Community

The Nazis claimed to be creating a new kind of society, a 'people's community', in which the class divisions that had previously rent the nation asunder would cease. Given the brief period of Nazi rule, long-term changes scarcely had time to take effect. While there was no fundamental redistribution of wealth, the Nazis did favour social mobility and new opportunities for advancement were opened up. Moreover, many Germans do seem to have felt an increased sense of comradeship, even if class identities were not eradicated.

d) Women's Role

Women were encouraged to leave work (they were squeezed out of professions like law and medicine) to marry and to bear children. Abortion was prohibited; access to contraception was restricted; and financial incentives were given to encourage people to have children. Mothers who had large families were held in esteem and given an award, the Mothers' Cross. Nazi birth-encouraging policies were successful: in 1936 there were over 30 per cent more births than there had been in 1933. To improve fertility women were encouraged to stop smoking and to do sport. Ironically, given the regime's goals, the number of employed women actually increased as labour shortage drew many females into work. Hitler worried about this. He continued to believe that a woman's place was in the home.

8 The Nazi Appeal

a) Were the Nazis Popular?

ISSUE

How popular were the Nazis, 1933–9?

The fact that there was little open opposition does not mean that most Germans supported what the Nazis did. Open opposition was difficult because:

▼ virtually all independent organisations in the Third Reich were dissolved;

▼ Nazi opponents were punished;

▼ by 1935 the Nazi Party had over 5 million members and over 500,000 officials. It was thus able to supervise virtually every citizen. Some 400,000 Block Wardens, for example, had the job of snooping on their neighbours and reporting suspicious behaviour.

However, Nazi rule does seem to have been popular:

▼ Evidence from Nazi agencies set up to track public opinion suggests that Hitler was very popular.

▽ In 1935 90 per cent of the people of the Saar voted to return to Germany.

▽ Germans in Austria, Czechoslovakia and Poland were keen to join the Third Reich.

Assuming Hitler was popular, the question must be asked – why?

b) Propaganda

In 1933 Goebbels became Minister of Popular Enlightenment and Propaganda. In time (although not immediately) his ministry was responsible for the control of books, the press, the radio and films. Realising the importance of radio as a medium for propaganda, Goebbels encouraged the mass-production of cheap radios. (By 1939 Germans owned more radios per head than any country on earth.) Goebbels also came to control the whole of Germany's art and culture. Painting, sculpture and architecture were all brought under government control. The notion of 'art for art's sake' was abandoned: instead art had to serve the state. Some works were condemned as 'degenerate'. Jazz music, associated with black people, was banned.

Figure 38 Joseph Goebbels.

Goebbels declared that no German in the Third Reich should feel himself to be a private citizen. The regime constantly urged people to work for the public good and to take part in Nazi activities. Efforts were made to create new kinds of social ritual. The 'Heil Hitler' greeting, for example, and the Nazi salute were intended to strengthen identification with the regime.

c) Control of Youth

The mobilisation of youth was a major goal of the Third Reich. By 1939 it was virtually compulsory to belong to one of the Hitler Youth Movements. The aim of these movements was to ensure that young Germans were loyal to fatherland and Führer. The Hitler Youth placed a strong emphasis on military training. The League of German Maidens emphasised fitness and preparation for motherhood. Education was also used to indoctrinate. Ideologically unreliable teachers were dismissed. Religious education was scrapped. Racial instruction became mandatory. Subjects like History were used as a vehicle for Nazi ideas. Great emphasis was also given to sport.

d) Popular Support

Hitler's position in Germany did not rest exclusively on intimidation and propaganda. Many aspects of his policy were popular.

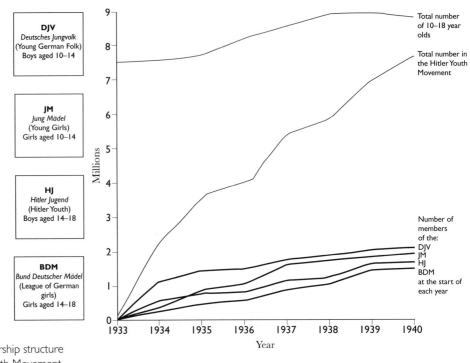

DJV
Deutsches Jungvolk
(Young German Folk)
Boys aged 10–14

JM
Jung Mädel
(Young Girls)
Girls aged 10–14

HJ
Hitler Jugend
(Hitler Youth)
Boys aged 14–18

BDM
Bund Deutscher Mädel
(League of German girls)
Girls aged 14–18

Total number of 10–18 year olds

Total number in the Hitler Youth Movement

Number of members of the:
DJV
JM
HJ
BDM
at the start of each year

Figure 39 Membership structure of the Hitler Youth Movement, 1933–40.

▼ Many Germans supported the idea of a united national community.

▼ Germans were proud of Hitler's foreign policy success (see Chapter 7).

▼ Most believed the Nazis had improved the economic situation.

▼ In some respects Germany was not a stereotypical totalitarian society. It was open to anyone wanting to visit it. (Many visitors were impressed by what they saw.) Germans could also travel freely abroad.

▼ Prior to 1939, Germans had almost a religious faith in Hitler. He was seen as a great leader, 'a man of the people' working tirelessly on Germany's behalf, the focus of loyalty and of national unity.

▼ Working on Germany: 1918–39

Why did Germany reject the democratic Weimar Republic?
Associated with national humiliation, the Republic struggled from the start. While it survived the early years of crisis, it was impossible to disguise its chief political weakness – the fact that coalition governments came and went with alarming regularity. When the depression brought economic ruin, faith in democracy collapsed. Perhaps Weimar-style democracy never had much chance of succeeding in

Germany post-1918. This is not to argue that Hitler's success was inevitable. But, given the lack of trust in Weimar and the fear of Marxism, it was always a possibility. The 44 per cent of Germans who voted for Hitler in 1933 did so for (what seemed at the time) rational reasons. Germany was in a hole. Hitler seemed to offer a way out of the hole.

How important was Hitler?

Hitler can be seen as the man who, almost single-handedly, brought the Nazis to power and thereafter directed Germany's affairs. However, there is a danger that too much focus on Hitler's personality can simplify complex developments. Nazism was surely more than Hitlerism. But as Ian Kershaw (who is generally against a Hitler-centred interpretation) says: 'No attempt to produce a comprehensive understanding of the phenomenon of Nazism without doing justice to "the Hitler factor" can hope to succeed.'

Was the Third Reich an aberration in German history?

Some think Hitler's dictatorship evolved from the authoritarian system of Bismarck and the Kaiser. (It is worth re-reading Chapter 1: Section 2 to see what Germany was like pre-1914). However, the Third Reich does seem to have been very different to the Second Reich. Hitler, of course, was intent on carrying out a – Nazi – revolution.

Answering Extended Writing and Essay Questions on Germany: 1918–39

Consider the question: 'Why did Hitler fail to gain power in 1923 yet succeed in 1933?'

A suggested line of response would be to compare the following:

▼ the economic and political situation in 1919–23 with that in 1930–3. Why was high unemployment a greater problem than high inflation?

▼ the strength of the Nazi Party in the early 1920s with the early 1930s. Why was the party much stronger in the early 1930s? What difference did this make to Nazi strategy?

Answering Source-Based Questions on Germany: 1918–39

1. We demand the union of all Germans, on the basis of the right of the self-determination of peoples, to form a Greater Germany.

2 We demand ... abolition of the Peace Treaties of Versailles and Saint-Germain.

3. We demand land and colonies to feed our people and to settle our surplus population.

4. Only those of German blood ... may be members of the nation. No Jew may be a member of the nation.

8. All further non-German immigration must be prevented.

11. We demand the abolition of incomes unearned by work.

14. We demand profit-sharing in large industrial enterprises.

16. We demand ... the immediate communalising of big department stores.

Source F Some of the 25 Points of National Socialism, 1920.

Fourteen years of Marxism have undermined Germany. One year of Bolshevism would destroy Germany. The richest and most beautiful areas of world civilisation would be transformed into chaos and heaps of ruins ...

The task before us is the most difficult which has faced German statesmen in living memory. But we all have unbounded confidence, for we believe in our nation and in its eternal values. Farmers, workers and the middle class must unite to contribute the bricks wherewith to build the new Reich.

The National Government will therefore regard it as its first and supreme task to restore to the German people unity of mind and will. It will preserve and defend the foundations on which the strengths of our nation rests. It will take under its firm protection Christianity as the basis of our morality, and the family as the nucleus of our nation and state. Standing above estates and classes, it will bring back to our people the consciousness of its racial and political unity and the obligations arising therefrom ...

Source G Hitler's 'Appeal to the German People', 31 January 1933.

▼ QUESTIONS ON SOURCES

1. Using the evidence in Sources F and G and your own knowledge, to what extent was the Nazi Party both a nationalist and a socialist party? **[10 marks]**
2. Which of the two sources best indicates what programme Hitler might put into operation in 1933? Explain your answer. **[10 marks]**

Points to note about the questions

Question 1 In your answer, it is worth stressing that Hitler was far more a nationalist than a socialist. That said, he did wish to create a national community in which (racially pure) Germans would pull together for the common good. Was this 'socialism'?

Question 2 Source G *should* be a better source for giving us information about Hitler's intentions. His views might have changed since 1920. However, Source F is far more specific. It *does* outline what the Nazi Party intends to do if it gains power. In Source G Hitler, while lambasting his enemies, avoids making too many commitments.

Further Reading

Books in the Access to History Series
For a more detailed approach to the Weimar Republic and Hitler's rise to power read Geoff Layton's *From Bismarck to Hitler: Germany 1890–1933* (Chapters 5–7) and *Germany: The Third Reich* (Chapters 2–4). On Hitler and the Third Reich, read *Germany: The Third Reich* (Chapters 5–6) by Geoff Layton and *Anti-Semitism and the Holocaust* (Chapters 2–3) by Alan Farmer.

General
For the Weimar Republic and Hitler's rise to power, Chapter 12 in *Years of Change, Europe 1890–1945* by Robert Wolfson and John Laver (Hodder & Stoughton) is a reasonable starting point. John Laver's *Imperial and Weimar Germany 1890–1933* in the History at Source series (Hodder & Stoughton) provides a good range of source materials. *Weimar and the Rise of Hitler* by A.J. Nicholls, 1991 (Macmillan) has withstood the test of time well. *Weimar Germany: The Republic of the Reasonable* by P. Bookbinder, 1998 (MUP) is more recent. Also try *The Nazi Voter* by T. Childers, 1983 (University of North Carolina) and C. Fischer's *The Rise of the Nazis*, 1995 (MUP). *The Nazi Seizure of Power: The Experience of a Single Town* by W.S. Allen, 1989 (Eyre & Spottiswoode) is fascinating.

While there was much more to the Nazi phenomenon than Hitler, you do need to understand the man. *Hitler and Nazism* by D. Geary, 1993 (Routledge) and *Hitler* by D. Welch, 1998 (UCL) are short introductions. *Hitler and Stalin: Parallel Lives* (HarperCollins) 1992, and *Hitler: A Study in Tyranny* (Penguin), 1962 by Alan Bullock are both classics. Anything by Ian Kershaw is worth reading. Try his *Hitler* (Longman) or (for the really ambitious) *Hitler: vol. 1, Hubris 1889–1936*, 1998 and *vol. 2, Nemesis 1936–1945*, 1999 (Penguin).

The Nazi Dictatorship: Problems and Perspectives by I. Kershaw, 1985 (Edward Arnold) provides analysis of the historiographical debates while M. Broszat, *The Hitler State*, 1981 (Longman) remains an important work. The following are good on particular topics: *A Social History of the Third Reich* by R. Grunberger (Penguin), *The Racial State: Germany 1933–1945* by M. Burleigh and W. Wippermann, 1991 (CUP) and *Nazi Germany and the Jews: The Years of Persecution 1933–39* by S. Friedlander, 1997 (Weidenfeld & Nicolson). For the definitive collection of documents refer to J. Noakes and G. Pridham, eds, *Nazism 1919–1945: A Documentary Reader*, 4 Vols, 1988 (Exeter University).

CHAPTER 6

ITALY, SPAIN AND FRANCE: 1918–39

POINTS TO CONSIDER

In this chapter you will be studying developments in Italy, Spain and France in the inter-war years. The chapter has been divided into an Introduction and five sections. The Introduction examines the meaning of fascism. Sections 1 and 2 examine Fascism in Italy. Sections 3 and 4 deal with the Spanish Civil War, examining to what extent this was fascist-influenced. Section 5 deals with events in France, asking why France did not 'go' fascist. Fascism is thus the central theme of the chapter.

In 1920 all but two of Europe's 28 states could be described as democracies in that they possessed a parliamentary system with an elected government. In the following two decades most of these democratic systems were replaced by dictatorships. By the end of 1940 only five democracies remained. The first dictatorship was that of the far left – Bolshevik Russia. However, the spectre of communism, which threatened many countries after 1918, failed to materialise. In the event all the dictatorships (the USSR apart) came from the right. While some of the dictatorships are usually seen as 'conservative', others (especially those in Italy and Germany) are seen as fascist. The first Fascist dictator was Benito Mussolini who came to power in Italy in 1922. (Throughout the chapter the convention is adopted of giving Italian Fascism a capital 'F' and the more general phenomenon of fascism a small 'f'.)

> **FASCISM**
> Derived from the Italian word *fascio* (plural *fasci*) meaning a group, it was a term associated with rebels. In Sicily in the 1890s *fasci* of left-wing workers organised strikes against absentee landlords. After 1918 nationalists set up their own local *fasci* to combat the left. When Mussolini formed the Fascio di Combattimento, Italians recognised that this was an anti-establishment organisation.

1 Introduction

a) What does Fascism Mean?

There is no generally accepted definition of **fascism**, nor any consensus about exactly which regimes qualify as being fascist. In the inter-war period Marxists claimed that virtually all right-wing dictatorships were fascist. Most historians today, however, choose to differentiate between fascist regimes and conservative (often military) dictatorships. But, historians do not necessarily agree about which dictator-

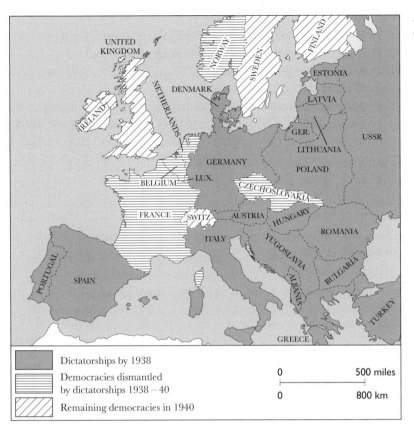

Figure 40 The European dictatorships, 1918–40.

Map legend:
- Dictatorships by 1938
- Democracies dismantled by dictatorships 1938 – 40
- Remaining democracies in 1940

0 ——— 500 miles
0 ——— 800 km

ships were fascist and which were conservative. Some sceptics even deny that there was such a thing as a general fascist phenomenon. They see each so-called fascist movement as separate and significantly different, claiming that only Mussolini's regime should be termed Fascist. Even Fascism and Nazism can be seen as very different doctrines. However, while there were certainly differences between them, Nazi Germany and Fascist Italy do seem to have had much in common. Assuming we accept that fascism has some wider meaning and that Fascism and Nazism (and possibly Franco-ism in Spain) were variants of the same movement, what do regimes need to have in common in order to be called fascist?

b) What were the Main Fascist Ideas?

Some historians insist that fascism was not a proper ideology, arguing that it had no great philosopher and was a hodge-podge of ideas. It can be seen as merely a 'style' of rule (focusing particularly on control of the media, political symbols, mass rallies, etc.) with little substance behind the style. However, fascists did share most of the following ideas.

ISSUE
Did fascism have an ideology, i.e. a relatively coherent set of political ideas?

▼ They were extremely nationalistic.

▼ They were anti-liberal and had no time for parliamentary rule.

▼ They hoped to create a new (more united) society.

▼ They were strongly anti-communist.

▼ They stressed the importance of youth.

▼ They had an ambivalent relationship with socialism. Some, like Mussolini, had once been socialists. Fascists often supported autarky (economic self-sufficiency) which implied the need for state direction.

▼ They emphasised military virtues and viewed war as a natural (even good) thing.

▼ They insisted on the importance of the leader, the heroic and infallible man of destiny who embodied the nation.

Given that these ideas did influence action, there was more to fascism than 'style'.

c) What Factors Led to the Rise of Fascism?

Fascist-type ideas developed pre-1914. However, the First World War was a vital catalyst in fascist development. Many countries emerged from the war with a profound sense of grievance. Fascism fed on nationalist grievances. It was boosted by economic misery and the perceived weakness of democratic regimes. Moreover, the war produced in Russia a communist revolution dedicated to fomenting class revolt across Europe. Fascists gained support by pledging themselves to resist communism. Indeed, fascism only attracted mass support when there was a serious communist threat.

d) Who Supported Fascism?

Fascism was particularly attractive to:

▼ ex-servicemen;

▼ young people who welcomed the opportunity for action and rebellion;

▼ the lower middle classes.

<table>
<tr><td>ISSUE
Why did Mussolini win power in Italy?</td><td>## 2 Italy: Mussolini's Rise to Power</td></tr>
</table>

a) What were the Problems Facing Liberal Italy?

Italy, unified in the 1860s, was far from a united state, and the Liberal regime had never had much popular support. Oddly, Liberal Italy had no strong liberal party or indeed any real party system. Instead, there existed a large number of factions, each clustering around a prominent individual. After elections, deals were struck and coalitions were formed. However, these were often short lived because politicians quickly fell out. To a growing number of left- and right-wing critics, democratic politics was a rotten game divorced from Italy's real needs.

i) The Legacy of the First World War

In 1915 Italy joined the war on the Allied side. Although nationalists hailed this decision, not all Italians were enthusiastic and socialists condemned the war. The expected easy victory did not materialise. Instead, Italy found itself involved in a deadly war of attrition against Austria. In 1918 Italians looked forward to enjoying the fruits of victory. These hopes were soon to be disappointed. The Versailles settlement did not give Italy all the territory it had been promised in 1915. Outraged nationalists deplored the 'mutilated victory'. Liberal politicians were blamed for failing to defend Italian interests.

ii) The Socialist Threat

As the economic situation worsened, industrial and agricultural workers flocked to join the Socialist Party. The 1919 Socialist Congress supported revolution, declaring that, 'The proletariat must have recourse to the use of violence for the conquest of power over the bourgeoisie'. Social unrest, and Socialist activity, was apparent everywhere in 1919–20. Industry was paralysed by strikes while in the countryside peasants seized land from large landowners. Italy's middle and upper classes feared a Bolshevik-type revolution, and the Liberals seemed to be doing nothing to meet the threat.

iii) Political Problems

In 1919 the Liberal regime introduced both universal manhood suffrage and proportional representation. The outcome of the November 1919 election, the first held under the new system, increased Italy's problems.

▼ The Socialists secured a third of the vote, winning 156 seats.
▼ The newly-formed Catholic Party, the Popolari, won over 100 seats.
▼ The Liberals could muster only about 180 seats.

Neither the Socialists nor the Popolari could provide the nucleus of a stable coalition. The Socialists were fragmented by disputes over whether to work within the system or not. (In 1921 the extremists broke away to form a Communist Party.) Thus factional groups of Liberals created precarious coalitions, usually relying on support from Popolari deputies. Between 1919 and 1922 there were five governments.

ECONOMIC PROBLEMS CAUSED BY THE WAR

▼ The national debt increased fivefold between 1914 and 1919.
▼ Inflation spiralled.
▼ After 1918, as government spending was cut back, unemployment rose.

D'ANNUNZIO AND FIUME

In 1919 a one-eyed poet and ardent nationalist, D'Annunzio, led 2,000 volunteers into the disputed city of Fiume (the population was largely Italian but the town had been given to Yugoslavia by the Versailles peacemakers) and claimed it for Italy. Nationalists hailed his action: he had acted whereas the Liberal government had done nothing. For over a year D'Annunzio ruled Fiume before Italian troops were sent to end the occupation. Italian Fascists adopted some of D'Annunzio's 'style' – not least the blackshirt uniform and the Roman salute.

Figure 41 Italy, 1918–24.

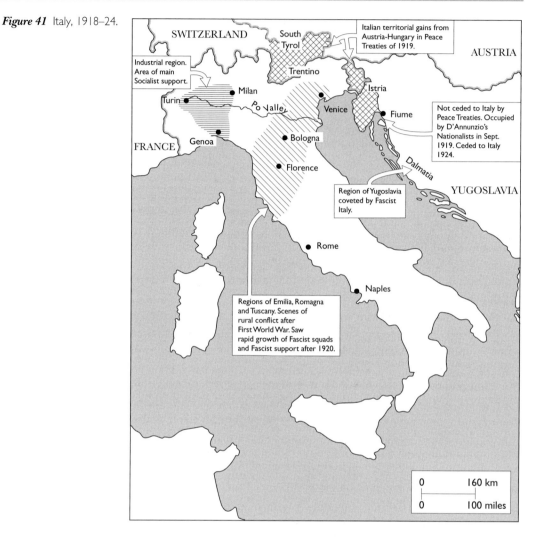

SWITZERLAND

South Tyrol

Italian territorial gains from Austria-Hungary in Peace Treaties of 1919.

AUSTRIA

Industrial region. Area of main Socialist support.

Trentino

Istria

Turin

Milan

Po Valley

Venice

Fiume

Not ceded to Italy by Peace Treaties. Occupied by D'Annunzio's Nationalists in Sept. 1919. Ceded to Italy 1924.

FRANCE

Genoa

Bologna

Dalmatia

Florence

YUGOSLAVIA

Region of Yugoslavia coveted by Fascist Italy.

Rome

Naples

Regions of Emilia, Romagna and Tuscany. Scenes of rural conflict after First World War. Saw rapid growth of Fascist squads and Fascist support after 1920.

| 0 | 160 km |
| 0 | 100 miles |

Figure 42 Mussolini in a typical pose.

Mussolini

Mussolini (1883–1945) was the son of a blacksmith and a school teacher. He had a difficult childhood (at school he was noted more for his bullying than for his academic prowess). In 1912 he became editor of the Socialist newspaper *Avanti* in which he advocated class struggle. In 1914 he supported intervention in the war and broke with the Socialists. Expelled from the party, he started a new paper *Il Popolo d'Italia* (The People of Italy). After joining, and then being invalided out of, the army, he returned to journalism. Claiming that Italy needed strong leadership, his paper sought to create a new political movement which would promote both nationalism and social reform.

Month of appointment	Name
October 1917	Vittorio Orlando
June 1919	Francesco Nitti
June 1920	Giovanni Giolitti
July 1921	Ivanoe Bonomi
February 1922	Luigi Facta
October 1922	Benito Mussolini

Table 15 Italian Prime Ministers, 1917–43.

b) Mussolini and the Rise of Fascism

i) The Formation of the Fascist Movement

In 1919 Mussolini founded the Fascio di Combattimento (or Combat Group) in Milan. The first Fascists represented a wide range of views and had little in common except a hatred of the Liberal state and a contempt for the socialist class struggle. They drew up a programme which contained both nationalist demands for an expansionist Italy and leftist demands, including worker control in the factories, the abolition of the monarchy, and the takeover of church property. In the 1919 election, the Fascists fared disastrously and won no seats. Mussolini won only two per cent of the vote in Milan.

ii) Italian Problems in 1920

In 1920 the veteran politician Giolitti became premier. He soon faced problems. In September workers occupied factories across northern Italy. Employers demanded government action. Fearing that the use of force would result in a bloodbath, Giolitti stood aloof, hoping that the occupation would collapse of its own accord. It did – but employers and conservatives did not forgive Giolitti for what they saw as cowardice and complacency. In rural areas, land occupations increased. Socialist power was shown in the 1920 local elections when the party won control of 26 of Italy's 69 provinces.

iii) A Change of Fascist Programme

After his failure in 1919, Mussolini discarded almost the whole of his programme, embracing instead big business, the Church, the landowners and the monarchy, while holding out carrots to the working classes with talk of employers and workers' unions cooperating to govern the country. Posing as bitter opponents of socialism, Fascists began to win support in north and central Italy. Many Fascist recruits were farmers who feared collectivisation of their land. Others were ex-soldiers who disliked the fact that Italy seemed to be falling into the hands of the Socialist revolutionaries who had done their best to sabotage the war effort.

iv) Fascist Squads

In late 1920, feeling abandoned by a do-nothing government, the right began to fight back. In Emilia and Tuscany, landowners and middle-class townspeople turned to local Fascist squads who needed little encouragement to burn down Socialist offices, beat up trade union leaders and intervene as strike breakers. As they proved their ability to intimidate the Socialists, the squads attracted new followers. Fascist violence in 1920–1 left hundreds dead and wounded. (Fascist opponents were sometimes humiliated by being forced to eat live toads or imbibe a dose of castor oil.) The government (and local police), loathing socialism, did little to prevent the violence.

Mussolini was not the guiding hand behind the squads. Many local Fascist bosses (or *Ras*) were virtually free of his control. But he quickly realised the political opportunities the squads offered in terms of winning support from landowners and big business. He added to his status by seeming able to control the violence while at the same time not being too closely associated with the squads. Most *Ras* accepted Mussolini's claim to be the undisputed leader of the Fascist movement. Without his leadership, Fascism would lack all coherence. With him as leader, it could be presented as a national movement with a vision of a new Italy.

v) The Situation in 1921–2

Mussolini justified violence as a painful necessity if Italy was to be saved from communism. However, he was careful to assure Liberals that he was not a revolutionary. In the spring of 1921 Giolitti, keen to absorb Fascism into the Liberal system, agreed an electoral alliance with Mussolini, and called for new elections. This alliance gave Fascists the stamp of respectability. Mussolini and 34 of his colleagues were elected after a violent campaign. The Socialists, with 123 seats, remained the largest party. But Mussolini, with 7 per cent of the vote and a foothold in parliament, was satisfied. Having no wish to be a junior partner in a Liberal coalition, he announced that the Fascists would not, after all, support Giolitti's government. Only the Fascists (he claimed) could provide strong government, stop the Socialist threat, and deal with Italy's economic problems. By 1922 the Fascist Party had over 300,000 members. Church leaders realised that Mussolini might well be a more effective defender of the Church against Socialist attack than the Popolari. King Victor Emmanuel began to be won over as Mussolini discarded his republicanism.

The Liberals, Popolari and Socialists, failing to appreciate the

Fascist threat, made no attempt to unite. Governments remained unstable. Giolitti was soon replaced by Bonomi who, in turn, was replaced by Facta. The fragile governments were unable to deal with the collapse of law and order. Over the winter of 1921–2, Fascist squads fought their way to power in many areas. Mussolini increased his efforts to appeal to the middle classes who, he stressed, had nothing to fear and much to gain from Fascism. His speeches concentrated on what Fascism was against – namely Socialism and Liberalism – rather than what it was for. His basic promise was strong government. That he managed to win conservative support and also avoid splits with the – revolutionary – *Ras*, was proof of his political skill.

c) The March on Rome

In October 1922, under great pressure from the *Ras* who wanted to gain power by force, Mussolini decided on a 'March on Rome'. On the night of 27–28 October, Fascist squads seized control in many towns and 30,000 blackshirts prepared to converge on Rome. Mussolini's hope was that a show of strength would cause the government to hand over power. The attitude of the King was now critical. As Commander-in-Chief Victor Emmanuel could order the army to crush Fascism. Prime Minister Facta sounded out the army leaders and was assured that the army would do its duty and defend Rome. At 2.00 a.m. on 28 October the King accepted Facta's request to impose martial law and 28,000 police and troops prepared to disperse the Fascist columns. However, by 9.00 a.m. the King fearing civil war – changed his mind and refused to sign the martial law decree. Facta resigned. Mussolini, invited to join a new government, refused to accept any office other than that of Prime Minister. On 30 October he was summoned from Milan and installed as premier.

d) Conclusion

Italy's problems – the left-wing threat, the sense of aggrieved nationalism, economic problems, and the weakness of democracy – had existed pre-1915. The war exacerbated the problems and created new grievances. To many Italians, the Fascists seemed the potential saviours of Italy and the only alternative to Bolshevism. In part Mussolini was lucky: Socialist and Liberal politicians played into his hands. But he also made his own luck. He showed skill and courage, not least in imposing leadership on the amorphous Fascist movement, which could well have collapsed through internal wrangles. Although he did not create the violent situation in the towns and countryside in 1920, he was quick to take advantage of it. He showed

1922 GENERAL STRIKE
In August 1922 Socialist trade unions called a general strike in protest at Fascist violence. The strike played into Mussolini's hands. He declared that if the government did not stop it his Fascists would. The strike proved a fiasco. Even in those cities where the strike call was obeyed, Fascist action limited its effect. When transport workers, for example, came out on strike, Fascists ran the trains. Within two days the strike had collapsed, leaving the Socialists in disarray and the Fascists triumphant.

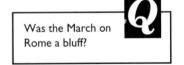
Was the March on Rome a bluff?

MUSSOLINI'S RISE TO POWER

1919 Fascist movement founded;
1920 Fascist squads take off;
1921 Fascist electoral alliance with Giolitti;
1922 spring/summer – Fascist violence at peak; August – failure of Socialist general strike; October – March on Rome; Mussolini became Prime Minister.

an opportunistic readiness to discard ideology and enter into agreements with big business, the Church and the monarchy – despite having once been a Socialist, an atheist and a republican. Careful to avoid committing himself to any clear programme (except the need for action) he forged a movement which could appeal to all classes. He also proved himself a brilliant propagandist, exaggerating the Socialist threat, denouncing Liberal incompetence, and depicting Fascists as selfless nationalists who had the youth and vigour to change Italy. Fascism brought some panache to Italian politics, motivating the masses and symbolising a new and (to many) refreshing dynamism. By October 1922 there was hardly any section of the establishment not ready to collaborate with Mussolini. Most Liberals, the King and Pope Pius XI thought there was no alternative to a Fascist entry into government.

ACTIVITY

Test your grasp of this section by considering the following question:
'The rise of Fascism was due more to the failures of Liberal Italy than to the qualities of Mussolini.' Discuss.
Below are some Liberal failures:
▼ Failure to deal with economic and social problems post-1918
▼ Failure to deal with the Socialist threat
▼ Failure to deal with Mussolini

Now make a list of Mussolini's main qualities. The two lists should enable you to write a conclusion to the question.

ISSUE
What impact did Mussolini have on Italy?

3 Italy: Mussolini in Power

a) The Parliamentary Dictator

Although Mussolini was now Prime Minister, his dream of complete personal power was still some way off. Although many of his black-shirts hoped that the Fascist revolution was about to begin, Mussolini knew that a wholly Fascist government could not command a majority in parliament, and the King would not yet allow him to dispense with parliament. He, therefore, formed a coalition cabinet in which only four of the 14 ministers were Fascists. This reassured many Liberals who hoped Mussolini would be 'transformed' into a respectable leader. Mussolini had a different agenda. Given the seriousness (or so he claimed) of the Bolshevik threat, he asked for extraordinary powers to deal with the situation. After a massive vote of confidence in parliament, the King gave him the right to rule by decree for one year. This meant he was effectively a dictator. Most Liberals believed his assurances that his new powers would be surrendered at the earliest opportunity. By the time this miscalculation was realised, it was too late. The dictatorship was largely in place.

Mussolini quickly moved to consolidate his position. Thousands of opponents were arrested or beaten up. Throughout 1922–3 there were changes of personnel in key jobs. In December 1922 Mussolini increased his power over his own party by establishing the Grand Council of Fascism, the supreme Fascist body, to which he made all appointments. In 1923 he reduced the influence of the *Ras* by converting the squads into a national militia. He also wooed influential groups, winning the approval of the employers' organisation and the tacit support of the Church. In November 1923 a new electoral law was enacted. Whichever party received most votes, would now obtain two-thirds of the seats in the Chamber. The new law was supported by Liberals (like Giolitti) who still believed that Mussolini was not an enemy of democracy. In the April 1924 election, the Fascists, aided by violence and some ballot rigging, obtained 66 per cent of the vote. With such support, it was hard for anyone, the King included, to prevent Mussolini doing as he liked.

In June 1924 the Socialist leader Matteotti, who had denounced Fascist abuses during the election and challenged the validity of the results, was murdered by Fascist thugs. Matteotti's death aroused a storm of indignation. Mussolini denied all knowledge of the crime. But with public revulsion against Fascism so strong, it seemed that the opposition had a chance to topple him. Socialist and Popolari deputies withdrew from Parliament and set up their own assembly, hoping to bring down Mussolini's regime. Their hopes and tactics failed. The King, the Pope and many Liberal politicians still supported Mussolini. There appeared to be no viable alternative.

b) Dictatorship

Mussolini moved to forestall any further opposition. In July 1924 he tightened press censorship and in August banned meetings by opposition parties. Most Liberal leaders now joined the opposition in protest. It was too late. In December 1924, leading Fascists, frustrated by Mussolini's lack of radicalism, presented him with an ultimatum. If he did not move decisively towards establishing a dictatorship, they would withdraw their support. He bowed to their demands. Opposition parties and newspapers were suppressed. A decree made Mussolini no longer accountable to parliament.

A new electoral law was introduced in 1928. The Fascist Grand

Council now chose 400 parliamentary candidates and presented them to the electorate for approval. (The Council merely approved what Mussolini had already decided.) The electorate could support or reject the entire 400. Only members of a Fascist syndicate and those who paid high taxes could vote, reducing the electorate from ten million to three million. In 1929, 136,000 voted against the listed candidates. The remaining 2,864,000 voters were obedient. Parliament was a sham: the deputies did not even bother to vote formally on legislation; they simply shouted assent. In 1939 parliament abolished itself altogether and was replaced by the equally meaningless Chamber of Corporations. Local democracy was also abolished. Elected mayors were replaced by officials appointed from Rome.

Il Duce (The Leader), as Mussolini now called himself, was in full control. Easily able to deter the King (who still had the theoretical right to dismiss him) from any political involvement, he also ensured that members of the cabinet were his loyal servants. His ministers' role was simply to obey his orders. In fact, Mussolini himself held the most important ministries for most of the time he was dictator. Since everything was centralised on him, and he himself was not the superman he pretended to be, there was inevitable delay and muddle. When decisions were taken, they were often made without proper thought or consultation. There was also a high degree of incompetence and corruption, caused partly by the fact that Mussolini liked to surround himself with yes-men.

There was no massive purge of personnel in the civil service or in the armed services. Realising that most civil servants and army officers were sympathetic towards him, he was ready to work with them provided they were loyal to him. They, in turn, soon realised that a pro-Fascist attitude enormously enhanced their promotion prospects. Only with the judiciary did Mussolini conduct a purge. The legal system soon lost all claim to impartiality.

c) The Church

In his youth Mussolini had been violently anti-clerical. While never really losing those attitudes, he realised that an accommodation with the Church would help him politically. Before 1922 he posed as an alternative to anti-clerical Liberals and 'godless' Socialists. After 1922 he tried for even closer relations with the Vatican. Restoring Catholic education in schools and increasing state payments to priests helped win the Pope's confidence. In 1929 the Lateran Agreement ended the conflict between Church and state that had existed since 1870. The Lateran Treaty restored the Pope's temporal power over the Vatican City in return for papal recognition of the Kingdom of Italy. Added to the treaty was a Concordat which defined the role of the

Church in the Fascist state. Catholicism was to be the state religion, clergy could not belong to political parties, Church marriages were recognised as legal by the state, and there would be no divorce without the Church's consent. The Concordat was Fascism's most enduring legacy to Italy.

While Pope Pius supported some of Mussolini's policies he was critical of others – not least the 1938 anti-Semitic laws. Anti-Semitism was not widespread either in Italian society or within the Fascist party. (There were only 56,000 Jews in Italy, one in three of whom were Fascist Party members.) Mussolini, himself, did not share Hitler's hatred of Jews (he had a Jewish mistress) but showed 'solidarity' by introducing laws prohibiting marriage between Aryan and Jewish Italians and banning Jews from some jobs. Pope Pius, who had once referred to Mussolini as the 'man of destiny', now criticised him for imitating the Nazis.

d) Control of the Fascist Party

Mussolini was determined that the Fascist party should serve him and not vice versa. Once he controlled the state, he was far less vulnerable to *Ras* pressure. His mastery of the party was demonstrated at its last congress in 1925 when he demanded that it should obey his orders. Purges of party dissidents followed. By 1928 all party posts were made from party headquarters in Rome. The party thus became totally subservient to its leader.

Fascists who had hoped to transform society and create a state in which the party controlled all organs of government were to be disappointed. Rather than Fascists taking over the state, state officials tended to take over the party as it opened its doors to all those who saw party membership as a way of advancement. The men who occupied senior party posts were soon notable less for their drive and ability than for their obedience and powers of flattery. The party became increasingly a bloated bureaucracy. However, its continued existence gave it some importance. In particular, it represented a potential rival authority to that of the state institutions. Rivalry between the two was particularly common in the provinces where local party secretaries competed for power with provincial prefects.

e) How Popular was Mussolini?

After 1924 the ban on political activity outside the Fascist Party, together with press censorship, denied opponents a platform for their views. Those who opposed Mussolini were likely to be spied upon by new secret police (the OVRA), beaten up and imprisoned. But although the regime set up penal colonies on remote islands, these were on a totally different scale to Nazi concentration camps or Stalin's gulag. Conditions were tough but the brutality was not systematic. Pre-1940 there were only nine executions of political prisoners.

The lack of significant opposition, in part a reflection of the strength of the regime's repressive measures, was also proof of Mussolini's ability to manipulate opinion. Journalists and intellectuals, who might have been expected to oppose a system which suppressed individual freedoms, were encouraged to join that system. Journalists had their pay doubled. The newly created Fascist Academy offered good salaries to leading academics. Well aware that dissent would lead to dismissal, most journalists and intellectuals kept silent.

The regime used extreme propaganda to build up support. Newspapers and films were censored. The radio was government-controlled. Posters insisted that the duty of every Italian was to 'Believe, Fight and Obey'. Italians were not wholly taken in by the incessant stream of propaganda. But they were not averse to the Duce's claims that Italy was – at last – successful.

f) How Successful was Mussolini's Economic Policy?

i) Agriculture

Mussolini concentrated on projects which would increase his personal prestige or help make Italy self-sufficient in food production. Calling for a victory in the 'Battle for Grain', he tried to reduce wheat imports. Farmers were guaranteed high prices for grain and offered grants to buy machines and fertilisers necessary for wheat production. The incentives worked. Wheat production doubled in the period 1922–39. However, wheat still remained Italy's third largest import. Fascism's second major initiative was land reclamation. The Pontine Marshes were the showpiece. These malarial swamps were drained and a network of small farms was set up. However, land reclamation schemes were limited in extent and serious problems of agriculture remained. Little was done to realise Mussolini's dream of creating a large class of prosperous peasants devoted to Fascism. Instead, a few wealthy landowners controlled most of the land. Rural poverty, especially in the south, remained widespread.

ii) Industry

Mussolini was fortunate to come to power just as industry was starting to 'boom'. His regime claimed the credit for the fall in unemployment. Finance Minister de Stefani brought in a simpler tax system, attracted foreign capital, tried to withdraw government from business, and – by reducing government expenditure – achieved a budget surplus for the first time since 1914. Despite this success, de

---

THE NEW CAESAR

A great effort was made to project a glorious image of Mussolini. He was portrayed as a new Caesar, a man of genius, action and culture. He claimed the credit for any successes and blamed others for any mistakes. He liked to be depicted as a virile, athletic, courageous man – a model for all Italian males. He was pictured horse riding, driving fast cars, and flying aeroplanes. His supposed dedication to duty led to stories that he worked up to 20 hours a day. In fact he usually went to bed early, but the light was left on in his study to give the impression that he was still working. Many Italians, uninformed about Mussolini's poor eyesight, ulcer and syphilis, were taken in by the cult of personality. Others were sceptical – but did not dare say so.

Stefani was dismissed in 1925. Convinced that a strong country should have a strong currency, Mussolini now revalued the lira. This enhanced his prestige but the economic effects were far from beneficial. Italian goods became more expensive abroad, making it harder to export. While the revaluation should have helped the Italian consumer, Mussolini prevented this by placing high tariffs on many imports.

Italy did not escape the effects of the Depression. By 1933 unemployment had risen to nearly 2 million. However, the government provided loans for industry and created jobs by funding public work schemes. New motorways (*autostrada*) were built and 5,000 km of railway were electrified. (Mussolini's famous boast that he had at least made the trains run on time had some substance.) As the Depression lifted, the emphasis in the economy shifted to military production and increased self-sufficiency. State control was expanded to the point where 80 per cent of shipbuilding and 50 per cent of steel production was directed by the state. Italian industry, however, remained comparatively backward and was heavily dependent on imported raw materials. The huge sums of money required for military adventures in Abyssinia and Spain meant that the government ran huge budget deficits in the late 1930s. Mussolini was forced to devalue the lira and increase taxes.

iii) The Corporate State

Fascism aimed to eliminate the struggles between employer and employee. Its goal was that everyone should work together for the common good. This was to be achieved by creating a new 'corporative system'. Everyone in a particular field of economic activity, workers and employers alike, would belong to a syndicate or corporation. These would meet separately and jointly to reach agreements on wages, hours and conditions of work. The government would then act as umpire, coordinating the corporations' work. A National Council of Corporations, representing workers, bosses, and party members, was created in 1930. Mussolini boasted that these developments were a constructive third way between capitalism and communism. However, it was soon apparent that the 'corporate revolution' was a myth. The corporations never achieved the pivotal role envisaged by Fascists. Essentially the state was in control and it ensured the pre-eminent position of employers. After 1926 workers no longer had the right to strike or to join free trade unions. Even great industrialists, who generally benefited from Fascist policies, soon lost faith in the corrupt and over-bureaucratic corporate system.

MUSSOLINI IN POWER

1922 creation of Grand Council of Fascism;
1923 new electoral law;
1924 April: Fascists won general election; June: Murder of Matteotti;
1929 Lateran Agreement with the Papacy;
1938 Anti-Jewish laws.

THE DOPOLAVARO
The Dopolavoro organisation was founded to provide leisure activities that would influence workers towards a Fascist view of life. By 1932 it controlled all soccer clubs, 2208 dramatic societies, and 3324 brass bands. Dopolavoro membership rose to nearly 4 million. Its popularity was partly due to the fact that emphasis was on having a good time, not on Fascist indoctrination.

ACTIVITY
Draw up a list of
a) differences, and
b) similarities between Fascism and Nazism.
(You may need to re-read chapter 5).

g) The Main Features of Mussolini's Social Policy

i) The Battle for Births
A 'Battle for Births', launched in 1927, was designed to increase the population from 40 million to 60 million by 1950. Italy would then have more men for its armies and more colonists for its empire. A married man with six children was exempt from all taxes. Propaganda suggested that good Italians had a duty to produce children for the Duce (who thought 12 children per family the ideal!). Bachelors faced heavy taxes and pressure was exerted on women to stay at home. Despite all the measures, the Battle for Births was lost. The birth rate actually fell in the 1930s.

ii) Control of Youth
Mussolini's dream of aggressive Fascists spreading Italian power overseas led to his interest in education and youth training. Teachers (who had to take an oath of loyalty to the regime) were ordered to stress the Duce's genius, and pupils were taught to take pride in Draly. In 1926 a Fascist youth organisation (the Balilla) was set up. Membership eventually became compulsory for all state school children. Members took an oath to follow the orders of the Duce and to serve the cause of the Fascist revolution 'with all my might, and, if necessary, with my blood'. Efforts to control Italian youth, however, were not totally successful. One loophole was that private and Catholic schools did not enforce Balilla membership. Another was that many children left school at the age of 11.

h) How Successful was Mussolini?

Mussolini achieved his main aim of gaining, and staying in, power. Until 1940 he enjoyed substantial support. He seemed to provide strong leadership and his foreign adventures gave Italians a pride in their country. He had some economic success: GNP grew by an average of over 1 per cent a year between 1922 and 1940 – not a bad record in view of the Depression. Many Italians overlooked the attack on political freedoms and individual liberties. However, Mussolini's success was limited. He was, in Denis Mack Smith's view, a 'stupendous poseur', more concerned with projecting himself as a superman than with administrative routine. This was apt because Fascism, in general, lacked the efficiency to dominate Italian society. Many Italians continued to view it with some scepticism. There was outward conformity but little inner conviction. Fascism's impact on the economy was also limited. Italy, far from self-sufficient in 1940, lacked the economic strength to compete with Germany or Britain. The Second World War, which brought him down, was final proof of Mussolini's failure.

4 Spain: The Origins of Civil War

a) Spain's Main Problems in the Early Twentieth Century

i) The Economy

Spain, overwhelmingly agrarian, was poor and backward in relation to most west European states. In southern Spain, a few landowners owned vast estates worked by landless labourers. In northern Spain, peasant farmers struggled against debt and insecure leases. Industry was largely restricted to the textile mills of Catalonia, the iron, steel and shipbuilding industries of the Basque area, and coal mining in the Asturias.

ii) The Political System

Spain was a constitutional monarchy. While real power resided in parliament (the Cortes), there was little real democracy. Elections were controlled by local notables by means of bribery, intimidation and ballot rigging. Governments were invariably coalitions of the two main parties, the Liberals and Conservatives. The corrupt system guaranteed that between 1876 and 1923 no government ever lost an election. (Occasionally over-zealous officials announced election results before the election had taken place!) In Catalonia and the Basque country there were growing demands for independence. Both regions had their own distinct language and culture.

iii) The Left

The Socialist party, with its trade union, the UGT, was generally moderate. It faced serious competition for working-class support from the Anarchists and their union, the CNT. Anarchists, well-supported in Catalonia and in Andalusia, aimed to destroy the state and to establish a new society based on self-governing communities. With Spain sharply polarised between 'haves' and 'have nots', unrest often erupted in rioting. This was brutally suppressed by the Civil Guard, an armed police force.

iv) The Right

▼ The Spanish Church usually opposed reform. Through its near monopoly of education, it instilled into those who did not rebel against it a conservative system of values. It was hated by radicals, and the burning of churches became a feature of left-wing disturbances.
▼ The army was a major prop of conservative Spain. It was far too large for Spain's diminished world role and was top-heavy with upper- and middle-class officers.

▼ Peasants in northern Spain, strongly Catholic, usually allied with the right.

Spain: The main events, 1898–1930

▼ In 1898, following a war with the USA, Spain lost most of its remaining colonies, including Cuba and the Philippines.

▼ Between 1898 and 1923 Spain stumbled from crisis to crisis. King Alfonso XIII (1885–1931) had no real desire for change.

▼ In 1917 there was a spate of serious strikes. Catalan separatists, Socialists and Anarchists demanded a new constitution. The crisis fizzled out but between 1918 and 1921 Barcelona was the scene of constant terrorism in which over 1,000 people died.

▼ In 1921 a Spanish army was defeated in Spanish Morocco. A parliamentary committee was set up to investigate responsibility for the disaster. To forestall its report, which was likely to blame the King, the military governor of Barcelona, General Primo de Rivera, in a bloodless coup, set himself up as dictator in 1923.

▼ Primo introduced martial law, dissolved the Cortes, censored the press, drove the CNT underground, and suppressed Catalan nationalism. He also initiated some public works including road building and irrigation schemes. In 1930, having lost the support of the army and the King, he resigned and fled into exile.

▼ In 1930–1 King Alfonso entrusted the premiership first to a general and then to an admiral. But the King and his governments faced bitter criticism from Socialists, Anarchists and Republicans. Accepting the need for change, the government called for local elections as the first stage in a return to democracy. In April 1931 there was a huge republican vote in the towns. When it was clear that the army would not support him, Alfonso abdicated without waiting for the results to come in from the rural areas (these showed an overall monarchical majority!) and fled from Spain.

---

b) The Left Republic, 1931–3

The local elections of April 1931 established the Second Republic. In June, elections were held for a Cortes which was to draw up a new constitution. The Socialists and an assortment of Republican parties won a resounding victory over the right. Until the autumn all forces favourable to the new regime were represented in the coalition government. Then power reverted to a left-Republican and Socialist coalition, led by Azana, leader of the left-Republicans.

A new constitution was finally agreed in December 1931. A single chamber Cortes was to be elected every four years. The head of state, the president, was to be chosen every six years by an electoral college. The most controversial clauses concerned the separation of Church and state. Payment of priests and religious education in schools were to end, religious orders could be dissolved if judged a danger to the state, and divorce was made easier. These reforms mobilised the Church against the Republic, motivating the right to reorganise more quickly than might otherwise have been the case. The granting of a large degree of autonomy to Catalonia in 1932 further alienated the right.

Another contentious area was land reform. With agricultural prices falling and unemployment rising, both the CNT and the UGT had gained huge support among agricultural workers in the south and their expectations were high. Despite serious divisions within the government (the Republicans wished to create an independent peasantry; the Socialists favoured setting up collective farms), land reform began in 1931 when eviction was banned, except for non-payment of rent. A 1932 law enabled the state to take over estates and to redistribute the land to peasants. Though land reform was largely ineffective, it alarmed not only great landowners but also small peasants and the middle classes generally. It was seen as a start to an all-out attack on property rights and made it seem as though Spain was copying the USSR.

Right-wing opposition to the Republic was soon evident.

▽ In Navarre the Carlists won support. They aimed to restore the monarchy and place Don Carlos on the throne.

▽ Army officers were hostile to the new Republic which 'encouraged' officers to retire and closed a number of military academies. In 1932, General Sanjurjo led a revolt. It failed but it indicated that disaffected elements in the army could be a potential problem.

▽ By 1933 the CEDA, an alliance of groups whose main purpose was to protect Catholic interests, was the strongest right-wing party. Funded by great landowners, it was supported by many Catholic peasants. While nominally supporting the Republic, its policies seemed anti-democratic and pro-fascist.

▽ While the right-wing thought the government was set on revolution, many on the left were dissatisfied with the slow pace of change and there were a spate of Anarchist-inspired strikes and riots. In January 1933 Azana used troops to put down an Anarchist uprising near Barcelona and subsequent widespread strikes. The government's unity was badly shaken by the Civil Guard's murder of an Anarchist group in the village of Casa Viejas. Further repressive measures by Azana led to the Socialists leaving the coalition.

c) The Right Republic, 1933–6

The right, benefiting from left-wing disunity, won a large majority of seats in the November 1933 election. The election ushered in what the left described as the 'two black years' when the reforms of the previous two years were reversed, and socialism and anarchism were suppressed. However, the right-wing bias of the government can be

THE COMMUNIST AND FALANGE PARTIES

The Communists:
Participation in the Asturias rising increased Communist prestige. The change of Comintern policy in 1934 meant that the party began to cooperate with other left-wing parties.

The Falange (Phalanx): This was founded by Jose Antonio Primo de Rivera, son of the former dictator, in 1933. By early 1936 the Falange had some 8,000 (mostly student) members and a distinctive blue-shirted uniform. The Falange advocated strong authoritarian leadership but was also committed to radical social change.

exaggerated. The CEDA, though the single largest party, did not have an overall majority and did not take office. Instead, a Radical government ruled – with CEDA support.

In December 1933 Anarchist-instigated risings in Barcelona and Saragossa were crushed. Undaunted, the Anarchists led a great strike in March 1934. The pretext for more revolutionary action came in October 1934 when three CEDA members joined the government. Socialist leader Caballero joined with the Anarchists and called for a general strike – precursor of revolution. Risings in Madrid and Barcelona were easily crushed. Efforts to declare Catalonia independent resulted in its autonomy being suspended. The army had to be sent into the Asturias coalfield to put down a serious left-wing rising. Thousands were killed, imprisoned or exiled. Events in the Asturias heightened left–right tensions. This was reflected in the growing importance of the Communist and Falange parties.

d) The Popular Front, February to July 1936

A series of financial scandals brought down the Radicals and new elections were held in February 1936. A small swing in the popular vote led to a great shift in power with the left-wing Popular Front, comprising Republicans, Socialists and Communists, winning a majority of seats. Azana took over the government which the Socialists refused to join. Fearing losing support to the Communists or the Anarchists, Caballero spoke as though he intended to launch a revolution, thus terrifying the right. Meanwhile Azana began by reintroducing anti-clerical laws and planning the restoration of Catalan autonomy.

The new government faced growing disorder. Some of the disorder was promoted by the right, especially by the Falange which engaged in street battles with left-wing groups. But left-wing activism also increased. The government's promise of land reform was pre-empted by many peasants who began to seize land. On 1 May the CNT called a general strike and in June there were strikes by various groups, including bullfighters and waiters. Scores of churches were destroyed. The right, convinced that Spain was in the midst of revolutionary change, began planning a counter-revolution.

The army was the right's best hope. Many officers hated the new government and were prepared to support an army coup. Plans were drawn up for army garrisons to establish military rule across Spain. There were persistent rumours of a conspiracy during 1936 but the government reacted with surprising nonchalance. Its main precaution was to transfer some of the disaffected generals to less central commands. Franco was sent to the Canary Islands, Goded to the Balearics, and Mola to Navarre. However, this did not greatly impede the conspiracy. The army conspirators could count on support from Alfonsist monarchists, the CEDA, the Carlists, and the Falange whose support surged after February 1936. There was little consensus as to what type of regime would replace the Popular Front. The exact timing of the rebellion was determined by the murder (on 13 July) of a popular CEDA leader. The murder persuaded many who were still vacillating (including Franco) that the time for action had come.

e) Why did the Second Republic Fail?

After 1931 there was a lack of consensus in Spain about almost everything and a reluctance to abide by the rules of democratic government. Spain had little experience of democracy, and there were groups on both extremes who were ready to resort to violence. Though the Civil War stemmed from the Spanish situation, there was a European dimension. The Spanish left was inspired by the example of the USSR and feared fascism: the right drew on Hitler and Mussolini and feared communism. Given the bitter divisions, Civil War may not have been inevitable but it was always a possibility.

SPAIN: 1931–6	
1931	start of the Second Republic: Left-Republicans in power;
1933	Right-Republicans in power;
1934	Asturias rising;
1936	February – Popular Front government elected; July – Army rising.

ACTIVITY

Consider the question: 'Why, after 1919, were both monarchy and democracy successively overthrown in Spain?' You might make the following points for the fall of the monarchy:

▼ Political, economic and social problems
▼ The failure of Primo de Rivera
▼ The events of 1930–1.

List the points you might make for the fall of democracy in 1936.

---

5 The Spanish Civil War

a) The Military Coup

The army coup had been set for 18 July. However, due to the discovery of the plot in Morocco, the army there rose on 17 July. The rebellion then spread, haphazardly, to mainland Spain. The rebels triumphed in northern Spain and in parts of Andalusia. But the rising failed in the main industrial centres and most importantly in Madrid. Several factors determined the rising's success or failure:

ISSUE
Why did the Nationalists win?

THE SPANISH CIVIL WAR, SEPTEMBER 1936– MARCH 1939

1936 September–October: advance of Army of Africa northwards; November: failure to capture Madrid;

1937 March: Battle of Guadalajara; April: northern campaign; June–July: failure of Republican offensives; October: northern Spain occupied by Nationalists;

1938 January: Republicans seize Teruel; February: recapture of Teruel and advance of Nationalists of Mediterranean; April; Mediterranean reached; Republican zone split in two; November: defeat of Republican Ebro offensive;

1939 January: capture of Catalonia; March; Madrid occupied; end of war.

▼ The army proved to be evenly divided, half supporting the rising and half remaining loyal to the Republic.

▼ Some of the Civil Guard and most of the Assault Guard (set up as a left-wing counterweight to the Civil Guard) opposed the rebellion.

▼ The attitude of the local population was important, especially where armed militias or paramilitary groups existed. For example, working-class militias contributed to the defeat of the rising in Madrid while Carlist support helped ensure its success in the north.

▼ Decisive action by individuals was also a factor. For example, General de Llano with few troops bluffed his way to control Seville.

b) Nationalists v Republicans

By late July Spain was divided between the Republican government and its opponents who described themselves as Nationalists. The population's loyalty often depended on the location Spaniards found themselves in when the war began. But in general the upper and middle classes supported the Nationalists while most of the working class supported the Republic. The peasants were divided. While the landless labourers of the south were pro-Republican, large numbers of peasants in north and central Spain were pro-Nationalist. The

Figure 43 General Franco, with General Mola on his left.

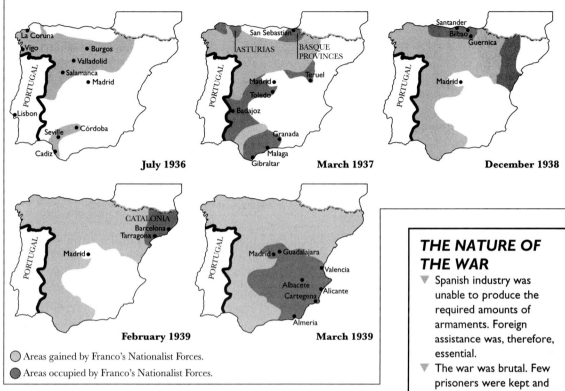

Areas gained by Franco's Nationalist Forces.
Areas occupied by Franco's Nationalist Forces.

Figure 44 The division of Spain in 1936, 1937, 1938 and 1939.

Catalans and Basques supported the Republic which had granted them autonomy. Ironically, in many parts of Spain the rising precipitated the very revolution it was trying to prevent. Across Spain, the left indiscriminately killed priests, landowners, and industrialists.

The airlifting to Spain of the 24,000 experienced troops of the Army of Africa, commanded by Franco, was a crucial development. In August Franco headed towards Madrid, capturing numerous towns and pursuing a deliberate policy of terror, designed to intimidate potential opponents. General Mola was also successful in the north. By September the Nationalists had a much stronger base. Nevertheless, the Republic still had some significant advantages:

▼ It controlled most of the major cities and the main industrial areas.
▼ It held the Spanish gold reserves.
▼ Most of the air force and navy remained loyal to the Republic.

THE NATURE OF THE WAR

▼ Spanish industry was unable to produce the required amounts of armaments. Foreign assistance was, therefore, essential.

▼ The war was brutal. Few prisoners were kept and little mercy was shown by either side to local populations caught up in the war. Of the 25 million Spanish population, some 175,000 Republicans and 110,000 Nationalists were killed in action. In addition, some 350,000 civilians were killed or died from malnutrition and disease. The atrocities included the bombing of civilians. The most infamous was the bombing of the Basque town of Guernica in April 1937 in which some 1,500 people probably died. The debate continues over who was to blame – the Nationalists, Germans or even Basque militias.

c) Republican Weaknesses

i) Political Disunity

Throughout the Civil War, the Republican government was beset by internal problems and crises. One problem was that its control was far from total. During the rising, workers' committees sprang up all over the Republican zone. Power shifted to the left and also to the regions, as Catalonia, the Basque region and the Asturias became virtually independent. Another problem was that Republican supporters subscribed to a wide variety of incompatible ideologies. In September 1936 Caballero became head of a coalition government. His rule, however, was undermined by conflict between the rival groups who proved unable to form a common front against the enemy.

The war encouraged the growth of communism. In July 1936 the Spanish Communist Party had only about 40,000 members. By October 1937 it had some 400,000 members. Tightly-knit and well-disciplined, it was able to exploit the divisions of the other parties and benefited from the fact that the USSR was the only major power to assist the Republic. From the start the Communists were in direct conflict with the Anarchists and **POUM.** The Communists, acting on Stalin's orders, believed that the revolution must be postponed until the war was won. The Anarchists and POUM, however, claimed that revolution, which would enthuse the population, was an essential prerequisite of Republican victory. In May 1937 there were four days of street fighting in Barcelona between the Anarchists and POUM on one side and Communists and Socialists on the other.

POUM
This was a small but very influential Catalan Marxist party which was critical of the Soviet system.

Negrin, the Communists' choice, replaced Caballero as Republican leader. Negrin's government was more united but it was also more dictatorial. POUM and Anarchist leaders were imprisoned or executed. Negrin's government survived until March 1939 when there was a military coup in Madrid. This second civil war within the Civil War reflected all the political conflicts which had plagued the Republic since 1936.

ii) Military Problems

In the first few crucial weeks of the war, the Republican government had neither an organised army nor central control of military operations. Improvised, and often ineffective, militia units mushroomed: the Republic waged a series of local wars rather than one concerted campaign. Not until autumn 1936 did the government begin to replace the militias with a more efficient Popular Army (which was far from popular with non-Communists).

iii) Economic Problems

In Anarchist-controlled areas, industries, transport and public utili-
ties were taken over and run by workers' committees while collective
farms were set up in the countryside. However, neither the industrial
collectives nor the collective farms were able to supply the needs of
the war economy and the Madrid and Catalan governments soon
introduced direct state control. Historians sympathetic to the collectives have argued that many of their problems cannot be disentan-
gled from the economic difficulties caused by the war. The general
consensus, however, is that the collectives hindered the Republic's
war effort. It was not practical to base a wartime economy on a series
of self-governing communities.

d) Nationalist Strengths

i) Political Unity

In July 1936 the Nationalists were almost as divided as the Republicans. They had few common aims except the overthrow of the
left-wing government. At this stage Generals Sanjurjo, Mola and
Goded seemed more important than Franco. Within weeks, however,
Franco emerged as the Nationalists' leader. He was fortunate that
most of his potential rivals either died or were discredited early
in the war. However, luck was not the only explanation for his
rapid rise to power. His control of the Army of Africa and the fact
that vital German aid was channelled through him helped his
cause. By September 1936 it was clear to most generals that they
needed a unified command. Most agreed to back Franco. He
was thus designated head of state with both military and political
powers.

In order to secure his position Franco needed to neutralise both
the Carlists and the Falange. By 1937 both were mass movements.
The Carlists possessed a militia of 70,000 while the Falange had
grown spectacularly with one million members. Franco had little
ideological common ground with the Falange. Fortunately for
Franco, the Falange lacked an effective leader. Jose Antonio de
Rivera, in prison in July 1936, was executed by the Republic in
November 1936. In April 1937 Franco announced the merger of the
Falange and the Carlists. The new party, the FET (Falange Espanola
Tradicionalista), was under his control. Some Falangists opposed
Franco's action but there was little they could do without disrupting
the war effort. While Franco was careful not to disillusion the
Carlists, the longer the war went on, the more unlikely a monarchi-
cal restoration became. The support of the Church helped Franco's
cause. Church leaders portrayed the war as a crusade to preserve
Christian civilisation against atheistic communism.

FRANCO

Franco was born into a middle-class family in 1892. He graduated from the Toledo Military Academy in 1910. After success in Morocco, he became Spain's youngest general. He was made Chief-of-Staff in 1934 after suppressing the Asturias rising. He was devoutly religious and his political ideas were simple. He felt that government was best run on military lines and he disliked democracy. After becoming the Nationalist leader, he remained in power in Spain until his death in 1975.

Was Franco a fascist or an old-style military dictator?

Fascist?
▼ Franco's regime was a one-party dictatorship.
▼ The cult of the *Caudillo* (as Franco was called) paralleled those of the Duce and the Führer. Posters and photographs of him appeared everywhere.
▼ Franco often praised Hitler and Mussolini.
▼ He tried to construct a corporate state. (As in Italy, it existed on paper not in reality.)
▼ Franco's regime controlled education and set up a youth movement.
▼ His regime was oppressive. Thousands of his opponents were executed or imprisoned.
▼ There was intellectual repression. Suspect books were banned and the press censored.

Non-fascist?
▼ Franco came to power through an army coup, not through the support of a fascist party.
▼ The army was always far more dominant in Franco's Spain than was the Falange.
▼ Franco lacked charisma and was not a great orator.
▼ The Church had a prominent role in Franco's Spain.
▼ Franco's regime drew much of its inspiration from the past, rather than looking to establish a new social system. Little was done to change economic or social life.
▼ Franco had no strong racial views.
▼ He did not pursue an aggressive foreign policy. When the Second World War began, he declared – and maintained – neutrality.
▼ He identified himself with European fascism simply because he needed fascist support.

ii) Military Unity

The Nationalists at first faced a situation similar to the Republicans with numerous 'columns' of Carlist and Falangist militias operating alongside regular army units. However, the militias were quickly absorbed into the regular army. As well as having plenty of junior officers, the Nationalists had, in the Army of Africa, Spain's best troops. This army shielded the rest of the Nationalist forces while they were trained and equipped.

iii) Economic Advantages

Favoured by the business community, the Nationalists were able to obtain the credit needed to purchase war supplies. By September 1936 the Nationalists controlled the main food-producing regions. Success in the north in 1937 meant that thereafter they also controlled Spain's main industrial area.

iv) The Leadership of Franco

Franco proved an able leader. While his cautious tactics were often the despair of his German and Italian advisers, his main aims were to ensure that each area was thoroughly subdued and to conserve men and resources. This strategy worked. His troops repaid his concern for their welfare by giving him unquestioning obedience.

e) Foreign Assistance

Was the Spanish Civil War a struggle between communism and fascism?

The Civil War evoked massive interest across Europe. The main powers responded to it partly in ideological terms but also in relation to how they could exploit it.

i) Non-intervention

Both Britain and France favoured neutrality and set up a Non-Intervention Committee which eventually had 27 members. Arguably the whole basis of the Committee was flawed since the practical effect of non-intervention was to deny the Republic, the legitimate Spanish government, the right to obtain arms, thereby placing it on the same footing as its rebel opponents. Even judged on its own terms, the Committee had little success. Germany, Italy, and the USSR all blatantly contravened its decisions.

ii) Support for the Nationalists

Portugal (which sent some 20,000 troops), Germany and Italy all gave help to the Nationalists. Without Hitler's help in August 1936 Franco would not have been able to transport the Army of Africa to Spain. Italy sent some 60,000 men, over 700 aircraft and 950 tanks.

Germany sent the Condor Legion, a combined air, tank and artillery unit comprising 10,000 men. This aid gave the Nationalists an important advantage.

iii) Support for the Republic

The USSR was the main supporter of the Republic. While Soviet aid was a major asset to the Republic, the number of Russians sent to Spain did not exceed 2,000. Some 35,000 men – mainly Communists – from various countries, eager to strike a blow against fascism, also volunteered to fight for the Republicans. They formed the International Brigades.

ACTIVITY

Consider the following question: 'To what extent was Nationalist success the result of foreign aid?' First decide what factors led to Nationalist success and then decide which factor(s) you think are most important. My conclusion might read something like this:

> While foreign aid was clearly in Franco's favour, it does not in itself explain his victory. In the last resort the war's outcome depended on the performance of the respective, largely Spanish, armies. The Republic suffered from its inability to organise as effective an army as the Nationalists or to establish central control over the various fronts.

What would your conclusion be?

ISSUES
Why did democracy survive in France?
Why was political life so unstable?

6 France: The Third Republic

The Third Republic in the inter-war period has been heavily criticised. It has been argued that a host of short-lived governments failed to tackle France's serious economic problems, discredited the country's parliamentary institutions, and were in part responsible for the deep divisions between right and left. Accordingly, the argument goes, by 1939 France was psychologically and materially unprepared for another major struggle with Germany. Is it possible to be more positive about the Third Republic in the inter-war years?

a) The Economic Effects of the First World War

France paid a high price for her victory. Given the lack of a proper system of direct taxation, she had met the cost of the war by massive borrowing. That cost would now have to be met. The recovery of Alsace-Lorraine and the right to administer the Saar coalfields went some way to help solve the financial problems. However, French governments relied on German reparations financing the costs of repairing the devastated northern provinces. If Germany did not pay, France would have to reform its tax system and increase taxation.

b) French Politics in the 1920s

In 1919 Clemenceau secured an electoral victory for the Bloc National, a coalition of centre and right-wing parties. Fear of revolutionary socialism contributed to right-wing success. There seemed a real risk of revolution in 1919–20. Clemenceau's decision to send men to fight the Reds in Russia led to serious agitation. Fortunately for Clemenceau the army remained loyal and the discontent was crushed. It was soon clear that French Socialists were divided. Some wanted to emulate Russia: others were horrified at this prospect. In 1920 the extremists set up a Communist Party. Bad blood between Socialists and Communists made it hard for the left to unite.

The strong Catholic bias of the Bloc National reawakened the pre-war struggle between the clerical right and the anti-clerical left. More significant than the religious issue, however, was the economic crisis, exacerbated by Poincaré's decision in 1923 to send troops into the Ruhr to force Germany to pay reparations. Poincaré resigned in 1924 when the Senate rejected his plans for tax increases. The 1924 election saw a swing to a Radical–Socialist coalition, the Cartel des Gauches. Herriot, a Radical, became premier. With large government debts, the franc falling in value, and inflation rampant, urgent action was required. Under pressure from the Socialists, Herriot finally proposed a 10 per cent tax on capital. When the Senate

> **FRENCH POLITICAL PROBLEMS**
> ▽ Party discipline remained loose. Deputies often voted independently.
> ▽ There was a multiplicity of parties, particularly of the right and centre.
> ▽ There were increasing divisions between right and left.

Table 16 The French Chamber of Deputies, 1919–40.

	1919	1924	1928	1932	1936
Right of centre parties	430	256	320	253	215
Radicals	86	139	113	155	109
Republican Socialists	26	43	40	36	55
Socialists	68	104	101	129	147
Left-wing Socialists	–	–	5	11	–
Communists	–	26	14	12	72
Total number of deputies	610	568	593	596	598

(Note that the size of the groups can vary even within the same parliament, and therefore the figures are only approximate.)

rejected this, Herriot fell from power in 1925. Five cabinets came and went in the next 15 months.

In 1926 Poincaré formed a government of 'National Salvation' to tackle the dire economic situation. Tax increases and foreign loans restored confidence. The recovery of the economy between 1926 and 1929 was remarkable. The huge sums spent on reconstructing the devastated areas of northern France began to pay dividends. France had an annual growth rate of 5 per cent, trade boomed and there was little unemployment. The government was able to introduce a national insurance scheme for old-age pensions and sickness benefits. However, it could be argued that Poincaré (who resigned due to ill-health in 1929) could have done more on the social reform front where France still lagged behind Britain and Germany.

c) French Politics in the 1930s

i) The Depression

By 1932 the French economy was stagnating. German reparations had ended and the franc's overvaluation made it hard to export. France soon had a balance of payments problem and growing unemployment. In 1932 the Socialists and Radicals reunited and won the election. Herriot again became premier. His attempts to devalue the franc met fierce opposition and he was forced to resign. Daladier's 1932 government alienated the Socialists by cutting the salaries of civil servants. The left's disunity resulted in rapid changes of government – six different cabinets in 20 months.

ii) The Right-Wing Threat: The Leagues

As the Depression worsened, support for right-wing **leagues** increased. Some of the leagues had traditional French roots: others sought to emulate Mussolini. Most were anti-Semitic. All were anti-communist, all opposed the Third Republic and all wanted strong government. The leagues offered right-wing sympathisers what communism offered to the left – an opportunity for action. However, the leagues' threat to the Republic should not be overstated. No right-wing charismatic leader emerged and the French right remained divided and fragmented. Total league membership was only about 150,000.

iii) The Stavisky Affair

Stavisky was a Jewish financial swindler. Arrested for fraud in 1927, he was released pending trial. He was still at liberty in 1933 having been granted 19 provisional releases thanks to friends in high places. After the failure of a new financial scam, he was arrested in January 1934 and died in suspicious circumstances. The right claimed that

THE LEAGUES

▼ Action Française, set up pre-1914, aimed at restoring royalist authority and national greatness. Its leader, Charles Maurras, was an intellectual rather than a man of action.

▼ Jeunesses Patriotes based itself on the Italian Fascist party.

▼ Solidaire Française was founded by talcum powder tycoon François Coty.

▼ Croix de Feu, the strongest of the leagues, led by Colonel de la Rocque. An ex-servicemen's organisation, its members were more patriotic conservatives than fascists.

Stavisky had been murdered to prevent him disclosing the names of his influential protectors. When Prime Minister Chautemps refused a committee of inquiry into the whole affair, the leagues organised demonstrations in protest at Republican corruption. On 27 January 1934 angry mobs frightened Chautemps into resigning. Daladier became Prime Minister and agreed to set up an investigative committee. However, to please the Socialists, he also dismissed the right-wing prefect of the Paris police. This dismissal sparked off serious trouble on 6 February. (The Communists, on Stalin's orders, joined with the leagues in the rioting.) Fifteen people were killed and hundreds were injured. Daladier resigned. The new premier, Doumergue, managed to prevent further violence by introducing right-wingers into his cabinet and by initiating an inquiry into the Stavisky affair. The inquiry put much of the blame on the real sinners, the police and judiciary.

The left, exaggerating the right-wing threat, saw the events as a fascist conspiracy to overthrow the Republic (conveniently forgetting the Communists' role in the riots!). But there is no evidence that the leagues had united to plot a coup and the events of February 1934 are best seen as a spasm of frustrated rage by the right against the hated Republic.

iv) The Popular Front

The most important consequence of league activity was the unifying effect it had on the left. By 1935 Radicals, Socialists and Communists (now under orders from Moscow to collaborate with Socialists and Liberals against fascism) formed a Popular Front. The Front's programme called for the dissolution of the leagues and economic and social reform. It particularly attacked the 'two hundred families', the Regents of the Bank of France, who embodied the power of organised wealth. In January 1936 the Front won a decisive election victory and the Socialist leader Blum became Prime Minister.

The Front's victory aroused hopes of better conditions among the workers. In May a wave of sit-down strikes paralysed economic life. Blum persuaded the employers to make major concessions. A 40-hour week was introduced and workers were given generous pay rises and holidays with pay. Blum also stated his intention to nationalise the armaments industry and exert closer control over the Bank of France. He went on to devalue the franc by some 25 per cent. Employers, not surprisingly, were reluctant to carry out new investment and unemployment (and inflation) remained high. The Spanish Civil War posed another serious problem. Blum realised that intervention on the Republican side would provoke the right and might spark civil war in France itself. (Blum had banned the leagues but they soon re-emerged with new names.) By not intervening,

Blum alienated the Communists who now withdrew their support from the Front.

In June 1937 Blum resigned when his demands for emergency powers to deal with France's financial problems were rejected by the Senate. Blum's supporters claimed that he was brought down by his capitalist enemies. It is certainly true that big business, and the right generally, had no faith in Blum's policies. But the right was not solely responsible for sabotaging Blum's government. Disunity on the left, a consistent feature of French inter-war politics, was also important. Left-wing historians still tend to see Blum's 1936–7 government as a significant turning point in modern French history, not least for its social reforms and its firm stand against the fascist threat. However, right-wing historians deny there was an internal fascist threat and accuse the Popular Front of weakening French industry with expensive reforms at a time when the country needed to rearm quickly.

France now experienced more rapid changes of government. Only in April 1938 when Daladier (a Radical who had been Prime Minister three times before and been in no less than 25 cabinets) became premier was some semblance of stability restored. Daladier moved sharply to the right, supporting a massive increase in armaments spending and revising some of the 1936 reforms. This created a feeling of security in financial circles and investment began to flow back into France. After years of decline, the economy showed signs of a revival. Many on the left, however, were incensed by Daladier's actions. In November 1938 the Communists called for a general strike. This was a total failure. Few workers came out and tough action was taken against those who did. Daladier, faced with the growing threat from Hitler, could now claim a new authority with the French people. Opinion polls in 1938–9 show a more optimistic mood and a desire to take a tougher line against Germany.

THE THIRD REPUBLIC: 1918–39

1919 victory of Bloc National;
1924 victory of Cartel des Gauches;
1926 Poincaré's government of National Salvation;
1934 Stavisky Affair: serious right-wing riots;
1936 election victory of Popular Front;
1938 Daladier became Prime Minister.

d) Conclusion

It is possible to see France as divided and enfeebled throughout the inter-war period and see its catastrophic defeat in 1940 as linked directly to political weakness. Arguably the real test of any regime is how well it can face up to crisis. In 1940 the Third Republic was tested and found wanting. However, the Third Republic can be viewed more positively. The short life of governments does not necessarily prove that government was chronically weak. While governments came and went the same ministers usually reappeared in different jobs in a sort of game of political musical chairs. The divided forces on the left and right, lacking a majority, had no alternative but to ally with the centre – especially the Radicals whose leaders were a constant in government. Thus, while left and right extremes made a lot of noise, they were really not that important. There was no internal revolution. Thanks largely to the fact that France had a solid democratic core the Third Republic survived (until 1940). Arguably defeat in 1940 was due more to military factors than inherent democratic weakness.

ACTIVITY

Consider the question: 'Why was French political life so unstable in the inter-war period?'

Suggested line of response:
▼ Examine the political, economic and social problems in the 1920s.
▼ Examine the impact of the Depression.
▼ Examine the Stavisky Affair.
▼ Examine the years 1936–9.
▼ Was political life really unstable?

▼ Working on Italy, Spain and France: 1918–39

It is clearly possible to examine each of the three countries studied in this chapter in isolation. It is also possible, and more difficult, to compare and contrast developments between them. Consider, for example, the following question: 'Why did Italy become a dictatorship while France remained a democracy in the inter-war period?'

Countries are often seen as abandoning democracy for the following reasons:
▼ a serious communist threat;
▼ nationalist grievances;
▼ serious economic problems;
▼ democratic weakness;
▼ charismatic right-wing leadership.

To what extent do these general factors explain Mussolini's rise to power? To what extent were the general factors at work in the Third Republic? Was there ever any possibility of democracy collapsing in France?

Answering Source-Based Questions on Italy, Spain and France: 1918–39

Our programme is simple: we wish to govern Italy. They ask us for programmes, but there are already too many. It is not programmes that are needed for the salvation of Italy, but men and will power . . .

Our political class is deficient. The crisis of the Liberal State has proved it . . . We must have a State which will simply say: 'The State does not represent a party, it represents the nation as a whole, it includes all, is over all, protects all.'

Source A a speech by Mussolini in Udine in September 1922.

Fascism . . . does not march against the police, but against the political class both cowardly and imbecile, which in four long years has not been able to give a Government to the nation. Those who form the productive class must know that Fascism wants to impose nothing more than order and discipline upon the nation and to help to raise the strength which will renew progress and prosperity . . .

We call on God and the spirit of our five thousand dead to witness that only one impulse sends us on, that only one passion burns within us – the impulse and the passion to contribute to the safety and greatness of our country.

Fascisti of all Italy! Stretch forth like Romans your spirits and your fibres! We must win! We will. Long live Italy! Long live Fascism!

Source B part of the order given to Fascists about to march on Rome in October 1922.

Source C from a speech made by Mussolini in Berlin in September 1937.

I have come among you in my capacity as head of a national revolution who has wanted to give proof of open and unequivocal solidarity with your revolution. And even if the course of the two revolutions has not been the same, the objective which both wanted to achieve, and have achieved, is the same: the unity and greatness of the people . . .

Just as fifteen years of Fascism have given a new material and spiritual countenance to Italy, so your revolution has given a new face to Germany: new, even if, as in Italy, it is based on the most noble and eternal traditions which can be reconciled with the necessities of modern life . . .

Not only have Nazism and Fascism everywhere the same enemies who serve the same masters, the Third International [i.e. communism], but they share many conceptions of life and history. Both believe in violence as a force determining the life of peoples, as the dynamo of their history . . . Both of us exalt work in its countless manifestations as the sign of the nobility of man; both of us count on youth, from which we demand the virtues of discipline, courage, tenacity, patriotism, and scorn for the comfortable life.

▼ QUESTIONS ON SOURCES

1. What is Mussolini's justification in Sources A and B for the Fascist takeover of power? **[6 marks]**
2. What can you deduce about Fascist principles from all three sources? **[12 marks]**
3. Using the evidence in Source C and your own knowledge, explain the main similarities and differences between Fascism and Nazism.
[12 marks]

Points to note about the questions

Question 1 What problems does Mussolini highlight? What does he promise to do?
Question 2 First work out what Fascism was against. Then, and this is a shade more difficult, work out what Fascism was for.
Question 3 In this type of two-part question it is best to give each a roughly equal treatment.

Further Reading

Books in the Access to History series

Start with *Fascism and Nazism* by Robert Pearce and *Italy, Liberalism and Fascism 1870–1945* by Mark Robson. *The Spanish Civil War* by Patricia Knight is splendid. Try also *France 1914–69: The Three Republics* by Peter Neville.

General

On Fascism and Italy, try Chapter 11 in *Years of Change: Europe 1890–1945* by Robert Wolfson and John Laver (Hodder & Stoughton). Chapter 10 of the same book provides a useful introduction to France.

On fascism the best single book is *A History of Fascism 1914–45* by S.G. Payne, 1995 (UCL Press). *Fascism: A History* by R. Eatwell, 1995 (Chatto & Windus) is also worth reading. On Italy *Mussolini and Fascist Italy* by M. Blinkhorn, 1994 (Routledge) is excellent. *Mussolini* by M. Smith, 1983 (Granada) is highly readable.

Democracy and Civil War in Spain, 1931–1939 by M. Blinkhorn, 1998 (Routledge) is a good, short introduction. Also valuable are *Spain's Civil War* by H. Browne, 1996 (Longman), *The Spanish Civil War*, 1993 (Blackwell) by S. Ellwood, *The Coming of the Spanish Civil War*, 1994 (Routledge) by P. Preston. On France try *Politics and Society in Twentieth-Century France* by J.F. MacMillan, 1992 (Arnold) and *A Concise History of France* by R. Price, 1993 (CUP)

7

THE CAUSES OF THE SECOND WORLD WAR

POINTS TO CONSIDER

In 1939, just over twenty years after the First World War ended, France, Britain and Germany were again at war. What went wrong? Given the enormous amount of material published on the origins of the Second World War, it is not surprising that there are fierce controversies. This chapter, which has been broken down into an Introduction and seven sections, will examine some of the key issues. If you are studying the causes of the war there is no easy way out: you will need to work through each section in turn.

ISSUE
To what extent was the Second World War 'Hitler's War'?

For years after 1945 most historians blamed Adolf Hitler for the outbreak of the Second World War. However, in 1961, A.J.P. Taylor argued that Hitler should not shoulder sole, or even major, responsibility for the war. Taylor focused attention not on Hitler himself but on German expansionist ambitions. According to Taylor, the First World War failed to satisfy – or crush – those ambitions. Taylor pointed the finger of blame at the Versailles peacemakers, claiming that a second war was 'implicit' since the moment the First World War ended. The peace settlement left Germany embittered but failed to reduce its latent power. Hitler, said Taylor, was simply a typical German statesman, pursuing typical German ends. Taylor's book aroused a storm of protest. Few historians were prepared to let Hitler off the hook. Most continue to believe that Hitler's policies were different in kind to those of his predecessors and did lead to war.

ISSUE
What were the main problems between 1919 and 1924?

1 Problems, 1919–24

a) The Problem of Enforcing the Peace Settlement

The Versailles peacemakers had done their best, in difficult circumstances, to construct a durable settlement (see Chapter 3). No one was entirely satisfied with the results. However, arguably the main defect of the peace settlement was not so much the terms of the treaties but the lack of agreement on how the terms should be enforced. The USA, which refused to ratify the treaty or join the

League of Nations, showed little inclination to uphold the peace settlement which it had done so much to create. Nor did Britain and
France, the two countries with the greatest responsibility for, and
interest in, upholding the settlement, always see eye to eye.

b) The Problem of Italy

Having failed to gain all the territory promised it in 1915, Italy felt
cheated by the peace settlement and was not committed to upholding it. In 1922 Mussolini came to power. He was intensely nationalistic and was determined to improve Italy's international status.
However, he was not sure how to do this. Italian efforts to expand in
the Mediterranean were certain to be opposed by Britain. (The
Mediterranean was a vital link in the British Empire's chain of communication.) Despite all his bombastic talk, Mussolini feared alienating Britain. Nevertheless, in 1923–4, he was prepared to indulge in a
number of diplomatic adventures hoping to score cheap victories
which would bolster his position in Italy. Thereafter Mussolini
calmed down and for most of the 1920s he generally sought prestige
by cooperating with Britain and France.

c) The Problem of Russia

The mere existence of Lenin's Bolshevik government encouraged
the possibility of communist revolution sweeping across Europe.
Moreover, the Bolsheviks' avowed aim was to spread that revolution
abroad. The Communist International organisation, the Comintern,
was set up in Moscow in 1919 for just that purpose. However, after
1920, Lenin accepted that for the time being he would have to
coexist with capitalist countries. Compromise rather than provocation was the order of the day. Lenin's death in 1924 made little difference to Soviet foreign policy. Stalin's main concern was domestic
affairs – socialism in one country rather than world revolution. Nevertheless, there was a great deal of mutual suspicion between the
USSR and the rest of Europe.

d) The Problem of Germany

Germany had been greatly weakened by defeat in the First World
War. Its army had been reduced in size, its fleet scuttled, and its overseas empire lost. Nevertheless, it remained potentially the strongest
power in Europe. Its population was nearly twice as large as that of
France and its heavy industry was four times greater. Moreover, the
war had left eastern Europe fragmented, economically weak and
politically unstable – open to German domination. Germany refused

to accept that the Versailles settlement was a fair and final outcome of the war. German foreign policy after 1919 was dominated by an unrelenting determination to revise Versailles. Some right-wing extremists insisted that Germany should refuse to pay reparations, reject the territorial clauses, and flout the disarmament terms. Most moderates, however, believed that cooperation with the West was the best way to revise the peace settlement. Perversely, many Western leaders believed that German cooperation was essential if it was to be maintained. Indeed the disarmament and reparations terms could only be maintained with German collaboration.

e) The Problem of French Security

France, fearing that a strong Germany would rise from the ashes of defeat, felt insecure. Thus, as well as maintaining the largest military force in Europe, French governments also sought alliances, particularly with Britain. Britain, however, was not prepared to underwrite French security by a military alliance. Britain's main concerns were the survival of its empire and the recovery of trade. The first consumed most of what force it had, leaving little to spare for guaranteeing French security. The second depended on a peaceful and prosperous Europe, which in turn necessitated a prosperous and contented Germany. Thus, while France insisted upon the most stringent enforcement of the peace terms, British leaders thought that a revision of the treaty was urgently needed.

By 1922 Germany had fallen hopelessly behind in its reparation payments. French premier Poincaré decided that enough was enough. In January 1923 French and Belgian troops occupied the Ruhr, the industrial heart of Germany, with the intention of forcing Germany to meet its obligations. German authorities responded with a policy of passive resistance with the result that industrial production in the Ruhr ground to a halt. (Britain disliked but did not openly condemn French action.) Although Poincaré faced strong British and US financial pressure, he held out stubbornly, forcing the Germans to call off passive resistance in the Ruhr and to pay reparations. However, the result was hardly a great triumph for France. In 1924 the Dawes Committee agreed that reparation payments should be reduced and phased over a longer period.

Having little success with Britain, France searched for allies elsewhere. As the newly-created east European countries also felt vulnerable, their interests coincided with those of France. The result was the construction of a far-reaching alliance system – the **Little Entente**. While seeming to secure both France and east European powers against attack, in many respects the alliance system lacked substance. The Little Entente nations had their own, often conflict-

---

THE LITTLE ENTENTE

A treaty (against Hungary!) between Yugoslavia and Czechoslovakia in 1920 was the basis. Both countries then signed treaties with Romania. In 1921 France and Poland promised each other help in the event of either being attacked. The Little Entente was first linked to France by the Franco-Czechoslovakian treaty of 1924 which provided for mutual aid if either country were attacked. French treaties with Romania (1926) and Yugoslavia (1927) strengthened the ties.

ing, interests. Yugoslavia regarded Italy as its chief threat, while Romania and Czechoslovakia most feared Russia and Germany respectively. Moreover, no combination of small powers could equal the power of Germany or Russia. The strength of the Entente system was thus the strength of France. It would survive while France had the strength and the will to defend its allies.

2 The Spirit of Locarno, 1925–9

ISSUE
Why and to what extent was there a more friendly international atmosphere in the late 1920s?

a) Gustav Stresemann

From 1923 to 1929 Gustav Stresemann, a pragmatic nationalist, controlled German foreign policy. In 1927 he wrote:

> In my opinion there are three great tasks that confront German foreign policy in the more immediate future:
>   In the first place the solution of the Reparations question ...
>   Secondly, the protection of Germans abroad, those 10 to 12 millions of our kindred who now live under a foreign yoke in foreign lands. The third great task is the readjustment of our eastern frontiers; the recovery of Danzig, the Polish corridor, and a correction of the frontier in Upper Silesia.

Source A

Stresemann believed that cooperation with Britain and France was the best way of achieving his aims. He was fortunate that his period in office coincided with that of French Foreign Minister Aristide Briand and British Foreign Secretary Austin Chamberlain, who were both keen to improve relations with Germany.

b) Locarno

In 1925 representatives from Britain, France, Germany, Italy, Poland, Czechoslovakia and Belgium met in Switzerland and accepted a number of agreements, collectively known as the the **Locarno Pact**.

This seen as a diplomatic triumph. It seemed that Germany and France had been reconciled. People talked of a new spirit, the 'spirit of Locarno' and Briand, Stresemann and Chamberlain were awarded the Nobel Peace Prize. In 1928 all the major powers signed the Kellogg–Briand Pact, outlawing war. In 1929 the Young Plan extended the period of reparations payments by 60 years, further easing the burden on Germany. As part of this deal, Britain and France agreed to end their occupation of the Rhineland five years ahead of schedule. The improvement in international relations,

THE LOCARNO PACT
▼ Germany was to be welcomed into the League of Nations.
▼ Germany's western frontiers with France and Belgium were accepted as final and were guaranteed by Britain and Italy.

However, Germany would not agree to the same recognition of its eastern boundaries.

THE MAGINOT LINE

A series of defensive fortifications built to secure the eastern border of France against a potential German attack. Partly as a result of Belgian protests and partly as a result of cost, it was not extended westwards to secure France's border with Belgium.

however, can be exaggerated. France retained its distrust of German intentions, so much so that in 1927 it began to build the **Maginot Line**. Regular meetings between Stresemann, Briand and Chamberlain after 1926 yielded little in the way of agreement.

c) The League of Nations

In the 1920s the League, based at Geneva, established itself as an international organisation capable of resolving disputes between minor powers and promoting a wide range of humanitarian and economic activities. It was a useful talking shop and its meetings provided good opportunities for statesmen to meet and discuss. It evoked enthusiastic support particularly in Britain. The British public came to believe, naively, that the League could solve peacefully all the world's problems. However, the League had little real influence. The important questions of the day were settled by the foreign ministers of Britain, France, Italy and (after 1926) Germany. While the League was capable of resolving disputes between minor powers, it was unable to deal with the aggressive actions of its leading members (for example, Italy's seizure of Corfu in 1923).

d) Disarmament

In 1919 the Allies had disarmed Germany, a move seen by some as the first step in the process of world disarmament. Disarmament efforts in the 1920s had mixed success.

EVENTS, 1923–9

1923 French and Belgian troops occupied the Ruhr;
1924 Dawes Plan reduced reparations;
1925 Locarno Conference;
1926 Germany joined the League of Nations;
1928 Kellogg–Briand Pact;
1929 Young Plan reduced reparations.

i) Naval

In 1922 the major naval powers concluded the Washington Naval Agreement under which capital warships (ships over 10,000 tons) would be in the following ratios: USA 5: Britain 5: Japan 3: Italy 1.75: France 1.75. No new capital ships were to be built for ten years.

ii) Military

Securing agreement about land armaments proved far more difficult. The main problem was the Franco–German distrust. French leaders, aware that Germany was not even complying with the Versailles disarmament terms, thought it would be national, as well as political, suicide to reduce France's own large forces.

e) Conclusion

In 1929 there seemed good reason for optimism. Both France and Germany seemed ready to settle disputes by negotiation rather than by force. If Mussolini's oratory was occasionally warlike, his escapades were minor. The USSR was an embarrassment rather than a serious problem. Almost all the major powers had agreed to renounce war and the League of Nations seemed to be an effective organisation that would ensure peace. Winston Churchill, writing in 1948, summed up the 1920s as follows:

> Although old antagonisms were but sleeping, and the drumbeat of new levies was already heard, we were justified in hoping that the ground thus solidly gained would open the road to a further forward march … At the end of … [1929] the state of Europe was tranquil, as it had not been for twenty years, and was not to be for at least another twenty. A friendly feeling existed towards Germany following upon our Treaty of Locarno, and the evacuation of the Rhineland by the French Army and Allied contingents at a much earlier date than had been prescribed at Versailles. The new Germany took her place in the truncated League of Nations. Under the genial influence of American and British loans Germany was reviving rapidly … France and her system of alliances also seemed secure in Europe. The disarmament clauses of the Treaty of Versailles were not openly violated. The German Navy was non-existent. The German Air Force was prohibited and still unborn.
>
> *Source B*

Sally Marks, a historian writing in 1976, had a different view:

> A few men knew that the spirit of Locarno was a fragile foundation on which to build a lasting peace. After all, the real spirit at Locarno behind the façade of public fellowship was one of bitter confrontation between a fearful France flanked by the unhappy east Europeans, trying to hide their humiliation and panic, and a resentful, revisionist Germany demanding even more alterations in the power balance to her benefit. Since Germany was potentially the strongest power on the continent, the private fears of her neighbours could only deepen.
>
> Yet the public faces remained serene and smiling, and the ordinary European did not know about the clashes behind closed doors … The public façade of the Locarno conference and the treaties themselves had created an illusion of peace, and ordinary men rejoiced. Misled by a false front Europe thankfully entered upon the Locarno years, thinking that real peace had arrived at last. Of all the interwar years these were perhaps the best years, but none the less they were years of illusion.
>
> *Source C*

ACTIVITY

Examine the two sources above and answer the following questions:

1. Why does Sally Marks refer to the Locarno years as 'years of illusion'? **[5 marks]**
2. In what ways, if any, does Churchill's account support the view of Marks? **[5 marks]**
3. Comment on the different perspectives of Churchill and Marks. **[10 marks]**

ISSUE

What impact did the Depression have on international affairs?

3 Depression, 1929–33

The collapse of the world economy following the Wall Street Crash in 1929 had a major impact on international relations. While the Great Depression made some countries more peaceful than ever, in others it led to governments coming to power which favoured foreign conquest as a means of alleviating the economic situation. As a result, the international climate became more menacing. The death of Stresemann and the removal from office of Austin Chamberlain and Briand in 1929 did not help matters.

a) Japan and Manchuria

Throughout the 1920s Japan was governed by a succession of liberal coalitions, most of which supported international cooperation. However, radical nationalists, strong in the army, wanted Japan to pursue its own interests and not be constrained by the 'rules' of the West. The Depression hit Japan hard and was a powerful incentive to military adventure. In September 1931 units in the Japanese army, acting without orders from the government, seized parts of the Chinese province of Manchuria. Aware of popular support for the army's action, the Japanese government did little to halt it.

This was the first real challenge by a major power to the League of Nations. Article 16 of the League's Covenant declared that if any member of the League should 'resort to war', this would amount to an act of war against all other League members. However, it was not clear that Japan had actually committed a 'resort to war' in an area where incidents between Chinese and Japanese soldiers were commonplace. Thus the League did little except appeal to China and Japan to refrain from further provocative actions. The Japanese army was not coerced by verbal warnings. By February 1932 it had occupied the whole of Manchuria and set up the puppet state of Manchukuo.

The League eventually set up a commission under Lord Lytton to inquire into the Manchuria situation. In October 1932 Lytton's Report condemned Japan's methods of redressing (some justified) grievances and recommended that Manchuria be returned to China. Japan, the only League member to vote against Lytton's recommendations, now withdrew from the League in protest and ignored its rulings. This was a critical moment for the League. How would it deal with a member who rejected its decision?

The League took no action. With hindsight, it is easy to condemn its failure to use force. It is even possible to claim that this ultimately led to the Second World War. However, the League's actions were, at the time, quite understandable. It had first to investigate the Japanese invasion. By the time Lytton had reported, it was too late to take action. The Western powers would have found it hard to justify to their electorates the need to 'punish' Japan for something it had done over a year earlier. Nor had they any wish to risk a major confrontation with Japan: their forces in the Far East were small and an economic blockade, without American support, was unlikely to achieve much.

Should the League of Nations have taken action against Japan in 1931–2?

b) Disarmament and Reparations

Given the economic problems, Britain in particular was not keen to spend money on armaments. Strongly adhering to the principles of disarmament and international cooperation through the League, Britain pinned great hopes on the World Disarmament Conference which met at Geneva in 1932. Sixty nations were represented, including the USA and Russia. However, it proved impossible to find a compromise between the German demand for equality and the French demand for security. Despite this failure, Britain hoped that other German grievances could be settled by negotiation. In June 1932 the Lausanne Conference did succeed in cancelling reparations.

EVENTS, 1929–33

1929 October: death of Stresemann; Wall Street Crash;

1931 Japanese troops began military operations in Manchuria;

1932 Disarmament Conference met at Geneva.

4 Increasing Problems, 1933–6

a) The Threat of Hitler

ISSUE
What were Hitler's aims? To what extent was he a threat to peace?

In 1933 Hitler came to power in Germany. This was a cause of alarm, if not panic, across Europe. It seemed certain that he would challenge the existing order. Historians continue to disagree about his ultimate intentions. A.J.P. Taylor has claimed that Hitler was a rather ordinary German statesman with a rather ordinary mission – that of increasing Germany's standing among the world's nations. In Taylor's view, Hitler was a man who took advantage of situations as they arose, rarely taking the initiative himself. He was no more unscrupulous or evil than most other statesmen. Hitler, Taylor argued, did not want a general war in 1939: the war broke out by accident. Few today accept Taylor's arguments in their entirety. While some **functionalists** (see page 155) believe that Hitler had little control of foreign policy and deny there was any consistency in Nazi policy, most historians believe that the ultimate direction of Nazi foreign policy *was* a reflection of Hitler's wishes. Clearly Hitler (like all statesmen) was at the mercy of events. Consequently, there was a large degree of opportunism in his policy: he probably did not have a stage-by-stage plan. Nevertheless, most historians think that Hitler had a clear and cold-blooded general purpose to overthrow Versailles, create a Greater Germany, win land in the east (*lebensraum*), and make Germany the strongest power in Europe.

b) Hitler's First Moves, 1933–4

Given that Germany was militarily, economically and diplomatically weak, Hitler's first moves in foreign policy were cautious. However, in October 1933, claiming that the other powers would not treat Germany as an equal, he withdrew from both the Disarmament Conference and the League. Aware that Germany was illegally rearming, France pushed ahead with building the Maginot Line. This had serious repercussions for France's allies in eastern Europe. France would be unable to offer much aid if its forces were going to cower behind defences in the event of war.

In *Mein Kampf* Hitler had argued that Germany should seek friendship with Britain and Italy. He believed that Imperial Germany had committed a grave error in alienating Britain. Voicing the hope that 'the two great Germanic nations' could work together, he tried – but failed – to achieve a formal agreement with Britain. Nor was Hitler any more successful with Italy. An official state visit by Hitler to Italy in 1934 was a disaster. He and Mussolini did not get on. Events in Austria in July 1934 further worsened relations. A Nazi-inspired putsch led to the assassination of the Austrian Chancellor, Dollfuss. Mussolini regarded Austria as an Italian satellite state and rushed Italian troops to the Austrian border as a warning to Hitler. Hitler did nothing and the Nazi putsch failed.

c) Germany Rearms

In March 1935 Hitler declared that Germany had an air force and announced that the German army would be increased to 500,000 men – five times the permitted number. Although Western governments were aware that Germany had been violating the military

GERMAN–POLISH PACT

In January 1934 Hitler surprised many of his own followers by signing a ten-year non-aggression pact with Poland, a country he despised. In the long term Hitler did not envisage any place for an independent Poland. The country was merely a gateway to winning *lebensraum*. But in the short term, the pact breached the French system of alliances in eastern Europe and forestalled any possibility of a Polish attack on Germany.

clauses of Versailles for many years, Hitler's announcement was a challenge which could not be ignored. Meeting at Stresa in April 1935, British, French and Italian leaders condemned Hitler's action and resolved to resist any future attempt to change the existing treaty settlement by force. This agreement was known as the Stresa Front.

Fearing the German threat, the USSR now adopted a radically different attitude towards the Western democracies. Entering the League of Nations in 1934, the USSR signed treaties of mutual assistance with France and Czechoslovakia in 1935. Instead of preaching hostility towards moderate socialist parties, the Comintern now encouraged communist parties to join 'Popular Fronts' against fascism. The gains which the new approach in Soviet foreign policy achieved proved largely superficial. Mussolini was hostile to any cooperation with the USSR. Britain was also suspicious of Stalin's motives. Right-wingers in Britain and France, unattracted by the idea of communist help to contain Hitler, preferred helping Hitler to contain communism.

Britain did not yet consider itself to be particularly threatened by Hitler. In June 1935 Britain and Germany signed a Naval Agreement by which Germany could build the equivalent of up to 35 per cent of Britain's capital ships and was allowed parity in submarines. This Agreement seriously damaged the Stresa Front. By sanctioning a much larger German navy than was permitted by Versailles, Britain seemed to be condoning German rearmament despite the Stresa Front's condemnation. However, British leaders thought the Agreement a realistic contribution to peace. Given the Japanese threat in the Far East, Britain had no wish to face a danger in home waters. The Agreement at least ensured that Britain had a naval superiority over Germany twice as great as in 1914.

d) Abyssinia

Britain and France hoped that Mussolini might be a useful ally against Hitler. There was some basis for these hopes. Italy had no wish to see a powerful Germany and particularly feared the prospect of a union between Germany and Austria. However, Mussolini had his own ambitions. He wanted to increase the Italian Empire by taking over Abyssinia (Ethiopia), one of the few countries in Africa still free from European control. A skirmish with Abyssinian forces in 1934 gave Italy an excuse to build up its forces. Recognising that an attack might damage relations with Britain and France, Mussolini made diplomatic efforts to ensure that they would accept his plans. In January 1935 France, anxious to keep on good terms with Italy, promised Mussolini a free hand in Abyssinia. In the summer of 1935, however, Britain made it clear that it was opposed to Italian

Figure 45 Abyssinia, 1934–6.

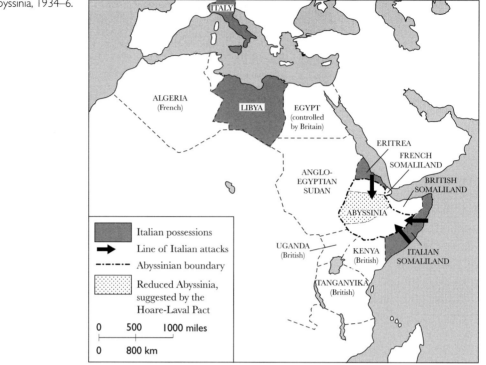

annexation of the whole of Abyssinia. Nevertheless, in October 1935 Italy invaded Abyssinia. The Abyssinian Emperor, Haile Selassie, immediately appealed to the League of Nations.

Britain and France now faced a terrible dilemma. Neither country had any real interest in Abyssinia and Haile Selassie was hardly a model ruler. To take action against Italy would wreck the Stresa Front and might force Mussolini into the arms of Hitler. But serious principles were at stake – not least whether the Western powers would honour their obligations under the League's covenant. British public opinion, strongly opposed to the Italian invasion, could not be ignored because there was a general election approaching. Despite its previous readiness to consider concessions, the British government now condemned the invasion and supported League action against Italy. France, more fearful of losing British than Italian support, did likewise. In October the League imposed economic sanctions. All imports from Italy and some exports to it were banned. However, the sanctions, which did not (initially) include an embargo on oil, had little effect. Fearing that Mussolini might resort to the 'mad dog' act of declaring war, Britain did not close the Suez Canal – the best way to damage the Italian war effort.

In December 1935, the British and French Foreign Ministers, Hoare and Laval, proposed a compromise settlement, whereby Italy would receive over half of Abyssinia. When details of the plan were leaked to the press, there was a storm of indignation in Britain. It seemed as though the government was betraying its commitment to the League. In the face of the outburst, Hoare resigned and the cabinet abandoned the plan. Meanwhile Italian forces overran Abyssinia. In May 1936 it became part of the Italian Empire. The sanctions against Italy were lifted but Britain still refused to recognise the Italian conquest, which infuriated Mussolini.

Arguably the failure to check Mussolini in 1935–6 was an important step on the road to war. Had Britain and France been ready to fight Italy, this might have strengthened the League and deterred Hitler. However, defeating Italy might not have been as easy as many have assumed. Italy was reasonably well-prepared for war in 1935. Even if it had been defeated it would have been left deeply embittered – a potential ally of Germany.

> ### THE RESULTS OF ABYSSINIA
> ▽ The crisis was a death blow to the League which had again failed to halt an aggressor.
> ▽ The crisis caused a major split between Italy and Britain and France.
> ▽ Mussolini began to move closer to Hitler who had consistently supported Italy's actions.

e) The Rhineland

In March 1936 Hitler sent German troops into the demilitarised Rhineland. By so doing he was cleary violating both the Versailles and Locarno treaties. Hitler knew he was taking a gamble. Germany was still too weak to fight a long war and the token forces that marched into the Rhineland had orders to withdraw at the first sign of opposition. However, Hitler's reading of the situation – that Britain and France would take no action – proved accurate. France did nothing, except pass the problem to Britain by asking if it would support French action. Britain had no intention of risking war against Germany. British opinion saw Hitler's move as regrettable in

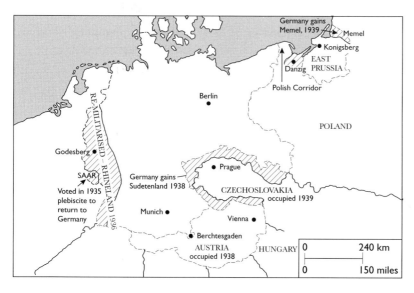

Figure 46 German gains, 1933–9.

Should Britain and
France have taken
action against Hitler in 1936?

**THE
ROME–BERLIN
AXIS**
The term used to describe
the growing friendship
between Germany and Italy.
Mussolini boasted that the
two nations would dominate
Europe and that all the other
states would revolve around
this 'axis'. In the Second
World War, 'Axis' was used
to describe all the powers
fighting on Germany's side.

EVENTS, 1933–6

1933 Germany left the League
and the Disarmament
Conference at Geneva;
1934 German-Polish non-
aggression treaty;
1935 March: Hitler announced
German rearmament; June:
Anglo-German Naval
Agreement; October: Italy
invaded Abyssinia;
1936 March: German troops
reoccupied the Rhineland;
July: start of the Spanish
Civil War.

ISSUE
**How sensible was
appeasement?**

manner but not threatening in substance. Most MPs probably agreed
with Lord Lothian's remark that Germany had every right to walk
into its own 'backyard'. While it can be claimed that France failed to
take action because Britain failed to offer support, it now seems
certain that there was no will in France to risk war with or without
British support. Germany began building fortifications in the
Rhineland, ensuring that from now on it would be even more difficult for France to take action. In retrospect, it can be claimed that
the Rhineland was 'the last chance' to stop Hitler without war and
thus the point at which Hitler could and should have been challenged. However, it probably was not the last chance to stop Hitler
without war. France might have stopped Hitler but only by going to
war. Had it taken this option, a French–German encounter might
not have been the easy French victory that many have assumed.

f) The Situation in 1936

In July 1936 the Spanish Civil War broke out (see page 187).
Germany benefited most from the war. As well as giving Hitler an
opportunity to test new weapons, the war also led to improved relations with Italy. In October 1936 Mussolini proclaimed the
Rome–Berlin Axis. In November 1936 Germany and Japan signed
the anti-Comintern pact, an agreement to stop the spread of
communism (Italy joined in 1937). Germany was rearming, Italy was
a threat in the Mediterranean and Japan was strong in the Far East.
In the circumstances Britain had little alternative but to begin extensive rearmament.

ACTIVITY

To test your understanding, consider the following question: 'Which
country – Japan, Italy or Germany – posed the greatest threat to
world peace in the years 1931–6?'

Suggested line of response:
▼ Examine Japanese aggression in Manchuria in 1931–2.
▼ Examine Italian actions in 1935–6.
▼ How much of a threat did Hitler pose in the years 1933–6?

5 The Tension Mounts, 1937–8

a) Neville Chamberlain and Appeasement

In 1937 Neville Chamberlain became British Prime Minister. He was
determined to play a leading role in foreign policy. His feeble

appearance belied his confidence and strength of purpose. The word now indissolubly linked to Chamberlain's name is **appeasement**. For many years after 1939, appeasement had a bad press. Those who supported it were seen as 'guilty men' whose misguided policies helped bring about war. Chamberlain was usually seen as the main guilty man. Some still insist that the only correct policy was to stand firm against Hitler: appeasement simply whetted his appetite, encouraging him to make fresh demands. However, appeasement is now often viewed in a more positive light. For hundreds of years it had been a cardinal principle of British policy that it was better to resolve disputes through negotiation and compromise than through war. Chamberlain loathed the prospect of war which in his view, 'wins nothing, cures nothing, ends nothing'. Sympathetic to Hitler's desire to unite the German-speaking people of Austria, Poland and Czechoslovakia, Chamberlain hoped that these changes could be effected without war.

Chamberlain did not trust either Hitler, Mussolini or the Japanese. For this reason he also favoured rearmament. Until Britain was adequately armed he accepted that, 'we must . . . bear with patience and good humour actions which we would like to treat in a very different fashion'. He had no confidence in France or the League of Nations. He had even less confidence in the USSR, distrusting Stalin as much as he distrusted Hitler. Given the strength of American isolationism, he knew there was little prospect of US involvement in world affairs. Nevertheless, he remained optimistic. He wrote in 1937, 'I believe the double policy of rearmament and better relations with Germany and Italy will carry us safely through the dangerous period.'

Appeasement was supported by the great majority of British MPs. Churchill was the most prominent anti-appeaser. He urged the need for a strong system of alliances and for extensive rearmament. He was later to acquire the reputation of having been right on Hitler whereas Chamberlain had been wrong. But Churchill's views derived essentially from his own anti-German prejudices and there were not many in Britain who cared to go along with the hunches of a warmongering maverick.

b) The Hossbach Conference

In November 1937, at a meeting with some of his leading commanders (the so-called Hossbach Conference), Hitler outlined the aims of German foreign policy and the possible courses it might follow. He asserted that he was set on winning *lebensraum* which could only be achieved by war. While Germany would not be fully prepared for war until the mid-1940s, he could not wait that long. If an opportunity arose before that date, he would take it. The first objectives were

APPEASEMENT
The name given to policies of giving in to threatening demands in order to avoid war. It is primarily associated with British foreign policy in the late 1930s.

THE SINO-JAPANESE WAR
In July 1937 Chinese–Japanese hostility escalated into full-scale war. Japanese forces took over large areas of China. Chamberlain appealed for an end to the conflict – in vain. In the circumstances the best British hope was that Japan would get bogged down in a war of attrition in China, which indeed was what happened. In the late 1930s British attention was focused more on Europe than the Far East. However, Chamberlain could not avoid the fact that European and Far Eastern problems often interacted. Fear of Japanese aggression was an important factor in understanding why Britain was keen to conciliate Italy and Germany.

the takeover of Czechoslovakia and Austria. The significance of the Hossbach Conference has become the focus of controversy. Some think it proves that Hitler was outlining a timetable for German aggression. Others think that, far from setting out precise plans, Hitler was simply daydreaming. Certainly events did not unfold exactly as he anticipated. Nevertheless, the winter of 1937–8 marked the start of a new phase in German policy. Several leading conservatives were removed from influential positions. Schacht resigned as Minister of Economics after differences with Hitler over the pace of rearmament. In February 1938, Ribbentrop replaced Neurath as Foreign Minister. Hitler's growing confidence led him to take the reins more firmly into his own hands.

c) The *Anschluss*

Despite the fact that it was specifically forbidden by the Treaty of Versailles, Hitler was determined to unite Austria and Germany. He was encouraged by the fact that many pro-Nazi Austrians held similar views. Since 1934 the Austrian government had struggled to keep the Austrian Nazis under control. As Hitler and Mussolini drew closer together it became obvious that Austria could no longer rely on Italian help. In early 1938 Austrian police discovered plans for a Nazi uprising, the repression of which would provide the pretext for a German invasion. In February 1938, Austrian Chancellor Schuschnigg decided to visit Hitler at Berchtesgaden, the Führer's home in Bavaria, hoping to persuade him to restrain the Austrian Nazis. This was a mistake. Bullied and threatened, Schuschnigg accepted Hitler's demands to include Nazis in his cabinet.

Hitler, confident that Austria would inevitably fall under Nazi control, planned to do little more at this stage. But Schuschnigg again precipitated events by announcing in early March that he intended to hold a plebiscite on whether Austria should join Germany. This was an attempt to destroy Hitler's claim that most Austrians wanted union. Hitler, fearing the vote might go against him, demanded the cancellation of the plebiscite and threatened war. (Invasion plans were hurriedly drawn up: none had previously been made!) Schuschnigg resigned. Austrian Nazis now took power and invited Hitler to send troops into Austria to preserve order. The German forces were enthusiastically welcomed. Hitler returned in triumph to his homeland and declared that Austria was to be fully integrated into the Third Reich. The union (or *Anschluss*) was approved by a massive majority in a Nazi-run plebiscite.

Britain and France had little warning of the crisis – not surprisingly because Hitler had only decided to act at the last minute. Chamberlain, recognising there was little he could effectively do, did

EVENTS, 1937–8

1937 May – Chamberlain became British Prime Minister; July – Start of Sino-Japanese War; November – The Hossbach Conference;
1938 The *Anschluss*.

nothing. France, without a government throughout the crisis, simply protested. It was hard to argue a great crime had occurred when so many Austrians expressed their joy at joining the Third Reich. From Chamberlain's point of view, the most worrying feature of the *Anschluss* was not that it had happened but how it had happened. If one frontier could be changed in this way why not others? Hitler's excuse for the *Anschluss* was that there were large numbers of German-Austrians demanding union with Germany. The uncomfortable fact was that there were German-speaking peoples in other countries who were also demanding union with Germany.

ACTIVITY

Discussion issues: Were there any real alternatives to appeasement? What action should Britain and France have taken over the *Anschluss*?

6 The Problem of Czechoslovakia, 1938–9

ISSUE
Was the Munich Agreement justifiable policy by Britain and France?

a) The Problem of the Sudetenland

The *Anschluss* immediately focused attention on Czechoslovakia, now partly surrounded by German territory (see Figure 48). Only about half the country's 15 million population was Czech. It also contained Slovaks, Hungarians, Ruthenians and Poles. But the largest minority group were some 3.25 million Germans who lived in the Sudetenland. By 1938 the Sudeten German Party (Nazi in all but name) was demanding either home rule or union with Germany. It received support from Germany where the Nazi press launched bitter attacks on the Czech government (with some justification) for victimising Sudeten Germans. Hitler hated the democratic Czech state. The fact that it had strong military forces meant it was also a potential threat. In March 1938, Hitler instructed Sudeten leaders to make demands on the Czech government which could never be satisfied.

President Beneš, the Czechoslovakian head of state, had no intention of accepting the Sudeten demands. He realised that if all the various ethnic groups within the country were given independence or self-rule, there would be no viable Czech state left. Confident that he would receive support from the Western powers, he determined to stand firm against German pressure. Most Western politicians had some sympathy with Czechoslovakia. Even if it did not treat its ethnic minorities particularly well, it had at least preserved a democratic constitution. A few politicians (like Churchill) thought Czechoslovakia worth fighting for. Chamberlain was not among that number. He regarded Czechoslovakia as a 'highly artificial' creation and had some sympathy for the Sudeten Germans. He was quite willing to see the Sudetenland handed over to Germany provided this was done peacefully. In March 1938 he told the Commons that British vital interests were not involved in Czechoslovakia. Britain had no treaty obligation to defend the Czech state and was not able to offer serious military aid. Chamberlain wrote, 'You have only to look at the map to see that nothing France or we could do could possibly save Czechoslovakia from being overrun by the Germans if they want to do it.'

Chamberlain's main concern was not so much Czechoslovakia but France. If Germany invaded Czechoslovakia, France might go to her aid. Britain might then be forced to help France. In fact, French leader Daladier had no wish to be drawn into war. His strategic view was similar to the British: Czechoslovakia could not be defended. He would be delighted if Britain gave him an excuse to avoid France's 1935 obligations.

In May after – false – reports of German troop movements, the Czechs mobilised some of their reserves and prepared for war. Both Britain and France warned Hitler against attacking Czechoslovakia. Hitler was outraged. The Western powers seemed to have won a diplomatic victory because he had stepped back from invasion, an invasion which he was not actually then planning! He now determined to destroy Czechoslovakia. German military leaders were ordered to prepare for an attack to begin in September 1938.

As the summer wore on, tension increased. The German press stepped up its campaign against the Czechs. Beneš still stood firm. In August, a mission led by Lord Runciman travelled to Czechoslovakia to try to resolve the crisis. Little was achieved: neither the Sudeten Germans nor the Czechs were prepared to compromise. By September opinion in Britain and France was divided. Some thought the Western powers should support the Czechs: others thought that war must be averted at all cost. Hitler kept up the pressure. In September, he demanded self-determination for the Sudeten Germans and assured them they would be neither defenceless nor deserted. Beneš declared martial law in the Sudetenland. Several Germans were killed: thousands more fled to Germany with tales of brutal repression. A Czech-German war seemed imminent.

b) The Munich Conference

On 15 September, in an effort to maintain peace, Chamberlain flew to meet Hitler at Berchtesgaden. The two leaders reached a rough agreement. Chamberlain accepted Hitler's main demand that the areas in Czechoslovakia in which Germans comprised over 50 per cent of the population should be handed over to Germany. In return Hitler agreed not to attack Czechoslovakia until Chamberlain had consulted with the French and Czechs. Hitler, assuming the Czechs would refuse to cede the Sudetenland and that Britain would then wash its hands of them, was delighted. Chamberlain flew back to

Britain and set about convincing his cabinet, the French and finally the Czechs that Hitler's demands, if met, would produce a lasting peace. The cabinet and the French were easily won over. The Czech government, appalled at the situation, had little option but to accept the loss of the Sudetenland.

On 22 September Chamberlain flew back to Germany to meet Hitler at Bad Godesberg. To his consternation, Hitler now said the previous proposals were insufficient. (Czech concessions were not what Hitler had wanted!) Polish and Hungarian claims to Czechoslovakian territory had also to be met and, in addition, to protect Sudeten Germans from Czech brutality, Hitler demanded the right to occupy the Sudetenland no later than 1 October. While Chamberlain favoured accepting Hitler's new proposals, many of his cabinet colleagues rejected them. Daladier now declared that France would honour its commitments to Czechoslovakia. Not surprisingly, the Czech government stated that the Godesberg proposals were totally unacceptable and mobilised its forces. Both Britain and France began to prepare for war. On 27 September Mussolini (following a British request) agreed to use his influence to persuade Hitler to reconsider. That same evening, Chamberlain broadcast to the British people:

> How horrible, fantastic, incredible, it is that we should be digging trenches and trying on gas masks here because of a quarrel in a far away country between people of whom we know nothing . . . I would not hestitate to pay even a third visit to Germany, if I thought it would do any good.

Source D

The next day, Chamberlain got his opportunity. Hitler accepted the suggestion of a Four Power Conference to be held at Munich to work out an agreement to the Sudeten question. It looked as though Hitler had backed down. Aware that his military leaders and the German people were not enthusiastic for war, in a sense he had.

On 29 September Chamberlain, Daladier, Hitler and Mussolini met at Munich. (Neither Beneš nor Stalin were invited to the Conference.) The Agreement, reached the next day, was very similar to Hitler's Godesberg demands. German occupation of the Sudetenland was to be carried out over a ten-day period rather than one. The precise borders of the new Czech state would be determined by a conference of the Four Powers. Beneš had to choose between accepting the terms or fighting Germany alone. He chose to surrender. Before returning home, Chamberlain persuaded Hitler to sign a joint declaration by which both Britain and Germany pledged to do all they could to preserve peace.

Figure 47 The Munich
Conference (l–r Chamberlain,
Daladier (Prime Minister of
France), Hitler, Mussolini and
Ciano (Italian Foreign Minister).

Figure 48 How Czechoslovakia
was divided, 1938.

c) Munich: Success or Failure?

Munich is often viewed as a terrible failure for the Western powers. Many historians think that they should have done the honourable thing and gone to war to save a friend. However, Chamberlain saw Munich as a victory. He could claim that from a position of weakness he had achieved most of his aims. War had been avoided, Germany's legitimate grievances had been settled, and Czechoslovakia remained as a sovereign state. Most people in Britain and France in 1938 also regarded Munich as a triumph. Both Chamberlain and Daladier were treated as heroes on their return home. Chamberlain announced to cheering crowds that he had brought back 'peace with honour'. Churchill, who described British policy as a 'total and unmitigated disaster', was in a minority.

The possible outcome of a war over Czechoslovakia in 1938 has intrigued historians ever since. Many have accepted Churchill's view that it would have been better for Britain and France to have fought Germany in 1938 than in 1939. Certainly Germany was not as strong in 1938 as British experts imagined. The French army, on paper, was still the best in Europe and Czech forces were far from negligible. Moreover, Russia might well have supported the Czechs. However, neither Britain nor France was ready for war. The Germans anticipated overrunning Czechoslovakia (whose forces were ethnically divided and whose defences were far from complete) in ten days. French forces, deployed along the Maginot Line, could have done little to help. Nor is it certain that Russia would have aided Czechoslovakia. Given that Poland was not prepared to allow Russian troops on Polish soil, it would have been difficult for Russia to have sent help.

Interestingly, Hitler did not view Munich as a great triumph. Although he had gained the Sudetenland, he had been denied a military triumph. He had not been bluffing: he had wanted a limited war against Czechoslovakia. He only accepted a negotiated settlement because he estimated that the risk of a continental war was too great. He soon regretted his decision. The existence of an independent Czechoslovakia still represented a troublesome wedge on Germany's south-eastern flank.

> **THE RESULTS OF MUNICH**
> ▼ Germany gained the Sudetenland and territory including 800,000 Czechs.
> ▼ Czechoslovakia lost Teschen to Poland and South Ruthenia to Hungary.
> ▼ Having lost most of her border defences and industrial capacity, Czechoslovakia was seriously weakened.

ACTIVITY

Test your grasp of this section by answering the question: 'To what extent was the conduct of British and French policy with regard to Czechoslovakia in 1938 a "total and unmitigated disaster?"'

Suggested line of response:
▼ Why was Czechoslovakia a problem in 1938?
▼ What was British and French policy? Was it the same?
▼ What happened pre-Munich and at Munich?
▼ Was Munich a 'total' failure?

---

7 The Coming of War

> **ISSUE**
> Why did Britain and France go to war with Germany in September 1939?

a) Uneasy Peace

Chamberlain was not convinced that Munich made peace more secure and was more determined than ever that the pace of rearmament should not slacken. At least Munich gave him a breathing space. With the Czech problem out of the way, it might be possible to make progress 'along the road to sanity'. A Franco-German agreement in December 1938 which expressed mutual goodwill and respect for frontiers seemed a positive step. Meanwhile Chamberlain tried, without much success, to improve relations with Italy.

In early 1939 Chamberlain received a number of (incorrect) intelligence reports predicting German moves against Poland, Czechoslovakia, Holland or Switzerland. In February, in a radical change of policy, Chamberlain agreed to detailed military talks with France and committed Britain to raising a large army which, if needs be, could fight on the Continent. French opinion also swung in favour of resisting Nazi expansion. Many Frenchmen feared that if Germany gobbled up more territory in the east it might ultimately prove too strong in the west.

b) The End of Czechoslovakia

After Munich Czechoslovakia faced serious internal problems. Many Slovaks had little love for the Czech-dominated state and Hitler deliberately encouraged them to seek independence. In early March President Hacha, who had replaced Beneš, proclaimed martial law. This desperate attempt to preserve the Czech state actually speeded its downfall. Hitler instructed Slovak leaders to appeal to Germany for protection and to declare independence. With his country falling apart, Hacha asked to meet Hitler hoping he might do something to help. Hitler, receiving Hacha on 15 March, told him that the German army intended to enter Czechoslovakia in a few hours time and that his only choice was war or a peaceable occupation. Hacha broke down under the threats and agreed to Hitler's demands. German troops now entered Czechoslovakia on the pretext that the country was on the verge of civil war. A German protectorate of Bohemia and Moravia was established while Slovakia became nominally independent.

While Hitler claimed to have acted legally, merely complying with the requests of the Czechs and Slovaks, he had clearly dismembered a small neighbour. This time, moreover, he could not claim that he was uniting Germans within one German state. There was no question of Britain or France going to war. Czechoslovakia had collapsed as a result of internal disruption which freed both countries from any obligation to it. However, Chamberlain (like British opinion in general) was outraged at the turn of events. He told the cabinet that his hopes of working with Hitler were over.

c) The Polish Guarantees

Hitler maintained the pressure. In mid-March he forced Lithuania to hand back the town of Memel, lost by Germany in 1919. Again

Britain and France took no action. It was inconceivable to think of going to war over Memel, a German city to which Hitler could lay reasonable claim. But Poland now seemed to be Hitler's next target – and this was another matter. There were some 800,000 Germans in Poland. Most lived in the Polish Corridor which divided East Prussia from the rest of Germany. Danzig was 96 per cent German. While it had been run by the Nazis since 1934, Poland controlled the city's trade and foreign relations. This arrangement was always liable to create friction. No German government, certainly not Hitler's, was ever likely to accept the Danzig solution or the separation of East Prussia as permanent. Polish governments were equally determined that things should remain as they were.

German relations with Poland had been remarkably friendly since the signing of the 1934 non-aggression treaty. On a number of occasions, Germany had suggested to the Poles that this agreement might be turned into an alliance against Russia. But Poland did not take up these suggestions. Polish policy was concerned with avoiding commitment either to Germany or to Russia. After Munich, Germany hoped that Poland would be drawn into the German orbit. In October 1938 Ribbentrop asked the Poles (in a friendly way) to give up Danzig. In return Poland would receive guarantees of its borders and the prospect of territory in the Ukraine. In January 1939 Hitler met Beck, the Polish Foreign Minister, and added a demand for a German-controlled road or rail link across the Polish Corridor. To Hitler's surprise, the Poles, unwilling to become a German satellite, refused to consider his proposals. German demands became more insistent. At this stage Hitler still hoped for a diplomatic rather than a military triumph. Nevertheless tension mounted. By late March there were rumours that a German attack on Poland was imminent.

On 31 March Britain took the unprecedented step of offering a guarantee to Poland: if it were the victim of an unprovoked attack, Britain would come to its aid. France offered a similar guarantee. Poland accepted both offers. The guarantees were widely condemned at the time and have been condemned since. Of all the east European states, Poland, a right-wing dictatorship, was probably the one that the Western powers liked least. In fact, until 1939 Poland had few friends – except Germany! Hitler's demands of Poland were more reasonable than his demands of Czechoslovakia in 1938. The guarantees can be seen as 'blank cheques' given to a country notorious for its reckless diplomacy. Moreover, in the last resort, the 'cheques' were worthless because there was little that Britain or France could actually do to help Poland.

However, there was a feeling in Britain and France that something had to be done. The guarantees were designed as a clear warning to Hitler. If he continued to push for expansion, he would face the

Should Britain and France have offered guarantees to Poland?

THE PACT OF STEEL

Determined not to be outdone by Hitler, Mussolini embarked on his own 'adventure'. In April 1939 Italian forces occupied Albania. He also announced that the Balkans and the eastern Mediterranean should in future be regarded as within the Italian sphere of influence. Mussolini's aggressive words and actions seemed to pose a further threat to east European stability. Britain and France now issued guarantees to both Greece and Romania in the same terms as those given to Poland. Hitler was pleased by Mussolini's action. Italy's Balkan ambitions might well preoccupy the Western powers while he settled the Polish question. It was a further bonus when Mussolini proposed a close military alliance. This 'Pact of Steel' was signed in May. This required each power to help the other in the event of war.

Source E

prospect of a war on two fronts. The guarantees were not a total commitment to Poland. Danzig's future was still thought to be negotiable and Chamberlain hoped that the right mix of diplomacy and strength might persuade Hitler to negotiate honestly and constructively. More angered than deterred, Hitler now abandoned any thought of accommodation with Poland and ordered his army leaders to prepare for war with Poland by the end of August.

In April conscription was introduced in Britain for the first time in peacetime. German diplomats, meanwhile, worked hard to secure support from (or improve relations with) a host of countries in Europe, including Hungary, Romania, Bulgaria and Finland. As the summer wore on there was increasing tension over Poland. The Germans claimed that the British and French guarantees resulted in Poland refusing reasonable terms. They also accused Poland of launching a reign of terror against Polish Germans. These stories, although exaggerated, had a foundation of truth.

d) Anglo-Soviet Negotiations

In the event of a German attack, only the USSR could offer Poland immediate military help. In consequence, the only sensible course of action for Britain and France seemed to be to ally with the USSR. In the mid-1930s the USSR had made some efforts to weld a powerful alliance capable of deterring Nazi aggression. However, these efforts had failed. In the late 1930s neither France nor Russia made any real efforts to strengthen the defence pact they had made in 1935. France had no wish to anger Britain, Italy and Poland, all of whom disapproved of the Franco-Soviet agreement. Throughout the 1930s Britain opposed any alliance with the USSR, suspecting that the real aim of Soviet policy was to embroil Britain and France in a war against Germany. In March 1939 Chamberlain expressed his thoughts about the USSR:

> I must confess to the most profound distrust of Russia. I have no belief in her ability to maintain an effective offensive, even if she wanted to. And I distrust her motives which seem to me to have little connection with our ideas of liberty and to be concerned only with getting everyone else by the ears.

In Chamberlain's view, there were many good reasons for not allying with Stalin who by 1939 had a far worse record of mass murder than Hitler. He believed that a policy of 'encirclement' of Germany, as in 1914, might lead to, rather than prevent, war. British intelligence indicated that Russian forces, after Stalin's purges, were of little military value. It was also likely that a Russian agreement might alienate the very east European countries that Britain was trying to win over. These states had no wish to ally with Russia, particularly if that alliance involved Russian troops occupying their soil. There was the added risk that an Anglo-Russian alliance might drive Spain and Japan into the arms of Hitler. However, by 1939 even those who viewed fascism and communism with equal distaste were more worried by Hitler than Stalin. Chamberlain, under pressure from France, from the press, and from parliament, agreed in late April to open negotiations with Russia. He did so without much conviction and favoured 'association', not a fully-fledged alliance. His main aims were to placate opposition at home and use the possibility of an Anglo-Soviet alliance as a further warning to Hitler.

Soviet policy in 1939 is a subject of great debate. Stalin's own thinking remains a matter of guesswork. On the surface his position was serious. Hitler was a sworn enemy of Bolshevism and Japan was a threat in the east. Stalin, therefore, faced a war on two fronts. However, the fact that Britain and France were committed to stopping Hitler advance eastwards gave him some room for manoeuvre. He could afford to press for favourable terms from Britain and France, and also to seek a deal with Germany. He was in a position to keep his options open and see who would make the best offer.

The Anglo-French-Soviet discussions were complex and slow. The talks finally deadlocked when the Russians asked whether Poland would accept the entry of Russian troops *before* the event of a German attack. The Poles, deeply suspicious of Russian intentions, would not budge on this issue. Chamberlain sympathised with Poland. He did not see why the presence of Russian troops in Poland was necessary or desirable. The Soviet government maintained that this attitude convinced them that Britain and France were not in earnest in their negotiations. But it is equally possible that the Russians made a series of demands that they knew Britain and France could not accept and that Stalin had no wish for an alliance with the West.

e) The Nazi–Soviet Pact

From 1933 the USSR had occasionally made approaches to Germany suggesting the need for better relations. Hitler had rebuffed each of these probes. The idea of a Nazi-Soviet agreement made no sense at all in ideological terms. But in 1939 Hitler realised that a deal with Stalin would strengthen his position, at least in the short term, and hoped that it would frighten Britain and France into backing out of their guarantees to Poland. Throughout the spring and summer Russian and German diplomats had been hard at work, trying to reach accommodation. With his planned attack on Poland less than a week away, Hitler sent a message to Stalin asking if Ribbentrop could visit Moscow to settle political matters. Stalin's response was favourable. Ribbentrop, therefore, flew to Moscow and on 23 August signed the Nazi-Soviet non-aggression pact. Secret clauses of the pact divided Poland and eastern Europe into spheres of German and Russian influence. The pact was a shattering blow to Britain and France.

Much criticism has been levelled at Chamberlain for his failure to secure a Russian alliance. Certainly he had little enthusiasm for it. But such an alliance was probably out of reach of even the most determined Western statesman. Just as Poland was not interested in a Russian alliance, so Russia had no wish for an alliance with the Western powers. The only thing the West had to offer Stalin was the prospect of immediate war, a war in which Russia would do most of the fighting. Hitler, on the other hand, offered peace and territory. From Stalin's point of view the pact seemed to best protect Soviet interests, at least in the short term. He was essentially playing for time. However, by giving the green light to Nazi aggression, he arguably made a serious mistake. While the pact sealed Poland's fate, it also brought nearer a German attack on Russia.

The Nazi-Soviet Pact was undoubtedly a decisive event. When Hitler heard news of its signing he banged the table in delight and shouted, 'I have them!' He realised that Poland could not now be defended and thought that Britain and France would realise the same. The way was thus open for the German attack on Poland, planned to start on 26 August.

f) The Outbreak of War

Hitler was prepared to risk, but still did not expect or want, a war on two fronts. He thought the Western leaders would wriggle out of their commitments to Poland. However, Britain and France made it clear that they had no intention of abandoning Poland. Hitler, surprised by their determination and shaken by Mussolini's announcement that Italy intended to remain neutral, decided to postpone his invasion until 1 September. He now made an extraordinary proposal to Britain. If it allowed Germany a free hand in Danzig and the Corridor, he would agree to guarantee the British Empire. Chamberlain saw this overture more as a divisive ploy than as a serious basis for negotiation and continued to support Poland. There were flurries of desperate last-minute diplomatic activity but the Poles refused to comply with any German demands. On 31 August Mussolini proposed that a conference should meet to try to resolve the crisis. This sounded like a second Munich. But this time the proposal came too late. That same evening Germany claimed that one of its wireless stations near the Polish border had been attacked by Poles. This claim, totally fabricated, was used as the excuse for war. On 1 September German troops invaded Poland.

Mussolini persisted with his conference proposal. While French leaders were reasonably enthusiastic, Britain insisted that a condition for such a conference was withdrawal of German troops from Poland. If Germany did not suspend hostilities Britain 'warned' Germany that it would fight. However, on 2 September Britain had still not declared war or even sent Germany an ultimatum. The reason for this delay was Chamberlain's wish to keep in step with French leaders who were anxious to complete their mobilisation plans before declaring war. But to many British MPs it seemed as though Chamberlain was trying to evade his commitments. On 2 September the Commons made it clear that war must be declared at once. Chamberlain accepted the inevitable. At 9.00 a.m. on 3 September Britain delivered an ultimatum to Germany. Hitler made no reply, and at 11.00 a.m. Britain declared war. France declared war at 5.00 p.m.

EVENTS IN 1939	
March	the end of Czechoslovakia; British and French guarantees to Poland;
May	Pact of Steel between Germany and Italy;
August	Nazi-Soviet Pact;
1 September	Germany invaded Poland;
3 September	Britain and France declared war on Germany.

g) How Guilty was Chamberlain?

Chamberlain may have been overconfident in his dealings with Hitler and may also have failed to recognise his ultimate intentions. But, in fairness to him, many Germans in the 1930s doubted that Hitler meant what he said and historians are still unable to agree about his precise intentions. Chamberlain, in fact, had few illusions about Hitler. He feared his ambition and unpredictability. He was aware, however, that the only alternative to working with him was war. Firmer action pre-1939 would not have prevented war: it would simply have precipitated it sooner. Appeasement, far from being a policy of shameful cowardice, seemed the best policy in the circumstances. The fact that it failed does not mean that it was not worth trying. Indeed, perhaps Chamberlain should be blamed not so much for his policy of appeasement but for his failure to stand by it to the end. Arguably, Britain had no moral obligation or self-evident interest to fight a major war over Poland. Hitler actually had a good case in 1939. Perhaps Chamberlain should have allowed, even encouraged, Hitler to go eastwards against Russia. Arguably the Western powers had little to lose and much to gain from a German-Russian war. But this was not the way that most British and French people saw matters in 1939. Most, distrusting Hitler, thought the time had come to resist German expansion.

ACTIVITY

Consider the following question: ' "A mistaken policy followed by honourable men for honourable ends." Discuss this view of the policy of appeasement as followed during the 1930s.'

Suggested line of response:
▼ Define appeasement.
▼ Was appeasement honourable? What were the alternatives to it?
▼ How was Hitler appeased post-1933?
▼ Was appeasement a mistake?

▼ Working on The Causes of the Second World War

By now you should also have a view as to who, or what, was responsible for the war. To what extent were the following to blame?
▼ The Versailles peacemakers (Reread pages 95–101 to refresh your memory of what they did.)
▼ The League of Nations (Should it have taken strong action against Japan and Italy?)
▼ Mussolini and Japanese militarists (Did they have central roles?)
▼ French inaction (Should France have taken action in 1936?)
▼ Chamberlain (Was appeasement a rational policy?)
▼ Stalin (Should he be blamed for the Nazi-Soviet Pact?)
▼ Hitler (Was the Second World War 'Hitler's War'?)

Consider the arguments for and against each of the above factors and then award each a mark out of ten. (Award a high mark if you think they were seriously to blame.) Which three factors do you think were most to blame for the war? Which was least to blame?

Answering Extended Writing and Essay Questions on The Causes of the Second World War

Consider the following question: ' "Hitler was a rather ordinary German statesman with a rather ordinary mission" '. Do you agree?'

A case can be made that Hitler was an ordinary German statesman who simply wished to redress the (perceived) wrongs of Versailles. Thus rearmament, the remilitarisation of the Rhineland, the

Anschluss, the takeover of the Sudetenland, and the demands for Danzig and the Polish Corridor can be seen as typical German policies. However, there is a counter-argument. Surely few previous German statesemen were prepared to gamble as recklessly as Hitler did? Surely few regarded war as a 'good thing'? Surely few had Hitler's racist aims of winning *lebensraum*? My view – that Hitler was far from 'ordinary' – need not be yours. You are in the good company of A.J.P. Taylor if you agree with the quote. Taylor was one of Britain's greatest historians – even if (or perhaps because) his views were often controversial. The main point is that you display your awareness of the debate and say why you think the evidence convinces you one way or the other.

Answering Source-Based Questions on The Causes of the Second World War

No one has been a more resolute and uncompromising struggler for peace than the Prime Minister. Everyone knows that ... Nevertheless, I am not quite clear why there was so much danger of Great Britain and France being involved in war with Germany at this juncture if in fact they were ready all along to sacrifice Czechoslovakia. The terms which the Prime Minister brought back with him could have easily been agreed, I believe, through the ordinary diplomatic channels at any time during the summer. And I will say this, that I believe the Czechs left to themselves, and told they were going to get no help from the Western powers, would have been able to make better terms than they have got after all the tremendous perturbation. They could hardly have had worse.

All is over. Silent, mournful, abandoned, broken. Czechoslovakia recedes into the darkness.

Source F Winston Churchill writing in *The Times*, 4 October 1938.

We appeared to have won the game when Chamberlain announced his visit to the Obersalzberg [Berchtesgaden] in order to preserve peace ... One could have reached an agreement without difficulty, on the basis of English mediation, about how the Sudetenland was to be split off and transferred to us in a peaceful manner.

However, we were dominated by the determination to have a war of revenge and destruction against Czechoslovakia. Thus we conducted the second phase of discussions with Chamberlain in Bad Godesberg in such a way that, despite our basic agreement, what had been decided was bound to fail. The group who wanted war, namely Ribbentrop and the SS, had nearly succeeded in prompting the Führer to attack. Among numerous similar statements made by the Führer in my presence during the night of 27–28 September was one to the effect that he would now annihilate Czechoslovakia. Ribbentrop and I were the sole witnesses of these words; they were not designed to have an effect on a third party.

Thus, the assumption that the Führer was intending a huge bluff is incorrect. His resentment stemming from 22 May, when the English accused him of pulling back, led him on the path to war. I have not quite managed to establish what influences then finally decided him to issue invitations to the four power meeting in Munich on 28 September and thereby to leave the path of war ...

Two factors were probably decisive: a) His observation that our people regarded the approach to war with a silent obstructiveness and were far from enthusiastic ... and b) Mussolini's appeal at the last moment, i.e. on the morning of the 28th, when the mobilisation was planned for 2 p.m.

Source G an entry from the diary of the German State Secretary in the Foreign Ministry, von Weizsacke, on 9 October 1938.

"MEIN KAMPF"

Source H a cartoon by David Low.

Source I a *Punch* cartoon of 1938.

▼ QUESTIONS ON SOURCES

1. How useful is Source F to historians? **[10 marks]**

2. What light does Source G throw on Hitler's actions? **[10 marks]**

3. Study the cartoons H and I and explain the cartoonist's message in each of them. **[20 marks]**

4. Using all the sources and your own knowledge explain why the Munich settlement continues to arouse controversy amongst historians. **[20 marks]**

Points to note about the questions

Question 1 This source gives us some indication of Churchill's opinion in October 1938. Did his views reflect the views of most British people?

Question 2 Source G, a diary entry from a German well-placed in the foreign office, is a useful source. While some of the views reflected in the source are simply speculations, they are still fascinating.

Question 3 Do the cartoonists support Chamberlain's actions?

Question 4 The sources give different views about Munich. Historians also hold different views. Obviously we will never know what would have happened if Britain and France had gone to war in 1938. That should not stop us speculating!

Further Reading

Books in the Access to History series

On international relations 1919–39, read *War and Peace: International Relations 1914–45* by D. Williamson. For more information on the foreign policy of individual powers, try *Germany: The Third Reich*, by Geoff Layton; and *Britain: Foreign and Imperial Affairs: 1919–39* by Alan Farmer.

General

On international relations 1919–39, start with Chapter 14 of *Years of Change: Europe 1890–1945* by Robert Wolfson and John Laver (Hodder & Stoughton). Try also *The Great Dictators: International Relations 1918–39* by E.G. Rayner in the History at Source series (Hodder & Stoughton).

The *Origins of the Second World War* by A.J.P. Taylor, 1961 (Penguin) is particularly worth reading but keep your critical wits about you. Much of the controversy raised by Taylor has been summarised in *The Origins of the Second World War Reconsidered*, edited by G. Martel, 1986 (Unwin Hyman). *The Origins of the Second World War in Europe* by P.M.H. Bell, 1986 (Longman) is excellent as is *The Illusion of Peace. International Relations, 1918–1933* by S. Marks, 1976 (Macmillan) for the years pre-Hitler. *Versailles and After*, 1995 and *The Origins of the Second World War* by R.Henig, 1985 (both published by Routledge) are nice summaries. *Nazism 1919–1945 vol. 3: Foreign Policy, War and Racial Extermination*, edited by J. Noakes and G. Pridham, 1988 (University of Exeter) has an excellent collection of documents on German foreign policy.

THE SECOND WORLD WAR AND THE HOLOCAUST

In this chapter you will be studying the most important event of the twentieth century – the Second World War – and one of the most horrific events that occurred during the war – the Holocaust (Hitler's attempt to kill all of Europe's Jews). Sections 1, 2, and 5 deal with the events of the war. Section 3 looks briefly at Hitler's New Order in Europe. Section 4 examines the Holocaust. Section 6 looks at why the Allies won. Section 7 examines some of the war's results. It is worth reading all the sections. An awareness of the Holocaust is essential if you are focusing on the war. Similarly you need to have some understanding of the war to appreciate the nature of the Holocaust.

The First World War was essentially a European war which spilled over into other continents and in which non-Europeans, especially the USA and Japan, intervened. The Second World War was different. Its first phase, 1939–41, was indeed European. Most European states were drawn into the struggle (only Spain, Portugal, Sweden, Switzerland, Turkey and Eire remained neutral). However, it was not really a genuine world war until December 1941 when Japan's attack on Pearl Harbor brought the USA into the war. The second phase of the war, 1941–5, ended with Europe in ruins, its economy crippled, and with the armies of the USA and the USSR meeting in the heart of the continent. This chapter aims to explain why the war became a world war and why it ended with Allied victory. It also seeks to examine why the Holocaust occurred and who was to blame.

1 The European War, 1939–41

ISSUE
Why was Germany successful, 1939–41?

a) The Defeat of Poland

Using *blitzkrieg* tactics to considerable effect, the Germans cut through Poland. Polish forces, poorly equipped and badly led, were effectively destroyed within a fortnight. To make matters worse, on 17 September the Russians invaded Poland from the east. Polish resistance collapsed and Germany and Russia divided Poland along

BLITZKRIEG

The German victories in 1939–40 were due in part to *blitzkrieg* or 'lightning war'. *Blitzkrieg* had several phases:

▼ The Luftwaffe, having won supremacy in the air, went on to bomb means of communication, troop concentrations and major cities.

▼ Motorised and light armoured divisions breached the enemy lines and kept pushing forward. Infantry and heavy tanks widened and secured the breach.

SIEGFRIED LINE

Germany's western line of defences.

the 'Ribbentrop–Molotov Line' (see Figure 49). A Polish government-in-exile was set up in London to try to continue the struggle but by the end of September Poland had effectively disappeared. The Germans now transferred the bulk of their army to the west.

France and Britain did little to help Poland. The slowness of French mobilisation and the defensive nature of French strategy prevented what might have been decisive action. In September less than a third of Germany's army was in the west and its **Siegfried Line** defences were not complete. In October Hitler offered peace proposals. Given that war against Germany was certain to be costly in terms of blood and money, there were good reasons for Britain and France to make peace. But few Western politicians were prepared to trust Hitler and sacrifice Poland.

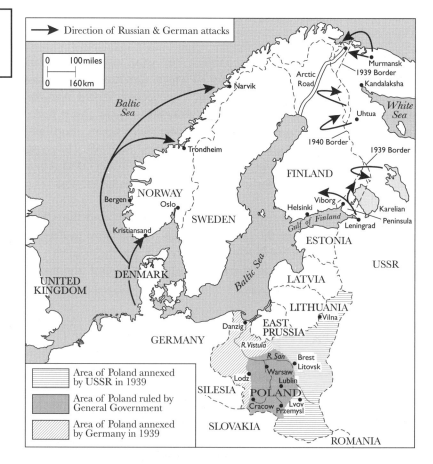

Figure 49 Poland, Finland and Norway, 1939–40.

Table 17 The balance of power in 1939.

	Great Britain	France	USSR	USA	Poland	Germany	Italy
Population (thousands)	47,692	41,600	167,300	129,825	34,662	68,424	43,779
National income ($m)	23,550	10,296	31,410	67,600	3,189	33,347	6,895
Reserves (millions)	0.4	4.6	12.0†	**	1.5	2.2	4.8
Peacetime armies (millions)	0.22	0.8	1.7†	0.19	0.29	0.8	0.8
Aircraft (first line)	2,075	600	5,000†	800	390	4,500†	1,500††
Destroyers	184	28	28	181	4	17	60
Submarines	58	70	150	99	5	56	100

**not available †approximate ††1940

GERMAN READINESS FOR WAR

German rearmament was by no means complete in 1939. Germany had few U-boats and its army was short of motor transport and tanks. In terms of equipment, weapons and numbers, Germany did not have a marked superiority over the combined forces of France and Britain (see Table 17). However, Germany had two key advantages:

▼ its air force (Luftwaffe) was stronger;
▼ senior German officers were willing to experiment with new weapons and new tactics.

FRENCH READINESS FOR WAR

The French army occupied a strong defence system, the Maginot Line. Perhaps the mind-set of its commanders, who failed to appreciate the power of tanks and aircraft, was France's greatest weakness.

b) The Phoney War

The period October 1939–April 1940 is known as the 'phoney war'. All the opposing armies waited behind their defensive lines. No country wished to be the first to launch massive aerial assaults on civilians. Germany did not yet have enough U-boats to pose a serious challenge to Allied shipping and Britain had the best of the naval war. Stalin exploited the situation. In October Estonia, Latvia and Lithuania were forced to accept Soviet garrisons. In November 1939 Russia invaded Finland after the Finns rejected Stalin's demands for territory. The Finns unexpectedly held up the vastly superior Russian forces. Many British and French politicians thought they should help

BRITISH READINESS FOR WAR

The Royal Navy was more than a match for the German surface fleet. The RAF had been strengthened in the late 1930s but the British army was weak.

Finland. An elaborate plan to send 100,000 troops to Finland, via Norway and Sweden, enabling the Allies to cut off Swedish iron ore supplies to Germany, was finally devised. But in March 1940, just as the Allied force was about to move, the Russo-Finnish war ended. Finland ceded strategic areas to Russia. French outrage at Allied inaction forced the resignation of Daladier. He was replaced by Reynaud.

Although the Allies could no longer help Finland, the idea of blocking Swedish iron ore to Germany was not abandoned. In April 1940 the Allies decided to block the winter supply route by laying mines in Norwegian waters. The day after they began mining, Hitler invaded Denmark and Norway. The Danes simply surrendered. Norway tried to resist and accepted the offer of Allied help. But the Allied campaign was a disaster and by the end of April most Allied troops had been evacuated. The Norwegian campaign led to the resignation of Chamberlain. He was replaced by Winston Churchill.

Figure 50 The German conquest of western Europe by July 1940.

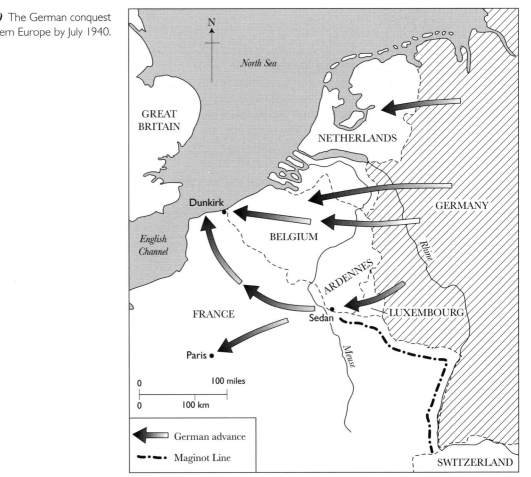

WINSTON CHURCHILL (1874–1965)

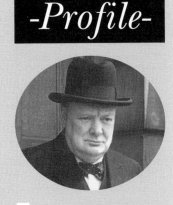

-Profile-

By 1940 Churchill had held most of the important ministerial posts in government. Most of those who knew him, and most historians who have studied him, stress his prodigious energy and his incredibly active mind. From the start, he struck a consistent pose of courage and resolve. Eccentric in dress, speech and gesture, he caught and kept the confidence of the public. Many have stressed the importance of his oratory. Churchill himself was more modest: 'It was the nation and the race dwelling all round the globe that had the lion's heart. I had the luck to be called on to give the roar.' Typical of his oratory was his speech to the Commons on the day he took office (10 May 1940):

> I have nothing to offer but blood, toil, tears and sweat . . . What is our policy? I will say: it is to wage war, by sea, land and air, with all our might and with all the strength that God can give us: to wage war against a monstrous tyranny, never surpassed in the dark, lamentable catalogue of human crime. That is our policy . . . What is our aim? I can answer in one word: Victory – victory at all costs, victory in spite of all terror, victory, however long and hard the road may be; for without victory there is no survival.
>
> *Source A*

While he is often seen as the twentieth-century's greatest Englishman, critics point out that he presided over the demise of Britain as a great world power.

The following two pieces, both written by American playwright Roger Sherwood, a speechwriter for President Roosevelt, give some idea of Churchill's style.

> Churchill always seemed to be at his Command Post on the precarious beach-head and the guns were continually blazing in his conversation; wherever he was, there was the battlefront. Churchill was getting full steam up about ten o'clock in the evening; often after his harassed staff had struggled to bed about 2:00 or 3:00 a.m. they would be routed out. Churchill's consumption of alcohol continued at quite regular intervals through most of his waking hours without visible effect . . . Churchill could talk for an hour or more and hold any audience spellbound. Here was one who certainly knew his stuff, who could recite fact and figure and chapter and verse, and in superb English prose.
>
> *Source B* From R Sherwood *Roosevelt and Hopkins: An Intimate History*, Grosset and Dunlap, Universal Library, 1950.

1874	born in Blenheim Palace, the son of Lord Randolph Churchill (himself a younger son of the Duke of Marlborough) and his American wife, Jenny;
1898	fought in the Sudan;
1899	became a war correspondent in the Boer War. Captured by the Boers and escaped;
1900	became Conservative MP for Oldham;
1904	joined the Liberal Party;
1910 –11	Home Secretary;
1911 –15	First Lord of the Admiralty;
1915	resigned after being blamed for the Gallipoli campaign;
1918 –9	supported British intervention in the Russian Civil War;
1924 –9	Conservative Chancellor of the Exchequer;
1930s	warned of the danger of Hitler's Germany;
1939 –40	First Lord of the Admiralty;
1940 –5	British Prime Minister;
1945 –51	Leader of the Opposition;
1951	returned as Prime Minister;
1955	resigned as Prime Minister;
1965	died.

CONSEQUENCES OF THE FALL OF FRANCE

▼ Germany now controlled most of western and central Europe.

▼ The USA suddenly feared that Britain might fall, handing Germany control of the Atlantic.

▼ The USSR, anxious to consolidate its power, annexed the Baltic States and Bessarabia.

c) How and Why was France Defeated?

On 10 May 1940 German forces invaded Holland and Belgium. Four days later German tanks *(panzers)* broke through the French defences near Sedan, north of the Maginot Line (see Figure 50). Within ten days the *panzers* had reached the Channel, driving a wedge between the Allied armies. Large numbers of British and French troops were cut off. Evacuation seemed the only alternative to annihilation. By early June around 350,000 Allied troops, leaving behind most of their weapons and equipment, had been evacuated from Dunkirk in a motley collection of vessels.

On 10 June the French government fled from Paris and Italy joined the war on Germany's side. Although French forces fought well against the Italians, elsewhere the Germans continued their advance. After anguished debate, the French government decided to surrender. Marshal Petain, at 84, became French leader and on 21 June accepted the German armistice terms. North-west France was put under German military occupation. The remainder of France kept its own government. This was sited at Vichy. It retained control of the French navy and the French colonial empire.

Historians once claimed that French morale had rotted almost to the point of collapse before the German blow fell. Recent research, however, suggests that this was not the case. The 1940 crisis resulted from the speed and intensity of the German attack: it was not caused by long-term political difficulties or divisions in French society. Military defeat quickly turned into political collapse. Reynaud's government failed to provide strong leadership and in the flight from Paris lost all administrative grip. While French generals and politicians blamed all sorts of factors – the Communists, sabotage, the British flight from Dunkirk – for France's defeat, most historians now agree that French failure was primarily a failure of military strategy.

d) Britain Alone

Britain had the support of all the Dominions (except Eire) and its Empire. Even so, its position seemed hopeless. There was little prospect of it defeating Germany. Instead it seemed possible that German forces would invade Britain. In July, Hitler launched another 'peace offensive'. He was ready to guarantee the British Empire in return for Britain accepting German conquests in Europe. Churchill rejected Hitler's proposal.

In July Hitler gave orders for an air offensive on Britain to be followed by a cross-Channel assault 'if we have the impression that the English are smashed'. Already contemplating a war against Russia, he did not have much confidence in Operation Sealion, as the invasion

Should Britain have made peace in the summer of 1940?

of Britain was code-named. However, if the Luftwaffe had destroyed the RAF, a German invasion would probably have been improvised. The Battle of Britain, therefore, was vital to Britain's survival. That battle lasted from July to September 1940. Although the Luftwaffe came close to victory, it failed to destroy the RAF. By remaining as a viable force, the RAF won the Battle of Britain. Any plans Hitler might have had to invade Britain were postponed. The Luftwaffe turned its attention to night bombardment of cities, especially London. Although some 45,000 people died in the '**blitz**' the Germans did not have enough bombers to shatter the British economy or civilian morale. Britain thus survived as the rallying point for others. Nevertheless, Hitler and the Germans had good cause for celebration. By late 1940 the war seemed as good as over.

> ### THE BLITZ
> The name for the German bombing of British towns in 1940–1. It is a shortened form of *blitzkrieg*.

e) The Search for Allies

Churchill was sure that the logic of events would eventually cause America and Russia to become engaged on Britain's side, and that this 'Grand Alliance' would triumph. In 1940–1, however, Stalin showed Britain no sympathy at all. Indeed the Russians were good business partners of Germany, supplying it with essential raw materials. The USA, by contrast, did offer some hope. President Roosevelt, like most Americans, sympathised with Britain. In 1939 he had persuaded Congress to allow the Allies to purchase arms on a 'cash and carry' basis. After the fall of France, Roosevelt was even more prepared to give aid and talked about the USA becoming the 'arsenal of democracy'. Following the Lend-Lease Act (March 1941), enormous quantities of US resources were made available to Britain. Soon the US navy was convoying merchant ships halfway across the Atlantic while US forces, countering possible German moves, occupied Greenland and Iceland. However, while the USA was far from neutral, most Americans still wished to avoid war.

In 1940 Germany did rather better at winning allies than Britain. Hungary and Romania became Nazi partners. In September Germany, Italy and Japan agreed to the Tripartite Pact. Fortunately for Britain, this was a vague expression of friendship rather than a fully-fledged alliance and Japan did not yet seem ready to join the war. Mussolini was more active. Italian forces invaded Egypt from Libya in September 1940 but were soon defeated by a much smaller British force. Britain followed this up by occupying Italian Somaliland and Ethiopia. An Italian invasion of Greece in October 1940 also failed. Hitler now sent General Rommel and the Afrika Korps to Libya to bolster the Italians. He also put increasing pressure on Greece to submit to humiliating terms. Greece refused. In April 1941 the Germans attacked and quickly overran both Yugoslavia and

Greece, driving out an ill-fated British expeditionary force and also capturing Crete. Meanwhile Rommel inflicted a series of defeats on British troops in North Africa.

ACTIVITY

Test your grasp of Section 1 by answering the question: 'Account for Germany's success between September 1939 and June 1941.'

Suggested line of response:
▼ German and Allied readiness for war;
▼ The Polish campaign and *blitzkrieg*;
▼ Allied failure and Nazi success in 1940;
▼ The situation by June 1941.

ISSUE

Why did Hitler declare war on the USSR and the USA?

2 The Grand Alliance

a) Operation Barbarossa

On 22 June 1941 Hitler launched Operation Barbarossa – the invasion of Russia. Stalin, disregarding warnings from Britain and his own intelligence sources, was taken by surprise. His trust in Hitler was a monumental miscalculation. Hitler's decision to attack Russia was rational (by his standards). It had always been his intention to win *lebensraum* at Russia's expense. He also longed to destroy communism. Over the winter of 1940–1 there was a set of acrimonious German-Soviet disputes in eastern Europe. By 1941 Russia was the last serious threat to Hitler. Defeat of Russia, moreover, seemed the surest way to end the war with Britain: once Russia was defeated, Britain must surely make peace. Hitler's advisers anticipated a two-month campaign. The Germans were so confident of success that they did not bother to lay up stores of winter equipment.

SOVIET STRENGTH

The USSR was strong on paper. It had over 5 million men under arms, 20,000 tanks and some 10,000 aircraft. However, many of its best generals had been killed during the purges. The army had performed poorly against Finland.

The sheer scale of the operations – 146 German divisions, 3,600 tanks and 2,700 aircraft – immediately made the Eastern Front the most important theatre of the war. Although Churchill hated communism, he realised the importance of Stalin as an ally. Within weeks Britain and Russia concluded an agreement for mutual assistance. Privately many British military experts predicted an early Russian collapse. This prediction came near to reality as the Red Army was cut to pieces by German armoured forces. By the end of September 1941 German troops had captured Kiev, besieged Leningrad and threatened to take Moscow.

Nevertheless, the Red Army continued to fight, and as Churchill

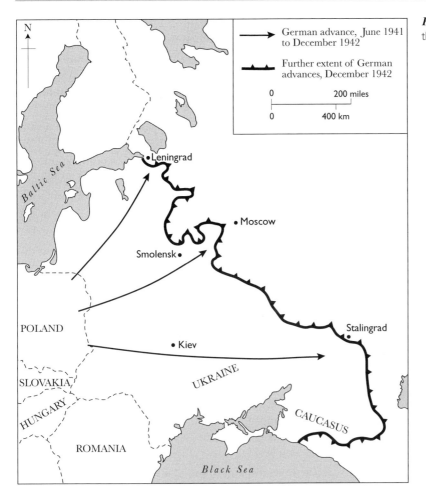

Figure 51 The German attack on the USSR, 1941–2.

said, what mattered was not so much where the Russian front happened to lie, but that the front was still in existence. By December German troops had reached Moscow's suburbs. That was as far as they got. On 6 December General Zhukov launched a Russian counter-attack. The Germans were driven back some 200 miles before their lines held. The campaign in the USSR would continue. It was to prove the decisive struggle in the war and its greatest killing ground.

b) Pearl Harbor

In August 1941 President Roosevelt and Churchill agreed to a joint statement of principles – the 'Atlantic Charter'. This committed the USA to the 'final destruction of the Nazi tyranny' and made it clear that the Allies were fighting for a wide range of 'freedoms', not for territorial goals. Churchill reported to the War Cabinet that Roosevelt had said he would wage war but not declare it. Roosevelt was cer-

THE WAR: 1939–41

1939 September: Poland was defeated; November: the USSR attacked Finland;

1940 April: Germany invaded Denmark and Norway; May: Hitler attacked Belgium, Holland and France; June: Italy joined the war. France surrendered; July–September: the Battle of Britain;

1941 April: Germany invaded Yugoslavia and Greece; June: Operation Barbarossa; December: the USA entered the war.

ACTIVITY

Consider the question: 'Why did Hitler declare war on the USSR and the USA in 1941?' Brainstorm the main points you would make. Note that it is easier to understand Hitler's reasons for attacking the USSR than it is to understand why he declared war on the USA.

ISSUE

How successful was the German New Order?

tainly edging nearer to war. Escort of convoys to the mid-Atlantic brought US ships into conflict with German U-boats.

However, it was events in the Pacific, not the Atlantic, which brought the USA into the war. After 1939 US-Japanese relations had deteriorated steadily as the USA tried to deter Japan from exploiting the situation in Asia. In 1941 the USA imposed an oil embargo on Japan after it took over French Indo-China. Japan had now to decide whether to withdraw from China and Indo-China, as the USA demanded, or seize more territory from which it could obtain the raw materials it needed to go on fighting. An expansionist policy was bound to lead to war with the USA. On 7 December 1941 the Japanese attacked Pearl Harbor in Hawaii, destroying a large part of the US Pacific Fleet. Japan also declared war on Britain.

On 11 December Germany and Italy, honouring the commitments of the Tripartite Pact, declared war on the USA. If Hitler had not declared war, America might have focused on the war against Japan rather than on the war in Europe. Why Hitler acted as he did is something of a mystery. Possibly he underestimated the USA's military potential. More likely he anticipated that war against the USA was only a matter of time. An early declaration of war might allow German U-boats to strike at American shipping before its defences were properly organised. Whatever his motivation, Hitler's declaration of war against the USA was a major error. Churchill rushed across the Atlantic to meet Roosevelt. Both leaders confirmed that overall priority should be given to defeating Germany.

The balance of strength had now shifted against the Axis powers. However, it would take the USA many months to prepare for war. Russia meanwhile was in a bad way. Its losses in 1941 had been staggering (5 million men, 8,000 aircraft, 17,000 tanks) while many of its main industrial areas and much of its best farmland was under German control. Early 1942 saw more success for the Axis.

▼ Britain and America suffered appalling defeats at the hands of the Japanese. By the summer Japanese forces controlled Malaya, the Dutch East Indies, the Philippines, much of Burma, and threatened India.

▼ Russian offensives against Germany in spring 1942 proved disastrous.

▼ In North Africa, Axis forces invaded Egypt.

▼ German U-boats threatened to starve Britain into surrender.

3 The New Order

By 1942 the Third Reich dominated Europe (see Figure 52). Greater Germany comprised all the German-speaking peoples and some annexed areas. Occupied France, Belgium, and large parts of Poland

and the USSR were under direct German military rule. Norway, Denmark and Holland were granted some rights of self-administration but, like Vichy France, Croatia and Slovakia, were very much German-dominated states. Hitler's intention was to create a **New Order** organised on racist principles.

> **NEW ORDER**
> Hitler boasted that he was going to create a New Order across Europe based on National Socialist principles.

a) Economic Exploitation

Economically, Europe was organised for short-term exploitation by Germany. Other countries were supposed to serve the German economy by providing food produce, raw materials and fuel while Germany concentrated on industrial production. Foreign workers were employed in Germany to make up for the Germans serving in the armed forces. (Hitler opposed conscripting German women into the war industries.) By 1944 there were 8 million foreign workers in Germany – 25 per cent of the workforce. While some of these workers came voluntarily from countries which were Germany's

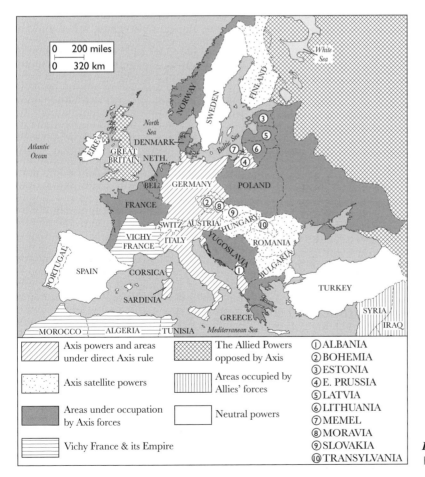

Figure 52 The German Reich, 1942.

allies, most came involuntarily from occupied countries. Foreign workers' treatment was largely determined by their racial origins. Many Russians and Poles worked in labour camps where discipline was harsh and food in short supply.

Yet the German economic war effort was inefficient. From 1939 to 1941 there was very little increase in Germany's military production. Hitler, confident that the war would be won by *blitzkrieg* tactics, rejected a total war effort – severe rationing, limitation of consumer goods and militarisation of the civilian labour force – believing this might damage morale. Nor was there any unified direction of the German economy. Instead, there were several organisations with independent (and competing) power over war production. Not until 1942–3 did Germany really begin to mobilise for total war. The Nazis thus made poor use of potentially enormous economic assets.

b) Collaboration

Why did many
Europeans
collaborate with Nazi
Germany?

Cooperation with Germany took on a variety of forms and varied from country to country and from time to time. At one extreme, there was simple acceptance of the German presence, a live-and-let live philosophy. At the other, there were local fascist groups, eager to take their place in the New Order. Though some fascists (e.g. Quisling in Norway) were placed in important positions, the Germans usually preferred to work with the existing structures of authority. Given that the purpose of the New Order was German predominance, few non-Germans were responsive to the idea. Hitler could and should have used the anti-Russian and anti-communist sentiment of many people in the areas overrun by Germany in 1941–2 to better effect. Many Ukrainians, hating Stalin and collective farms, welcomed the German invaders. However, Hitler's racial fanaticism stood in the way of utilising this potential support. The Slavs were regarded as 'subhumans' and treated accordingly. The early welcome soon turned to hatred. Only later, in 1943–4, did German policy change. By then it was too late.

c) Resistance

Not all Europeans were willing to accept the German presence. Some fled abroad and created forces such as the Free French, led by General de Gaulle. Others, despite the threat of brutal punishment, joined resistance groups within their country. In the east the barbarity of the Axis forces stimulated immediate resistance. Resistance in the west took longer to develop. The fact that the resistance movements were divided into left (generally pro-communist) and right (more nationalistic) was a major problem. While resistance activity, particularly that of Tito who ultimately led some 250,000 partisans in Yugoslavia, tied down large numbers of enemy troops, in general it had only limited success. Open risings against the Germans (for example in Warsaw in 1943 and 1944) proved to be disastrous.

4 The Holocaust

By late 1941 Hitler was committed to a plan to murder all of Europe's Jews. This plan is usually referred to as the **Final Solution** or the Holocaust. While the Holocaust was possibly not the worst crime against humanity of the twentieth century (Stalin and Mao Zedong probably killed more people in the name of economic determinism than Hitler killed in the name of racial determinism), it was a terrible lapse into barbarism. There are still some who deny that it happened, claiming that it was a myth created by Jews and communists to damn the Nazis. The 'deniers' case collapses, however, because there is overwhelming evidence, from survivors and from perpetrators, that the Holocaust did occur.

a) What were Hitler's Intentions in 1939–41?

i) The Madagascar Plan
In July 1940 the Germans began to promote the notion of sending German and western European Jews to Madagascar, a large island off the east coast of Africa. There was apparent enthusiasm for the Madagascar plan at every level, from Hitler downwards. The plan was far from humane. The Nazis anticipated that many Jews would die on the journey or as a result of the inhospitable climate when they arrived. The continuation of the war with Britain, however, ensured that the plan was never put into effect.

ii) The Situation in Poland
The German conquest of Poland was to have dire consequences for Poles in general and for Polish Jews in particular. Hitler made his brutal intentions clear from the start. In 1939 a special task force – or Einsatzgruppen – was set up, comprising men from police and SS units. Its role was to combat 'all anti-German elements' and to 'render harmless' the leadership class in Poland. The Einsatzgruppen executed thousands of Polish doctors, teachers, lawyers and landowners. By defeating Poland, Germany won territory containing over 17 million Poles, 2 million Jews and 675,000 Germans. Roughly half this area was incorporated directly into the Reich. The rest became known as the General Government.

ISSUE
Who was to blame for the Holocaust?

THE FINAL SOLUTION
A term the Nazis used to describe whichever Jewish policy was in vogue. There were thus several 'final solutions', not all of which intended to annihilate the Jews, before the 'Final Solution'.

Himmler's first priority was settling some 200,000 ethnic Germans from the USSR, the Baltic States and the General Government in the incorporated territories. To make room for the Germans, Himmler set about deporting Poles and Jews to the General Government. In the General Government, where Governor Hans Frank shared power with the SS, German rule was based on terror. Polish Jews had to wear the Star of David on pain of death. There was large-scale expropriation of Jewish property and many Jews were sent to labour camps. Himmler hoped to create a reservation for Jews within the General Government and over the winter of 1939–40 thousands were deposited in the Lublin area – the furthest corner of the Reich. However, transportation problems (arising from the build-up for Operation Barbarossa) resulted in the Lublin plan being postponed.

iii) The Polish Ghettos

The concentration and isolation of Jews in Polish cities became part of Nazi policy in 1939. Intentionalist historians think the 'ghettoisation' policy was a conscious first step for annihilation. Functionalist historians, by contrast, while accepting that ghettoisation eventually did help the implementation of the Holocaust, believe that the Nazi leadership had not really thought through its policies. It seems almost certain that there was no master ghettoisation plan in September 1939 or for many months thereafter. Historian Christopher Browning, convinced that ghettoisation was not designed to decimate the Jews, has shown that it was carried out at different times in different ways for different reasons on the initiative of different local authorities. The first 'sealed' ghetto was established in Lodz in April 1940. The Warsaw ghetto was not finally 'sealed' until November 1940. It soon housed about 500,000 Jews. This resulted in six people sharing an average room. In Warsaw, the food rations for Jews fell below an average of 300 calories a day (compared with 2,310 for Germans). Fuel was also in short supply. In consequence, the health of most Jews steadily deteriorated. Some 500–600,000 Jews probably died in the ghettos and Polish labour camps in 1939–41.

iv) The Situation by June 1941

Hitler had shown no mercy to the Polish elite or to handicapped Germans. Given that he regarded the Jews as far more dangerous, he was unlikely to find it hard to order the Holocaust. However, Nazi policy does not yet seem to have been set on genocide. The forced emigration of Jews, whether to the General Government or to Madagascar, remained the 'final solution' until 1941. Hitler's speeches and actions give no indication of any genocide plans in 1939–40. Himmler in 1940 regarded extermination as 'impossible'. If he was not thinking of genocide, it is unlikely that anyone else was.

Euthanasia

The euthanasia programme was a euphemism to camouflage the killing of mentally and physically handicapped people. The aim was partly financial: it would help conserve medical resources. But Hitler's desire to create a pure race was probably more important than economic considerations.

Concerned about negative world and German opinion, Hitler refused to introduce a euthanasia law. However, he did sign a document in 1939 empowering certain doctors to grant 'a mercy death' to those suffering from 'incurable' illnesses. A central office was established in Berlin at Tiergarten Strasse No. 4 to oversee the euthanasia programme: it thus became known as Operation T-4 or simply as T-4. All institutions holding mental patients had to provide specific information about their patients. On the basis of this information, three 'experts' decided who should die. Those selected for death were transferred to wards in six special hospitals. Killings got under way in the autumn of 1939. At first most victims died by means of a drug overdose. But T-4 doctors soon decided that carbon monoxide gassing was more efficient. The first gassing took place in 1940. Most of the T-4 staff, managers, doctors and nurses, were loyal Nazis: they seem to have felt no moral qualms about what was going on. While great efforts were made to maintain secrecy, the deaths of so many people aroused suspicion. In 1941 a number of church leaders denounced the killings. Fearful of alienating public opinion, Hitler ordered a stop to the gassings. By then over 70,000 people had been killed. Hitler's stop order, in fact, had little effect. Adult euthanasia resumed but out of public view.

CHILDREN'S EUTHANASIA

1939 a small team of doctors and bureaucrats worked out the methods of secretly implementing child euthanasia. The planners set up a fictitious organisation, the 'Reich Committee', to camouflage their activities. In August 1939 a decree ordered midwives and doctors to report to the Reich Committee all infants born with severe medical conditions. The impression was given that this information would be used for medical research: it was used instead to determine who should die. Those babies selected to die were transferred to special clinics where they were given drug overdoses or starved to death.

b) Operation Barbarossa

In June 1941 German forces attacked the USSR. Hitler was now set on destroying 'Judeo-Bolshevism'. In March 1941 he had issued a directive to his Army High Command insisting that 'the Bolshevik/Jewish intelligentsia' must be 'eliminated'. Germany's army leaders accepted Hitler's call for unprecedented brutality. Most shared Hitler's hatred of Bolshevism and Judaism (which they saw as one and the same) and his belief that the enemy had to be beaten, whatever the cost.

Implementation of most of the initial dirty work was left to four Einsatzgruppen, each of about 1,000 men. Although the officers had been briefed by Heydrich in June, the precise content of their orders is a matter of controversy. Einsatzgruppen actions in June/July suggest that there was no pre-invasion genocide order. Generally they rounded up and shot communist leaders and some, but by no means all, Jewish men. Relatively few Jewish women and children were killed. Historian Phillippe Burrin has pointed out that a few thousand policemen, untrained in mass killing techniques, were unlikely to be thought sufficient to kill 5 million Russian Jews.

c) The Final Solution: The Decision

Browning thinks that an elated Hitler, confident that victory over the USSR was at hand, ordered the mass killing of Soviet Jews in mid-July 1941 and at the same time asked Himmler to come up with plans to kill all of Europe's Jews. (Once he resolved to kill all Russian Jews it was but a small step to decide to kill all Jews.) On 31 July Goering, who was still officially responsible for the Jewish question, charged Heydrich with 'making all necessary preparations . . . for bringing about a complete solution of the Jewish question within the German sphere of influence in Europe'. Browning thinks this is evidence that a genocide order had been given. According to Browning, Hitler then vacillated for several weeks, his mood changing as the fortunes of war in the USSR changed. Between mid-September and mid-October the fighting swung in Germany's favour. At some stage in this period Browning thinks Hitler gave the green light for the killing of all European Jews.

Other historians (e.g. Burrin and Kershaw) believe that Hitler finally decided on total genocide more out of a sense of desperation than of elation. By September, Operation Barbarossa was not going to plan. According to Burrin, Hitler decided, in late September or early October, that the Jews should pay for the spilling of so much German blood. His decision, claims Burrin, 'arose from a murderous rage increasingly exacerbated by the ordeal of the failure of his campaign in Russia'. Given the scarcity of documentation, debate about the factors which led to the decision is likely to continue. However, there is little doubt that the decision was Hitler's. Himmler was not acting on his own initiative, although it is conceivable that Hitler authorised him to produce a solution of the Jewish question without enquiring too closely into what would be involved.

d) The Killing in the USSR

From mid-August the killing of Soviet Jews was on a different scale to what it had been before. Jewish women and children were now routinely massacred. In July most of the victims were shot individually by firing squad. By August hundreds of victims at a time were forced to lie in or kneel at the edge of a trench before being shot in the back of the head. Karl Jager, head of a unit of Einsatzgruppen A, kept extensive execution records. In July 1941, his unit killed 4,293 Jews of whom only 135 were women. In September 1941, by contrast, his unit killed 56,459 Jews – 15,104 men, 26,243 women and 15,112 children. Perhaps the most notorious killing took place at Babi Yar on the outskirts of Kiev: over a three day period, 33,771 Jews were shot. Not only the Einsatzgruppen carried out the killings. Auxiliary forces, recruited from people of the Baltic States and the Ukraine, were also willing executioners. So were ordinary German soldiers. The savage fighting in the USSR seems to have had a brutalising effect on German troops: few had serious misgivings about killing Jews. The killing continued through 1942–3. Those Jews who were given a stay of execution for labour purposes did not last long. By 1943 over 2 million Russian Jews had probably been murdered.

Figure 53 The main concentration and extermination camps.

e) The Killing of Non-Russian Jews

In August 1941, Himmler commissioned his SS technical advisers to test different ways of killing and recommend those which were more efficient and more 'humane'. Not surprisingly they soon hit upon the idea of gas: the T-4 programme had ensured that the executioners were trained, the technology proved, and the procedures worked

THE WANNSEE CONFERENCE

Coordination of various agencies, both within Germany and in the occupied countries, was required if thousands of Jews were to be transported to the killing centres in Poland. Accordingly, a meeting of top civil servants was held at Wannsee in January 1942 to discuss logistical and other matters. The conference, chaired by Heydrich, formulated common procedures whereby all of Europe's Jews were to be 'resettled' in the east. The conference minutes, prepared by Eichmann, did not spell out extermination. At his trial in 1960, Eichmann was franker about the conference than he was in the minutes: 'the gentlemen . . . talked about the matter without mincing their words . . . The talk was of killing, elimination and liquidation'. The Wannsee Conference was not the starting point of the Holocaust: that was already underway. It was, however, the moment when it was endorsed by a broad segment of the German government.

out. Jews of the Lodz ghetto were among the first to be gassed. Over the winter of 1941–2 an SS team converted an old mansion at Chelmno into a barracks and gas chamber. Chelmno began operations on a large scale in January 1942. It was a pure killing centre: it had no labour camp. By the time it was destroyed in March 1943, some 140,000 Jews (and a few thousand Gypsies, Poles and Russians) had died there. Meanwhile Himmler selected Odilo Globocnik to oversee the killing of Polish Jews. Dozens of SS and ex-T-4 men were assigned to Globocnik in the autumn of 1941. Their task was to construct and run a number of death camps in the Lublin region.

The mass gassing of the Jews in the General Government is usually known as Operation Reinhard, after Reinhard Heydrich who was assassinated by Czech partisans in May 1942. Belzec, the first functional Operation Reinhard camp, opened in March 1942, Sobibor in May, and Treblinka, a much larger camp, in July. The basic layout and procedures were the same at all three camps. Each camp was divided into two parts. Camp 1 contained barracks for undressing. Camp 2 contained the gas chambers. A path known as the 'tube', bordered by a wire fence, linked the two camps (see Figure 54).

Jewish leaders had the job of finding people for 'resettlement' (Warsaw had to supply 10,000 a day from July 1942). The transportation experience was horrific. People were crammed into freight cars without food, water or toilets. Once the transports arrived at Belzec, Sobibor or Treblinka, the camp authorities aimed to kill all but a few of the deportees within two hours. Males and females were separated and herded into barracks to undress. Then the victims were forced to run down the 'tube' to the building signed 'Baths and Inhalation Rooms'. The victims were pushed into chambers which could hold hundreds of people. A diesel engine pumped in carbon monoxide gas. After 30 minutes, the engine was switched off and the Jewish 'death brigade' (or Sonderkomando) had the job of disposing of the bodies. Although the Operation Reinhard camps were simply death camps, a several hundred-strong Jewish workforce was soon being employed in the various steps of the killing process. Most work-Jews, poorly fed and ill-treated, found that their reprieve from death seldom exceeded a few months.

By 1942–3 Himmler's goal of exterminating all the Polish Jews had been largely achieved. By November 1943 all the Operation Reinhard camps had been dismantled. Some 500,000 died at Belzec, 150–200,000 at Sobibor, and 900–1,200,000 at Treblinka. Himmler thanked Globocnik 'for the great and unique service which you have performed for the whole German people by carrying out Operation Reinhard'.

The transportation of Jews to the death camps added extra pressure to Germany's railway system. More importantly, the killing

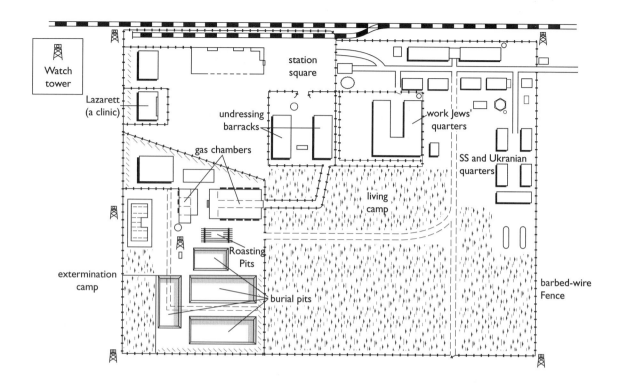

Figure 54 A plan of Treblinka concentration camp.

reduced Germany's potential labour pool at a time when it was suffering from a desperate shortage of labour. As a result of protests by the army, industry and civilian authorities, there were phases during which the extermination programme was slowed to permit the exploitation of Jewish labour. In 1941–2 two camps, Majdanek and Auschwitz, began to serve a dual purpose. On the one hand they were extermination centres: on the other they were labour camps in which some Jews received a temporary stay of execution.

f) Auschwitz

By 1941 Auschwitz had expanded into a vast labour camp, mainly for the utilisation of Soviet prisoners. Camp commandant Rudolf Hoess, told by Himmler that Auschwitz was to be a principal centre for killing Jews, had no moral qualms. A fanatical Nazi, he was determined to carry out his orders to the best of his ability and hit upon the idea of using Zyklon B as the gassing agent. First tested on Soviet prisoners, it killed in half the time required by carbon monoxide.

Figure 55 The Jewish dead.

Hoess shifted the gassing to a new, more secluded camp at Birkenau. It began operations in 1942. With good railway connections, Auschwitz-Birkenau quickly grew into the largest of the Nazi death camps.

The process of killing was slick and streamlined. As the trains arrived, an SS doctor decided who was fit and unfit. The unfit, the old, sick and young children, were condemned to immediate death in the gas chambers. The fit (usually about a third of each transport) were taken to one of Auschwitz's many labour camps (most of the inmates of which were non-Jews). As in camps across German-occupied Europe, inmates were stripped of their individuality, poorly fed and brutally treated. Few survived for more than a few months. In total, over one million Jews from all over Europe probably died at Auschwitz.

g) The Situation in 1945

By 1944–5 German concentration camps, hitherto used mainly for non-Jewish prisoners, were used to house Jews evacuated from the east. (Tens of thousands lost their lives on the marches, perishing from cold, hunger, disease and periodic shootings.) Allied soldiers who liberated these camps were appalled at what they found.

RESEARCH ACTIVITY

Divide into groups. Each group should research the extent to which each of the folllowing helped contribute to the Holocaust.

▼ European anti-Semitism;
▼ West European collaborationists;
▼ East European 'willing executioners';
▼ Neutral responsibility;
▼ Papal responsibility;
▼ Allied responsibility;
▼ Jewish passivity.

Each group should then report back to the rest of the class.

---

h) Hitler's Responsibility

Immediately after 1945 most historians believed, as some intentionalist historians still believe, that it was Hitler's intention all along to exterminate European Jewry. He simply sought the right moment to act. Functionalist historians, however, have a different view. They claim that improvisation was usually the name of the game in the 'authoritarian anarchy' that was the Third Reich. Behind the Nazi propaganda façade, functionalists think that Hitler was not really in control. They claim that Nazi Jewish policies evolved as a result of pressures from radical anti-Semites at local level or from initiatives taken by other Nazi leaders. They see the Holocaust resulting from the chaotic situation in eastern Europe after 1939, not from Hitler pursuing long-term ideological aims.

HOW MANY DIED?

The exact number of Jews who died in the Holocaust will never be known. Most historians, accepting the findings of the Nuremberg War Crimes Tribunal, think that over 5 million died. Most of the killing was in 1942. In mid-March 1942 some 75 per cent of all the eventual victims of the Holocaust were still alive: some 25 per cent had already died. By mid-March 1943, 75 per cent of all the eventual victims were dead.

OTHER DEATHS

Millions of non-Jewish Poles and Russian civilians died as a result of German occupation, reprisal and deportation policies. Of 5.7 million Soviet prisoners some 3.3 million died in German custody; 25,000 Gypsies and 6,000 Jehovah's Witnesses were also killed by the Nazis.

THE HOLOCAUST

1939 Hitler authorised the euthanasia programme;
1940 June–July: Madagascar Plan;
1941 June–July: Einsatzgruppen started killing communists and Jews in the USSR;
1942 January: Wannsee Conference; March–July: Belzec, Sobibor and Treblinka began operations; May: Start of mass gassings at Auschwitz;
1943 October: end of Operation Reinhard;
1945 January: Soviet troops liberated Auschwitz.

Most historians position themselves at some point between the intentionalist and functionalist poles. Few now think that Hitler envisaged and planned the Holocaust from 1933 onwards. However, most agree that his fervent anti-Semitism played a central role in the evolution of Nazi policy. While not always personally concerned with the detailed moves to achieve a 'solution of the Jewish question', he gave signals that established priorities and goals. Hitler's actions pre-1941 do not indicate that he was planning genocide. Nevertheless, given his hatred of Jews, the potential for a Holocaust was always present. Once Germany was at war with the USSR, it made sense (by Hitler's standards) to kill all Russian, and then all Europe's, Jews. No order signed by Hitler containing an explicit command to exterminate the Jews has ever come to light. It is unlikely to do so. Incredible though it may seem, the order to kill millions of people was probably little more than a nod from Hitler to Himmler.

i) Himmler and the SS

While Hitler was the ideological and political author of the Holocaust, it was translated into a concrete strategy by Himmler, a fanatical racist and the ultimate bureaucrat. As a result of the SS's powerful position in Poland and Russia, he was able to take almost complete control of anti-Jewish initiatives. It could be that the SS has become Germany's 'whipping boy'. In truth, relatively few SS men were directly involved in the Holocaust. Nor was the SS the only organisation responsible for the killings. Nevertheless, it played a crucial role and was a perfect instrument for mass murder.

j) The German Army and Police

The Army High Command accepted the need for harsh measures against Jews in Russia. Both the fear and reality of partisans increased the army's readiness to cooperate with the SS. German officers and men believed that Jews were behind the partisan activity and were happy to shoot Jews in retaliation. Police battalions also played a crucial role. Their task was to scour occupied Russian territory, shooting every Jew they could find. Christopher Browning and Daniel Goldhagen have focused attention on the members of Reserve Police Battalion 101. The men were a good cross-section of German society. Few were fanatical Nazis. Some were devout Christians. Thus they were not a promising group from which to recruit mass murderers. Yet this is what most became – killing women and children not in a depersonalised way but at very close quarters. Most killed without pity, sometimes tormenting and torturing their victims in the process. They were not forced to act in this way. Refusal to take part in the slaughter did not result in punishment. Most of the men actually seem to have been proud of their actions. Goldhagen thinks that because the men of Police Battalion 101 were so typical of German society, the 'inescapable truth' is that most of their fellow Germans would also have served as 'Hitler's willing executioners'.

k) Were the Germans 'Willing Executioners'?

i) The Case for the Germans

▼ Hitler tried to preserve the secrecy of the Holocaust presumably because he was not sure that he could rely on popular support.

▼ The killing, involving small numbers of men, occurred out of sight of most Germans.

▼ Those directly involved in the killing claimed they had little choice but to obey orders.

▼ The war produced a blunting of moral feeling among Germans, as it did with Britons and Americans, few of whom felt any qualms about bombing German cities.

ii) The Case Against the Germans

▼ Very few Germans were critical of anti-Semitic action at any stage between 1933 and 45.

▼ Knowledge about the mass shootings in the USSR was fairly widespread. Germans who took part in the killings often told their families.

▼ Goldhagen claims that 500,000 Germans may have been directly implicated in the Holocaust and that many Germans approved of it.

l) Conclusion

Although the Holocaust was an enterprise to which countless people throughout Europe contributed, it was essentially a German enterprise. The best way for the Germans to escape responsibility after 1945 was to lay all the blame at the door of Hitler. He was a convenient scapegoat simply because he was the main guilty individual. German anti-Semitism may have been a necessary condition for the Holocaust but it was not a sufficient one. It was Hitler who made the difference. He was largely responsible – and would wish to be remembered – for what happened. What to most people now seems totally irrational and evil seemed to Hitler logical and good. At the end of his life he claimed that the extermination of the Jews was his legacy to the world.

> **Q**
>
> If Hitler had died in the summer of 1941, would the Holocaust have taken place?

5 Allied Victory

a) The Turn of the Tide

i) The Battle of the Atlantic

The war at sea was crucial. Success for the U-boats would have meant the starvation and surrender of Britain. Thanks to the application of radar technology, code-breaking, and the use of long-range aircraft and aircraft carriers, from May 1943 Allied shipping losses were greatly reduced while U-boat losses were severe. Henceforward the Atlantic became a relatively safe seaway. This meant that a huge American build-up of men and supplies in Britain could proceed largely unhindered.

ii) North Africa

In October–November 1942 General Montgomery defeated Rommel at the battle of El Alamein in Egypt. Rommel was now forced to retreat across Libya and Axis hopes of capturing the Suez Canal ended. In November 1942 an Anglo-American force, under the command of US General Eisenhower, landed in French Morocco. Vichy French resistance to the invasion soon crumbled. By May 1943 Axis forces were cornered around Tunis and some 250,000 prisoners were taken. The fighting in North Africa was over.

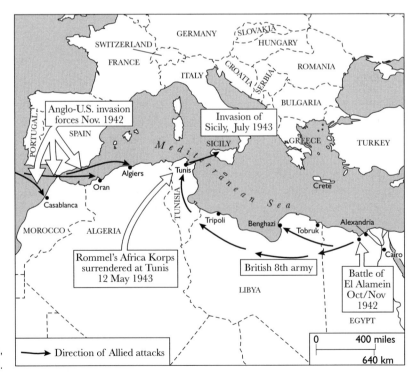

Figure 56 The Mediterranean, 1942–3.

iii) Russia

In the summer of 1942 German forces pushed deep into southern Russia. By September 1942 they had reached Stalingrad. Capture of the town could lead to German control of the Caucasian oil fields, crippling the Soviet capacity to wage war. The battle for Stalingrad raged for five terrible months. In November General Zhukov encircled the Germans in a large pincer movement, tightening the ring as winter set in. In February 1943 the 91,000 surviving Germans surrendered. Stalingrad is often seen as the decisive battle of the war. This can be questioned. The Germans managed to stabilise their lines and Russian losses had been heavy. (They lost more men at Stalingrad than the USA lost in the entire war.) The results of the battle were as much psychological as physical: the Russians had proved to themselves they could defeat the Germans. Stalingrad was followed by other Soviet victories. The Russian victory at Kursk in July 1943, the largest tank battle of the war, was arguably more decisive than Stalingrad. After Kursk German forces in Russia began a slow retreat. In January 1944 the Russians finally lifted the siege of Leningrad. By March 1944 they had reoccupied the whole of the Ukraine.

iv) Anglo-American Strategy: 1943

Stalin continued to press the Allies to open up a Second Front to divert German forces from the east. Roosevelt supported the idea of an immediate attack on France, believing the Allies should not waste time and effort on subsidiary theatres of war. But Churchill, fearing huge casualties, resisted the Second Front pressure. He favoured military action in the Mediterranean. Given that so many Allied troops were already in North Africa, the logical next step was an attack on Sicily and then Italy. In January 1943 Roosevelt and Churchill met at Casablanca. Churchill persuaded Roosevelt to agree to an Allied landing in Sicily. The two leaders also agreed that the Axis powers must unconditionally surrender. Some historians criticise this decision, arguing that it led to the Japanese and Germans fighting desperately to the last. But in reality unconditional surrender probably made little difference, given that German and Japanese leaders were determined to fight to the end.

v) Italy

In July 1943 Allied forces occupied Sicily. The Fascist Grand Council now deposed and arrested Mussolini and the new Italian government began secret negotiations for an armistice. It now made sense, even to those US military chiefs who wanted an immediate attack on France, to invade the Italian mainland. The Allied invasion began in September 1943. The Italian government immediately announced that it had changed sides. The Germans rushed forces into Italy, rescued and restored Mussolini but henceforward treated the country as occupied territory. The Allied advance up the Italian peninsula developed into a long slogging match as the Germans fell back from one defensive position to the next. But the Allies did push northwards (entering Rome in June 1944) forcing the Germans to divert men and resources from the Eastern Front.

vi) The Bombing of Germany

In 1943 Allied air raids began to inflict damage on German cities. The US adopted a policy of daylight raids aimed at precise targets. This led to high casualties among the air crews. Britain bombed German cities by night, sometimes wreaking enormous havoc. By 1945 Germany had received over 300 tons of explosive for every ton dropped on Britain. However, Britain's massive effort in building up a huge Bomber Command fleet was probably not cost-effective. Although attacks on some industrial targets, such as oil refineries, did take their toll, Germany's economy was not seriously crippled until the last months of the war. Even though over half a million Germans died from bombing, civilian morale did not crack.

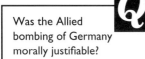

Was the Allied bombing of Germany morally justifiable?

b) The Grand Alliance

The cooperation of Britain, the USA and the USSR was amazing if only because their leaders had relatively little in common.
▼ Roosevelt, wedded to democracy and capitalism, disliked communism and imperialism.
▼ Stalin hated capitalism, liberal democracy and imperialism.
▼ Churchill was a staunch imperialist and anti-communist.

However, the leaders were prepared to sink their differences to the collective goal of defeating Hitler. The personal friendship between Churchill and Roosevelt created the idea of a 'special relationship' between Britain and the USA. Their correspondence and frequent meetings illustrate a form of cooperation rarely seen among allies. The two men and their staffs worked out a common strategy, which was put into effect by the Combined Chiefs of Staff. However, Britain and the USA did not have identical interests. A great deal of friction arose over the fact that US policy was geared to promoting British decolonisation. By 1944 Roosevelt tended to dominate the alliance and did not always act in ways which Churchill perceived to be in the best interests of both powers.

Anglo-American relations, albeit sometimes strained, were always far friendlier than Anglo-Soviet relations. Churchill had little trust in Stalin and no strategic cooperation of any depth or closeness was

THE TEHERAN CONFERENCE

The Teheran Conference, held in November 1943, was the first attended by Roosevelt, Churchill and Stalin. For Churchill it was something of a disaster. Roosevelt dealt directly with Stalin, and it was clear that British influence was fading. The main outcome of the Conference was that Churchill and Roosevelt agreed to invade France in May 1944. (Churchill would have preferred an invasion of the Balkans, thereby preventing the Red Army taking all of eastern Europe.)

achieved. A major problem was Russia's post-war borders. While Churchill was prepared (grudgingly) to acknowledge Russia's position in the Baltic States, Poland was a real sticking point. In 1943 the USSR proposed that the eastern frontier of Poland should be the same as that agreed between Germany and the USSR in 1939. Poland

Figure 57 The 'Big Three' at Teheran: Stalin, Roosevelt and Churchill.

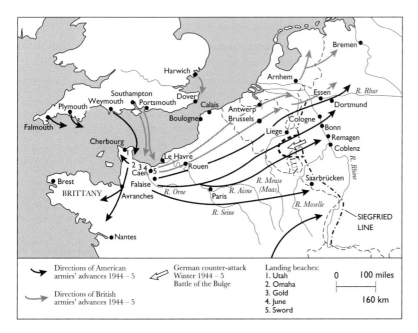

Figure 58 The Second Front. 1944–5.

would be compensated for its losses in the east by gaining territory at Germany's expense in the west. The anti-communist Polish government in exile in London opposed giving away any Polish territory and its relations with the USSR rapidly deteriorated. The discovery, by the Germans in April 1943, of a mass grave of 10,000 Polish officers in Katyn forest made matters worse. These officers, the Germans (correctly) declared, had been murdered by Russians in 1940. The Russians announced (wrongly) that the Germans were responsible for the atrocity. The London Poles proposed that the International Red Cross should investigate the matter. The USSR responded by breaking diplomatic relations with the London Poles. Aware that the German revelations were probably true, Churchill realised that Hitler hoped to use the Katyn discovery to drive a wedge between the Allies. Britain, therefore, largely ignored the Katyn massacre. Morality took second place to expediency.

c) Operation Overlord

Massive preparations for 'Operation Overlord', the Allied attack on France, continued through 1943–4. By the summer of 1944, 10,000 planes, 80 warships and 4,000 other craft had been assembled and there were over 500,000 US servicemen in Britain. The Germans knew that an attack was coming but did not know where or when. Eisenhower, the Allied Supreme Commander, did all he could to keep them guessing. On 6 June 1944 – D Day – Anglo-American forces landed on the Normandy beaches and established a bridgehead. Within three weeks over 1 million men had been landed. Allied air superiority played a crucial role in Germany's failure to repel the invasion. After weeks of hard fighting, German resistance, first in Normandy and then throughout France, collapsed. Paris was liberated on 25 August. In mid-September Allied troops advanced into Belgium and Holland. As the Allies prepared for the final assault a major difference of opinion arose between Eisenhower and the British commander Montgomery. Montgomery advocated a single 'powerful and full-blooded thrust' aimed at the Ruhr, Germany's main industrial area. Eisenhower, however, opted for a broad front strategy. A British attempt to leap the Rhine in Holland ended in failure at Arnhem. By the autumn the Allied advance ground to a halt as a result of supply problems and German defences.

d) The Situation by 1944–5

By 1944 Germany was facing catastrophic defeat. In July 1944 some high-ranking German officers made an attempt on Hitler's life by means of a time-bomb concealed in a briefcase. The bomb exploded but Hitler escaped. His only hope now lay in Germany's batch of new weapons, including flying-bombs (V-1s) and rockets (V-2s). They killed thousands of Londoners but did not seriously damage the Allied war effort. Rockets apart, by 1944–5 Allied aircraft enjoyed almost complete control of the air and Germany was bombed unmercifully. In December 1944 Hitler launched a surprise attack against the Americans in the Ardennes region. After some initial success, the German attack soon stalled. Meanwhile, the Russians continued their inexorable advance in the east. In August 1944 Romania surrendered, followed by Finland and Bulgaria. Hungary surrendered in January 1945 and Poland was cleared of German troops by February 1945. By 1945 the Russians had five soldiers, six tanks and 17 aircraft to every one German.

e) Allied diplomacy, 1944–5

Poland remained a major area of British concern. The London Poles were still unwilling to work with either the Russians or the Russian-backed Polish 'Committee of National Liberation' – the so-called Lublin Poles. Events in Warsaw in August–September 1944 aggravated the situation. Expecting Russian aid, Poles in the capital rose up against the occupying Germans. The Russians gave no help and the rising was brutally crushed.

Churchill was increasingly worried about Russian aims and apparent US aimlessness with regard to eastern Europe. He tried to salvage the situation by forging an old-fashioned balance of power agreement with Stalin in October 1944. Essentially, Churchill recognised Soviet dominance in eastern Europe while Stalin recognised British dominance in Greece. Stalin's good faith was soon demonstrated. He made no effort to help local communists in Greece and a pro-Western government, backed by British troops, was set up. Even so Churchill still feared the ambitions of the Soviet leader as more and more of eastern Europe was occupied by the Red Army. Churchill's fear intensified his desire to see a resurrected France that could stand with Britain against the USSR – essential if US troops withdrew from Europe at the end of the war.

In February 1945 Churchill, Roosevelt and Stalin met at Yalta. Agreement on several matters, such as the division of Germany into three occupation zones, had been reached before the meeting. The 'Big Three' were also able to resolve a number of issues. Churchill won acceptance for the proposal that a military zone for France should be carved out of the area proposed for Britain. There was agreement that there should be free elections in the countries of liberated Europe. Stalin agreed to join both the United Nations and

THE WAR: 1942–5

1942 June: German summer offensive in southern USSR commenced; October: British victory at El Alamein; November: Allies landed and occupied French North Africa;

1943 January: Casablanca conference; February: Germans surrendered at Stalingrad; May: Axis forces surrendered at Tunis; July: Russian victory at Kursk; Allies invaded Sicily; September: Allies invaded Italy: Italian surrender: German occupation of Italy; November: Teheran Conference;

1944 June: D-Day landings; August: Paris liberated;

1945 February: Yalta Conference; March: Allied forces crossed the Rhine; April: Deaths of Roosevelt, Mussolini and Hitler; May: Germany surrendered; August: Japan surrendered.

the war against Japan within three months of the war against Germany ending. Agreement was even reached on Poland's frontiers. Its eastern border was essentially that of September 1939. Its western border was to be the Oder-Neisse river which meant that a good deal of Germany would come under Polish rule.

Since 1945 there have been many criticisms of the Yalta agreements. Some historians, echoing the views of Churchill, have argued that a dying Roosevelt was misled into making too many concessions to Russia. However, it is hard to see how the Western Allies could have better terms. Soviet forces already controlled much of eastern Europe. Roosevelt's main concerns were to end the war as quickly as possible and to remain on good terms with Stalin after the war. At least Stalin had committed himself to the United Nations (Roosevelt's great hope for the future) and to war against Japan. Roosevelt had not really been duped. While he spoke in public of Yalta as a triumph, in private he was far more doubtful about Stalin's intentions.

Churchill, who had returned from Yalta saying he had 'every confidence in Stalin', was soon concerned about the situation in Poland. Polish communists seemed more concerned with arresting enemies than with civil liberties. In March 1945 Churchill wrote to Roosevelt urging him to take a tougher line on the USSR. But Stalin held all the cards. Determined that countries like Poland, Romania, Bulgaria, and Hungary should be 'friendly' to the USSR, he insisted that the West had no business to interfere in the east, any more than he himself should interfere in France, Italy, Belgium and Holland.

f) German Defeat

By March 1945 Germany's position was hopeless. In that month Allied forces crossed the Rhine and pushed into Germany. Montgomery and Churchill wished to press on and capture Berlin ahead of the Russians but Eisenhower refused to pursue what he saw as a purely political objective. By this stage in the war the Americans were calling the tune. US armament production was six times as great as Britain's and the USA had more troops in Europe than Britain. Eisenhower had no wish to suffer unnecessary casualties. Plans for dividing Germany into occupied zones had already been worked out. Berlin was in the Russian sector: it was therefore left for the Russians. By April Soviet forces had captured Budapest and reached Vienna. In mid-April Zhukov launched the final attack on Berlin. Roosevelt, Mussolini and Hitler all died in April. Roosevelt had a heart attack, Mussolini was executed by Italian anti-Fascists, and Hitler committed suicide in Berlin. Germany finally surrendered on 8 May.

THE DEFEAT OF JAPAN

The Japanese advance in south-east Asia and the Pacific was checked in 1942 by American naval victories in the Coral Sea and off Midway Island. By the end of 1943 New Guinea had been recaptured and in 1944 the Americans won a decisive victory at the naval battle of Leyte. By 1945 US planes attacked Japan almost at will. Even so, it seemed likely that Japan might continue fighting for many more months. President Truman, fearing the Allies might sustain more casualties than in the war against Germany, determined to use a new weapon. On 6 August the first atomic bomb was dropped on Hiroshima, killing tens of thousands of people. Although there has been much criticism of the dropping of the bomb, a decision not to drop it would have been hard to make and even harder to justify in 1945. Two days later Russia declared war on Japan. The next day a second atomic bomb was dropped on Nagasaki. The Japanese government at last agreed to surrender.

6 Why Did the Allies Win?

a) Economic Factors

The Allies combined human and industrial war potential was much greater than that of their enemies. Italy, bedevilled by corruption and administrative incompetence, failed to harness its limited resources effectively. Germany's economy also underperformed. One problem was its lack of key natural resources, especially oil. Nazi ideology, especially the failure to use non-Aryans and German women efficiently, was another factor. A third factor was the inefficiency arising from the overlapping agencies within the Third Reich. A fourth factor was the lack of standardisation and the failure to mass produce. German manufacturers produced relatively small quantities of very good weapons: its enemies simply produced much more. In 1943, for example, the USSR turned 8 million tons of steel and 90 million tons of coal into 48,000 heavy guns and 24,000 tanks. Germany, by contrast, turned 30 million tons of steel and 340 million tons of coal into 27,000 heavy guns and 17,000 tanks. Not until Speer became minister in 1942 did Germany begin to rationalise its war production. By then it was too late.

The Allies were far more successful in organising war production. By 1940 Britain had a more thoroughly militaristic economy than Germany. The USSR, despite losing a great deal of its economic resources, managed to create a strong war economy in which all labour, male and female, was ruthlessly mobilised and directed. The US war economy was by far the most successful of all the belligerents. By 1943 it was out-producing the combined war efforts of all the Axis nations. It was not only able to equip its own forces but also, through Lend-Lease, to give substantial help to its allies.

b) Technology, Science and Invention

The capacity to produce high-quality weapons and detection systems was just as important as the ability to produce large quantities of war material. On land German equipment was often of superior quality to Allied counterparts. In the air, by contrast, it was the Allies who usually possessed a technological advantage. German developments in jet- and rocket-engine technology came too late to challenge Allied command of the air. At sea the Allies ultimately deployed more advanced detection devices and weaponry, enabling them to defeat the U-boat threat. In general, the Allies had more resources they could deploy for research and development purposes. Significantly, the Americans were able to produce the most scientifically advanced weapon of them all – the atomic bomb.

c) Intelligence and Deception

Allied advantages included:
▼ Allied air superiority helped aerial observation.
▼ Resistance groups passed on useful information.
▼ Germany suffered from a lack of coordination between rival intelligence agencies.
▼ The USSR spy services were highly effective.
▼ British code-breakers' success in intercepting and deciphering German radio messages, was an important advantage.
▼ Both sides tried to mislead the enemy about the timing and strength of major operations. Perhaps the Allies' greatest success came in 1944: the Germans were convinced that the Allies would attack Calais, rather than Normandy.

Table 18 Weapons production of the major powers, 1939–45.

	1939	1940	1941	1942	1943	1944	1945
Aircraft							
Britain	7,940	15,049	20,094	23,672	26,263	26,461	12,070
USA	5,856	12,804	26,277	47,826	85,998	96,318	49,761
USSR	10,382	10,565	15,735	25,436	34,900	40,300	20,900
Germany	8,295	10,247	11,776	15,409	24,807	39,807	7,540
Japan	4,467	4,768	5,088	8,861	16,693	28,180	11,066
Major vessels							
Britain	57	148	236	239	224	188	64
USA	–	–	544	1,854	2,654	2,247	1,513
USSR	–	33	62	19	13	23	11
Germany (U-boats only)	15	40	196	244	270	189	0
Japan	21	30	49	68	122	248	51
Tanks‡							
Britain	969	1,399	4,841	8,611	7,476	5,000	2,100
USA	–	*c.*400	4,052	24,997	29,497	17,565	11,968
USSR	2,950	2,794	6,590	24,446	24,089	28,963	15,400
Germany	*c.*1,300	2,200	5,200	9,200	17,300	22,100	4,400
Japan	*c.*200	1,023	1,024	1,191	790	401	142
Artillery pieces§							
Britain	1,400	1,900	5,300	6,600	12,200	12,400	–
USA	–	*c.*1,800	29,615	72,658	67,544	33,558	19,699
USSR	17,348	15,300	42,300	127,000	130,300	122,400	31,000
Germany	*c.*2,000	5,000	7,000	12,000	27,000	41,000	–

Dashes indicate reliable figures unavailable.

‡ Includes self-propelled guns for Germany and the USSR

§ Medium and heavy calibre only for Germany, USA and Britain; all artillery pieces for the USSR. Soviet heavy artillery production in 1942 was 49,100, in 1943 48,400 and in 1944 56,100.

d) Leadership

Axis defeat was hastened by the disparity in the quality of leadership. Mechanisms for effective joint planning by the Axis powers never emerged. Germany, Italy and Japan pursued largely independent strategies that were in some respects at cross purposes. Given the predominance of German power on the Axis side, strategic decision-making within Germany was crucial. Hitler was the key figure. While he was an effective war leader from 1939 to 1942, thereafter he was out of his depth. Key decisions were made intuitively, with partial or complete disregard for professional advice. His almost pathological desire to act offensively probably hastened Germany's defeat.

On the Anglo-Allied side, strategy was well thought out via bureaucratic mechanisms such as the Combined Chiefs of Staff. While there were serious differences of opinion about how the war should be fought, the differences were invariably resolved. The work of the US Chief of Staff, General George Marshall, and Sir Alan Brooke, Chief of the Imperial General Staff, was particularly effective.

Churchill has long been regarded as one of Britain's greatest prime ministers. Recently, however, historians such as John Charmley have questioned his 'greatness'. Certainly the Churchill of myth was not always the Churchill of history. Roosevelt said of him: 'He has a hundred [ideas] a day and about four of them are good.' However, Churchill has more defenders than critics. His constant probings, suggestions and demands at least imparted a sense of urgency to all who came under his scrutiny. To his credit, he forged a military team that eventually had considerable success. Roosevelt proved a brilliant war leader. He delegated well, interfered far less than Churchill and had an extraordinary grasp of the overall direction of the war. Throughout the war, he got most of the main strategic decisions right. Stalin made some serious errors in 1941–2. Subsequently, however, he learned to place some trust in the judgement of proven field commanders (like Zhukov), thereby increasing the effectiveness of Soviet military operations.

e) Will

All the belligerent states maintained ministries of propaganda or information, using the widest possible range of means available, films, radio, press and posters, to try to maintain national morale. Not all were successful. Italians showed little will for victory. Japanese morale, on the other hand, remained high until 1945. Victory and limited calls for sacrifice sustained German morale in the early years of the war. After 1941 Nazi propaganda effectively played on the fears of what would happen in the event of German defeat. Hitler's regime was also ready to kill anyone who opposed the war effort. Thus Germans, in contrast to 1918, fought on until the bitter end. Japanese and German tenaciousness might well have negated Allied material advantages if the peoples of the Allied states had not been willing to make the necessary sacrifices. They were willing. Morale in Britain was high from start to finish. Hitler's view that the Americans

THE POTSDAM CONFERENCE

The Potsdam conference in July–August confirmed, and exacerbated, the distrust between East and West. On the first day President Truman claimed that the Russians had violated the Yalta agreements and demanded 'free' elections across eastern Europe. Stalin replied that these were domestic affairs and not the concern of the conference. Once Truman knew that the USA had a successfully-tested atomic bomb, he was less inclined to make concessions. Little was decided: almost every issue was referred to the Council of Foreign Ministers.

lacked the moral fibre to sustain a savage war proved incorrect. The Soviet people, spurred on by a brutal state apparatus, made almost superhuman sacrifices to achieve victory.

7   Some Results of the War

At least 36 million Europeans lost their lives – about three times the figure for the First World War (see Table 19). Almost two-thirds of the dead were civilians. The bulk of the casualties occurred in eastern Europe. Poland suffered most, as a proportion of her population. Some 6 million Poles died – a total loss of 15 per cent.

The physical destruction was enormous. Aerial bombing had caused immense damage in some British and most German cities. In the east, practically every town from Moscow to Berlin had been bombed, shelled, and laid waste. Across Europe transportation systems had largely broken down and industrial and agricultural production had fallen. Of all the belligerents only the USA came out of the war richer than it entered it.

The war resulted in a movement of peoples, the scale of which Europe had not seen for centuries. The process started early in the war when Germans living outside the Reich were settled within it. But it was at the end of the war that the greatest movement came

	Mobilised (thousand)	Military killed (thousand)	Civilians killed (thousand)
Germany	11,000	3,250	3,810
Italy	4,500	330	500
Japan	6,095	1,700	360
British Empire	8,720	452	80
France	6,000	250	360
Poland	1,000	120	5,300
USSR	12,500	9,500	21,500 (estimated)
USA	14,900	407	Small
China	8,000	1,500	7,800
Total from above countries	72,700	15,600	35,800

Table 19 Casualties in the Second World War.

about. Over 12 million Germans were driven – or fled – westwards. In Poland and Czechoslovakia only tiny German populations remained. The German minorities' problem was thus brutally 'solved'.

Europe lost its old dominance to the USA and the USSR. The pre-war colonial powers were so weakened that they could no longer easily sustain their overseas empires. Despite popular myth, the war was hardly a glorious success for Britain. If it was fought to save Poland, it failed. If it was fought to keep totalitarianism out of Europe, it failed. By 1945 Britain was bankrupted by its 'victory' and had ceded its world power to the USA. It is thus possible to claim that Britain's finest hour was its gravest error.

> ### ▼ Working on The Second World War and the Holocaust

Your reading of this chapter should ensure that you now have opinions on all the following areas:
▼ Why was Germany so successful in the years 1939–41?
▼ Why did the war become a real 'World War' in 1941?
▼ How successful was the Nazi New Order?
▼ Did Hitler always intend the Holocaust?
▼ Hitler apart, who else was to blame for the Holocaust?
▼ Why and how did the Allies win the Second World War?

Answering Extended Writing and Essay Questions on The Second World War and the Holocaust

Consider the question: 'Which Allied country contributed most to Germany's defeat in World War Two?'

Brainstorm the main points you might make. For example:
▼ Britain fought the longest and made use of the resources of its Empire.
▼ Although the USA paid the least in terms of lives expended, its economic and military contribution was massive.
▼ The peoples of the USSR eventually ground down their adversary, losing over 30 million lives in the process. Seventy-five per cent of German casualties were on the Eastern Front.

THE NUREMBERG TRIAL

The surviving Nazi leaders were tried, at Nuremberg before a tribunal of judges from Britain, the USA, France and Russia, on charges of committing war crimes and crimes against humanity. Such a trial was unique in history and many have questioned its justice. However, the trial did at least put on record the appalling story of Nazi inhumanity. Of the 22 accused, 12 were sentenced to be hanged, three were given life imprisonment, four were given long prison sentences and three were acquitted.

Answering Source-Based Questions on The Second World War and the Holocaust

We men of Germany must be strict with ourselves ... For we must finish matters once and for all and finally settle accounts with the war criminals, in order to create a better and eternal Germany for our heirs ... There are three or four operations a week. Sometimes Gypsies, another time Jews, partisans and all sorts of trash ... I am grateful for having been allowed to see this bastard race close up. If fate permits, I shall have something to tell my children. Syphilitics, cripples, idiots were typical of them ... We are ruthlessly making a clean sweep with a clear conscience.

Source C this letter, written in June 1942 (in the Ukraine) was sent by a young policeman to an SS chief, a friend from his home district.

I also want to talk to you quite frankly about a very grave matter. We can talk about it quite frankly among ourselves and yet we will never speak of it publicly ... I am referring to the Jewish evacuation programme, the extermination of the Jewish people. It is one of those things which are easy to talk about. 'The Jewish people will be exterminated', says every party comrade ... Not one of those who talk like that has watched it happening, not one of them has been through it. Most of you will know what it means when a hundred corpses are lying side by side, or 500 or a 1,000 are lying there. To have stuck it out and – apart from a few exceptions due to human weakness – to have remained decent, that is what has made us tough. This is a glorious page in our history and one that has never been written and can never be written .... We had the moral right, we had the duty to our people, to destroy this people which wanted to destroy us.

Source D an extract from a speech by Himmler to SS leaders in October 1943.

I asked Hoess how it was technically possible to exterminate 2.5 million people. 'Technically?' he asked. 'That wasn't so hard – it would not have been hard to exterminate even greater numbers' ... it was possible to exterminate up to 10,000 people in one 24-hour period ... 'The killing itself took the least time ... it was the burning that took all the time. The killing was easy; you didn't even need guards to drive them into the chambers; they just went in expecting to take showers and, instead of water, we turned on poison gas. The whole thing went very quickly'. He related all this in a quiet, apathetic, matter-of-fact tone of voice ... 'But what about the human – ?' I started to ask. 'That just didn't enter into it', was the pat answer before I could finish the question.

Source E Hoess, the Auschwitz Commandant, interviewed by a US psychologist, after the war.

▼ QUESTIONS ON SOURCES

1. How do Sources C and D justify the Holocaust? **[10 marks]**
2. To what extent do the sources help our understanding of the
Holocaust? **[20 marks]**

Points to note about the questions

Question 1 What do the two sources have in common? To what
extent do they differ?
Question 2 All the sources give us some indication of German attitudes to the Holocaust. Do you think the attitudes betrayed in the
sources were commonly-held German attitudes?

Further Reading

Books in the Access to History series

For background on the Second World War, try *War and Peace: International
Relations 1914–45* by David Williamson. On the Holocaust, read Chapters 4–7
in *Anti-Semitism and the Holocaust* by Alan Farmer.

General

Start with Chapter 15 in *Years of Change Europe 1890–1945* by Robert Wolfson
and John Laver (Hodder & Stoughton). Excellent general accounts of the
war may also be found in *The Second World War* by J. Keegan, 1989 (Viking),
The Second World War in Europe by S.P. MacKenzie, 1999 (Longman), *Struggle
for Survival: The History of the Second World War* by R.A.C. Parker, 1989 (OUP)
and *A World in Flames* by M. Kitchen, 1990 (Longman). Try also *Why the Allies
Won*, 1995 (Norton) and *Russia's War*, 1997 (Penguin), both by R. Overy.

   Concerning the Holocaust, *The Holocaust in History* by M. Marrus, 1989
(Penguin) and *Hitler and the Jews* by P. Burrin, 1994 (Arnold) are good, short
introductions. *The Final Solution: Origins and Implementations* by D. Cesarani,
ed. 1996 (Routledge) is a splendid collection of essays by many of the main
Holocaust scholars. *Nazism 1919–1945: Foreign Policy, War and Racial Extermination: A Documentary Reader* by J. Noakes and G. Pridham, 1988 (University
of Exeter) contains a tremendous collection of documents. *Hitler's Willing
Executioners: Ordinary Germans and the Holocaust* by D.J. Goldhagen, 1996
(Little, Brown and Company) is a powerful indictment of the German
people. *The Path to Genocide*, 1992 (CUP) and *Ordinary Men: Reserve Police Bat-
talion 101 and the Final Solution in Poland*, 1992 (HarperCollins), both by
C.R. Browning, are 'musts'. And finally you really ought to read the novel
Schindler's Ark by T. Keneally, 1983 (Penguin).

CHAPTER 9 · EUROPE AND THE COLD WAR: 1945–90

POINTS TO CONSIDER

After 1945 Europeans found themselves under the domination of the two 'superpowers' – the USA and the USSR – who enjoyed an immense military superiority over all possible rivals. Britain, the only former European great power to survive the war uninvaded, lacked the resources to compete. So did France. Germany was in ruins and occupied by Allied armies. Europe's fate for decades to come was to be shaped by decisions taken in Moscow and Washington. This chapter is divided into an introduction and six sections. Sections one and four examine the **Cold War**; sections two and five focus on the USSR; section three concentrates on developments in western Europe; while section six examines the situation in 1990. Each section can be studied in 'splendid isolation'. Alternatively you may wish to read the entire chapter to get an overview of the period.

COLD WAR

A term, first used in 1947, to describe the emerging tensions between the USSR and its eastern European satellite states on the one hand and the USA and its western European allies on the other.

During the war relations between the west (Britain and the USA) and the USSR were never very cordial. The differences that had been played down during the war became increasingly evident as hostilities drew to a close. In particular there was concern about who would fill the power vacuum in the centre of Europe. By 1945 the Red Army was in occupation of most of eastern Europe and there was little the west could do about it. The Potsdam Conference in July/August achieved little. President Truman left the Conference alarmed at what he believed was the failure of Stalin to uphold either the agreements made at Yalta in February 1945 or the principles embodied in the Declaration of the United Nations (for example, that all people should have the right to choose their own forms of government). Truman and British leaders feared that Stalin was bent on communist expansionism. Disagreements about the future of Europe led to the **Cold War**. While the Cold War had a major effect on the world as a whole, it arose because of the situation in Europe, had a profound impact on Europe, and ended as a result of developments in Europe. The Cold War is at the heart of this chapter.

1 The Start of the Cold War

a) What were Stalin's Intentions?

After 1945 the USSR took control of much of eastern Europe. Was this a step towards a Soviet take-over of the whole of Europe (as the West feared), or was it a defensive move (as Stalin claimed)? On balance, Stalin's motives seem to have been more defensive than offensive. Given the huge damage the war had inflicted on the USSR, Stalin may have been less aware of his country's strength than of its weakness. Above all he was determined to prevent another invasion of Russia. Before 1941 most east European states had been governed by right-wing regimes which had allied with Germany. In Moscow it seemed likely that if these states became independent, they would again become anti-communist. Stalin particularly feared German reunification unless it was under a government he could control. He also regarded the USA, with its tremendous economic strength and its possession of the atomic bomb, as a threat. He believed it was his job to stop American capitalism from dominating the world. Given all these factors, Stalin calculated that his best policy was to ensure that the USSR had a buffer zone of friendly states.

After 1945 the West interpreted Soviet moves as expansionist. Western leaders possibly exaggerated the Soviet threat: the reality of Russian weakness was not fully appreciated. Nevertheless, Western fears were rational. Stalin's take-over of eastern European was a clear violation of previous agreements. Moreover, he was a brutal dictator whom it was dangerous to trust. Given the ideological differences between the West and the USSR, the Cold War was always an accident waiting to happen. However, if blame has to be apportioned, then Stalin was probably more guilty than anybody. His actions in eastern Europe helped to create an atmosphere of distrust which conditioned Western attitudes towards the USSR. In 1945 Stalin was much more suspicious of the USA than the USA was of him. There was little cause for his suspicion. While many Americans disliked communism, most hoped for improved relations with the USSR.

b) The Soviet Take-over of Eastern Europe

As the Red Army drove westwards in 1944–5, the Soviet leadership made sure that occupied territory came under the control of pro-communist governments. Encouraged by Moscow, these governments nationalised industry, established collective farms, controlled the media, arrested leading opponents, and rigged elections. Eventually all opposition was destroyed. The process was more rapid in

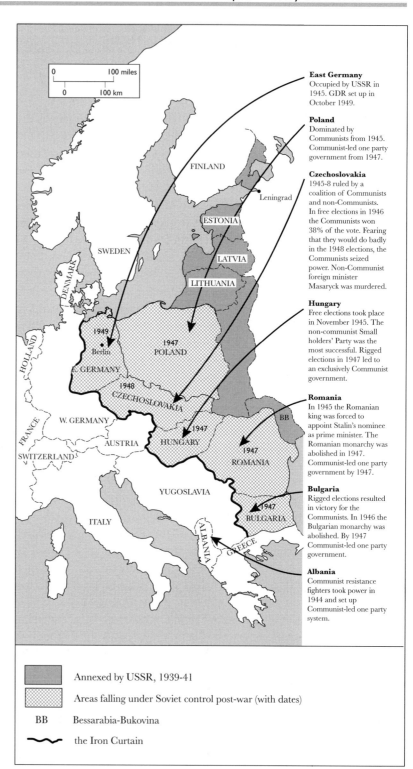

Figure 59 Soviet expansion, 1939–49.

some countries than in others (see Figure 59). By 1948 all the communist states – except Yugoslavia – took their orders from Moscow. The Yugoslav communist leader Tito had no intention of being Stalin's puppet. In 1948 Stalin took political and economic action to try bring Tito 'into line'. Tito – who dealt effectively with internal opposition and won support from the West – survived.

c) The USSR: 1945–53

Given the devastation caused by the war, Stalin regarded reconstruction as a priority. His basic economic strategy after 1945 was the same as before 1941. The aim of the Fourth Five Year Plan was fast growth in all parts of heavy industry. Even allowing for inflated claims, the aims seem to have been achieved. By 1950 Russia's industrial structure was probably stronger than it had been pre-1941. The major weaknesses were the inability to increase agricultural productivity and the failure to raise living standards.

Stalin's regime did not become any less repressive. Propaganda became more intense and ideological control much stricter, especially in education. Totalitarian terror remained. In 1945 the Allies agreed that all released prisoners-of-war should be returned to their country of origin. These included many Soviet citizens who had fought for Germany in an attempt to break free of Stalin. They were forcibly repatriated by the Allies and most were executed. Even genuine Soviet prisoners were treated harshly. Many were transferred from German camps into Soviet labour camps on the grounds that their survival somehow indicated that they had collaborated with their captors. In 1949 Stalin initiated another party purge, comparable in scale to those in the 1930s. He then purged Soviet Jews. Only his death in 1953 prevented a purge of the medical profession.

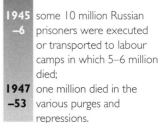

STALIN'S VICTIMS: 1945–53

1945 –6 some 10 million Russian prisoners were executed or transported to labour camps in which 5–6 million died;
1947 –53 one million died in the various purges and repressions.

d) The Iron Curtain

A tough Western policy towards Russia was not possible in 1945. The public in the West would not have tolerated a new confrontation with their ex-ally. Nor were the Western powers able to negotiate from a position of strength. The huge Red Army was as great a threat as the atomic bomb, especially as the USA quickly demobilised. (Many Western Europeans feared she might retreat back into isolation.) The Red Army, as well as controlling much of eastern Europe, occupied northern Iran, Mongolia and northern Korea. It also seemed possible that Greece and Turkey might fall to communism. In March 1946 Winston Churchill made his famous 'iron curtain' speech at Fulton, Missouri.

> From Stettin, in the Baltic, to Trieste, in the Adriatic, an iron curtain has descended across the continent. Behind that line lie all the capitals of the ancient states of Central and Eastern Europe: Warsaw, Berlin, Prague, Vienna, Budapest, Belgrade, Bucharest and Sofia. All these famous cities, and the populations around them, lie in the Soviet sphere, and all are subject in one form or another, not only to Soviet influence, but to a very high and increasing measure of control from Moscow. Athens alone ... is free to decide its future ...
>
> However, in a great number of countries, far from the Russian frontiers and throughout the world, Communist fifth columns are established and work in complete unity and absolute obedience to the directions they receive from the Communist centre ...

Source A

Many thought that Churchill was exaggerating the Russian menace. However, events soon seemed to prove the accuracy of his opinion.

ACTIVITY

Answer the following questions:

1. What did Churchill mean by the term the 'iron curtain'? **[5 marks]**
2. Churchill mentions ten capitals. Link the capitals to European countries. **[10 marks]**
3. What did Churchill mean by the term 'fifth column'? **[5 marks]**
4. What do you think were Churchill's motives for making the speech? **[10 marks]**

Figure 60 President Harry S. Truman.

e) The Truman Doctrine

President Truman, like Churchill, was worried by Soviet policies. Relations between the superpowers deteriorated and by 1946–7 there was a strong feeling in Washington that the USA needed to take a tough line to stop Soviet power spreading further. The lesson of the 1930s suggested that appeasing dictators did not work.

In February 1947 Britain warned Truman that it could no longer afford to pay for the upkeep of its troops in Greece. If the British forces withdrew, there was a real possibility that Greece would fall to communist insurgents. Nor could Britain afford to give aid to Turkey – similarly threatened. Truman decided to fill the vacuum. Asking Congress for $400 million for Greece and Turkey, he argued that the money was essential if democracy was to triumph over totalitarianism.

At the present moment in world history nearly every nation must choose between alternative ways of life. The choice is too often not a free one. One way of life is based upon the will of the majority, and is distinguished by free institutions, representative government, free elections, guarantees of individual liberty, freedom of speech and religion, and freedom from political oppression. The second way of life is based upon the will of a minority forcibly imposed upon the majority. It relies upon terror and oppression, a controlled press and radio, fixed elections, and the suppression of personal freedoms.

I believe that it must be the policy of the United States to support free peoples who are resisting attempted subjugation by armed minorities or by outside pressures.

Source B

The so-called 'Truman Doctrine' marked a major change in US foreign policy – from one of attempted cooperation with the USSR to one of confrontation. Few decisions by American politicians have had such momentous consequences for Europe. In the short term, Congress agreed to fund Greece and Turkey – neither of which went communist. In the long term, the USA was now committed to resisting communism in Europe and across the globe.

f) The Marshall Plan

In early 1947 there was a severe economic crisis in Europe. A poor harvest in 1946, followed by an unusually harsh winter, meant that people were cold as well as hungry. In France and Italy discontent led to massive support for local communist parties, which benefited both politically and morally from their prominent role in wartime resistance movements. US leaders reckoned that the best way to avert the danger of communists being voted into power was to end the poverty and despair on which they thrived. The USA thus decided in June 1947 to offer massive economic aid to those European countries which made an acceptable application. This project, organised by US Secretary of State George Marshall, became known as the Marshall Plan. In theory, even the USSR was able to apply for help. But Stalin, unwilling to make the USSR economically dependent upon the USA, refused to have anything to do with it.

The Marshall Plan was a great success. Leaders of 16 west European countries met in Paris in the summer of 1947 and bid for US money. Over the next four years $13 billion of help was provided. By 1952, when the Plan officially ended, western Europe was well on the road to economic prosperity. Churchill called Marshall aid 'one of the most unsordid acts of history'. Actually, it served US interests rather well. It ensured that Western Europe did not go communist. It also benefited the USA economically. By rebuilding Western Europe, America was creating trading partners who could buy US goods and provide investment opportunities for US capital.

g) Germany and the Berlin Blockade

At Yalta it was agreed that Germany would be divided into four zones, controlled by Britain, the USSR, the USA and France. At Potsdam the Allies agreed that Germany would eventually be reunited. In the meantime, German political life was to be reconstructed on a 'democratic basis' in order to prepare Germany 'for eventual peaceful co-operation in international life'. However, the West and the USSR were soon at odds over the treatment Germany was to receive. Stalin wanted Germany permanently crippled and demanded huge reparations. The West, by contrast, dithered. In 1944 the so-called Morgenthau Plan had envisaged turning Germany into a primarily agricultural country. However, this idea was soon discarded. As Cold War divisions increased, Germany became an intractable problem, dividing the USA and the USSR. Both knew that whoever controlled Germany would control Europe.

In 1945 the Russians set about stripping their east German zone of industrial equipment, using it to repair damage in the USSR. Given that most of Germany's food had been produced in the east, the western zones were short of food. The problem was made worse by the arrival of over ten million extra Germans fleeing from Russian-controlled areas. Britain had to divert grain to Germany at the cost of bread rationing at home. In 1947, the USA and Britain linked their zones together in an effort to restore the German economy. The Marshall Plan provided an essential injection of capital. Between June 1948 and December 1949 industrial production rose 125 per cent and the West German economic miracle was under way.

By 1948 western Germany, with its own elected executive, was functioning as if it was a separate country from the eastern sector. The creation of an industrially powerful West German state, closely allied to the USA, was of great concern to Stalin. News of a new currency for West Germany in June 1948 further alarmed him. Stalin thought he had one powerful weapon. West Berlin, controlled by US, French and British forces, was a Western 'island' deep inside the Soviet sector of Germany. On 23 June the USSR closed the road, canal and railway links between West Berlin and West Germany. The Soviet blockade took the Western allies by surprise. Some American generals thought that tanks should be used to blast a way through. In the event, Truman decided to keep the two million West Berliners supplied by aircraft. During the airlift (which lasted 318 days) allied planes flew nearly 200,000 missions, supplying West Berlin with over 1.5 million tons of fuel, food and equipment. Far from backing down (as Stalin had hoped), the USA had shown that it was prepared to risk war in order to preserve the post-war settlement as it stood in 1948.

In May 1949 Stalin called off the blockade. It was a major defeat. He had been outfaced in a trial of strength. The Berlin blockade had also done much to damage the Soviet image in Europe. Moreover, the blockade, far from averting it, accelerated moves towards the creation of a West German state. The new state, the Federal Republic of Germany (FDR), formally founded in May 1949 held its first elections in August. Adenauer, a conservative who hated communism, became the new Chancellor. Resolute and astute, he was to rule until 1963. The development of a stable and prosperous West Germany was the last thing that Stalin wanted. In October 1949 he cut his losses and set up the communist-led German Democratic Republic (GDR) in East Germany. For the next 40 years there were to be two Germanies. The Cold War ran along the line dividing them.

h) The North Atlantic Treaty Organisation (NATO)

The Berlin blockade encouraged the western allies to form NATO in 1949. Those signing the treaty – Belgium, Britain, Canada, Denmark, France, Iceland, Italy, the Netherlands, Norway, Portugal and the

THE COMMUNIST THREAT: 1949–50

▽ In 1949 the USSR tested its own atomic bomb.

▽ In 1949 Chinese communists, led by Mao Zedong, took power in China. The USSR proposed that Mao's China be admitted to the United Nations (UN) in place of the American-backed Nationalist China, led by Chiang Kai-shek, now outcast on Formosa. The failure of this proposal led to the Soviet delegation staging a protest walk-out from the UN Security Council.

▽ In 1950 communist North Korea invaded South Korea, with Stalin's approval. With the Soviet delegation absent, the United Nations agreed to set up a UN army to defend South Korea. The bulk of the UN forces were American but several other nations (including Britain) sent contingents to help. By autumn 1950 China was drawn into the war. Although the USSR was not involved militarily, Stalin gave North Korea and China diplomatic support. The war dragged on until 1953 but UN-US forces ensured South Korea did not fall to the communists.

Frontiers of Germany before the war

Figure 61 The division of Germany, 1945–9.

USA – agreed that 'an armed attack against one or more of them in Europe or North America shall be considered an attack against them all'. (Turkey and Greece joined NATO in 1952.) NATO's formation was a milestone in US foreign policy. Never before had the USA been a member of a peacetime military alliance.

j) NATO v The Warsaw Pact

In 1950 US military leaders believed that the Korean War was a diversionary strategy and feared Stalin intended to attack Western Europe. This led to three major developments.

▼ The US committed four combat divisions to Europe.
▼ General Eisenhower was appointed as Supreme Allied Commander of all NATO forces.
▼ The US pressed for the inclusion of West German forces in NATO. France, in particular, feared reviving German militarism so soon. Not until May 1955 did West Germany join NATO. The USSR responded five days later by setting up its own military alliance – the Warsaw Pact.

Thus by the mid-1950s Europe was divided into two hostile camps, sustained by different economic systems and protected by military pacts. The east–west division remained until the late 1980s.

2 Developments in Eastern Europe: 1953–64

a) Khrushchev

ISSUE
What impact did Khrushchev have on the USSR and eastern Europe?

THE H-BOMB
In 1952 the USA tested an even more deadly device than the atomic bomb – the hydrogen bomb. The USSR followed in 1953. The nuclear arms race was on.

A period of collective leadership, which turned into a power struggle, occurred after Stalin's death. By 1955 Nikita Khrushchev had emerged as victor. Once an enthusiastic supporter of Stalin, Khrushchev determined to change his policies. In 1956, at the 20th Congress of the Communist Party, he attacked Stalin's memory. Under Stalin's regime, said Khrushchev, Soviet citizens 'had come to fear their own shadows'. He denounced the purges and Stalin's failures in foreign policy. Khrushchev's speech had a considerable impact, not just in Russia but across the eastern bloc. Images of Stalin disappeared from public places and de-Stalinisation seemed the order of the day. De-Stalinisation, however, was – and is – easy to misinterpret.

i) More Liberal?

While the outgoing and jocular Khrushchev presented a sharp personal contrast to the paranoid Stalin, he was a resolute upholder of

Communist rule. While his regime was more humane than Stalin's, it was still authoritarian. Thousands of political prisoners were released, but the Gulag remained.

ii) An Improved Standard of Living?

Boasting that the USSR would soon be as rich as the USA, Khrushchev put more emphasis on agricultural production and on producing consumer goods. A Seven Year Plan, introduced in 1959, was intended to promote light industry, chemicals and plastics. Incentives rather than coercion were offered to get people to work hard. While the Plan had some success, it failed to deal with the housing shortage. There were also problems with agriculture. In 1954 Khrushchev introduced the 'virgin lands' policy which aimed to exploit previously unused areas of the USSR for crop production. Massive financial investment was put into the scheme. However, short-sighted planning and poor management led to mistakes and targets were not met. 1963 was a disastrous year and the USSR had to import American grain. By the mid-1960s Soviet living standards still lagged far behind the West.

iii) Different Roads to Communism?

In 1955 Khrushchev claimed that the USSR believed in: 'equality, non-interference, respect for sovereignty and national independence.' In 1956 he announced that there were many different roads to communism which the different national parties must choose for themselves. It seemed to many east Europeans that the USSR was moving towards tolerance and freedom. These hopes were soon to be dashed.

b) The Hungarian Rising

After the rigged 1947 election, Communist leader Rakosi ruled Hungary with considerable brutality. In 1956 there were increasing disturbances and demands that Hungary should break away from the Soviet bloc. Rakosi was forced to resign in July 1956. The new ruler, Gero, was just as unpopular. Student demonstrations in October called for his removal and the reinstatement of the reformer Nagy. Soviet troops attacked the students who were joined by the Hungarian army as fighting spread across the country. A new government, which included non-communists, was formed with Nagy at its head. Khrushchev withdrew Soviet troops from Budapest, hoping that this would end the disturbances. It did not. When Nagy's government supported free elections and a free press and proposed to leave the Warsaw Pact, 200,000 Soviet troops and 2,500 tanks invaded Hungary in November. The Hungarians fought back and Nagy's government

Figure 62 Nikita Khrushchev.

THE START OF THE COLD WAR

1946 Churchill's 'iron curtain' speech;
1947 March: President Truman outlined the Truman Doctrine; June: Marshall called for a European recovery programme;
1948 USSR blockaded Berlin;
1949 April: formation of NATO; May: end of Berlin blockade; May: West Germany came into existence; October: East Germany formed;
1950 start of Korean War;
1953 death of Stalin;
1955 West Germany admitted to NATO: Warsaw Pact signed.

Table 20 Grain production in the USSR, 1953–65.

Grain harvest in millions of tonnes	
1953	82.5
1954	85.6
1955	103.7
1956	125.0
1957	102.0
1958	134.7
1959	119.5
1960	125.5
1965	121.1

Based on A. Nove, *An Economic History of the USSR.* 1969, and Soviet sources

Table 21 Industrial output in the USSR, 1955–65.

Industry	1955	1965
Oil (million tonnes)	170	507
Coal (million tonnes)	390	578
Iron (million tonnes)	33.3	66.2
Electricity (billions of kW)	170	507
Tractors (thousands)	163	355

Based on A. Nove, *An Economic History of the USSR*, 1969, and Soviet sources.

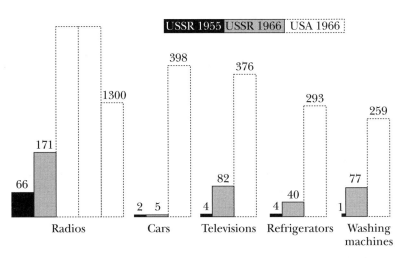

Figure 63 Living standards in the USSR and USA, 1955–66.

ANTI-
COMMUNIST
RIOTS

▼ Riots in East Germany in 1953 were put down by the security forces. Hundreds of rioters were killed.

▼ In 1956 Polish workers clashed with police and scores of people were killed. Gomulka, a communist imprisoned by Stalin, became Polish leader. He calmed the situation and his regime toed the Soviet party line.

made desperate appeals to the West for help. While the UN General Assembly condemned Soviet action, no Western help was forthcoming. Soviet forces took control of Hungary and imposed a new pro-Soviet government. As many as 30,000 Hungarians may have died in the fighting; 200,000 fled abroad.

c) A Thaw in the Cold War?

Khrushchev hoped to improve relations with the West. The ending of the Korean War in 1953 helped ease tensions. In 1955 the USSR recalled its army of occupation from Austria, and there was a friendly summit meeting of the main powers at Geneva. Although the Hungarian rising and the Suez crisis (see page 284) damaged relations, Khrushchev continued his policy of co-existence with the West, embarking on a series of visits to countries outside the eastern bloc – including the USA. He was able to boast of Soviet achievements in space, especially the launching of the world's first satellite, Sputnik, in 1957. However, co-existence proved hard to sustain in the face of recurrent crises over such unresolved issues as Germany and the arms race.

d) The Problem of Berlin

The existence of West Berlin remained annoying to Soviet leaders. Much more prosperous than the GDR, it was an advertisement for the economic success of Western Europe. Moreover, East Germans could move freely into West Berlin and from there to West Germany. Between 1949 and 1960, some 3 million people left the GDR via Berlin. The situation was complicated by the fact that the West refused to recognise East Germany as a sovereign state. In 1958 Khrushchev called for recognition of the GDR, the end of the four-power control of Berlin, and set a time limit of six months for the settlement of Berlin's future. The USA stood firm, reasserting the right of free access to West Berlin. Khrushchev backed down somewhat, accepting the rights of the Western occupying powers in Berlin. In return, President Eisenhower indicated that he was prepared to make concessions on Berlin's future. The two leaders agreed to meet for further discussions in 1960. As the meeting was about to start, Khrushchev announced that an American U-2 spyplane had been shot down over Soviet territory. Khrushchev made an issue of Eisenhower's refusal to apologise and stormed out of the conference – missing a chance to do a deal over Berlin.

   John Kennedy, the new US president, was determined to stand firm against communism. In June 1961 he and Khrushchev met in Vienna. Khrushchev demanded that Berlin should be neutral and threatened war. Kennedy conceded nothing. After the meeting Khrushchev repeated his demands, insisted that the USA must act within six months, and increased Soviet defence spending by 30 per cent. Kennedy rejected the Soviet demands and ordered a massive increase in the US armed services. War suddenly seemed a real possibility. However, Khrushchev found a different solution to the crisis. On 13 August 1961 barbed wire and barricades were erected around West Berlin, sealing off the city from the GDR. The barbed wire was soon replaced by a more substantial barrier – the Berlin Wall. There was little the West could do except protest.

e) The Cuban Missile Crisis

In 1959 the Marxist Fidel Castro seized power in Cuba and began to take steps to end the USA's economic domination of the island. Khrushchev, recognising the possibility of a major Cold War coup, arranged to buy up Cuba's sugar crop and offered economic help. The USSR hoped, and the USA feared, that the creation of a Marxist

---

THE RESULTS OF THE HUNGARIAN RISING

▼ The leaders of the rising were severely punished. Nagy was executed in 1958.

▼ The rising showed that while the USA was ready to fight to stop the spread of communism, it was not prepared to intervene in eastern Europe.

▼ Communists around the world were dismayed by the way that the USSR acted. Many western European communists left the party in disgust.

THE RESULTS OF THE BERLIN WALL

▼ The Wall averted the threat of nuclear war.

▼ The flow of refugees from East to West Germany stopped almost completely. In this way the Wall saved East Germany from a possible economic collapse caused by the loss of key workers.

▼ The Wall was a gift to Western propagandists who could (legitimately) argue that communism was so awful that people had to be walled in to prevent them escaping.

state in Cuba would mark the prelude to the rapid spread of communism throughout Latin America. US attempts to support a counter-revolution at the Bay of Pigs in 1961 ended in total failure.

Khrushchev now increased Russian involvement in Cuba, culminating in the secret installation of Soviet nuclear missiles. In October 1962 US photographic reconnaissance confirmed that missile sites were being built. The missiles, supposedly there to defend Cuba against US intervention, almost caused US intervention. But instead of invading, Kennedy announced a naval blockade of Cuba until the missiles were removed and placed US forces on nuclear war alert. Khrushchev, aware that the USA had a superiority in inter-continental ballistic missiles of more than six to one, chose not to risk war and agreed to remove the Soviet missiles in return for the US withdrawing its missiles from Turkey and promising not to invade Cuba. Given that the USSR had backed down, the outcome seemed like a diplomatic victory for the USA. After 1962 Khrushchev pursued a more peaceful policy. In 1963 the Washington–Moscow 'hotline' was established – a direct telephone link from the White House to the Kremlin. A Test Ban Treaty banned all but underground nuclear tests.

f) USSR v China

There had never been much harmony between the two great Communist powers and Sino-Soviet animosity increased throughout the 1950s. Disagreements over foreign policy and Marxist ideology were deepened by disputes over territory. Both countries stationed large numbers of troops along their joint borders. Incidents were frequent and threatened to lead to war. By 1964, when China exploded its first nuclear device, Sino-Soviet relations were at an all-time low. International communism had thus become a divided force.

THE USSR: 1953–64

1955 Khrushchev in full control;
1956 Hungarian uprising;
1961 Berlin crisis: building of Berlin Wall;
1962 Cuban Missile Crisis;
1964 Khrushchev overthrown.

g) Khrushchev's fall

By the 1960s Khrushchev's policy failures, both at home and abroad, tended to outweigh his successes. He had promised – but failed to deliver – a more productive economy. The virgin land policy seemed to have failed. The Cuban Missile Crisis was a personal disaster. General irritation grew with his unpredictable style of leadership. In October 1964, while he was on holiday, his enemies proclaimed Brezhnev as first Party Secretary. Khrushchev retired into peaceful obscurity. The Khrushchev years were relatively good ones for Russia with some economic progress and more freedom. However, Khrushchev did not leave the USSR in a particularly strong economic or international position and the country was still subject to the rule of a repressive Communist Party.

ACTIVITY

What impact did Khrushchev have on a) the USSR and b) the world?

Suggested line of response:
a) The USSR
▼ How far did de-Stalinisation go?
▼ How successful was the Soviet economy 1953–64?
b) The world
▼ Examine Khrushchev's attempts at co-existence pre-1960?
▼ Examine the Berlin and Cuban crises?

---

3 Developments in Western Europe: 1945–90

ISSUE
How successful was
Western Europe in the
period 1945–90?

a) Why was Western Europe so Successful Economically?

From 1945 to 1948 most western European states experienced economic hardship. However, after 1948 western Europe enjoyed two decades of sustained expansion. The reasons for this 'golden age' of economic growth include:

▼ Scientific and technical progress, in some cases sparked by the war, continued apace after 1945.
▼ Taking to heart the ideas of British economist J.M. Keynes, many governments acted positively to promote economic growth.
▼ Marshall Aid played a vital role in aiding the western European recovery.
▼ A spectacular rise in the mechanisation of farming and the use of fertilisers led to increased yields per hectare. Much of the agricultural labour force was thus released for use in industry or services. By 1960 only 17 per cent of western Europe's working population was employed in agriculture compared with 50 per cent in 1914.
▼ A 'baby boom' occurred after the war. By 1970 western Europe's population had risen from 264 million in 1940 to 320 million. This encouraged economic growth.

b) The End of Empire

Britain, France, Belgium, the Netherlands, Portugal and Spain still had overseas empires in 1945. These empires all collapsed after 1945. In 1939, 500 million people in Asia and Africa were ruled by Europeans. By 1970 the number had fallen to 21 million.

i) End of Empire in Asia

In the late 1940s there was a wave of de-colonisation in Asia and the Middle East. French forces left Syria and the Lebanon in 1946. At first the Dutch tried to fight nationalists in the Dutch East Indies but by 1948 the Dutch admitted defeat and granted independence to the new state of Indonesia. Britain gave up control of the Indian sub-continent in 1947 and granted independence to Burma (Myanmar) and Ceylon (Sri Lanka) in 1948. The French waged a savage war against communist guerrillas in Indo-China in an attempt to maintain their empire. When Vietnamese communists defeated French forces in 1954 at Dien Bien Phu, France abandoned Indo-China. Vietnam was divided between the communist North and the 'free' South. Laos and Cambodia also became independent.

ii) The Suez Crisis

In 1956 the Egyptian leader, Abdul Nasser, seized the Suez Canal from the private Anglo-French company which owned it. Britain and France protested and, in collusion with Israel, plotted Nasser's overthrow. In October 1956 the Israelis invaded Egypt to destroy the bases from which guerrillas harassed their borders. Britain and France called for a cease-fire. When Nasser rejected this, they launched air attacks and a seaborne landing. The USA, angered at not being informed and alarmed at the USSR's threatening reaction, used its financial pressure to force Britain to accept a cease-fire, negotiated by the UN. Nasser retained control of the Canal. The Suez affair was essentially symbolic: it indicated that Britain and France were no longer great world powers.

iii) Algeria

In 1954 a serious revolt broke out in Algeria against French rule. While some Frenchmen wanted to quit Algeria, others opposed any retreat on the grounds that it was the home of 1 million French people. When in 1958 it seemed that the government was considering granting independence, the French army came out in open revolt, demanding that General de Gaulle be called to head the government. De Gaulle, leader of the Free French during World War II, had helped restore order in France in 1944–5. He resigned in 1946 after his proposals to create a strong presidency were rejected. His hopes for an early return to power were disappointed. Although there were various political crises between 1946 and 1958 – and 25 different governments – the Fourth Republic survived. De Gaulle accepted leadership in 1958 on condition that he was given a free hand to draft a new constitution which gave more power to the president. (The Fourth Republic thus came to an end.) The army and settlers in Algeria presumed that de Gaulle would fight to keep

Algeria French. Instead he decided to grant it independence (in 1962), defeating revolts by the French army in the process. De Gaulle had got France out of a hole. Probably no other French leader could have achieved as much without a civil war.

iv) Sub-Saharan Africa

In 1945 the only independent countries in Africa were Liberia and South Africa. By 1961 24 new African states were already in existence. De-colonisation was a surprisingly quick and relatively bloodless process. Only Portugal fought a long – and ultimately unsuccessful – war in an effort to retain its African colonies, (see Figure 64).

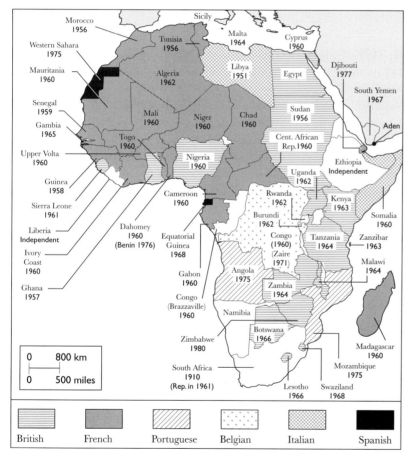

Figure 64 African independence.

c) Moves for West European Unity

i) Support for Unity

The situation in 1945 (and after) encouraged and gave opportunities to those who sought a new way of organising Europe. Many European

ISSUE
Why and how did western Europe become more unified?

politicians blamed nationalism for causing both World Wars. The onset of the Cold War persuaded many in the western democracies that European reconstruction would require a common economic, political and military effort. Some governments supported inter-governmental cooperation for defined and specific ends. Others, in contrast, supported the creation of a United States of Europe – a new superpower to rival the USA and the USSR. After 1945 a number of organisations were created in which European states cooperated. These included NATO and the OEEC (the Organisation for European Economic Cooperation) which administered the Marshall Aid programme. In 1949 ten countries formed the Council of Europe. At Britain's insistence, its role was vague and its power negligible. Britain was convinced that her true interests lay more with the Commonwealth and the USA. She was not attracted by the idea of European unity.

ii) The European Coal and Steel Community

Many supporters of European union believed that economic unification was the best, and first, step to political unification. In 1948 Belgium, the Netherlands and Luxemburg formed the Benelux Union. In 1950 two Frenchmen, Robert Schuman and Jean Monnet, drew up a plan to 'unite' Europe's coal and steel industries. (Monnet was one of the most enthusiastic proponents of a united Europe.) The Schuman Plan provided the impetus for the establishment of the European Coal and Steel Community (ECSC). A treaty translating this idea into reality was signed in 1951. There were six members of ECSC – France, West Germany, Belgium, Holland, Luxemburg and Italy. All duties on coal and steel between the Six were removed, and a 'high authority', in which all Six were represented, was charged with organising the joint programme. Monnet believed that ECSC was the start of a 'united Europe'.

iii) The Treaty of Rome

The success of ECSC in increasing coal and steel production persuaded its members that free trade should be extended to all industries in order to establish full economic integration. In 1955 delegates from the Six met at Messina and agreed to form the European Economic Community (EEC) or Common Market. In 1957 the Treaty of Rome, setting up the EEC, was signed. This provided for the abolition, over a 12–year period, of all customs duties on mutual trade. Obstacles to the free movement of persons, services and capital were to be abolished and a common agricultural policy was to be introduced. However, something much wider than a common market was envisaged. The signatories of the treaty agreed that they were 'determined to lay the foundations of an ever closer union among the peoples of Europe'. Five main bodies were to govern the

EEC's activities: the Commission, responsible for formulating policy; the Council of Ministers, a decision-making authority; a Parliament, with advisory powers only; a Secretariat; and a Court of Justice.

iv) French-German agreement

The EEC proved a remarkable success. Its first decade saw the creation of a common market with all internal tariffs abolished and a single external tariff established against outsiders. At the heart of the EEC was a remarkable entente between France and Germany. For Adenauer, West German Chancellor from 1949 to 1963, friendship with France was as great a priority as the containment of communism. He was thus prepared to accept the EEC on French terms. Preferential treatment for France's colonies was allowed and the **common agricultural policy** suited the interests of France's peasant

> **THE COMMON AGRICULTURAL POLICY**
> This was introduced to protect European farmers from foreign competition and keep farm prices high. It did this by fixing prices and buying up any produce which farmers could not sell at those prices. The EEC thus built up huge stores of unwanted produce, including butter 'mountains' and wine 'lakes'.

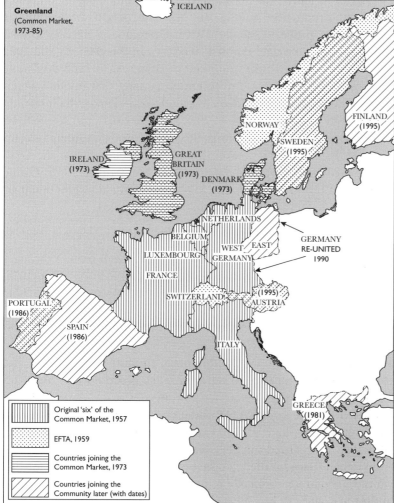

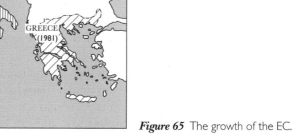

Figure 65 The growth of the EC.

farmers. Although France determined the framework of the EEC, West Germany's economic strength was central to its success. From 1950 to 1964 the country's gross national product rose threefold, faster than any other European state. By 1960 West Germany accounted for one-fifth of world trade in manufactured goods.

v) Britain and the EEC

The Six initially wanted Britain to join. Britain, which still saw itself as a world power rather than a European one and which wanted to go on buying cheap Commonwealth foodstuffs, refused. In response to the EEC's formation Britain took the lead in forming the European Free Trade Association (EFTA) in 1959. This was composed of seven countries – Britain, Switzerland, Austria, Portugal, Sweden, Denmark and Norway. Its object was to establish a free market between its members. It soon became clear that membership of EFTA (for Britain) was no substitute for membership of the EEC. Industrial production among the Six rose nearly three times as quickly as in Britain in the late 1950s. Therefore in 1961 the British government announced that it wished to join the EEC. By late 1962 negotiations seemed near completion. However, in 1963 de Gaulle came down firmly against British entry, claiming that Britain was not sufficiently European-minded. Wartime experiences had left de Gaulle with a deep distrust of the 'Anglo-Saxons' and he disliked Britain's special relationship with the USA. Equally important was his fear that Britain would weaken France's influence inside the EEC. France's partners favoured British entry but yielded to de Gaulle rather than risk breaking up the EEC. When Britain sought membership again in 1966–7 de Gaulle remained inflexible.

vi) The Influence of De Gaulle

De Gaulle appeared to dominate western European politics throughout the 1960s. The new constitution, which he introduced in 1958, gave the French president wide powers. He was elected by the people every seven years, and had the right to appoint the prime minister, dissolve parliament, and call referenda. France now seemed to have strong leadership – welcome after the chaotic politics of the Third and Fourth Republics. De Gaulle's main interests lay in defence and foreign policy. His desire to restore French greatness and break US influence in Europe amounted to an obsession. (In 1966, he extracted France from NATO's integrated command, claiming that the organisation had become an instrument of US domination.) Although he regarded the EEC as a means of freeing western Europe from dependence on the USA, de Gaulle was concerned that Europe should remain an association of sovereign national states whose authority would not be replaced by supra-national organisations such as the European Parliament. Throughout the 1960s de Gaulle opposed further moves towards political union. Only after he retired in 1969 could further moves towards European unity be made.

vii) Greater Unity

In 1969 at The Hague, the Six committed themselves to foreign policy coordination, monetary union, and enlarging EC membership. (By 1969 the word 'Economic' had been – significantly – dropped from the EEC.) Britain, Denmark and Ireland were finally admitted in 1973. Greece, Spain and Portugal also applied to join. These three countries were very different from the industrialised core of the EC and posed huge problems of assimilation. The pressures for their inclusion were essentially political. In the mid-1970s all three countries were struggling to establish democracies (having been ruled by authoritarian regimes) and their admission to the EC was intended to consolidate that process. Greece joined in 1981, Spain and Portugal in 1986. By the late 1980s there were moves towards even greater unity. In 1987 the Single European Act came into force, getting rid of many frontier controls. In 1991 the Maastricht Treaty gave the European Parliament greater powers over EC legislation and made plans for a single European currency by 1999. Whether most Europeans felt truly 'European' – or whether their main loyalty was to the country of their birth – remained to be seen.

WESTERN EUROPEAN UNITY

1951	Paris Treaty established the European Coal and Steel Community;
1957	The Treaty of Rome;
1963	de Gaulle vetoed Britain's EEC entry;
1973	Britain, Denmark and Eire joined the EC;
1981	Greece became an EC member;
1986	Spain and Portugal joined the EC.

ACTIVITY

Brainstorm: What were western Europe's main a) successes and b) failures in the years 1945–90?

4   The Search For Detente: 1968–80

By the late 1960s the two European blocs seemed to be facts of life. The Cold War no longer threatened to become hot war but had frozen hard. While some progress had been made to improve relations, the two superpowers continued to confront one another. The USA's determination to prevent communist North Vietnam from conquering South Vietnam led to it becoming involved in a draining war. The USSR and China both sent huge amounts of aid to North Vietnam and enjoyed US embarrassment.

a) The Arms Race

The two superpowers continued their 'arms race', building up bigger stockpiles of nuclear weapons and military hardware. Britain and France both had their own nuclear weapons – although after 1962 Britain was increasingly dependent on buying her 'hardware' from the USA. While the USA retained its nuclear lead, the USSR retained its lead in conventional forces. By the mid-1970s the Warsaw Pact had nearly twice as many men and three times as many tanks in Europe as NATO.

ISSUE
To what extent was there a thaw in the Cold War in the period 1968–80?

DETENTE
The word is used to mean a relaxation of tensions between East and West.

INTERNATIONAL RESULTS OF CZECHOSLOVAKIA

▼ After the invasion Brezhnev said the USSR was not prepared to let any communist country abandon communism: if it did, the USSR claimed the right to impose communism by force. This policy became known as the Brezhnev Doctrine.

▼ The Czech invasion appalled most Western countries.

▼ Communists around the world were critical. Yugoslavia, Albania and China condemned the Soviet action. In western Europe many communists stopped looking to Moscow for guidance. In the 1970s the strong Italian and French communist parties called for a new style of communism that allowed free speech and free elections.

b) Soviet Problems

In 1964 Brezhnev became Russian leader. At first he shared power with others but by 1971 he was in full control. He faced growing problems. The USSR's industries and most of its farming were inefficient and living standards remained low. Dissent and criticism were becoming more audible.

c) Communist Independence

Some Balkan dictators, while remaining grimly Stalinist at home, adopted a more independent foreign policy. In Albania, Hoxha (1945–85) aligned himself with China. Romanian dictator Ceausescu (1965–89) played the same game and also opened up trade with the West. Both leaders resented Moscow's attempts to keep them as Russian colonies. But Ceausescu was careful to remain within the Warsaw Pact. Moscow did not feel threatened by developments in Albania or Romania and took no action.

d) 1968: Czechoslovakia

After 1966 many Czechs, disappointed with their poor standard of living and lack of freedom, called for greater democracy. In 1968 Dubcek became Czech leader, replacing the hard-line Novotny. The early months of 1968 became known as the 'Prague Spring' as Dubcek supported a number of reforms, including giving more responsibility to individual farms and factories, allowing trade unions greater freedom, and abolishing censorship of the press. While Dubcek declared that his country would remain a loyal member of the Warsaw Pact, Brezhnev feared that the reforms were the first step towards Czechoslovakia becoming a Western-style country, allied to the USA. He was not prepared to allow this. Czechoslovakia was important strategically. Moreover, if free speech was allowed in Czechoslovakia, people in other eastern bloc countries would demand the same rights. This would lead to the collapse of communism. By July Soviet tanks and troops were massed on Czechoslovakia's border. On 15 July the Soviet leadership sent a letter of warning to the Czechoslovakian Communist Party:

Source C

> Developments in your country are causing deep anxiety among us . . . We cannot agree to have hostile forces push your country away from the road of socialism . . . This is something more than your own concern . . . It is the common concern of our countries, which have joined in the Warsaw Treaty to place an insurmountable barrier against the imperialist forces.

Dubcek's response to the Soviet threat made matters worse. He invited Yugoslavia's leader, Tito, to Prague and also signed a pact of friendship with Romanian leader Ceausescu. To Brezhnev this seemed like a signal that Dubcek was moving away from the Warsaw Pact. On 20 August Warsaw Pact troops, crossed the Czech frontier. A day later these forces were in Prague. The Czech government decided not to resist. People took to the streets to protest peacefully but there was none of the bloody street fighting that had taken place in Budapest in 1956. (Nor were there any of the brutal reprisals.) A pro-Soviet leader, Husak, took Dubcek's place and all anti-Communist political activities were banned. Dubcek was thrown out of the Communist party but kept his life and his freedom.

e) Strategic Arms Limitation

Strategic Arms Limitation Talks (SALT) between the superpowers began in 1969. Negotiations dragged on for three years and did not seem to be getting anywhere. Then, in 1972 Brezhnev invited Nixon to Moscow and the two leaders signed the SALT 1 treaty which limited the number of long range missiles each side could have. Although only a temporary measure, it appeared to herald a new attitude on both sides.

In 1974 representatives from the USA, Canada and every European state except Albania met in Helsinki to try to resolve a number of Cold War issues. In 1975, in return for the recognition of Europe's post-war frontiers, the USSR agreed to sign a guarantee of human rights and political freedom. There were hopes that detente might go further. However, President Carter's attempts to link new SALT talks with human rights failed. Despite the Helsinki agreement the USSR continued to take a hard line against leading dissidents and hopes of a new agreement foundered. The arms race continued.

f) US Problems in the 1970s

In 1973 Nixon finally accepted a ceasefire in Vietnam. Though Nixon described it as 'peace with honour' it was in fact a thinly disguised American defeat. In 1975 communist forces took control of all of Vietnam. Communist governments were also established in Laos and Cambodia. American defeat and the Watergate scandal which forced Nixon to resign in 1974 shook confidence in the political system. Moreover, the USA now faced serious economic problems. A rise in oil prices, arising from the 1973 Arab-Israeli war, contributed to inflation and growing unemployment in the USA.

In the late 1970s communism seemed to be on the march. Africa

---

REASONS FOR DETENTE

▼ Both sides feared of a catastrophic nuclear war which neither could win.

▼ By the 1970s both superpowers were suffering from economic difficulties and were anxious to reduce defence spending.

▼ Relations between the USA and China began to improve in 1971. Fearing the results of US-Chinese friendship, Brezhnev determined to improve relations with the USA. President Nixon hoped that better US relations with both China and the USSR, might force North Vietnam to make peace, enabling the USA to pull out of South Vietnam with some honour.

▼ Western European leaders favoured detente, particularly Willi Brandt, Chancellor of West Germany, 1969–74. Brandt worked for better relations with eastern Europe, including the GDR. His period in office saw the recognition of the GDR and acceptance of the 1945 border with Poland.

KEY EVENTS: 1964–80

1964 Brezhnev became Soviet leader;
1968 Prague Spring: Soviet invasion of Czechoslovakia;
1972 SALT 1 Treaty;
1975 Helsinki agreement;
1979 Soviet troops invaded Afghanistan.

THE SPACE RACE
The USA and USSR also competed in space. The USSR seemed to be well in the lead, sending the first man, Yuri Gagarin, into space in 1961. President Kennedy took up the challenge and announced that the USA would aim to have a man on the moon before the end of the decade. The USA spent huge resources on space development and quickly overtook the USSR. In July 1969 the USA landed a manned rocket on the moon.

saw the establishment of Marxist governments in Mozambique and Angola. In 1978 the USA faced another setback when its ally the Shah of Iran was overthrown and replaced by a hostile Islamic regime. In 1979 Soviet forces were sent to Afghanistan to support a puppet regime against Muslim rebels. Carter, worried that the USSR might pose a threat to Middle East oil, called on the world's athletes to boycott the 1980 Moscow Olympic Games. The SALT II talks collapsed and detente was over. In 1980 the USA faced further humiliation when it could not obtain the release of US diplomats held as hostages by Iran.

ACTIVITY

Consider the following question: Why were attempts at detente not more successful in the period 1968–80?

Suggested line of response:
▼ Why did both superpowers want detente?
▼ What efforts were made on the detente front?
▼ Why did USA–USSR relations not improve more?

ISSUE
To what extent was Gorbachev responsible for the collapse of the Soviet empire?

5 The Collapse of the Soviet Empire

a) What Problems did the USSR Face in the 1980s?

The USSR seemed to be in a strong position in 1980. However, appearances were deceptive. In 1980 Ronald Reagan became US president. His administration brought about a remarkable recovery in the confidence of Americans. Convinced of the evils of communism, Reagan encouraged a policy of confrontation with the USSR. He increased US military spending and challenged the USSR to join a new arms race. This competition was symbolised by Reagan's 'Star Wars' project (officially known as SDI: the Strategic Defence Initiative). This project involved research into ways of giving America nuclear superiority by destroying Soviet missiles in space. The USSR could only keep up with the USA by diverting a huge proportion of its national income to defence. This had a detrimental impact on living standards, not just in the USSR, but across eastern Europe.

Eastern Europeans were beneficiaries as well as victims of communism. After 1945 most eastern Europeans (outside the Balkans) were transformed from peasant farmers into industrial workers. The provision of free education, basic health care and full employment suggested that the lot of the average person had improved under communism. However, rigid communist central planning proved unable to build sufficient houses or meet a growing thirst for consumer goods. By the 1970s east European industries were grossly uncompetitive in world terms while their unrestricted growth had created appalling pollution. The Eastern bloc was unable to compete with the West in new industries like computers and telecommunications. Agricultural output remained low. On average each US farmer produced seven times more food than each Soviet farmer. The USSR had to import millions of tons of grain, much of it from the USA. Thus, by the 1980s all the Eastern bloc countries, increasingly dependent on Western aid, were (to varying degrees) in a state of economic crisis.

The USSR also faced problems in Afghanistan where Muslim rebels waged an effective guerrilla war. The USSR's situation in Afghanistan in the 1980s was similar to that of the USA in Vietnam in the 1960s. The ten-year war led to the death of 15,000 Soviet troops and cost the USSR about $8 billion a year. It also led to hostility between the USSR and much of the Muslim world, a major problem given the large Muslim population in the USSR.

By 1980 not a dictatorship survived west of the Iron Curtain. Across eastern Europe, by contrast, corrupt dictatorships ruled over increasingly sullen populations. Communist rule rested ultimately on (Soviet) force. The communist system was not totally monolithic. Leaders accommodated themselves to local circumstances. In many respects East Germany was the most successful communist state. Hard-liner Ulbricht worked hard to create a sense of East German national consciousness, using sport as one of his main weapons. Huge amounts of money (and steroids) were pumped into GDR athletes, who performed well at Olympic Games. Yet the GDR remained an artificial state: its living standards were poor compared with those in West Germany. The appeal of its neighbour was enhanced by the accessibility of West German TV in most of the GDR. (Thanks to improved television broadcasting and a virtual end of radio jamming, it became difficult to bar east Europeans from Western information.) Dissident voices grew louder as awareness of contrasts with the West grew.

b) The Leaders of the USSR

The founders of communism had promised a new kind of state based on fairness and equality. Under the leadership of Brezhnev, Soviet communism moved a long way from these ideals as politicians became more corrupt and the secret police (the KGB) wielded more power. There was a new elite composed of government officials and senior members of the armed forces. Brezhnev's last years were years of economic stagnation and growing social problems – alcoholism, drug abuse and crime. Following his death in 1982, Andropov became the new leader. He favoured reform, attacking corruption at home and calling for an end to the arms race. His influence was limited. Within a few months of coming to power he became desperately ill and he died in 1984. Chernenko, his successor, died in 1985. His replacement as General Secretary was Mikhail Gorbachev – at 54 the youngest member of the Politburo.

MIKHAIL GORBACHEV

-Profile-

In some respects Gorbachev seemed a typical communist. When nominating him as leader, the veteran hard-liner Gromyko told his colleagues: '*This man has a nice smile but iron teeth*'. In 1985 Gorbachev declared that the USSR would prevail by '*force of example in all fields of life – economic, political and moral*' and said there must be a crackdown on '*idle talk, swagger and irresponsibility, in fact anything which contradicts Socialist norms*'. However, British prime minister Margaret Thatcher, an ardent anti-communist, declared after meeting Gorbachev: '*I like Mr Gorbachev. I can do business with him.*'

In 1992 Gorbachev described the USSR's problems in 1985:

I knew that an immense task of transformation awaited me. Engaged in the exhausting arms race, the country, it was evident, was at the end of its strength. Economic mechanisms were functioning more and more poorly. Production figures were slumping. Scientific and technical developments were cancelled out by an economy totally in the hands of the bureaucracy. The people's standard of living was clearly declining. Corruption was gaining ground. We wanted to reform by launching a democratic process. It was similar to earlier reform attempts.

Source D

1931 born in a small farming village in southern Russia;
1950 started studying at Moscow State University;
1950s onwards: worked for the communist party;
1980 became the youngest member of the Politburo;
1985 became Secretary General of the Soviet Communist Party;
1989 announced, with President Bush, that the Cold War was over;
1991 fell from power.

c) *Glasnost* and *Perestroika*

Gorbachev was determined to support policies of *glasnost* (openness) and *perestroika* (economic reconstruction). His hope of radically reforming the Soviet economic system, however, failed. The levels of

Soviet Economic Growth, 1986–91 (% figures, from official Soviet sources)							
	1986–90	1986	1987	1988	1989	1990	1991
National income produced (%)	4.2	2.3	1.6	4.4	2.4	−4.0	−15.0
Industrial output (%)	4.6	4.4	3.8	3.9	1.7	−1.2	−7.8
Agricultural output (%)	2.7	5.3	−0.6	1.7	1.3	−2.3	−7.0

Table 22 Economic growth in the USSR, 1986–91.

corruption and inefficiency were too great. If anything, the economic situation deteriorated (see Table 22). As the economy collapsed, freedom to protest grew.

In an effort to reduce arms spending, Gorbachev set about improving relations with both China and the USA. His efforts to reach agreement with Reagan resulted in a series of summit meetings in 1985, 1986 and 1987. The result was the INF (intermediate nuclear forces) Treaty in 1987. Both the USA and the USSR agreed to remove medium-range nuclear missiles from Europe within three years. Although the Treaty only led to a four per cent reduction of existing nuclear weapons, it marked the end of the nuclear arms race. In 1988 Gorbachev began withdrawing troops from Afghanistan, a move completed in 1989. In 1988 he announced huge cuts in the Soviet armed forces and also made it clear that the Brezhnev doctrine was now abandoned. The countries of eastern Europe could do what they liked.

d) 1989: Year of Revolution

Gorbachev hoped that liberalisation throughout the Soviet bloc would create a new framework for economic cooperation, thereby strengthening Russian influence. Instead, across eastern Europe his policies resulted in revolution. Reconstruction became deconstruction. In 1989 communism was swept away by a rising tide of popular opposition. The process began in Poland.

i) Solidarity in Poland

With a population of 35 million, Poland was, after the USSR, the largest country in eastern Europe. By 1980 Polish opposition to communist rule was increasingly evident.

In 1980 new price rises led to widespread unrest. Striking workers at shipyards in Gdansk, led by Lech Walesa, set up a new – and free – trade union called Solidarity. Soon it had 9 million members and was demanding not only better conditions for workers but also political and religious freedom. Polish communist leaders were now in a difficult position: if they tried to destroy Solidarity, they would be despised by most Poles; if they accepted its existence they risked provoking a Soviet invasion. Having failed to reach agreement with Solidarity, the new Prime Minister, General Jaruzelski, declared a state of martial law in 1981. Solidarity leaders (including Walesa) were arrested. Meetings and demonstrations were forbidden. In 1982 Jaruzelski's government tried to replace Solidarity with new communist unions. However, no one took these unions seriously and Solidarity – although hit hard – survived underground. Jaruzelski's government could not win popular support or prevent further economic deterioration.

The rise to power of Gorbachev undermined old-style communism in Poland. In 1988 Walesa and the still illegal Solidarity organised a nationwide series of strikes against price rises. Jaruzelski finally agreed to legalise Solidarity and to hold free elections. The June 1989 elections were a disaster for the Communists. In the Polish Senate, Solidarity won 99 out of 100 seats. In August Mazowiecki, a leading Solidarity member, became Prime Minister. He was the first non-communist to lead an Iron Curtain country since 1948. Gorbachev expressed support for a peaceful handover of power. In 1990 Walesa was elected President. The Solidarity takeover was complete.

ii) The Rebellion Spreads

The importance of events in Poland and the fact that the USSR was no longer ready to use force to control its empire were quickly perceived in other communist countries. In 1989 revolution quickly spread (see Table 23). From start to finish the drama of liberation was played out on Europe's television screens. Indeed, TV images were a revolutionary force in themselves, inspiring acts of emulation. All over eastern Europe in 1989–90 there were free elections. Nowhere did the Communists get more than 16 per cent of the vote. Communism had collapsed in eastern Europe.

e) German Reunification

In March 1990 free elections in East Germany gave the Alliance for Germany Party an easy victory. Unity, a primary aim of West German Chancellor Kohl, was in principle no longer in doubt. All that remained was to settle procedures and timetable and to reassure non-Germans who feared the prospect of a reunified Germany. In September 1990 Britain, France, the USA and the USSR signed a treaty bringing an end to the post-war occupation of Germany. On 3 October 1990 Germany was reunified. With a population of 71 million and the largest economy in Europe west of the USSR,

Table 23 The year of revolutions: 1989.

1989	Poland	Hungary	East Germany	Czechoslovakia	Bulgaria	Romania
January	Crisis talks between Solidarity and the communist Government.	Parliament passes laws permitting opposition parties to be formed.		Police break up protesters seeking Gorbachev-style reforms.		
February					Free trade union like Solidarity formed.	
March		Demonstrations for freedom.				
April	Ban lifted on Solidarity; elections to be held in June.					
May		Remains of Nagy given State Funeral.		May Day rally broken up by police.		
June	Solidarity wins most seats in election.					
August	Non-communist Tadeusz Mazowiecki is made Prime Minister.		Thousands travel to Hungary hoping to flee to the West.			
September		Barbed wire on Austrian border removed; thousands of East Germans fled to the West; free elections agreed.	Massive protest demonstration broken up by police in Leipzig.		Demonstrations for freedom.	
October		Non-communist republic comes into being.	Huge protest meetings Erich Honecker orders use of force but Egon Krenz refuses. Krenz takes over from Honecker.			
November			10th: Hated Berlin Wall comes down on orders of Egon Krenz.	24th: Massive protests. Milos Jakes and other Party officials resign but Communists still rule country. 27th: General strike brings country to a standstill.	10th: Communist hard-liner Todor Zhivkov forced out of office. 18th: Demonstrations by protesters wanting free elections and the sacking of Communist hard-liners.	
December			Communist Party leadership resigns; free elections to be held next May.	Non-communists dominate the new government. Vaclav Havel, a former dissident, elected President.	Reforms approved – including free elections and formation of opposition parties.	17th: Riots. Ceaucescu orders use of force. Many killed. Riots spread to Bucharest. Government falls. 25th: Ceaucescu and wife Elena executed.

Germany would be once more capable of playing a great power role as other Germanies had done in the past. However, the new Germany was not quite the old Germany revived. Shorn of the old east German lands, it was no longer dominated by Prussia. More reassuring was the fact that Germany was now a fully democratic state with nearly 40 years' experience of democratic politics to build on.

f) The Last Days of the USSR

After 1989 Gorbachev was in a difficult position. His plan to reform communism had failed. The Soviet economy was deteriorating rapidly. Communism had been rejected by eastern Europeans – and by many Russians. In February 1990, following protests in Moscow, the Communist Party agreed to allow other political parties to contest elections. Within the USSR different nationalities now demanded home rule. Civil war or a military coup seemed a distinct possibility. In May Boris Yeltsin, the leader of the reformists, was elected President of the Russian Republic. A month later he left the Communist Party. In late 1990 Gorbachev tried to stop the disintegration of the USSR by using force against nationalists in Latvia, Estonia and Lithuania. At the same time he appointed old-style communists to key positions of government.

While Gorbachev was attacked by hard-line communists for going too far, others (like Yeltsin) attacked him for not going far enough along the road to democracy and a free-market economy. The struggle for control came to a head in 1991. By 1991 parliaments in nine of the fifteen Soviet republics had asserted a substantial degree of independence from the Union government. The Russian Republic, challenging Gorbachev and the Communist Party, set out to run its own economy separately from that of the Union, and Yeltsin supported the Baltic republics whose leaders were seeking total independence from the USSR. Hard-liners, on the other hand, believed the Union had to be preserved. Gorbachev tried to compromise, supporting a treaty which, while retaining the Union, loosened the ties between the republics and granted them considerable independence. An attempted coup by leading hard-liners (who took Gorbachev prisoner for a few days in August) quickly collapsed. The defeat of the coup brought little joy to Gorbachev. It simply reinforced Yeltsin's authority. It also meant an end to the Union Treaty. Although Russia, Ukraine, Belarus and eight other republics formed the Commonwealth of Independent States in December 1991, the Baltic Republics and Georgia opted for total independence. The Soviet Union no longer existed. Gorbachev's position as Soviet president thus disappeared and he became a private citizen. Yeltsin remained as President of the Russian Republic.

6 The Situation in 1990

The events of 1989–90 marked a great upheaval in European – indeed world – history. In 1989 Presidents Bush and Gorbachev met in Malta to declare that the Cold War was over. In 1990 the countries of NATO and the Warsaw Pact signed a treaty agreeing that they were 'no longer adversaries'. However, those who hoped that the world's problems would miraculously disappear with the collapse of communism were to be disappointed. Instead a new range of problems surfaced.

a) The Problem of Nationalism

National and ethnic divisions, which had been suppressed by communism, emerged, or re-emerged, in the former states of the USSR and elsewhere in eastern Europe – most tragically – within the former Yugoslavia. Tito had managed to hold the six republics and two autonomous provinces that made up Yugoslavia together. But after his death in 1980, his successors were mainly concerned with cultivating ethnic support within their own republics. The secession of Slovenia in 1991 proved relatively bloodless but elsewhere – in Croatia, Bosnia and Kosovo – complex civil war broke out. 'Ethnic cleansing' – a euphemism for the elimination of a local population by means of murder, deportation and terror – was commonplace through the 1990s.

b) Problems in Eastern Europe

All the former communist states faced serious economic problems as they tried to change to 'free-market' economies. Establishing Western-style democracy also proved difficult in former police states with few democratic traditions. As economic problems mounted, many hankered after (what they saw as) the good old Soviet days of secure employment, cheap food and international respect.

c) European Unity?

After 1989 Europe was far from a single entity. Once the artificial east–west divide ended, older divisions in Europe became visible again, such as the divide between Catholic and Orthodox Europe. Even in western Europe nationalism remained strong. By no means all people wanted greater European unity and at work within most nation-states were strong regionalist tendencies.

EAST EUROPEAN JEWS

While national and minority problems remained alive across Europe, one of the most ancient seemed to have been solved. The fate of east European Jewry had been in part determined by the Holocaust. After 1945 many of Europe's surviving Jews were drawn to the new state of Israel. East European communist parties, keen to make use of traditional popular anti-Semitism, encouraged emigration – often by minor persecution. In some countries (such as Poland) the outcome was a virtual elimination of the Jewish population.

THE EUROPEAN UNION

The EC (now called the European Union or EU) continued to grow. Austria, Finland and Sweden joined in 1995. Former communist states such as Poland and Hungary also pressed for admission.

d) European Prosperity

Despite all the problems, Europeans were much better off in 1990 than at any previous stage in history. While there were huge disparities (particularly between east and west), economic growth was widely shared after 1945. By 1990 Europeans were better educated, lived longer, were less isolated as a result of telecommunication developments, and were far more mobile. Higher living standards had not necessarily made them happier. The decline in church attendance and the collapse of communism had eroded old certainties. Figures for drug addiction, suicide and crime continued to rise steeply.

▼ Working on Europe and the Cold War

Your reading of the chapter should ensure that you now have opinions on all the following areas:
▼ Who – or what – was to blame for the Cold War?
▼ When did the Cold War really start?
▼ What impact did the Cold War have on western Europe?
▼ What impact did the Cold War have on eastern Europe?
▼ What efforts were made to ease Cold War tensions in the 1960s and 1970s?
▼ Why did the Cold War end?

Answering Extended Writing and Essay Questions on Europe and the Cold War

Consider the following question: 'Why had the Soviet empire collapsed by 1991?' On the long-term front, stress the strains particularly economic, within the USSR. On the medium-term front stress Gorbachev's aims and actions between 1985–9. To what extent did his policies raise – but not realise – expectations? On the short-term front examine events in eastern Europe and in the USSR from 1989–91. In conclusion you will have to decide whether the Soviet empire's break-up was inevitable even before Gorbachev came to power. To what extent did his actions alter the timescale of the process?

Answering Source-Based Questions on Europe and the Cold War

PEEP UNDER THE IRON CURTAIN

Source E *Daily Mail* cartoon, 6/3/1946.

Source F The Truman Line, *Punch* cartoon, 1947.

" WHO'S NEXT TO BE LIBERATED FROM FREEDOM, COMRADE ?"

Source G 'Who's next to be liberated from freedom, comrade?', cartoon in the *Evening Standard*, 1948.

▼ QUESTIONS ON SOURCES

1. What points are the three sources trying to make? **[10 marks]**
2. What, if anything, do the three cartoons have in common?
[10 marks]

Points to note about the questions

Question 1 In Source E, what does the cartoonist suggest is happening? In Source F, what is Truman symbolically doing? In Source G, what are Stalin and Molotov doing?
Question 2 Point out that all the cartoons are British. Do they show any common bias? What is their common concern?

Further Reading

Books in the Access to History series
Stalin and Khrushchev: The USSR 1924–64 by Michael Lynch and *Stagnation and Reform: the USSR 1964–91* by John Laver are excellent.

General
Among the best books available on this period are *Years of Division: Europe since 1945* by John Laver, Chris Rowe and David Williamson, 1999 (Hodder & Stoughton), *Europe since 1945: A Concise History* by R.J. Wegs and R. Ladrech, 1991 (Macmillan), *Cold War Europe, 1945–1989: A Political History* by J.W. Young, 1991 (Edward Arnold) and *Europe in our Time 1945–92* by W. Laqueur (Penguin). Perhaps the best book on the USSR 1945–91 is *The Last of the Empires. A History of the Soviet Union 1945–1991* by J. Keep, 1995 (OUP). The last chapters of *A History of the Soviet Union* by G. Hosking, 1985 (Fontana) are also very useful.

GLOSSARY

INDEX